# GALVESTON

# GALVESTON

## A HISTORY OF
## THE ISLAND

# GARY CARTWRIGHT

TCU PRESS

FORT WORTH, TEXAS

Copyright © 1991 Gary Cartwright; epilogue copyright © Gary Cartwright 1998

All uncredited photographs appear through the courtesy of the Rosenberg Library, Galveston, Texas.

First published 1991 by MacMillan Publishing Company

Number Eighteen: The TCU Press Chisholm Trail Series of significant books dealing with Texas, its life and history

**Library of Congress Cataloging-in-Publication Data**

Cartwright, Gary, 1934–
    Galveston : a history of the island / Gary Cartwright.
       p. cm—(Chisholm Trail series ; no. 18)
    Originally published: New York : Atheneum : Toronto : Maxwell
Macmillan Canada, 1991.
    Includes bibliographical references (p.  ) and index.
    ISBN 0-87565-190-9
    1. Galveston Island (Tex.)—History. I. Title. II. Series.
F394, G2C38   1998
976.4'139—dc21                       98-3289
                                                CIP

*For Warren and Kay Burnett; and for Pam Diamond;*
*and for Phyllis again, and always.*

# *AUTHOR'S NOTE*

LET ME MAKE clear right off the top that I'm a journalist, not a historian. I'm not even sure that I know the difference, except that a journalist doesn't use footnotes and historians hardly ever get sued for libel.

*Galveston* is my attempt to write the profile of a place. I've written a lot of profiles of people, using place as a substratum to put the subject in perspective and give it texture; but in this book I'm reversing the process. The place is the main character. I want the reader to understand the way it looks, how it feels, what it represents, the many ways it has been used and misused over the years, and how it has responded. This place is different from other places, and it was my mission to examine and explain why this is so.

I am indebted to so many people that I don't know where to start thanking them. I spent hours and days and weeks in the Rosenberg Library archives, and I'm deeply grateful to Jane Kenamore, Casey Greene, Lisa Lambert, Julia Dunn, and all the other staff members for their patience and courtesy.

I need to thank all the native and adopted Islanders who guided me along the way, especially Steve Long, whose defunct and deeply lamented *In Between* magazine was a font of information; and of course my great friend and confidante Pam Diamond, who was always there when I needed her, and to whom this book is partially dedicated.

I read the works of many historians and authors, but I particularly want to thank David McComb, whose *Galveston: A History* was my Rosetta stone and my Bible. I slept with McComb's book under my pillow, and I hope I absorbed enough to ensure that this book is at least fair and accurate.

The following is a partial list of books and authors to whom I owe a debt of gratitude:

*Living with the Texas Shore*, by Robert A. Morton; *Galveston: History of the Island and the City*, by Charles W. Hays; *The Early History of Galveston*, by Joseph O. Dyer; *Galveston: A Different Place*, by Virginia Eisenhour; *Bob's Galveston Reader* and *The Port of Galveston's Bicentennial Appointment Calendar and Compendium for 1976*, both by Bob Nesbitt; *Gail Borden: Dairyman to a Nation*, by Joe B. Frantz; *Samuel May Williams: Early Texas Entrepreneur*, by Margaret Swett Henson; *Tales of Frontier Texas*, by John Q. Anderson; *Galveston in Nineteen Hundred*, by Clarence Ousley; *The Galveston Era*, by Earl W. Fornell; *Six Decades in Texas*, by Francis R. Lubbock; *Adventures of a Blockade Runner*, by William Watson; *Lone Star*, by T. R. Fehrenbach; *Commodore Moore and the Texas Navy*, by Tom Henderson Wells; *Norris Wright Cuney: A Tribune of the Black People*, by Maud Cuney Hare; *Papa Jack*, by Randy Roberts; *When the Heavens Frowned*, by Joseph L. Cline; *Storms, Floods, and Sunshine*, by Isaac Cline; *A Weekend in September*, by John Edward Weems; *Progressive Cities: The Commission Movement in America, 1901–1920*, by Bradley Robert Rice; *The Shame of the Cities*, by Joseph Lincoln Steffens; *The Man Who Stayed in Texas*, by Ann Nathan and Harry I. Cohen; *Galveston: Ellis Island of the West*, by Bernard Marinbach; *Houston: A Twentieth-Century Urban Frontier*, by David G. McComb; *Lafitte the Pirate*, by Lyle Saxon; *Jean Lafitte*, by Mitchell Carnley; *The Galveston That Was*, by Howard Barnstone; *The Browns of Ashton Villa*, by Suzanne Morris; *Taken at the Flood: The Story of Albert D. Lasker*, by John Gunther; *The Dethronement of the City Boss*, by John J. Hamilton; *Recalled Recollections*, by I. H. Kempner; *Report on the Seawall*, by the Galveston Board of Engineers; *The Port of Houston; A Brief History of the Galveston Wharf Company; Memoirs of Alfred Horatio Belo*, by Alfred H. Belo; *The Galveston Community Book*, edited by Samuel Graham; *Report of Red Cross Relief, Galveston, Texas; The Handbook of Texas*, edited by Walter Prescott Webb; *The Narrative of Alvar Núñez Cabeza de Vaca; The Odyssey of Cabeza de Vaca*, by Morris Bishop; and *Lest We Forget*, by Jane and Rebecca Pinckard.

In researching the Karankawas, I read papers and essays by Charles Hammond, Alice W. Oliver, Albert S. Gatshet, B. C. Stuart, and Roy Bedichek. A number of unpublished manuscripts and theses were studied, including "A Sociological Study of a Segregated District," by Granville Price; "Partners in Progress," by Thomas T. Baker, Jr.; "The Battle of Galveston Bay," by Bert C. Armstead, Jr.; "A Blockaded Seaport," by Brother Raymond Ogden; "Norris Wright Cuney," by Virginia Neal Hinze; the autobiography of Louisa Christine Rollfing; the papers of George Sealy; "The Grande 1894 Opera House," by C. M. McConnell; the letters of I. H. Kempner.

I am indebted to Alan Waldman for his series of articles, "Big Sam and Papa Rose," published in *In Between* magazine, and to numerous articles and pieces of information gleaned from the *Southwestern Historical Quarterly*, *Texas Monthly*, the *Texas Observer*, the *Texas Almanac*, the *Galveston Daily News*, and other publications. Finally, I want to thank all the people who volunteered bits and pieces of information, and who sat still for interviews.

If I have forgotten anyone, I apologize. I told you I wasn't a historian.

# 1

I NEVER GO back to the Island without sensing the ghosts. I can't think of a place where they run thicker. The cannibalistic Karankawa Indians occupied the Island at least as far back as 1400. Cabeza de Vaca, La Salle, and Jean Lafitte all visited it before Texas was a republic. The Battle of Galveston wasn't the greatest sea battle of the Civil War, but it was one of the most poignant. Galveston has about 550 structures listed on the National Register of Historic Places, and many more that could be. When I visited the Island in the late spring of 1990, I had just about completed this book, but I wanted one more look at the Island—Galvestonians always use a capital *I*—one more frolic with the spirits, just to make sure I hadn't missed anything or dreamed all this up.

Coming down the coastal prairie from Houston on Interstate 45, you can smell the ghosts before you see or hear them. They smell sweet and moldy, like the unfocused memory of some lost sensation jarred unexpectedly to mind. It's the scent of tangled gardens of jasmine, honeysuckle, and magnolia, maybe. Or the smell of decaying timbers of shipwrecks half-buried in sand, or the weathered, salt-caked planking of abandoned cotton warehouses stretching between the highway and the wharves. Encoded in the smells are secrets so ephemeral that just thinking about them causes them to vanish.

Off to the left like the bleached bones of some hideously deformed reptile are the petroleum refineries of Texas City, and off to the right, at the water's edge, small sailboats and a few derelect shrimpers. The causeway humps up and over marshlands and bayous, and then begins to span the bay. Galveston Bay is enormous, a body of water seventeen miles wide and more than thirty miles long. It is fed by numerous creeks and bayous and two major rivers, the San Jacinto and the Trinity. The causeway spans the narrowest part, about three miles from mainland to Island. It is the Island's umbilical cord. Except for the Bolivar Ferry and the toll bridge across San Luis Pass, the causeway is the only way on or off the Island.

At the crest of the causeway you can see the Island, or at least some of its major landmarks—the American National Insurance Company (ANICO) Building, the sprawling University of Texas Medical Branch (UTMB), the cranes and elevators of the port of Galveston, the superstructures of some of the ships tied up there, one or two high-rise hotels on Seawall Boulevard. The Island itself is flat as a penny, a thin string of sand thirty miles long and so narrow you can walk across its widest part in half an hour. It runs northeast to southwest, parallel to the Texas coastline, part of an almost unbroken chain of barrier islands that stretches ten thousand miles, from the south shore of Long Island, down the Atlantic coast, around the tip of Florida, and west all the way to Mexico. Galveston Island sits at the mouth of Galveston Bay like half of a double gate, its backside to the mainland and its face toward the Gulf of Mexico. The other half of the gate is Bolivar Peninsula. Between the Island and the peninsula is a gap through which the ships of the world pass, called Bolivar Roads. Because the bay is so large, Bolivar Roads appears as a tiny cut between barrier islands, but in fact it is nearly a mile across. Except for San Luis Pass, which was used by a few shallow-draft blockade runners during the Civil War, Bolivar Roads is the only passage from the Gulf to the bay.

When the Spanish navigator Hervía charted Galveston Bay in 1783 he reported that people were living on the Island, though he didn't say if they were Indians or white men. Hervía named the bay "Galvestown" in honor of the viceroy of Mexico, Don Bernardo de Gálvez, who never saw the Island. People are not supposed to live on a sandbar, and the fact that they choose to live on this one tells you something about the collective psyche. These are people who like to be different, who see themselves as select, and maybe even a little invincible. There is an unmistakable attitude of tolerance on this Island, too, similiar to the liberal atmosphere one experiences in San Francisco—another seaport that survived a devastating natural disaster at the turn of the century. "People who putatively may die together learn to live together," remarked one of Galveston's great civic leaders, the late Harris K. "Bush" Kempner.

There is also an unmistakable snobbishness in Galveston society. Indeed, the provincialism of these people gives one a rough sense of the infinite. A bride is expected to send wedding invitations to total strangers if *her* grandparents spent the night with *their* grandparents during the 1900 storm. There is even an acronym to set natives apart—BOI, meaning "born on the Island." The local newspaper uses BOI without further definition. A friend of mine, Gail Rider, moved to the Island twenty-nine years ago and is still viewed with suspicion by some of the old families. Her social standing is assisted only slightly by the fact that her great-great-great-grandfather was Thomas Borden, who with his brother Gail ran one of the first newspapers in Texas and helped finance the Texas War of Independence. When a historical group decided to erect a plaque beside an oak tree in front of Gail Borden's family home on 35th Street (it was one of the few trees to survive the 1900 hurricane), Gail Rider and her lawyer husband were invited, because she was a Borden. But the group didn't choose to invite the current owners of the house on 35th Street, whose tree was being celebrated.

Islanders are resourceful, too, and resilient. They are the descendants, literally and spiritually, of eight generations of Europeans, Asians, Hispanics, Africans, and Creoles who somehow made do on this small sandbar where there is no drinkable water and hardly any agriculture. It is easy to forget, but the weather here can be relentless and cruel. Islanders claim that the temperature is usually ten degrees more comfortable than it is on the mainland, and that's true, as far as it goes. What they forget to mention are the occasional Arctic storms, called blue northers, that roar down the plains and slam into the coast with the force of runaway trains. Some winters are so severe the bay freezes over. In the summer the wind blows straight out of the tropics, hot, wet, and mean. West Indies winds bring hurricanes, tornadoes, and brain-boiling heat and humidity. Major hurricanes wrack the Island on an average of one every twenty years—the last big one was in 1961 and Islanders are still waiting. It's a game they play with death.

*   *   *

THE CAUSEWAY empties onto Broadway, and the ghosts take form
and begin to murmur. Broadway runs down the spine of the Island,
flanking a handsome esplanade of palms, oaks, and oleanders, separating the bay side from the Gulf side. Along the way are monuments to the war dead, dating back to the Texas Revolution.

Things change slowly in Galveston, when they change at all—a
pace that gives Island life its musty old-wine flavor. It is a few
minutes after ten on a weekday morning. I tune my car radio to
station KGBC-AM (1520) and retreat into my reverie as Frances
Kay Harris plays big-band music of the 1930s and tells women
whether they'll need furs for transatlantic cruises. You wouldn't
know it by listening to her today, but Frances was one of the movers
and shakers of the civic-reform movement in the late 1950s and
early 1960s, when Galveston was one of the most progressive cities
in Texas.

On the bay side you pass rows of warehouses where families like
the Sealys and the Moodys made their fortunes. As you head toward
downtown, the street numbers diminish—45th, 44th, 43rd. The city
was laid out in a simple, easily understood gridiron pattern in 1837
by eccentric surveyor and inventor Gail Borden, who rode around
town on a pet bull, and tried to market jelly made out of the horns
and hooves of oxen. Over the years the names of some of the lettered
or numbered avenues and streets have been altered to flatter the
Island's ruling families—for example, 21st Street is now Moody
Street, 22nd is Kempner, and that part of Avenue I in the downtown
district is Sealy. There is a Borden Street, but it's way out in the
boondocks.

The old city cemetery, on Broadway (Avenue J) between 43rd
and 40th, predates the Civil War. I stop there to seek the grave
of a Union officer, Lieutenant-Commander Edward Lea, second
in command of the gunship USS *Harriet Lane*. Lieutenant-
Commander Lea's death was one of many sorrows of that tragic
and stupid war. He died at the Battle of Galveston, in the arms
of his father, Major A. M. Lea, a Confederate engineer under General John B. Magruder, whose forces had just disabled and captured the *Harriet Lane*. As he died, the young lieutenant-
commander whispered to one of his mates, "My father is here."
Those words are supposedly carved on his headstone.

On this particular day I can't locate the grave of Lieutenant-

Commander Lea. But old cemeteries can't be still, and soon I'm hearing new, unsolicited tales. In the oldest part of the cemetery, near the 40th Street entrance, I squat to read the faded inscription on a modest headstone: MARGARET ANN, WIFE OF STEPHEN KIRK-LAND. She died May 30, 1844, at the age of twenty-one. On the adjacent grave is an identical headstone: MARY W. KIRKLAND, SEC-OND WIFE OF STEPHEN KIRKLAND. She died June 30, 1847, at twenty-two. A few feet away I discover a fifteen-foot high marble, phallus-shaped monument, marking the grave site of Stephen Kirkland, who died in 1859, at forty-four. Apparently, the monument was erected (no pun intended) by his third wife, Mary A. Kirkland, who died in 1906, at the decent age of seventy-eight. You may be surprised that there are so few headstones from September 8, 1900, considering that on that terrible weekend more than 6,000 Islanders died in the most devastating hurricane in American history. Many of the bodies were never recovered, and those that were were hurriedly dumped at sea or burned in giant funeral pyres.

Islanders have a passion for monuments—and mansions built to look like monuments. The old Moody Mansion, at 26th and Broadway, purchased for ten cents on the dollar after the 1900 hurricane, sits vacant, soon to be a museum. The impressive structure rising from the corner of 24th and Broadway is the Sealy Mansion, designed by the famed New York architect Stanford White. At 25th Street (also called Rosenberg), the statue of Victory atop the Texas Heroes Monument points toward the bay, and past that, toward the San Jacinto Battlegrounds on the mainland. Generations of young men who visited the Island in the thirties, forties, and fifties believed that the statue was positioned to point the way to the old Postoffice Street red-light district.

Turn north at 24th, toward the bay and the Strand. A hundred years ago, the Strand was the greatest banking and finance center between New Orleans and San Francisco—the Wall Street of the Southwest. Today it's a tourist street of souvenir and antique shops, boutiques, art galleries, bars, and restaurants. But the feeling is timeless. The Strand was—is—one of the country's finest examples of Victorian architecture. The late Howard Barnstone, critic and professor of architecture, wrote that while the Strand never achieved the urban quality of the Avenue de l'Opéra in Paris, "it came as close to this sense of city as anything in Texas and, probably, as anything in the west." Fifteen years ago the Strand was skid row, but since then many of the great buildings have been restored. You can read the names of Galveston's ruling families on the parapets and cornices—the Hutchings, Sealy & Company Building, the W. L. Moody Building (one-story shorter since the 1900 hurricane sheared off the top floor), the Marx & Kempner Building (one story shorter since the 1915 storm did likewise). My favorite is the Trueheart-Adriance Building, on 22nd, just off the Strand. Wedged between two larger buildings, this little crazy-quilt gingerbread structure is right out of Dickens: you almost expect to see Scrooge and Marley looking out one of the narrow Romanesque windows.

I always suggest that visitors get oriented at the Strand Visitors Center between 21st and 20th streets. They've got free maps and pamphlets describing points of interest, and there is always someone available to answer questions or give directions. I need directions to a famous grove of oaks known as Three Trees. I first read about the grove in Cabeza de Vaca's diary. When the Spaniards washed up somewhere on West Beach in 1528, they discovered an Indian camp beside a grove of trees, on a ridge near the center of the Island. Three Trees is the Island's earliest landmark: for at least three centuries it was a gathering place for the Karankawas. In the fall of 1817, according to my research, the tribe fought a bloody three-day battle there with Jean Lafitte's pirates. In 1821, after Lafitte abandoned Galveston, a twenty-man party headed by a doctor named Purnell came to Three Trees looking for buried treasure. Instead, the treasure hunters found a hundred Karankawas, dancing and singing. Assuming that the Indians had found the treasure and were celebrating, Purnell attacked, and once again the earth beneath the grove was soaked with blood.

I have been looking for Three Trees for a long time. So have a lot of others, I learn at the Visitors Center. "Legend has it that Lafitte buried some gold there," said a young historian named Richard Eisenhour. "People spent so much time digging out near 13-Mile Road that for years there was a deep trench. I think it's overgrown by now. But nobody ever found the location of Three Trees." I make a note to drive out West Beach. If Cabeza de Vaca's ghost is there, I'll know.

The Visitors Center is part of a group of buildings called Hendley Row, the oldest commercial block (1855) on the Island. During the Civil War it was, at various times, a lookout post and headquarters

for both Union and Confederate troops. Islanders claim you can
still see marks of cannonballs on the 20th Street side, though I've
never been able to find them. Hendley Row is owned now by Sally
Wallace, a leader in the Galveston restoration movement and owner
of the Hendley Market, where you can browse through an amazing
collection of old maps, books, bottles, buttons, lace dresses, shawls,
and silk-trimmed frock coats. The building once housed a cotton-
factoring firm, owned by Colonel Moody. Notice the impressive
skylight. The old cotton factor's offices upstairs are now apartments.
For the first three months that I was researching this book, I lived
up there, with a fun-loving crowd of would-be actors, writers and
musicians, and the ghosts of the Sacred Order of the JOLO (nobody
knows what the letters signified) who stood watch on the roof of
the Hendley Building during the Civil War.

While you are in this part of town, walk over to 20th and Postoffice, to the 1894 Grand Opera House. It was modeled after the
great opera houses of Europe, and on its scale it is the equal of any
of them. Sarah Bernhardt and Al Jolson performed here, and so
did the great Russian ballerina Anna Pavlova.

At its west end, the Strand dead-ends into the old Santa Fe Building, now known as Shearn Moody Plaza. While you're here, take
time to tour the Railroad Museum, a time-warp experience where
you almost inhale history. In the waiting room are life-size, ghost
white statues of men, women, and children in 1930s dress, reading
newspapers, checking luggage, frozen in the postures of daily life.
In the yard outside, vintage locomotives and passenger cars sit for
inspection. Have lunch in Dinner on the Diner, the museum's stain-
less-steel Pullman dining car. Better yet, have dinner: the service
is more elegant at night, with soft lighting and piano music. Also,
the feeling that you are actually moving through the countryside is
not interrupted in the evening by touring groups of schoolgirls
pressing their faces against the window.

One of the waitresses in the dining car is a friendly, gray-haired
woman named Madge Saenz, who came to Galveston in 1935 to
work as a Harvey Girl at the train station café. In those days Fred
Harvey had train station cafés all over America, famous for coffee,
apple pie, and ham sandwiches, served by pretty young Depression-
era girls in starched white outfits. Madge still wears hers fifty-five
years later. She used to average two dollars a week in tips, she tells
me, of which forty cents went for her mother's burial plot and

twenty cents for her own plot. "A lot of people back then were buried in pauper's graves," she explains.

A block south of the Strand, on Water Street (also called Port Industrial Boulevard), is the port of Galveston. Unlike Houston or most other ports I've visited, you can walk or drive along the bay-front and see the ships up close. There are usually three or four in port, from the USSR or Norway or Germany or some distant and exotic locale. From the 1870s until World War II, this was one of the busiest ports in the world. Today it's not even one of the busiest in Texas. Galveston's tall ship *Elissa* is docked at Pier 21 beside what will soon be the Texas Seaport Museum. The Island's main body of shrimp boats—the Mosquito Fleet—ties up at Pier 19. In the late afternoon when the shrimpers return to the pier, seabirds so thick they blot out the sky skim in their wake. If you're looking for fresh seafood to take home, Pier 19 is the place. It is also where you charter fishing or party boats. Just east of here, at the foot of 15th Street, you can see the ruins of Lafitte's wine cellar.

Up Water Street at 28th, I visit the Quonset-hut studio of an artist named Mark Muhich. I come to inquire after the condition of Mu-hich's most controversial Island icon, an abstract statue of former heavyweight boxing champion Jack Johnson that sits in a small park on Seawall Boulevard at 29th. "It's been shot and hit about a hundred times," Muhich tells me. "Sometimes it gets splashed with paint." Jack Johnson grew up on the Island, in a tiny house at 808 East Broadway, and established his reputation in the 1890s as a dockside fighter and a participant in vicious free-for-all bouts known as battles royal. Anyway, Muhich, who is white, was fasci-nated by the story of the world's first black champion, and he crafted an enormous black steel spiral, which since 1984 has been on dis-play at a park frequented mainly by blacks.

Some believe that blacks are responsible for the vandalism, that it's a form of protest because Muhich's work doesn't look anything like Jack Johnson. Muhich thinks the protestors are whites who are incensed that Johnson married a white woman. "Several times I've peeled off Ku Klux Klan stickers," Muhich says.

The Galveston Historical Foundation offers an annual tour of historic homes the first two weekends in May, but I can tell you how to take your own private tour, at your own convenience. First, supply yourself with pamphlets and maps from the Visitors Center. Then rent a bicycle from one of those places along Seawall and ride north on 19th Street to Sealy. The heart of the East End Historical District is located between 19th and 14th, from Sealy to the Strand. Mainlanders who envision the Island as a barren sandbar are invariably amazed at the canopy of great oaks and the wall of stately palms that grace Galveston's historic neighborhoods. Many of the homes are identified by markers: the "castle" of the Danish immigrant John C. Trube, at 1627 Sealy, is one of the Island's strangest and most intriguing homes. It looks as though it were designed by a committee of architects. Trube, once the gardener of a Danish nobleman, had the house designed to resemble a castle in Kiel, Denmark, with battlement towers, and a mansard roof with nine gables. The house on the northwest corner of 17th and Winnie is the boyhood home of King Vidor, one of Hollywood's best directors in the 1930s.

The single most spectacular home is the old Gresham Mansion, now called the Bishop's Palace, at the corner of Broadway and 14th. In silhouette this immense place looks like a medieval town. This was once the home of Colonel Walter Gresham, whose lobbying efforts secured federal money to widen and deepen the ship channel after the Civil War. Ashton Villa, a more delicate Victorian structure at 2328 Broadway, was once the home of Miss Bettie Brown, who scandalized Islanders in the 1880s by smoking cigarettes in public and racing unchaperoned along Broadway in a carriage pulled by matching teams of stallions—a black pair for day and a white pair for evening. It is said that on occasion Miss Brown's ghost appears in the dead of night and plays the piano in the villa's Gold Room.

Seawall Boulevard has to be one of the most impressive marine drives anywhere. In its halcyon days, from the 1920s to the mid-1950s, the Boulevard was a glittering strip of casinos, nightclubs, and pleasure piers. You can still see the old Balinese Room extending out over the Gulf. Though no gambling has gone on for years, the B-Room hosted the biggest names in show business, and highest-rolling gamblers. It was almost impossible to raid because the casino area, where the illegal activity took place, was situated on the T-head of the long narrow pier. When raiding parties of Texas Rangers appeared, someone up front pushed a button, the band struck up "The Eyes of Texas," and the gambling paraphernalia folded into the walls like Murphy beds.

The pier next to the B-Room, which advertises itself as "the original" Murdoch's Pier, isn't the original, by the way. The original was three stories high and much wider, with a steep Churchill Downs–style roof and a lot of pennants. Island merchants sometimes play fast and loose with history. I should point out that the Tremont Hotel, on Ship's Mechanic Row, is the third hotel to bear that name, and that, except for the block that passes in front of the hotel, the road is known less elegantly as Mechanic Street. However, the Old Galveston Club on 21st and Postoffice is—as the sign on the building suggests—"the last of the old speakeasys." You can almost smell the beer on the ghosts' breath. The bartender, Santos Cruz, claims to have invented the margarita in honor of Peggy Lee, when he was mixing drinks at the Balinese Room in 1948. The club is dark and smells faintly rancid, like the pulverized popcorn ground into the floor of old movie houses. From the glow of a beer sign you can see the oil portraits of seven nude beauties hanging on the south wall. The models were all local girls, some of them quite respectable, most of them grandmothers today. One of the models, Candy Russo, owns an Italian restaurant a few blocks away.

I like to stay on the Boulevard, where I can hear the ocean and taste the salt breeze. My favorite hotel is the Galvez, one of those wonderfully grand and imposing old resort hotels that you used to see pictured on postcards in your grandmother's attic. FDR stayed there, as did Douglas MacArthur and Dwight D. Eisenhower. Phil Harris and Alice Faye were married there, in the penthouse suite of gambler-gangster Sam Maceo. It was built in 1911, by I. H. Kempner, John Sealy, Jr., and other Galveston businessmen, to demonstrate their faith in the Island's recovery after the disaster of 1900. When the next really big storm hit in 1915, legend has it, Islanders sipped champagne and danced the night away in the Galvez ballroom.

The best seafood restaurant in Galveston—and maybe in the world—is Gaido's, on the Boulevard at 38th. This is an Island institution. Founder San Jacinto Gaido opened the family's first seafood canteen on Murdoch's Pier in 1919. (One of his associates and customers was the barber and future crime syndicate kingpin Rose Maceo.) You can't miss Gaido's: the building takes up most of the block, and a plaster King Kong–size crab appears to be eating the roof. Everything on the menu is fresh and expertly prepared, but the soft shell crabs—broiled, deep fried, or fried in heavy iron skillets with butter, almonds, and other succulent variations—are good enough to be illegal. Be prepared to wait for a table.

Clary's on Offatt's Bayou is where Islanders go to get away from tourists. It's relaxed, intimate, unpretentious, yet there is a white-table-cloth elegance that makes you feel like dressing up. The sea-food is local and prepared individually according to the rigorous culinary discipline of Mr. Clary Milburn, who moved here a quarter of a century ago from Louisiana. His unique cuisine might be called "down home up bayou." The seafood gumbo is world-class, and there is a spectacular dish called Oysters 32, baked and served in a hot muffin tin, covered with a variety of sauces. On a winter evening when the fog rolls in, there is no finer place to be.

The merits of Gaido's and Clary's notwithstanding, my favorite eating spot on the Island is an unpretentious Cajun joint called Benno's. Located on the Boulevard, at 12th Street, Benno's must date all the way back to the early 1980s. You order at a counter and eat on picnic tables, inside or on the patio. Benno's Cajun oysters, grilled with a little butter and spices and served with garlic bread, are the best I have ever had—and I thought I had tried them all.

A perfect spot for a family outing is Seawolf Park on Pelican Island, across the 51st Street Bridge. There is a pavilion with a snack bar, a huge grassy play area for kids, and a World War II destroyer escort and submarine, open for inspection. A promontory of the park juts out just north of Bolivar Roads, exactly where the Galveston Ship Channel forks away from the Houston Ship Channel. You can sit on the rocks or the pier and watch the ships of the world glide past. Every fifteen or twenty minutes, the Bolivar Ferry slips across the channel. Take a ride: it's free, it's fun, and with luck a school of dolphins will follow you across. Off the end of the pier you will note one of the Island's curious landmarks, the wreckage of a 421-foot concrete ship called *Selma*. It's been there since 1920. In the 1940s a hermit named Frenchy LeBlanc lived aboard, catching most of his meals in the shallow water around his home.

My friend Aubrey Thompson, a researcher at UTMB, tells me that Seawolf Park is one of the best fishing spots on the Island. "The best time to fish is an hour or two before or after the tide is turning," he advises. "Fish hit better in moving water." You can purchase bait and rent fishing gear at the pier. On a warm, blustery day in May, when the fishing should have been terrible, we caught eleven different species, including one pompano and enough flounder for dinner the next night.

As happens so often on the Island, my discovery of Three Trees is pure serendipity. I am talking to Sam Popovich, Galveston's seventy-two-year-old constable, when he mentions that as a young man he used to punch cattle on the old Ostermeyar Ranch. "That's out by Lafitte's Grove," he says. "What they used to call Three Trees." Half an hour later we are driving out West Beach, on what used to be the stagecoach road between Galveston and the old port of Velasco (now Freeport). At 10-Mile Road, we turn back toward the bay, then continue west on Stewart Road. Finally, Popovich stops beside a small pond, near a grove of oaks. We climb over a gate, onto private property. "Old man Ostermeyar and his wife Emmie are buried over there," he says, pointing to a tiny family grave plot beside a barn.

Then I see the marker, identifying Lafitte's Grove, "the site of the Battle of Three Trees." Of the fifteen or twenty trees there today, at least two appear to be hundreds of years old. Who can say if these are the original trees, or the offspring? But I'm certain this is the place. Lafitte burned the settlement of Galveston (which he called Campeachy) and sailed away forever in the spring of 1821. Shortly before his departure, legend has it, Lafitte was heard to remark: "I have buried my treasure under the three trees." A group of pirates who remained behind supposedly dug up a long wooden box near the grove, and when they pried off the lid they found . . . not treasure, but the body of a woman. Who she was nobody knows. Over the years Islanders have turned up small caches of treasure, a few doubloons here, a few coppers there, nothing to speak of. I dig the toe of my boot into the soft dirt, not really expecting to find anything but unable to resist the temptation.

Later I go looking for the spot where Cabeza de Vaca and his wretched crew crawled ashore. Passing a subdivision, I walk along a narrow beach littered with shells and driftwood from a recent tide. It is early on a Saturday, and the beach is nearly deserted. I stand on top of the dunes, my back to the surf, trying to see what Cabeza de Vaca must have seen. Countless storms and flood tides have rearranged this beach since the 1500s. By my rough calculation, Three Trees would have been five or six hundred feet farther inland. Nevertheless, from the dunes I can see the trees clearly. A breeze ripples the pages of my notebook, and for an instant I think I hear a voice. *If you were shipwrecked*, it asks, *what would you do?* But of course! I'd head straight for that grove of trees.

# 2

ONE HUNDRED thousand years ago when there were no boundaries or known civilizations and when strange creatures wandered the face of the earth, the sea level was about the same as it is today. Then a cataclysm of unknown duration and origin altered the earth's angle to the sun. Maybe Zeus sneezed, or maybe some cosmic upheaval caused the earth to wobble slightly on its axis. More likely, the cataclysm was the product of an arcane blip of physics, an aberration within the earth's own rotation sufficient to tilt the planet a degree or two away from the sun and affect temperatures over a large part of the earth's surface. This sort of aberration happens from time to time, and is called the Milkanvotich Cycle in recognition of the scientist who first observed the relationship of the earth's climate to variations in its rotation. Whatever happened one hundred thousand years ago, it caused the earth's temperature to drop a few degrees, which was enough to freeze the planet from its poles halfway to its equator.

The big freeze extracted enormous volumes of moisture from the atmosphere, dropping sea levels all over the world and creating glaciers and ice sheets of unimaginable size and form. In the northern hemisphere the glacier field spread as far south as the present states of Illinois and Kansas. As the earth's supply of water was redistributed to form glaciers, what had been ocean bottom became dry land. The shoreline of what we now call Texas would have been

150 miles out into the Gulf of Mexico, compared to its present location.

Then the cycle began reversing itself about eighteen thousand years ago. The earth warmed, melting glaciers and elevating sea levels. Trillions of tons of water rushed down ancient riverbeds, flooding coastal valleys along the Atlantic and Gulf coasts: the Pacific coast, because it was mostly lined with mountain ranges, had few coastal plains to flood. In time, the coastal valleys became jagged inlets called bays. Nature's relentless response to a jagged shoreline is to straighten it out, and that's what happened: the pounding surf began eroding piles of river sediment (called head-lands) that had collected between the bays. Longshore currents carried the sand from these headlands laterally along the coast, forming dunes and sandbars. The sea level continued to rise, flooding the low areas behind these sandbars, or spits of sand, and separating some of them from the mainland. The spits of sand that remained attached to the mainland became peninsulas like Bolivar, and those that were separated became barrier islands like Galveston.

One of the interesting things about barrier islands is that they are constantly migrating toward the mainland. When Galveston Island was formed at the end of the last ice age, it was located a hundred miles or more south of its present location. Because the sea level was rising, the Island was constantly eroding on the ocean side and building up on the bay side, always advancing toward the mainland—which was also eroding. Then about five thousand years ago the acceleration of the tides slowed and the Island stopped migrating. That is to say, it stopped eroding. But it continued to grow on its bay side, becoming wider and higher.

In 1930 scientists made a surprising discovery: not only was the sea level rising again, it was accelerating at an amazing pace, a foot or more each century. This was particularly significant to low-lying islands along the Gulf coast because their gently sloping coastal plains caused the tide to move more rapidly than it would up a steeper incline. A one-foot rise in sea level can gobble up a thousand feet of Galveston shoreline.

Evidence of the Island's inexorable march toward the shore is scattered along any beach. Those oyster, clam, and snail shells that you see are native to the brackish waters of the bay. So what are they doing over here on the Gulf side? Answer: the Island moved, literally passed over the lagoon where they were born. The majority of the shells found on the beaches of any barrier island are fossils, revealed by radio carbon dates to be prehistoric.

To measure exactly how far Galveston Island has traveled since the last section of the seawall was completed in 1962, drive to where the wall ends, near 7-Mile Road. Look west, toward a group of condominiums near the water's edge. That two-to-three-hundred-foot area between the condominums and the end of the sea-wall represents thirty-six years of erosion. In another ten to fifteen years, the first floor of those condos will be under water. So will a lot of extremely expensive vacation homes on West Beach, if a major hurricane doesn't get them first.

The dynamics of shoreline erosion are misleading—beaches don't disappear, they just move somewhere else. There is only so much sand to go around, and every coastal resort on the Texas Gulf shares the supply. Geologists speak of "sediment budgets" in what is essentially a zero sum game. One man's loss is another's gain. The seawall that has saved God knows how many lives since it was constructed after the killer storm of 1900 has simultaneously destroyed much of Galveston's beaches. Seawalls work by reflect-ing the energy of waves; unfortunately, they reflect it back on the beach, which is washed out to sea and carried away by currents. Bolivar Roads' set of parallel jetties, which prevent sand from clog-ging the ship channel, also trap sediment that would otherwise nourish neighboring beaches. Along the Texas coast as much as 50 percent of the sand supply is held prisoner by jetties.

This has been a boon to developers on East Beach, where sand trapped between the jetty and the seawall has caused the beach to accrete rather than erode. Dr. Ed Henderson, a Galveston veteri-narian turned land speculator, bought 368 acres of marshland near the Island's east end in the 1950s, and when he sold it in 1984, the tract was 472 acres of prime beachfront. But the feats of engineering that brought a windfall to Dr. Henderson cause immeasurable grief to those who own property west of the seawall. Every major storm cuts a fringe off somebody's property. Most West Beach homeown-ers are wealthy and savvy enough to calculate the risk They know that major storms come about twenty years apart. If they guess right, that's how long they have to recover their investment. Property owners with sufficient insurance coverage actually made money on Hurricane Alicia in 1983. Alicia was only a medium-size hurricane. The last really big blow was Carla in 1961. For a time after Carla, homeowners couldn't *buy* insurance. One of these days, as sure as the sun sets and the wind blows, the condo market in Galveston is going to crash.

Scientists predict that sea levels will not only continue to rise in the future, but may accelerate dramatically. By the year 2100, tides may be four feet higher than they are today. Factor in other phenomena such as the greenhouse effect, which figures to raise temperatures and melt more glaciers—*and* cause a thermal expansion of ocean waters already in place—and you begin to understand the scope of the global problem. But there is yet another factor peculiar to the Texas coast. It's sinking, especially in the Greater Houston area. This is the downside of Houston's long and profitable exploitation of petrochemicals: as oil, gas, and water are pumped out of the ground, subterranean pressure decreases, sediment compacts, and the earth sinks. There are places in Houston where the surface level is eight or ten feet lower than it was in 1930. Entire subdivisions have slid beneath the water and been abandoned. Wellheads that were once flush with the ground stick out of the prairie like iron scrub brush. The reflecting pool in front of the San Jacinto Monument has settled and tilted so noticeably that water runs over one edge.

Galveston is on the periphery of this sinking landmass. The Island city has sunk about half a foot since 1930. From a vantage point on the back side of the Island, it is difficult to determine if the land is sinking or the tide is rising. Either way, there is water halfway up to your knees. Some geologists believe that the solution to the problem—if indeed it is a problem—is to let nature have her way. As the shoreline retreats, either move buildings to higher ground or let them take their turn falling into the Gulf of Mexico. The only other solution, short of a new ice age, is to build a seventeen-foot-high wall along the entire 367 miles of the Texas coast and forget the beach.

# 3

THE ISLAND'S first residents were a remarkably antisocial tribe known as the Karankawas. The Karankawas patrolled a 350-mile stretch of coastline from the Rio Grande to Galveston Bay, but they lived about half the year on the Island. Except when they were raiding other villages, stealing maidens to marry and children to eat, the Karankawas went out of their way to avoid contact with other tribes. They were one of the few coastal tribes that refused to take part in the Truce of the Tunas, an annual spring mingling of otherwise hostile tribes in South Texas. When the sweet purple fruit of the prickly pear cactus—the "tunas"—ripened each May, Indians from all along the coast declared a truce. They put away their tools and their weapons of war and migrated to the scrubby cactus and mesquite country near the present town of Alice. There they gorged themselves on the succulent fruit, danced, frolicked, and generally conducted themselves like fools rather than warriors for as long as the fruit lasted. Then they returned to their own dwelling places and life returned to normal. Even the ferocious Mariames observed the Truce of the Tunas. But not the Karanka- was.

Although the Karankawas were virtually extinct by the time Texas became a republic, no tribe in the state archives—not even the better known Apaches and Comanches—are more maligned. One author refers to the Karankawas as "the meanest, greediest, laziest, most treacherous, lecherous, vicious, cowardly, insolent aborigines of the Southwest."

That is putting it a bit strongly. Many of the coastal tribes had what, to us, would seem behavioral quirks. Historian Morris Bishop writes of an unnamed tribe of peyote-eating, sexually promiscuous cannibals who deflowered their maidens at age ten. The Mariames established their vicious reputation partly because of their practice of marrying slave women bought from other tribes (price: a bow and two arrows) while feeding their own newborn daughters to their dogs. Compared to these people, the Karankawas were model citizens. That said, it should also be noted that the Karankawas were sometimes less than perfect hosts. When a Spanish treasure fleet went down off the coast of Padre Island, the Karankawas forced the three hundred survivors, many of them women and children, to take off their clothes and march naked. Though priests sent the women ahead so the men wouldn't see their nakedness, several women are said to have "died from shame." Eventually, only two of the castaways survived.

Historians and archaeologists have argued for years whether the Karankawas were cannibals. No doubt they were. Most of the tribes that lived near the Texas coast practiced ritualistic cannibalism. Indians believed they could absorb an enemy's strength by devouring his flesh. Eating an enemy was also regarded as the ultimate humiliation, particularly if a warrior hacked off a piece of flesh and ate it while the enemy was still alive. Some tribes ate human flesh just because they enjoyed it, and the Karankawas appear to have been among them.

On Christmas Day 1686, the Karankawas massacred the remnants of an expedition that had followed La Salle to what they thought was the mouth of the Mississippi River. The expedition had overshot the Mississippi by a good three hundred miles and ended up halfway down the Texas coast, in a bay that La Salle called La Vaca (the cow) in tribute to a herd of buffalo observed feeding on the prairie grass. The Indians spared two brothers who were members of the expedition and held them prisoner for six years, during which time the Frenchmen witnessed numerous acts of cannibalism among their captors.

Early Anglo-American settlers of Austin's colony told of seeing human hands and feet, hardly choice cuts, roasting over Karankawa campfires. There are other reports, none well documented, of shipwrecked Spanish sailors being eaten, but the main body of evidence suggests that the Karankawas dined mostly on members of enemy tribes. The French explorer Simars de Belle Isle was marooned on Galveston Island in 1719. He lived for a while on shellfish, boiled sedge grass, and maggots before being taken prisoner by the Karankawas. In the Indian camp, Belle Isle witnessed a ritual that must have made a dinner of maggots seem like a blue plate special. His captors peeled the skin off the arms of a still-living Toyal tribesman and devoured yellow globs of fat while their women danced about shaking human bones and fingernails.

The credibility of such reports is suspect. The Spanish, French, and Anglo-Americans who explored the Texas coast were not famous for their adherence to truth and fair play. Most Europeans considered Indians to be a subhuman species, probably agents of the devil. Sixteenth-century conquistadors reckoned captured Indians by the head, like cattle. An officer assigned a project would report to the quartermaster and check out so many head of savages. Spare Indians were used for sport. One sport enjoyed by these knights of the Spanish realm was betting which one of them could cut off an Indian's head with the cleanest stroke of his sword. In New Grenada, the Spanish raised their dogs on Indian flesh, in the belief that it made the dogs better hunters.

Still, there doesn't seem to be any question that the Karankawas practiced cannibalism, in all its various forms. According to the diary of a Spanish priest, the tribe had a taste for young children. Karankawa warriors interviewed at a Spanish mission at Refugio told the priest that it was their custom to capture children old enough and strong enough to walk and herd them along as meat on the hoof. Until fairly recently, archaeologists tended to discount the priest's story. Then Herman Smith of the Corpus Christi Museum discovered among a pile of bones excavated from an Indian campsite north of Corpus Christi the elbow bone of a six-year-old Indian child. The bone had been butchered and cooked, and then snapped apart the way Indians snapped deer bones to suck the marrow. "That doesn't absolutely prove the priest's story," Smith said. "But somebody cooked and ate that child."

The Karankawas were a physically imposing race, strongly built and magnificently formed. The men sometimes approached six feet in height, which made them appear as giants to the much smaller Europeans. Their skin was lighter than other coastal tribes and their coarse hair, bleached cinnamon red by the sun, hung to the waist. Even in old age they had splendid teeth and appeared remarkably robust, not that many reached old age: old people were routinely killed for the practical reason that they could no longer contribute to the general well-being. The menacing appearance of the Karankawas was accentuated by their broad, flat foreheads, a result of the tribal practice of strapping babies to boards and suspending them from the ceilings of their lodges, a flat forehead being considered beautiful in this culture.

Except when they were hunting or fishing, the men sat cross-legged on grass mats, chewing tar balls washed up from the floor of the ocean—the same gooey asphalt that sticks to the feet of modern-day beach-goers and is wrongly assumed to be pollution from offshore oil rigs. Sometimes the men swam in the surf or amused themselves by wrestling and slamming each other with sharkskin saps. Women dug roots, toted, fetched, cooked, and cared for the the camp and the children. The women were shorter than the men and tended to be dumpy and unattractive.

Women wore few ornaments, but men covered their faces with distinctive tattoos and decorated their bodies by threading slender pieces of reed through the skin of their their chests. The men went naked or wore breechclouts, and the women made do with flimsy skirts of Spanish moss. Children went naked summer and winter. Only the maidens of the tribe wore modest deerhide skirts. There appear to have been precious few maidens, possibly because they were carried away by enemy warriors.

The Karankawas traveled in packs of thirty or forty, in expanded family groups or clans. There probably were never more than a few thousand of them in Texas. Not only did they refuse to associate with members of other tribes, they sometimes refused to associate with other Karankawas. One group that lived on the Trinity River side of Galveston Bay, for example—they were apparently the offspring of Karankawa braves and slave women—never dared approach the camp of a much larger clan of Karankawa purebloods, who spent much of the year on the same bay, near the San Jacinto River.

All things external to their culture were rejected out of hand. Though they knew about agriculture from inland tribes they had raided, they never practiced it, even when the alternative was starvation. Almost every other tribe on the coast hurried to embrace symbols of the white man's lifestyle—whiskey, firearms, horses, clothing, religion—but in nearly every case the Karankawas resisted.

The only substantial material possessions treasured by the tribe were their weapons and their canoes—sturdy twenty-five-foot dugouts that the Karankawas carved from tree trunks. The dugouts were their equivalent of the frontiersman's horse. Without them, they could not have survived.

Karankawas followed no leader, had no discernible religion, and exercised a system of justice that was swift and terrible. Adultery was punished by mutilation. Blood vendettas were required. La Salle's men may have foredoomed themselves when, on their first day among the seemingly friendly Karankawas, they stole nine canoes. When some of Jean Lafitte's pirates kidnapped a Karankawa squaw in the 1820s, the Indians retaliated by massacring a hunting party of pirates. Among early Anglo settlers—who referred to the tribe derisively as the Kronks—the Karankawas were notorious for stealing cattle. Archaeologists joke among themselves that the tribe had some kind of genetic flaw that made it impossible for them to distinguish between a cow and a deer. The truth was, the Karankawas couldn't conceive of anyone "owning" an animal.

The Karankawas were generous and affectionate, and practiced the simple virtue of fidelity, though neither the explorers nor the settlers seemed to notice. Karankawas doted on their children. When a child died, the entire village indulged in ritual wailing that lasted a full year. Day after day, month after month, the parents woke before sunrise and started crying. They cried again at midday and once more at dusk. At the end of a year they observed the anniversary by washing and cleaning themselves of all paint.

When a son or brother died, there was more ritual weeping and members of the dead warrior's household refused to gather food for three months. They either starved or lived off provisions given by neighbors. In freezing weather there was never enough food anyway, but in the lodges of grieving relatives starvation was by choice.

La Salle's men referred to this tribe contemptuously as "the weepers," but these crying fits were not a sign of weakness. Indeed, they were as much a part of the culture as saluting or bowing or making the sign of the cross was in Western culture. Conversation within the Karankawa culture must have attained a high art: even a simple request or complaint among tribal members was preceded by the shedding of mutual tears. When a Karankawa visited the hut of a neighbor, the visitor and the host went to the middle of the room and squatted on mats. Without speaking a word, both wept bitterly for half an hour. At the end of that time the host gave the visitor everything he owned and the visitor took the gifts back to his own lodge, still without speaking. (Ritual weeping wasn't unique with the Karankawas. The phenomenon has been observed among certain tribes in South America, Africa, and Indonesia. No one knows its origin or meaning.)

The tribe moved about the coast in a body, navigating the creeks, bayous, and inlets with skill and daring. Their migratory patterns seemingly defied logic. The canebrakes and dense forests of the river bottoms would have made ideal winter camps. The forests sheltered an abundance of bear, rabbit, and wild turkey; deer were so plentiful that settlers later shot them from windows. By the same reasoning, when the woods became unbearably hot and unhealthy in the summer, it would have seemed natural for the tribe to migrate to the seashore. For some reason the Karankawas usually did it backward—wintering on the Island and spending their summers in the woods.

Whenever their inner vision told them it was time to cross over to the Island, the Karankawas put their fleet of canoes in from a narrow promontory on West Bay still known as Carancahua Point: there are at least thirty different spellings of the tribal name, and many estimates of how many branches divided this band of Indians. The passage from Carancahua Point to Carancahua Cove—near the present site of Galveston Island State Park—was two miles across, and passed near a succession of oyster beds known as Carancahua Reef.

Even in ancient times the Island was no tropical paradise. True, it *was* usually more pleasant than the mainland, with its afternoon breezes blowing in from the Gulf, cooling in the summer and warming in the winter. In warm months mosquitoes were a problem after dark: French explorers told of spending the night neck-deep in bay water to escape the torment. The Karankawas covered their skin with a foul-smelling repellent extracted from the livers of sharks and alligators, which kept away insects and probably discouraged their enemies as well. The Indians drank the brackish subsurface water when they had to, and stored rainwater in clay pots. After torrential rains it was possible to dip fresh water from the bay, sometimes for several weeks. There was also a small sweet-water lake about halfway down the Island, near several clumps of live oak trees.

The tribe normally camped at the grove they called Three Trees, on a ridge about equidistant between the Gulf and the bay, at the center of an unimaginably rich biomass of potential food sources. Edible roots grew along the marshes, and there were deer and game birds on the Island. The bayous and creeks brimmed with an amazing variety of sea life—trout, redfish, flounder, pompano, shellfish, turtles. Texas naturalist Roy Bedichek wrote that "ancient oyster production (in Galveston Bay) staggered the imagination."

The Karankawas were such skilled archers that they fished with bows and arrows. Like their canoes, these weapons were prized personal possessions. Bows were fashioned from red cedar and were exactly as long as the man was tall. Bowstrings were twisted strands of deer sinew. One historian observed that Karankawa war bows were as "useless in the hands of a man of ordinary strength as was the bow of Ulysses in the hands of the suitors." With his weapon in hand the Karankawa hunter waded into the transparent water and stood frozen in place, poised like a heron, naked legs as sensitive to the subsurface undulations of fish as heron's legs are said to be. The bowman rarely missed, but if he did, the flint point of the arrow plunged into the sand, and the staff stood quivering in plain sight, its wild goose feathers above water. Smaller fish were trapped in cane weirs and oysters and clams scooped up with bare hands.

Under such conditions it seems beyond comprehension that the tribe could ever experience hunger, but the Karankawas experienced it almost constantly.

The Karankawas were relative latecomers to the coast of Texas. Indians have lived along this coast for at least forty-five hundred years, but this tribe apparently arrived about 1400, less than a century before Europeans discovered the New World. Many archaeologists believe the tribe originated in the Caribbean. The language, the impressive physical size, and the cultural traits (particularly the antisocial behavior) of the Karankawas are strikingly similiar to those of the Carib Indians, a tribe of cannibal warriors who traveled in sturdy dugout canoes and regularly raided and conquered neighboring islands.

Karankawa is not the name this tribe gave itself. Like most other North American Indians, they called themselves men, people, genuine people, human beings, or bodies. Other South Texas tribes assigned various names to these newcomers. The Lipan-Apaches knew them as "people who walk in the water," and others called them "wrestlers" or "without moccasins." But the name that stuck came from two Indian words—*karan* (dog) and *kawa* (to love). Since the tribe traveled with small, barkless, foxlike dogs, it became known as the dog lovers, Karankawas. Archaeologists note that this breed of dog has been discovered only two places in the Western Hemisphere: among the Karankawas and among the Armwak population of the Lesser Antilles.

Somewhere around 1400 the Caribs sent a fleet of dugout canoes across the Caribbean and conquered the Armwak, probably taking home an assortment of Armwak women and maybe their dogs, too. Some of the Caribs may have been caught in a storm and blown across the Gulf of Mexico. It is equally possible that a group of Caribs decided to see what was over the northwestern horizon, and just started paddling and never came back. Either way, Galveston Island must have looked like home after such a perilous trip.

# 4

THE FIRST white men to set foot on Galveston Island and encounter the Karankawas must have been a sorry sight. There were forty of them, nearly naked, nearly starved, and completely delirious. They washed ashore in a storm in the early morning hours of November 6, 1528. They were Cabeza de Vaca and the remnants of the ill-fated expedition of Don Pánfilo de Narváez. The expedition had started out in Florida five months earlier with three hundred men and forty horses, and this pitiful collection was all that remained.

Alvar Núñez Cabeza de Vaca was in his mid-thirties when the Spanish fleet set sail from Cuba to conquer the Florida peninsula. His family traced its ancestry (and its ludicrous name) to a humble shepherd who carved a place in Spanish history by showing the troops of King Sancho of Navarre a shortcut through the mountains north of Seville. The shepherd's name was Martin Alhaja and he marked the mountain pass with the skull of a cow—*cabeza de vaca*—thus enabling the Spanish to rout the Moors during the Reconquest of 1212. As a reward, the king gave Martin Alhaja the noble name of Cowhead. In the centuries that followed, the family distinguished itself as builders, civil servants, and explorers. Cabeza de Vaca's paternal grandfather led the conquest of Grand Canary Island in the late 1400s.

By 1500 the island of Cuba had become headquarters for Spanish conquistadors. Cortés had sailed from Cuba in 1521 to conquer the Aztecs of Mexico (which he called New Spain). Six years later,

Charles V gave permission for an expedition to conquer and populate the region from the Rio de las Palmas in northeastern Mexico to the Isle of Florida. The Spanish greatly underestimated how much territory this included, or what an incredible effort would be required to conquer and populate it. Don Pánfilo de Narváez, who financed the expedition out of his own pocket, was appointed its governor and commander in chief. The emperor appointed Alvar Núñez Cabeza de Vaca as royal treasurer to the expedition, a bright young man with a head for numbers, a gift for command, and an extraordinary measure of faith and courage.

On April 7, 1528, after seven weeks at sea, the fleet sighted the landlocked Bay of Espíritu Santo. The vessel commanded by Cabeza de Vaca landed at St. John's Pass, just north of St. Petersburg. In all, four ships, four hundred men, and eighty horses survived the crossing. Fifteen years earlier Ponce de León had discovered and named the mainland of Florida, but now it was the task of Don Pánfilo and his compadres to claim it in the name of the crown.

But the cove where they landed was not the sheltered bay their pilots had charted. The real bay (Tampa Bay) was just to the south. The smart move would have been to stay with the ships and explore the coastline until they found suitable anchorage, but the governor was impatient to start marching north. He had been in Mexico a few years earlier and heard tales of enormous treasure somewhere north of Vera Cruz. Don Pánfilo didn't know where he was, but his heart told him he was close to the cities of gold. At worst, he figured, it was only a few days' march to the Spanish settlement of Pánuco. This was a tragic and monumental error in his geography. The Spanish expedition was standing on the coast of Florida and the village of Pánuco (now Tampico) was on the northeast coast of Mexico, more than half a continent away.

Ignoring the advice of his senior officers, Don Pánfilo and the main body of the expedition started overland, trooping over dunes, sand flats, swamps, and marshes. They had carried only two pounds of hardtack and a half-pound of bacon per man, and after a week their rations were depleted and they lived on fruit from dwarf fan palms. At the end of the second week they discovered an Indian village on the banks of what was probably the Withlacoochee River. The Indians seemed friendly enough. They led the starving Spaniards to fields of ripe corn and gave them water. Falling to their knees, the conquistadors thanked God, though it didn't occur to them to thank the Indians. Their real mission was gold, the Spaniards managed to convey. The Indians made the Spanish understand that though they had no gold, plenty of it could be found by marching north to the empire of the Apalachee tribe. It wasn't far, the Indians indicated.

The trip to the village of Apalachee turned out to be a march of nearly six weeks, 250 miles or so, to the shores of Micosukee Lake near the present Georgia border. They were expecting golden temples and possibly casks of wine and legs of mutton. What they found were forty thatched huts and a small store of corn and deerskins. A few wretched women and children huddled near a campfire, but the men had vanished into the forest. The Spaniards were bitterly disappointed and near exhaustion. Their faces and arms were ripped by thorns and infected from insect bites, and their bodies blistered under their heavy shirts of mail. Scouting parties reported that beyond this village the country was barely passable, nothing but lakes, marshes, fallen trees, tangles of underbrush, and hostile Indians.

For the next month the expedition made its headquarters in the village, enjoying a hospitality had not been necessarily offered. The Apalachee weren't openly hostile, but they practiced a kind of guerrilla warfare that drove the Spaniards mad. A conquistador would be minding his own business, picking dewberries, and suddenly an arrow from nowhere would graze his ear and bury itself six inches deep in the trunk of a tree. A detachment of soldiers watering the horses would hear a rustling, and a volley of arrows would erupt from the underbrush. Several of Don Pánfilo's men were killed from ambush. Sensing that they had overstayed their welcome—the Apalachee food supply was exhausted anyway—the expedition turned south toward the sea, hoping against hope that their ships might be waiting there.

The march south was the worst yet. A merciless July sun turned the woods into a furnace, and the bone-tired and dispirited conquistadors stumbled like zombies through lashing branches and putrid bogs, conquering nothing, not even the terror in their own hearts. They crossed creeks in which alligators were indistinguishable from clumps of green scum, hauling their sore bodies over fallen tree trunks as wide as barrels. Flies swarmed over their bleeding, sweating faces, while ticks and redbugs crawled beneath the blistering metal of their armor and made nests. Each step brought them palpably closer to death. As the Spaniards were attempting to ford a lake, a band of large, naked Indians attacked. Arrows pierced their armor as though it were goose down, wounding a number of the men, including Cabeza de Vaca.

After a number of days the expedition reached the mouth of the Ocklockonee River, two hundred miles down the coast from Pensacola Bay. The coastal prairie was low and marshy, barely rising above the lagoon, a purgatory that was not quite land and not quite sea. There was no Spanish ship waiting there, of course, not that anyone truly believed there would be. Cabeza de Vaca and a few of the officers still strong enough to think clearly decided that their only salvation was to build some boats as best they could.

Though they had no food, no tools, no iron, no smithery, no oakum or pitch, and not the slightest idea how to build a ship, the Spaniards went about the business of constructing five barges. At least one-third of the men were too sick to work and the number increased daily. They found a few oysters in the lagoon and some maize in a nearby Indian village, and every third day they killed a horse and rationed out servings of meat.

In building their crude barges, the Spaniards showed marvelous ingenuity. They fashioned bellows out of deerhide and cane pipes. In an earthen forge they melted down their stirrups, spurs, and crossbows and made nails, saws, and axes. Fibers and husks from palmettos and hair from horses' manes and tails were twisted into rope; sails were created from raggedy shirts. A Greek soldier in their ranks showed them how to make pitch and oakum from pine sap. They flayed the legs of horses, tanned the hide, and made leather canteens for carrying water. By September 20, seven weeks after they started building, five 35-foot barges were ready to sail. Though nobody knew how to navigate, they slaughtered their last horse and put to sea, 247 desperately frightened, nearly naked Spaniards, crammed three and four abreast, praying that Pánuco was just down the coast.

The pitiful little fleet hung close to the shore, exploring an occasional inlet for food and fresh water but finding only a few birds' eggs and a lot of bad Indians. Anchored at one island waiting out a storm, some of the men drank salt water and five of them went mad from the drink and died in agony. With the storm still raging, they put back to sea, determined to find a miracle or die.

They fought an all-night battle with Indians at Pensacola Bay, and later tried without success to find food and water at Mobile Bay. By the time the fleet reached the mouth of the Mississippi, the Spaniards were crazed with thirst and almost too weak to man the oars. They dipped fresh water from the river, drinking themselves sick, then landed on the east side of the river, only to discover there was no firewood to roast their small supply of corn.

This was a river unlike any the expedition had encountered. It was so wide they couldn't see the opposite bank, and currents and eddies collided in boiling swirls, sucking under great bodies of debris and spitting them into erratic patterns. When they tried to cross the great river, a rising north wind pushed them toward the open sea. For two days they struggled against a treacherous tide, losing sight of land and, for a while, of each other.

At dawn of the third day Cabeza de Vaca's vessel hooked up with two other barges, including the one that carried the governor—the other barges apparently were swept away. The governor had despaired of command and at this point issued his final order: every man for himself. Exhausted and close to starvation, straining against hope, the remaining members of the expedition rowed all day against the current, never reaching land. Sometime before sunset, Cabeza de Vaca looked back and realized that the governor's boat had vanished. Now there were only two boats, one commanded by Cabeza de Vaca and a second commanded by two captains named Panalosa and Tellez. Four days later there was another storm and the second boat vanished. Three hundred proud and ambitious Spaniards had started out from Florida nearly five months before, and now Cabeza de Vaca could count only himself and about forty others, all more dead than alive.

For two weeks the men battled heavy seas, existing on a daily allowance of half a handful of raw maize. By the night of the fifteenth day Cabeza de Vaca and his boatswain were the only two strong enough to work the barge and they took turns steering. Certain that they were at death's gate, Cabeza de Vaca closed his eyes and slumped over the bodies of his fallen men, too weary to protest.

"Near dawn," he wrote many years later, "it seemed to me I heard the tumbling of the sea; for as the coast was low, it roared loudly. Surprised at this, I called to the boatswain, who answered me that he believed we were near an island." Sounding the bottom, they found themselves in seven fathoms. Cabeza de Vaca grabbed an oar and began to row, then a wave lifted the barge out of the water, flipped it upside down, and flung it toward shore. Roused from their stupor, the men began to stumble and crawl up the beach.

Cabeza de Vaca dispatched the hardiest of his men, Lope de Oviedo, to climb a tree and survey this place. Indeed, they had landed on an island, Oviedo reported. A scouting party was sent in the direction of a grove of trees, and returned shortly with a supply of dried mullet, a small dog, and a cooking pot. They had found an Indian village but no Indians. Warming themselves by the fire, parching their corn and dividing the mullets and dog meat, the Spaniards must have experienced the wondrous sensation of people brought back from the dead. They were too busy eating to hear the movement, but when the Spaniards looked up from their meal, they were surrounded by a hundred giant archers.

The Spaniards were far too weak to fight; some of them were too weak to stand. But the Indians made no move to attack. They waited at a discreet distance like so many apparitions. They were tall, naked, well-formed men, Cabeza de Vaca wrote in his diary, and their lips were pierced with sections of quarter-inch cane that gave the illusion of perpetual grinning. The nipples of their bare chests were perforated, and foot-long pieces of cane ran under the skin. The Spaniards must have appeared equally bizarre to the Karankawas, who had never seen a white man or even a beard. The white men weren't dressed much better than the Indians, covered as they were with just a few gritty rags.

Cabeza de Vaca offered the savages beads and bells, and each Indian responded by giving the Spanish captain an arrow. The Indians had no food with them, but they made signs indicating that they would return at sunrise with provisions, which they did. Then they disappeared again. Over the next few days the savages appeared at sunrise and again at sunset, always with food and pledges of friendship. Their diet apparently consisted of fish and nutlike roots that they dug with some effort from the bayside marshes.

Their strength and their sense of mission returning, the Spaniards gathered a supply of fish and roots and decided to continue their journey to Pánuco. They stripped away their rags to keep them dry, then dug their barge from the sand and launched it in the shallow surf. The weather was cold and blustery, and their hands were so sore and numb they could barely grip the oars. Still in sight of land, a wave turned the barge broadside to the breakers and flipped its occupants into the sea. Three men drowned in the tumbling current and the others were flung out onto the beach.

"We survivors escaped naked as we were born," Cabeza de Vaca wrote, "with the loss of all we had; and although the whole was of little value, at that time it was worth much, as we were then in November, the cold was severe and our bodies were so emaciated the bones might be counted with little difficulty, so that we looked like the picture of death. . . ." In this entry in his journal, Cabeza de Vaca revealed that since May he hadn't eaten anything except maize and a few fish. Horsemeat was more than he could handle. Now they had nothing—no maize, no clothing, no weapons, no boat. Three more men had drowned in this latest disaster and two others died a short time later. There were still a few sparks from their campfire, and they rekindled it and sat close, the north wind howling and their despair beyond mortal comprehension.

As had become the pattern, the Karankawas appeared at sunset with food. They didn't realize that the Spaniards had tried to leave the island. When they saw the wretched survivors praying and crying, and observed the bodies of their comrades rolling in the surf, the Indians fled. Cabeza de Vaca called them back and in sign language tried to explain what had happened. The Karankawas apparently understood because they sat down and began to weep. For half an hour their wails could be heard all across the island. Cabeza de Vaca recalled: "Verily, to see beings so devoid of reason, untutored, so like unto brutes, yet so deeply moved by pity for us, it increased my feelings and those of others in my company for our own misfortune."

The Spaniards debated what to do next. In their present state, most of them would be dead by morning. The savages might agree to take them back to their village, but those who had served in New Spain feared they might end up as sacrifices to some pagan idol. Either way, Cabeza de Vaca pointed out, they were going to die. They might as well die warm and well fed.

While a small party of Indians stayed on the beach with their guests, others gathered firewood and hurried off toward their lodges. After dark the Indians carried the remnants of the expedition along a trail, literally lifting them by their arms so that their feet barely touched ground. On their way to the village they stopped four or five times to revive and warm themselves by fires built by the advance party. An hour later the Spaniards were secure inside a hut, with many fires and plenty of fish and roots. The Karankawas danced and celebrated throughout the night, which the Spanish took as a sign they were about to be sacrificed. But when the sun rose again over the narrow island, they were still alive.

That same morning Cabeza de Vaca made an extraordinary discovery. An Indian showed him a trinket and said he got it from "other men like ourselves." This had to mean that at least one other barge from the expedition had washed up on the island and that there were survivors. A short time later there was a joyous reunion with captains Andrés Dorantes and Alonso del Castillo and all their crew. Their barge had stranded on a reef a league and a half (3.9 miles) northeast of the village. They had escaped with only the clothes on their backs, which was more than Cabeza de Vaca and his crew had done, but their barge was wrecked beyond repair. The three captains agreed that they had no choice except to spend the winter on the Island. In the meantime, a four-member scouting party went ahead to search for Pánuco.

Either Cabeza de Vaca's memory was faulty or the winter of 1528–29 was about as bad as it gets on Galveston Island. The bay didn't freeze over, but no sooner had one blue norther ripped down from the prairie than another was on its way. The Karankawas had divided members of the expedition into small groups and placed them in various villages along the Island. The weather was too cold and stormy to fish or even pull roots, and the eighty surviving Spaniards went days without food. So did the Indians, of course, but they suffered without complaint.

Cabeza de Vaca was gaining a strange respect for these savages on whom he and his men depended, a stirring that he couldn't quite articulate. The Spaniards prayed out of habit, and out of fear, never daring to doubt that there was a divine presence overseeing all that happened. The Indians seemed to recognize a presence too, one as unyielding and merciless as any Old Testament deity. But it wasn't the same. Maybe it wasn't even a religion—maybe it was something as simple as an accord with nature—but the Karankawas surrendered themselves to the reality of constant sorrow.

And yet their generosity and compassion was unequivocal. "Of all the people in the world," Cabeza de Vaca wrote, "they are those who most love their children and treat them best." When their young died, as they did in great numbers that winter, the Indians seemed not only willing but absolutely fanatical in their determination to risk their own lives in ritual fasting. The Catholic religion was harsh, but no Spaniard would starve himself to death if he had a choice. And yet these savages unfailingly shared what little they had with these pitiful castaways, so superior in their attitude and yet so loathsome.

Something happened that winter that dramatically altered the relationship between the Spanish and the Indians and prompted Cabeza de Vaca to reflect again on who were the true savages. Five Spaniards had taken refuge alone down the Island; then one day there were only four. Then there were three, then two, until finally one poor wretch survived, surrounded by the well-picked bones of his comrades. They had eaten each other, all but one.

When the Karankawas learned what had happened, they were horrified. This tribe that has been so maligned by historians might understand a symbolic Last Supper in which the bodies of enemies were devoured, but eating a friend was an act so intolerable that they had never considered a response. "There was such an uproar," wrote Cabeza de Vaca, "that I verily believe if they had seen this at the beginning they would have killed [us] all."

The Indians didn't kill the surviving Spaniards, but they no longer considered them guests. Since the Spaniards had no skills with the bow and arrow, they were given women's jobs of pulling submerged roots from the rushes. It was backbreaking work under bitter cold conditions, and the sharp reeds of the marsh sliced Cabeza de Vaca's fingers until they bled. He was naked except for the rags taken off the bodies of fallen comrades. Hunger and abject misery were his only companions, and his only choice was to submit himself in total obedience to the savages. Ten months earlier he had landed on the coast of Florida under the banner of the sovereign, the emperor Charles V, vowing to subject such savages to the cross and sword; now he himself was subjected to an even harsher imperialistic mandate, the law of nature. To his credit, Cabeza de Vaca accepted his fate with courage and humility.

Starvation and cannibalism weren't the only tribulations in paradise that winter. A plague—probably cholera—killed half the Indians on the island and more than half of the Spaniards. By January only fifteen of the eighty castaways had survived. The Indians blamed the Spanish for their misfortune. Surely these visitors were sorcerers, most members of the tribe agreed, and the safe course would be to sacrifice those still alive. Then one Indian stepped forward with an appeal to reason: if the Spaniards had so much power, why was it that they had suffered and died, too? This was the first bit of European-style logic that the Spaniards had heard since their arrival on what they now called Isla de Malhado—the Island of Bad Luck.

Instead of killing the Spaniards, the Karankawas made them medicine men. This made no sense to Cabeza de Vaca, but he was cagey enough to keep quiet. Though the Indians recognized no chief or priest, they put enormous trust in their shamans and gave them special privileges. Shamans didn't pull roots or beg for fish heads. They were permitted to take two or even three wives, and the wives were expected to live together in harmony and friendship. Ordinarily, a Karankawa was limited to only one wife and was required to closely observe custom and tradition. Shamans on the other hand were free to do about anything they wanted. Shamans made the rules as they went along.

It didn't take Cabeza de Vaca and his men long to learn the new trade. Shamans cured the sick by breathing on their wounds or laying on hands or sometimes heated stones. First, the medicine man made a few cuts where the pain was located and sucked the skin around the incisions. Then he cauterized the wound with fire, a practical method to arrest infection. Finally, he breathed on the spot where the pain had been and the disease supposedly went away. The Spaniards added a few touches of their own, making the sign of the cross and reciting a Pater Noster and Ave Maria or two. The methods of the shamans weren't all that different from practices used by European physicians, who still treated gunshot wounds with boiling oil. To Cabeza de Vaca's surprise, most patients professed to be cured, at which time the patient was expected to give everything he owned, and everything he could borrow from relatives, to the shaman.

At the end of February the clan of Karankawas with whom Cabeza de Vaca had lived paddled back to the mainland, taking him with them. He went with mixed feelings. He realized now that the four-man party he had sent to find Pánuco had never made it, but he still held out hope that a Spanish ship might sail close enough to the Island to notice the castaways. He had lost track of the other members of the expedition by this time.

For the next two months the Karankawas lived beside an inlet to the mainland, subsisting on oysters and brackish water. At the end of April they migrated to the shore and ate blackberries and herbs, dancing and celebrating the entire month. Everywhere there were signs of new life. Fragrant weeds and wildflowers spread over the coastal prairie, and ducks and geese nested in the marshes, so thick you could have killed them with a stick. Why the Karankawas didn't is anybody's guess. According to the journal of Cabeza de Vaca, the Indians didn't hunt or fish or do much of anything else to sustain their existence during the rites of spring.

It is possible he didn't remember much about the spring of 1529: he became deathly ill, probably with malaria. During Cabeza de Vaca's delirium, captains Andrés Dorantes and Alonso del Castillo gathered the other survivors of the expedition—about a dozen remained—and made plans to start again for Pánuco. Finding Cabeza de Vaca near death, they decided to go without him. When he awoke days later, Cabeza de Vaca learned what had happened and realized that he had been abandoned.

For the remainder of the spring and throughout the summer, the Karankawas migrated from one campsite to another, moving every three or four days. Recovered now, Cabeza de Vaca was put to work carrying lodge mats, fetching firewood, and performing any other menial chore his masters could devise; apparently, he had lost his license to practice medicine during his own illness. When the black-berries played out, the tribe lived on wild onions, fish, and the meat of an occasional deer. Sometimes they caught lizards, snakes, rats, and giant spiders. His Majesty's royal treasurer, who had once turned up his nose at horsemeat, fell shamelessly on servings of roasted rat and baked tarantulas. But he was already devising a plan to escape.

On those rare occasions when his particular clan of Karankawas encountered other Indians, this white man with the bushy beard was always the center of attention. A constant state of warfare prevented most tribes from trading or bartering with each other, but he learned in conversations that they had no objection to his acting as their broker or intermediary. This was a role he courted with great enthusiasm, but he would have to wait for the right moment to break away.

When the Karankawas returned to the Island in October, Cabeza de Vaca made a discovery that was to sidetrack his escape for nearly three years. He wasn't the only Spaniard left behind: Lope de Oviedo had stayed by choice, though Cabeza de Vaca hardly recognized him. Less than a year before, Lope had been the only crewman strong enough to climb a tree. Now he looked numb and hollow, a walking dead man interested in nothing except the bare rudiments of survival—a dry place to sleep, some fish and roots, and an occasional romp with a squaw. He wanted no part of Cabeza de Vaca's escape plan.

Cabeza de Vaca found his chance to break away when the tribe returned to the mainland in 1530. For the next two years he lived alone in the wilderness, free to travel as he pleased. All things considered, life as a trader was infinitely better than life as a slave. He roamed 150 miles or more along the coast—always wondering what lay just to the south—and he ventured well into the forests of the interior. His stock was seashells and cockles, and beanlike fruit and herbs used in medicine and ritual dances. Indians saw him as a bearded curiosity who stayed among them at various times of the year, bringing news and trade goods and a manner that was unfailingly ingratiating. Wherever he went, Cabeza de Vaca was welcome and well treated. He was like one of them. He was as naked as they were, and he understood their customs and common phrases. He took part in their raids and moonlight rituals and learned to drink a bitter, mildly hallucinogenic tea that the Indians brewed from yaupon leaves and evergreen branches. He could have headed for Pánuco anytime he wished but Cabeza de Vaca couldn't bring himself to desert his addled and cowardly crewman, Lope de Oviedo. Each year he returned to the Island and each year Lope found a new excuse to stay put.

At last, in the summer of 1532, Lope agreed to follow Cabeza de Vaca down the coast, along his familiar trade route. Near Port O'Connor, on the southern tip of Matagorda Bay, Cabeza de Vaca discovered that three other members of the expedition long given up for dead were actually prisoners of the Quevenes. Andrés Dorantes, Alonso del Castillo, and the Moorish slave Estebanico had endured more than three years of cruel captivity but were at least alive and well. Joining them would mean that Cabeza de Vaca and Lope de Oviedo would also be prisoners, at least temporarily.

The prospect was too much for poor Lope. Preferring the familiar agony of the Island of Bad Luck to whatever lay ahead, Lope fled back in the direction he had come, never to be heard of again. Cabeza de Vaca was long past caring what happened to Lope. He described his reunion with the two Spanish captains as "the greatest pleasure we had enjoyed in life."

Using their old medicine-man cures to make their lives as comfortable as possible, the remaining four members of the expedition marked time and waited for their chance to run. They found it in the spring of 1535, during the Truce of the Tunas. While the various tribes were feasting on the sweet purple cactus fruit, Cabeza de Vaca and the Spaniards slipped away in the desert and headed south toward the Rio Grande.

Near the present Mexican border town of Reynosa they made another strategic error in navigation. Instead of turning southeast to the Gulf where they would have found Spanish settlements in another few weeks, they journeyed west into the rugged Sierra Madres. From Monclova, Mexico, they veered northeast, crossing the Rio Grande again and wandering through the hauntingly beautiful Big Bend Country. From there they went north along the the volcanic plains and limestone ridges of the Chihuahuan desert, crossing the Rio Grande a third time just downstream from El Paso del Norte. It was a circuitous route to salvation that took them two thousand miles out of their way.

During the long journey Cabeza de Vaca learned the fate of other members of the Narváez expedition. The barge carrying Don Pánfilo had washed up on the Texas coast near the San Bernard River, Dorantes and Castillo told him. Following an argument with his crew, Don Pánfilo had gone into one of his infamous sulks and insisted on spending the night aboard the barge; sometime during the night a storm carried the governor's barge out to sea for the last time. Crewmen from yet another barge had wintered near Rockport on Copano Bay, and, like their comrades on the Isla de Malhado, had eaten each other until only one remained, a man named Esquivel, who was subsequently captured by Indians. As for their long quest to reach the Spanish settlement of Pánuco, the settlement had been abandoned long ago, according to Dorantes' information.

Cabeza de Vaca's remarkable experience was nearly complete, but one final revelation was yet to take place, perhaps the bitterest one of all. In December 1535, as they made their way along the backside of the Sierra Madres, they began to hear stories of other Christians just beyond the mountains, toward the Gulf of California. Presently, they saw evidence with their own eyes. First, they noticed clusters of buzzards drifting high above the bean fields of adobe villages. As they drew closer, Cabeza de Vaca and his companions saw that the villages had been sacked, ravished, and burned. Skeletons hung from trees, Spanish rope twisted about their necks. Soon they found the survivors of these villages, chained together and whipped along by mounted and armored conquistadors. They had found their way back to Christian civilization.

# 5

AFTER THE departure of Cabeza de Vaca, the Karankawas had the Island mostly to themselves for nearly two hundred years, though Dutch pirates used it as a rendezvous point in the early 1600s. All the famous pirates operated in the Gulf of Mexico—Henry Morgan, Captain Kidd, Edward (Blackbeard) Teach. Hundreds of Spanish treasure ships passed along the Texas coast in the seventeenth century, bound for Cuba and Spain, and legend has it that pirates sometimes tied lanterns to the backs of burros and led them along the beach, hoping seamen would mistake them for passing ships and pile up on the reefs.

By the time Jean Lafitte arrived on the Island, just after the War of 1812, the pirate profession had assumed a quasi-legal status. Pirates preferred to be called privateers, the distinction being that, unlike pirates, privateers carried letters of marque from this or that nation, authorizing them to attack vessels with whom the nation was at war. In those days of revolution and Napoleonic conquest, nearly every nation was at war with someone. The three leading powers of Europe—France, England, and Spain—had extensive holdings in the Americas, as well as the Indies, and the Gulf became a particularly attractive hotbed for freebooters. The French preyed on the British, the British preyed on the Spanish, and a few freebooters preyed on any ship that happened along. In the early part of the nineteenth century, none was more dashing than Jean Lafitte.

To this day he endures as a folk hero of near-mythological pro-
portion.

A devilishly handsome man who dressed all in black and moved
with the grace of a dancer, Lafitte went out of his way to create a
mystique. He first showed up in New Orleans in 1806, with a man
named Pierre, who passed himself off as Lafitte's brother. Some
said that Lafitte's parents had been guillotined during the French
Revolution, and that Pierre was the son of a trusted servant who
smuggled the two boys to safety. Lafitte didn't deny the story. Others
said that Lafitte had killed a man in Charleston in a duel over a
woman, and had been forced to flee the United States and live as
a fugitive. Lafitte didn't deny this either. The brothers shared a
cottage in what is now the French Quarter, and entertained frequently and lavishly. Their parties were attended by everyone who
was anyone in Creole society. Jean spoke fluent French, Spanish,
and English, and was considered a bon vivant and connoisseur of
all things New Orleans' upper class held dear—food, wine, art,
fashion, table appointments. Pierre was a quiet, thickset man who
gave the appearance of stupidity because his eyes crossed, but who
was in fact a shrewd businessman. The brothers operated a small
blacksmith shop at the corner of Bourbon and St. Philip streets,
but most people understood that their true businesses were piracy
and smuggling.

Piracy and smuggling were largely a matter of legal semantics
in the early 1800s. An international treaty adopted in 1750 had
sought to reform the practice of privateering, requiring that any
sea captain who received letters of marque be a citizen of the country issuing the documents. Pirates flying the flag of France, for
example, didn't have to be citizens of France necessarily, but they
had to be citizens of a country that flew the French flag. That became
a problem in the late 1700s when the British fleet began capturing
French ports.

When the Leeward Islands port of Guadeloupe fell to the British
in 1810, there wasn't a single French seaport remaining in the West
Indies. What there were in great numbers, however, were ports that
flew the flag of Spain, nearly every one of them part of a newly
declared republic in open revolt against Spanish greed and domi-
nation. Jean Lafitte acquired citizenship and letters of marque from
the Colombian port of Cartagena, as did many other pirates. Getting
a commission from any of these Hispanic republics was almost as

easy as asking. What's more, the fleets of Spain were the fattest prizes in the Indies. They carried silver from Mexico; sugar, coffee, and spices from Jamiaca; gold and cotton and tropical fruit from South America. Nothing was more popular or more profitable than preying on Spanish ships, and nothing was easier.

As long as a privateer carried a letter of marque, he could loot and plunder any enemy vessel he captured and keep the ship and cargo as his prize. He could even scuttle the vessel and kill the crew if he wanted—these were legitimate acts of warfare. But there was one catch. Before the privateer could clear his cargo through customs and sell it legally, he needed approval from a court of admiralty. That meant first taking the cargo to some port that flew the same flag his man-of-war flew. Cartagena was a long way from the Gulf. On the other hand, the mouth of the Mississippi was a short voyage; and just upriver was the bustling port of New Orleans, where merchants were not picky about customs laws or the formality of courts of admiralty. Smuggled goods fetched lower prices than legitimate merchandise, but then smugglers didn't have to pay duty. In this milieu nobody asked a lot of questions.

Two years after Lafitte opened his blacksmith shop in New Orleans, the business of piracy and smuggling received a leg up from an unexpected source—the Congress of the United States. When Congress passed a law in 1808 prohibiting the importation of slaves, the price of slaves went out of sight and so did the rewards of smuggling them into the country. Before the law was enacted, a plantation owner could buy a good slave for $100; with the supply cut off, the price shot up to $1,000. Blackbirders (as slave smugglers were called) bought slaves on the coast of Africa for $20, but pirates got them free, simply by boarding and looting the blackbirders' vessels. When crooks stole from crooks, no letter of marque or court of admiralty was expected, and no authorities notified. Blackbirders and pirates were businessmen and both understood the cost of doing business. A new term was introduced among traders—black ivory.

Always the entrepreneur, Jean Lafitte put the slaves that he captured to work in his blacksmith shop: a black who knew the rudiments of the smith's trade had added value. Lafitte's true base of operation wasn't New Orleans, but a barrier island called Grand Terre, near the mouth of the Mississippi. Grand Terre was one of the islands that separated Barataria Bay from the Gulf, and it was

the home for a colony of the hardest and most black-hearted buccaneers anywhere in the world, a motley collection of French, Italian, Spanish, Portuguese, Dutch, and assorted other outcasts,
refugees, and adventurers. Lafitte organized them into a colony, a
sort of commune with himself as first among equals. He assigned
crews to the colony's fleet of low, fast schooners and feluccas, sent
them to sea in search of prizes, and logged them in again on their
return, dividing the loot among all hands and retaining a share for
himself and the organization. Lafitte had just one rule, but he enforced it without mercy: only ships flying the flag of Spain were to
be taken. Pirates who violated this rule were summarily executed.
Public opinion was on his side, Lafitte knew, and would stay that
way so long as his corsairs limited their raids to attacks against the
hated Spanish. But there was something else, something Lafitte did
not discuss. His own hatred of the Spanish was obsessive. No one
knew why.

With Pierre serving as a broker in New Orleans, Lafitte filled
orders from merchants as far away as New York and Philadelphia.
One of his most ingenious marketing strategies was the creation of
a way station called the Temple, located on an oak-clustered shell
mound along one of the countless bayous. When there was merchandise to be auctioned, Lafitte himself strolled across the Place
d'Armes, New Orleans' main plaza, passing out handbills: 1400
PRIME SLAVES AND LARGE QUANTITIES OF MERCHANDISE AT AUCTION!
The auctions attracted the best, the richest, and the most interesting
people in New Orleans. Planters, traders, and merchants—their
bejeweled Creole ladies outfitted in low-cut gowns—mingled with
pirates and comely quadroon maidens in dazzling head scarves.
They came, as though on command, to bid on a dazzling array of
merchandise—linens, silver, cinnamon, black ivory. Items sold at
bargain prices, but the purchaser also took on the obligation of
smuggling the goods back to New Orleans.

Governor William C. Claiborne, who had made it his mission to
rid Louisiana of Lafitte, occasionally sent dragoons to the Temple.
In January 1812 there was even a brief skirmish in which a customs
officer was killed. But Claiborne was little more than an annoyance
to Lafitte. A tactless and spiteful man, Claiborne had been appointed
to his post by President James Madison, and was regarded as an
outsider by the Creole population. He was constantly writing proclamations denouncing Lafitte, and Lafitte was constantly making

the governor an object of ridicule. Once, Claiborne issued a proclamation offering a $500 reward to anyone who would deliver
Lafitte to the sheriff of Orleans Parish. Two days later Lafitte issued
his own proclamations, offering $1,500 to anyone who would de-
liver the governor to Grand Terre. While Claiborne's dragoons were
searching the maze of bayous and creeks and swamps, Lafitte attended a birthday party for General Humbert at the Hotel de la
Marine, right under Claiborne's nose.

The War of 1812 made Jean Lafitte an American hero, but it also
ended his days as a pirate at Grand Terre. By offering his men and
arms to General Andrew Jackson, Lafitte helped turn the Battle of
New Orleans. Lafitte's Napoleon-trained artillery men in particular
inflicted terrible damage on the enemy. But in the swell of patriotism that gripped the city once the victory was secure, Lafitte's
reputation as a pirate was suddenly socially embarrassing. Stories
of pirate atrocities in the Indies, some of them greatly exaggerated,
turned public opinion against him. Merchants who once boasted
of their close relationship with the fabulous Lafitte snubbed him,
and society matrons dropped him from their must-invite lists. In
his own mind Lafitte was a privateer, not a pirate. He was without
question a patriot. Shortly before the battle he had refused a British
bribe to betray his adopted country, and in letters to the governor
and to General Jackson had vowed never to oppose the American
flag. Nevertheless, Lafitte now faced ostracism from all sides.

The most famous snub, and the one that convinced Lafitte that
his run of luck in Louisiana had ended, came during a lavish celebration party at the French Exchange. As Lafitte approached a
group of dignitaries that included Andrew Jackson and William
Claiborne, the governor looked at one of the generals and asked,
"Do you know Mr. Lafitte, General?" There was a moment of
stunned silence in which several members of the group turned their
backs, a slight that Lafitte could not mistake. His hazel eyes went
cold, then Lafitte said, "You know, Lafitte the *pirate!*" The general
laughed and extended his hand, but the humiliation of the incident
was permanent and decisive.

In the days that followed, Lafitte's officers began to drift away,
one by one, preferring retirement or a career in the Republic of
Venezuela or one of the other insurgent ports of the Gulf or the
Caribbean. Now that there was peace between the United States
and Great Britain, no major nations were at war. The only place a

corsair could obtain papers was from one of the colonies that had overthrown Spanish rule. Jean and Pierre Lafitte and a few of their most loyal men sailed to Haiti and tried to set up a new base of operation at Port-au-Prince, but they were refused papers.

At that propitious moment in history Lafitte learned through his network of agents that another island on another bay on the Gulf coast was about to be available for occupancy: Snake Island, the Indians called it. For several years the Island had been controlled by a band of corsairs under the command of a privateer named Don Louis d'Aury. But in April 1817, d'Aury decided to join an expeditionary force that was invading Mexico. Nine days after his departure Lafitte and forty buccaneers in seven ships sailed into Galveston Harbor and took control. When d'Aury returned to the Island in July, his own forces depleted by the unsuccessful invasion, he denounced Lafitte and his men as "a nest of pirates," but it was too late for complaining. Lafitte, the hero of the Battle of New Orleans, had already taken command in the name of the Mexican republican government and set up his own court of admiralty. D'Aury wisely decided to move his operation to New Grenada.

Lafitte had aged noticably in the last two years. Once so gay and dashing, he appeared now as a bitter and frustrated man, nearing forty, a little heavier, a little slower, his raven hair touched with gray, his shoulders slightly stooped as though he were carrying around an invisible sack of grain. He had grown a mustache, too, and taken to signing his name "Laffite," as if to acknowledge that he wasn't the man he used to be. His left eyelid drooped when he was tired, and closed when he engaged in conversation. His hazel eyes had lost their temper and showed the strain of command. Lafitte seem to realize that the day of the pirate was nearly finished.

The fortress town that Lafitte called Campeachy was built on the ruins of d'Aury's village, on the east end of the Island. Most of the houses were constructed of sailcloth and scrap timber, but Lafitte's own house was an impressive two-story structure of heavy masonry, painted red, its tower facing the bay and the noses of two cannons jutting from portholes. The wine cellar of La Mansion Rouge is still apparent today, beneath the ruins of a later structure at the foot of 15th Street.

Lafitte and his senior officers, several of whom had served under Napoleon, insisted on luxuries and refinements: wine and cognac were imported from New Orleans, along with provisions, building materials, and ammunition. A French physician was also brought in, though some of the men believed he was inferior to the Indian medicine men: when food poisoning devastated a shipload of French colonists, General Lallemand, who had commanded the artillery of Napoleon's imperial guard, ignored the French physician and called in a shaman from the mainland.

Campeachy resembled a boom town, a single main street lined with houses, taverns, gambling parlors (equipped with billiard tables), and the inevitable Yankee boarding house. At the edge of the bay were an arsenal, a dockyard, and a ship's repair shop, all stocked with the best examples of nineteenth-century technology. Lafitte's flagship, the *Jupiter*, armed with a 28-pound swivel gun and six 32-pounders, was said to be the fastest vessel in the Gulf.

The government created by Lafitte was the same sort of communistic arrangement used on the island of Barataria, with each man sharing the work and the profits. Strict discipline and adherence to rules was required of outsiders as well as members of the colony. Every pirate who sailed to Campeachy had to present his letters of marque and submit to the formality of Lafitte's court of admiralty, which he had created by executive decree shortly after his arrival on the Island.

There was also a local court to try crimes within the settlement, composed of a chief judge and thirteen jurymen. Murder, robbery, mutiny, and piracy were capital offenses. Lafitte, of course, was a one-man Supreme Court. It is possible—even likely—that Lafitte's colony never received formal recognition from the Mexican Republic; its court of admiralty was a sham to pacify Lafitte's need to be seen as a patriot. Indeed, there is ample evidence that Lafitte operated as a double agent, looting Spanish ships for the insurgents while selling information about the insurgents' movements to Spanish officials in Havana. One of Lafitte's greatest talents was the ability to talk out of both sides of his mouth.

The customs collector in New Orleans certainly did not regard Lafitte as a patriot. In letters to his superiors in Washington, the customs collector warned that Lafitte's smuggling operation was again in full swing. Under the Spanish-American treaty, the *Jupiter* and other vessels of the Galveston fleet were officially classified as pirate ships. On the pretext of ridding the Island of pirates, Washington offered to invade, but the Spanish delicately refused the offer: permitting American forces to set foot in Texas would have been tantamount to surrendering Spain's claim to control.

The colony on Galveston Island prospered beyond anyone's wildest dreams. As word spread throughout the Indies, sailors, and soldiers of fortune hastened to join. By the end of 1817 there were two hundred buildings in Campeachy and the settlement had a population of nearly a thousand, equal to Grand Terre at its peak.

Everyone was getting rich: ordinary deck hands made the fantastic sum of $150 a month. Buyers from nearly every port in the United States sailed to Campeachy to take advantage of the bargains, and still loot from Spanish ships piled up on the docks. Lafitte devised a plan to swap the excess to fur traders from the Texas interior. This may have been history's first example of money-laundering: the furs that Lafitte received in trade for the Spanish contraband were perfectly legal and easily sold in Jamaica, Martinique, or any American port.

The Island became the largest slave market in the New World. Blacks captured from Spanish slaving vessels were sold wholesale for $1 a pound. The average black weighed 140 pounds, and could be resold to Louisiana planters for as much as $1,000 dollars. One of the more energetic and clever traders of the frontier was James Bowie, who with his brothers made several trips to the Island in 1818–19. The Bowies bought slaves from Lafitte in lots of forty and transported them overland by way of Bolivar Point to Louisiana. Though the slave trade had been outlawed in the United States, there was a loophole that allowed smuggled slaves confiscated by the government to be sold at auction like any other contraband. The law also rewarded informers with payments equal to half the value of whatever was seized. Bowie delivered the slaves to a customs officer, becoming in effect an informer against himself. When the slaves were sold at auction, Bowie bought them back and resold them to planters at a price agreed on in advance. Profiting from both ends of this operation, Bowie and his brothers made $65,000 in two years.

Though the pirates traded with the Indians from the mainland and even married Indian women, they seldom saw the Karankawas, who lived on the opposite end of the Island at Three Trees. During a carnival celebrating the latest arrival of Spanish prizes in the fall of 1817, some of the pirates slipped down the Island and kidnapped a Karankawa maiden. A few days later the tribe retaliated by murdering a hunting party of four pirates, at which point Lafitte marched on Three Trees with two hundred men and two artillery pieces. In a series of bloody skirmishes, thirty warriors were killed and many on both sides wounded. After three days the Karankawas retreated across the shallow lagoon of West Bay, carrying their dead and wounded. Lafitte's men stayed away from Three Trees after that, and the Indians permitted pirates to hunt in peace.

A slave trader named Randall Jones who visited the Island in the summer of 1818 reported that a number of foreign schooners were anchored in the harbor, including a Yankee Clipper from Boston that came to swap potatoes and cured pork for sugar, cocoa, coffee, and wine. More buccaneers were arriving daily, some with women. Many seamen took black mistresses from the populations of slaves kept in Galveston to do domestic chores and handle cargo. New huts were being constructed all across the eastern end of the island; the population had swelled to nearly 2,000.

A hurricane that hit late in the summer almost wiped out the colony. At the storm's approach, Lafitte ordered that the women be evacuated to the Island's highest point, the ridge occupied by La Mansion Rouge and the fort. Then Lafitte and some of his officers went aboard a schooner anchored in the bay to ride out the storm. It was clear that this was a major hurricane. By midnight most of the Island was under water. More than a dozen ships were blown across the bay and torn to splinters. Houses vanished under walls of water. The fort collapsed. La Mansion Rouge stood against the gale, but sometime that night a cannon crashed through the tower floor into a room where the women were huddled. Many were killed and many more maimed, including a quadroon girl named Jeannette, who was either Lafitte's mistress, his housekeeper, or his daughter, depending on which story one believes. By dawn the storm had passed, but the settlement was in ruins, and hundreds of corpses were strewn along the beach. One historian estimates that at least half the members of the colony died.

In the face of that horrible adversity, Lafitte was magnificent. He formed the men into details, gathered timber from the wreckage of ships, constructed huts to shelter the wounded, and buried the dead in sand dunes. The major problem was lack of provisions. Little food remained and their supply of fresh water had been contaminated by the flood. While a party went to the mainland to look for food and water, Lafitte made a decision that horrified the population of Campeachy. The only way the colony could survive, he decided, was for all the blacks to go, even those who had married among Lafitte's men. Three days later all the blacks were herded aboard ship—some of them kicking and screaming—and sent to the slave market in New Orleans.

Lafitte also sailed for New Orleans, aboard the *Jupiter*, one of three ships that escaped the storm. There he secured a loan, which he used to buy provisions and material to rebuild the colony. But when he returned to the Island, Lafitte discovered Colonel George Graham, an officer of the United States government, waiting with an ultimatum. Depredations against Spanish shipping would no longer be tolerated, even in the cause of Mexican independence, Graham informed Lafitte. Washington was prepared to back up this order with force if necessary. Always the gentleman, Lafitte brought out his best wine and reaffirmed his loyalty to the United States. If Washington wanted him to go, he told Colonel Graham, then he had no choice except to go. But he didn't say when.

In the spring of 1819 Lafitte saw an opportunity to buy time. He learned from his agents in New Orleans of a bold plan to send an expeditionary force to capture and colonize Texas. The plot had been hatched by Aaron Burr. Embittered by his loss of the presidency to Thomas Jefferson—and cast out of American politics after killing his chief rival Alexander Hamilton in a duel—Burr intended to claim all the territory from the Mississippi to the Pacific Ocean and set himself up as emperor. In New Orleans, Burr sold the idea to General Wilkinson, commander of United States forces in the Southwest. Wilkinson eventually betrayed Burr, who was tried for treason, but Burr's grandiose scheme was passed on to other conspirators.

The conspirators selected as their leader an officer who had distinguished himself under Andrew Jackson, General James Long. Lafitte discovered that Long and an army of four hundred had already established a civil government in the East Texas settlement of Nacogdoches. Ostensibly, the purpose of Long's expedition was to assist the cause of Mexican independence—and it was, except not in the manner envisioned by Mexican patriots. Long assumed that Lafitte worked for the Mexican patriots and wrote asking the pirate to join his cause.

Lafitte replied with characteristic elegance and guile. He wrote to Long, assuring him that the emancipation of the Mexican provinces was his sole reason to exist, that he had defended the cause with his life for eight years and would never abandon it, but that since three major expeditions had already attempted and failed to invade Mexico, Lafitte would be negligent if he did not urge caution. Lafitte's letter—signed "your humble and very obedient servant"— promised everything and said nothing, but it convinced Long that Lafitte was his ally. Long personally traveled to the Island and formally declared it to be the port of entry of the new Republic of Texas. Then he appointed Lafitte governor of Galveston. Lafitte expressed gratitude in his usual flowery terms. No doubt he was sincere: he needed time to study the situation in the Gulf and Long had provided it.

A few months later, when it became apparent that Spanish pressure on Washington truly threatened the pirate trade, Lafitte wrote another of his famous letters—this one to the Spanish governor in Havana. Lafitte reported details of Long's plot and swore loyalty to Spain, suggesting that he would even welcome a Spanish flag flying over Galveston. This letter was signed "Jean Lafitte, Spanish Spy." The letter had its desired effect. Long's men were attacked and scattered by the army of the Spanish royalists and the leader was forced to flee for his life into Louisiana.

By early 1820 the pirate trade had about bottomed out in the Gulf. Fewer and fewer Spanish ships sailed out of Mexican ports, and those that did operated under the protection of heavily armed armadas. Morale was low among Lafitte's men. Quarrels and killings and desertion were common, and so were hangings. Bodies of men who had been hanged were left dangling for weeks, as a reminder that Lafitte was still in charge.

An incident in the fall of 1819 forecast Lafitte's doom. He sent two pirate cruisers into the Gulf under the command of a disreputable, mean-tempered captain named Brown. Though Brown was under explicit orders to attack only Spanish shipping, he landed instead on the coast of Louisiana, and sent a raiding party ashore to ransack the plantation of a wealthy planter named Lyons. The pirates terrorized the Lyons family, captured several slaves, and retreated to their ship with what they could carry—jewelry, linen, even wearing apparel. As it happened, the U.S revenue schooner *Lynx*, under the command of Captain Madison, was cruising nearby.

Brown ran his cruisers south, toward Galveston, with the *Lynx* in hot pursuit. Brown grounded his ships near Bolivar Point and escaped across the channel to Galveston Island. The *Lynx* promptly sent a landing party to the Island under the command of Lieutenant James M. McIntosh.

Lafitte treated McIntosh with great courtesy, offering wine while his men constructed a gallows to hang Captain Brown. Having hung Brown, Lafitte then ordered members of Brown's crew flogged and turned over to the Americans. Before the *Lynx* departed, Lafitte organized a banquet in honor of its officers and treated them to a day of hunting. In an article published later, McIntosh praised Lafitte and noted that "we passed a week with no common man; with one who, if he had his vices had also his virtues, and who possessed a courteous and gentlemanly deportment seldom equalled and not to be surpassed."

Early in 1821 the U.S. brig *Enterprise* was dispatched to Galveston with orders to disperse Lafitte and his pirates. Lafitte asked for two months to wind up his affairs, and in those two months settled accounts with his officers and men. Everyone was paid in full, and each man was given the opportunity to decide his future. Some wanted to follow Lafitte, though Lafitte seemed to have no idea where he was going from here. Others wanted to settle in Texas. Whatever each man decided, he had to agree to leave the Island. Lafitte intended to burn the colony.

When the *Enterprise* returned to Galveston Bay in the spring of 1821, Lafitte was packed and ready to sail. Work parties were dismantling the fort and carrying ballast aboard the ships of the flotilla. The pirate fleet had been reduced to three ships: the others had already been scuttled. Lafitte and most of his men had gone aboard a black, clipper-built schooner. An old seadog chewing the stub of a cigar told the officers of the *Enterprise* that Lafitte was waiting to entertain them aboard the schooner.

Lafitte met them at the gangplank. He was dressed simply, in foraging cap and blue frock. The officers of the *Enterprise* found it hard to believe that this rumpled, overweight figure was the legendary pirate, Jean Lafitte. With a wry smile Lafitte called their attention to the body of a pirate dangling from a gallows on the beach, and to two fresh graves in the dunes just beyond. "That villain plundered an American ship," Lafitte explained. "As for the graves, those men were caught in a plot to murder my steward." Lafitte shook his head at the injustice of it all and said, "They call me a pirate, but I might have done them some good service when I lay at Barataria."

The aging pirate led them to his cabin where a feast of wild turkey, stew, sun-dried fish, and French wine had been laid out. Several toasts were offered. As the men began to eat, they were astonished by the sudden appearance of a strikingly beautiful quadroon woman who smiled and joined them. One officer described her later as "a full and voluptuous form of faultless outline, beautiful features and sleepy black eyes, with the blackest and most luxuriant hair that ever curled."

Lafitte didn't introduce her. He was telling a story of cannibals who had killed and eaten two of his men at Matagorda Bay, and seemed hardly aware that she was in the room. The woman sipped wine and divided oranges into quarters, which she gave to the young officers around her. Beguiled by this enchanting creature who "flirted dreadfully," the crew of the *Enterprise* barely heard Lafitte. Then there was a single glance from Lafitte, a look so sharp that it crackled. Without a word the quadroon woman set her glass on the table and disappeared into her stateroom. Lafitte called for more wine and filled everyone's glass. "Come, gentlemen," he said. "You do not like my wine?"

"I should like very much to hear your life, Captain," one officer said.*

Lafitte smiled and shrugged his shoulders. "It is nothing extraordinary," he said. "I can tell it in very few words. But there was a time"—he paused and drew a long breath—"a time when I could not tell it without cocking both pistols. Bah. I tell you my life.

"Eighteen years ago I was a merchant in San Domingo. My father before me was a merchant. I had become rich. I had married a wife. She was rich and beautiful." Lafitte stifled a sigh and took a sip of wine, then continued. "I determined to go to Europe, and I wound up all my affairs in the West Indies. I sold my property there. I bought a ship, and loaded her, besides which I had on board a large amount of specie, all that I was worth. Well, sir, when the vessel had been a week at sea, we were overhauled by a Spanish

*In an article written by one of the officers from the *Enterprise* and published years later, Lafitte offered the only firsthand account of his background known to exist, supplying among other things a reason for his obsessive hatred of the Spanish.

man-of-war, commanded by Señor Chevalier d'Alkala. Yes, I remember his name, for I settled my debt with him afterwards. At any rate, the Spanish captured us. They took everything—goods, specie, even my wife's jewels. They set us on shore upon a barren sand key, with just provisions enough to keep us alive a few days, until an American schooner took us off and landed us in New Orleans. I did not care what happened to me. I was a beggar. My wife took fever from exposure and hardship and died three days later. I met some daring fellows, who were as poor as I was. We bought a schooner and declared a war against Spain. So long as I live I am at war with Spain, but no other nation. Although they call me a pirate, I am not guilty of attacking any vessel of the English or French. I showed you the place where my people have been punished for plundering American property. At New Orleans I refused to be the enemy of America. Captain, will you take coffee?"

That night Lafitte burned Galveston and sailed away forever. The crew of the *Enterprise* watched as Lafitte's three ships cleared the harbor bar, their billowing sails dappled from the firelight and the deep shadows of the sea. They moved silently before the wind until they were three specks on the horizon, then they seemed to drop off the face of the earth.

Nobody knows what happened to Jean Lafitte. Some say he died at sea, off the coast of Yucatán, after rescuing Napoleon from St. Helena. That sounds like something Lafitte might have done. The problem is, Napoleon died at St. Helena shortly before Lafitte left Galveston. Another story claims that Lafitte was the illegitimate son of John Paul Jones, and that these two old pirates, Lafitte and Uncle John Paul, are buried together in an unmarked grave on Goose Bayou in Louisiana.

In the decades after Lafitte's disappearance he was portrayed in popular magazines as a dashing young adventurer, maligned and misunderstood by authorities. "Mayhap 'tis true," wrote one gushing reporter in an 1831 issue of *Casket* ("a magazine for young women"). A young woman named Emma Hortense Mortimore Laflin, who lived in Charleston, South Carolina, read that article, or one like it, and became so enamored of Lafitte that she fantasized that she ran away from her husband, John Laflin, and became Lafitte's bride. This fascinating theory is advanced in a book titled *Great Forgers and Famous Fakes*, by Charles Hamilton.

A family Bible that turned up a century later in New Orleans is inscribed: "To Mademoiselle Emma Hortense Mortimore, Jean Lafite"—that's how the pirate's named was usually misspelled in print back then. On the inside front cover of the Bible, a handwritten family history records that Lafitte married Emma Hortense Mortimore in 1832, and that he died in 1854 and was buried in Alton, Illinois.

Hamilton writes that in the late 1940s, a con man and forger named John Laflin, who claimed to be Lafitte's great-grandson, breezed through Texas, peddling letters, documents, a journal, and even a family Bible that supposedly belonged to the infamous pirate. The curator from the archives of former Texas Governor Price Daniel forked over $20,000 for a portion of the collection: some of the papers are still stored in the Sam Houston Regional History Center at Liberty, and others show up from time to time on the philographic markets of New Orleans or St. Louis.

Hamilton and other experts exposed Laflin as a con man and forger, but the interesting part of this story is that he may have inherited these bad habits from his well-intended great-grandmother—Emma Hortense Mortimore Laflin.

# 6

COLONEL STEPHEN F. Austin, not General James Long, is known as the Father of Texas. But Long got close. He married the Mother of Texas.

Undeterred by Lafitte's betrayal and the humiliation of his first failed expedition—survivors were arrested by government officials in New Orleans and paraded down Charles Street—General Long assembled another army and established a fort on Bolivar Peninsula, across the channel from Galveston Island. When Lafitte departed, the general moved some of his troops to the Island. Galveston was still to play a strategic role in his obsession to invade Mexico.

Long had hoped that his vainglorious scheme would attract thousands of volunteers, but only a few hundred came forward. It was a measure of Long's ego and ambition that he continued to believe he could conquer a country the size of Mexico, and a testament to his foolhardiness that he believed he commanded loyalty. Some of Long's men were patriots to the cause of Mexican independence, but many more were soldiers of fortune or fugitives; Long had trouble distinguishing between the two.

The more the general's invasion plans were delayed, the more they were imperiled by his own stupidity. First, there was trouble with Karankawas. Long decided to teach the Indians a lesson after they attacked and butchered the crew of a French sloop that ran aground on the Island. With only thirty men Long attacked a much

larger force of Indians. Forced to retreat, Long left behind his dead
and wounded, which hardly endeared him to his men. A short time
later the general hanged one of his officers for insubordination. The
victim was a popular young colonel named Modellio, and his execution was viewed by other Mexicans under Long's command as
an act nearly tantamount to murder.

In the fall of 1821, Long learned of a rebellion at La Bahía Pres-
idio (the present town of Goliad), and, with a contingent of troops,
marched off to help, leaving his wife and fifty men at Fort Bolivar.
Mrs. Long never saw her husband again. Months later she learned
that he had led his men into Mexico and been assassinated in Mexico City, probably in retaliation for the murder of Colonel Modellio.

Jane Wilkinson Long was a gentle and refined woman, the niece
of General James Wilkinson, who had been deeply implicated in
Aaron Burr's plot. In the fall of 1821, a few weeks after Long
marched off on his final expedition, the troops that he left behind
to protect Fort Bolivar and his family began to drift away. Jane
Long could have gone with them, but she had promised the general
that she would wait for him at the fort. And that is what she did.

Pregnant and alone with her young daughter, a black servant
girl, and a dog, Jane Long waited all winter. The winter of 1822
was one of the worst ever: for a quarter of a mile out from shore
Galveston Bay froze solid. Across the narrow channel Jane Long
could see the campfires of the Karankawas and hear their bloody
yelping. To prevent attack she hoisted her red flannel petticoat on
the fort staff and fired cannons.

She chopped a hole in the ice and caught fish with a handline,
and when her fishhooks were lost, she seined with an old hammock
and stored her catch in a pickle barrel of brine. Sometime that
winter she gave birth to a child. General James Long is a footnote
in Texas history, but in honor of the fact that her child was the first
born to an American settler on the Texas frontier, Jane Long will
always be known as the Mother of Texas.

Over the next fourteen years Long's dream of an independent
Texas became a reality under Stephen F. Austin and his followers.
What Long tried to do by force, Austin attempted by means of
diplomacy. Austin had a contract with the Mexican government to
colonize land between the watersheds of the Brazos and Colorado
rivers. The ongoing revolution in Mexico made all agreements tenuous, but Austin kept the faith and insisted that his colonists ob-

serve strict neutrality. If the empresario had any thoughts of an independent Texas, he kept them to himself.

Shiploads of settlers began arriving at the port of Galveston in 1822. People crowded the decks to get a look at the ruins of the fort occupied by Lafitte and later by General Long. Galveston Bay was still largely uncharted—six hundred square miles of deceptively placid water. One of the first schooners to arrive, the *Revenge*, piled up on Red Fish Bar and sank with all its stores. The eighty colonists aboard were able to reach the west bank safely, however, and started the first permanent settlement on the San Jacinto River.

The bay had changed in the three hundred years since Cabeza de Vaca explored it. Directly north of Lafitte's fort, across a narrow channel, a shell bank called Pelican Island had risen out the water. Off to the west near Virginia Point a marsh was beginning to transform into what would later be called Deer Island. South of the bay, a rifle shot from the western tip of Galveston Island, was the mouth of the Brazos River, which led inland to Austin's colony at San Felipe, just west of Houston. But there was no harbor at the mouth of the Brazos in those days (Freeport is there today) and so the route to the San Felipe colony was across Galveston Bay and up Buffalo Bayou. Though Galveston was the official port of entry and thus part of the colony, immigrants were encouraged to settle inland and leave the the Island to the Karankawas.

LOOKING BACK, it is obvious that the Karankawas were already doomed to extinction. The Island was too attractive for white settlers to ignore. It abounded with game, and there was supposed to be buried treasure. Hunters prospered by selling meat and game to mainlanders—deer, geese, teal and canvasback ducks, red fish (settlers called them the cod of the Gulf), perch, trout, oysters, crabs, shrimp, turtles.

Most hunters coexisted peacefully with the Indians, but treasure seekers were another breed. In 1821 a twenty-man party headed by a doctor named Purnell came looking for gold and found a hundred Karankawas dancing and singing at Three Trees. The Indians had stripped the sails from a ship abandoned by pirates and were using them as shelter. If the Indians had found a ship, Purnell reasoned, they must have found gold, too. He waited until dark and then attacked. After a brief battle the Indians retreated, carrying off their dead and wounded.

Over the next decade there were numerous battles with the Karankawas along the coast, and each time the tribe diminished. It wasn't just their numbers that were dwindling. The Karankawas began to lose their hold on the traits and customs that had sustained them since before the time of Columbus—their self-reliance and self-respect, and their disdain for the white man's ways and his material possessions.

Samuel May Williams, Austin's trusted assistant, traded tobacco to the Karankawas in 1821. Spaniards who occupied La Salle's old fort on Lavaca Bay tried to Christianize them, and sent a number of Karankawas to the Spanish mission in Refugio. The family of Mexican empresario Martín de Léon, who had settled near Victoria, tried to exterminate the tribe with poison, which they mixed with boiled corn (hominy) and distributed among the Indians. To the astonishment of the de Léons, the tribe appeared again the following morning, begging for more. Apparently, the trader who was supposed to supply the arsenic substituted cream of tartar.

Gradually, the Karankawas forgot the clannish ways of their ancestors and took up with any group that would feed and protect them. Squaws begged sacks of flour and matches to start their fires. Warriors coveted the weapons of whites and took European names. Chief Antonio, who was born and baptized in the Spanish mission at La Bahía, negotiated a treaty with Stephen F. Austin in 1824, promising that the Karankawas would abandon their traditional hold on Galveston Island and move 150 miles down the coast, west of the San Antonio River. Many ignored the treaty and were butchered by settlers or by other Indians.

One group of Karankawas fleeing the Apaches surrendered themselves to members of DeWitt's Colony in Gonzales, preferring to survive as indentured servants rather than risk life in a hostile wilderness. Another band was annihilated by Mexican cattlemen near the Kinney Ranch, southwest of Corpus Christi. And still another was caught stealing cattle on Padre Island, where they were lined up against a sand dune and shot. The few who survived migrated into Mexico and became part of the greater mestizo population. By 1847 the tribe was extinct.

AS EMPRESARIO of the colony in San Felipe, one of Stephen Austin's toughest jobs was convincing his Anglo-American settlers to stay out of Mexican politics. Various factions were struggling for control of the Mexican government, but Austin preached a policy of strict neutrality. Most of the colonists were able to live with that part of the bargain that required that they become citizens of Mexico. Their capital was Saltillo in the Mexican state of Coahuila, which was a long way from San Felipe, roughly seven hundred miles to the southwest. The Texans had little in common with the citizens of Coahuila: their commercial, cultural, linguistic, and religious ties were with the United States. As long as the Mexican belligerents concentrated on fighting each other, Austin believed, the colony was secure.

The other part of the deal was irresistibly sweet. A family man could buy 640 acres for 12.5 cents an acre, about a tenth of the cost of similiar land in the United States. Some of the more avaricious Americans purchased enormous tracts: Colonel Samuel May Williams, Austin's clerk, had acquired 48,000 acres by 1831, and was looking to buy a lot more. Whatever the drawbacks of Mexican citizenship, most of the colonists were content at first. If the rulers of Mexico had made a nominal effort to govern Texas with justice and fair play, there probably wouldn't have been a revolt.

For nearly ten years Austin played a dangerous double game with the warring factions in Mexico. Two sides had emerged—the Centralists, composed of the artistocracy, the clergy, and most of the military, and the Federalists, who favored a pragmatic self-ruling republic modeled after the government of the United States. Santa Anna had become the Centralist dictator, reorganizing the party to suit his own ambitions.

In 1830 Santa Anna rammed a bill through the Centralist congress designed to Mexicanize the Anglo settlements of Texas. The new law restricted immigration to native Mexicans and Europeans and required all Texas immigrants to embrace the Catholic faith. Worse yet, it imposed stringent duties on commerce—a customs house was built on the east end of Galveston Island—and prohibited Texans from organizing a militia. Military oppression and unfair taxation sounded a particularly ominous note: just fifty years earlier, in 1776, the grandfathers of these settlers had revolted against the British over similiar injustices.

In 1833 Austin traveled to Mexico City to petition Santa Anna to repeal the noxious law of 1830, but Santa Anna had him arrested and imprisoned. This is when it finally occurred to the empresario that war with Mexico was the only recourse for Texas.

With Austin in jail, his clerk and chief assistant, Samuel May Williams, assumed control of the land office at San Felipe. Colonists viewed Williams as brusque and cold-hearted, a man interested chiefly in lining his own pockets. The empresario had hired Williams as his clerk in 1822, shortly after Williams and a woman companion arrived in Galveston aboard the sloop *Good Intent*, registered under the alias of Mr. and Mrs. E. Eccleston. An arrogant and cunning man, Williams had lost his fortune in New Orleans in the Panic of 1818 and escaped owing large sums of money. His was not an unfamiliar story. Many Americans seeking to escape harsh debtor laws sought asylum in Texas—the epithet GTT (Gone to Texas) was tacked to the doors of farmhouses and small stores all across the South and Midwest. Few of the financial fugitives had Williams' talent or background for recovery, however.

The nephew of a Baltimore financier, Samuel May Williams had learned banking, insurance, and the techniques of commerce in his uncle's commission house. The Williams family made a fortune shipping foodstuffs to Argentina and the rebellous Spanish colonies in exchange for hides and specie. In Argentina, Sam Williams learned Spanish and French and observed firsthand the sort of Latin republicanism that required playing both ends against the middle.

He had had several dealings with Jean Lafitte, first in Baltimore, where Lafitte had come to buy sails from Williams' brother, then later in Washington, D.C., and New Orleans. Sam Williams lived in New Orleans in 1818 and served in a volunteer militia that tracked down the fugitive survivors of Long's first expedition. Three years later Williams himself was a fugitive. Stephen F. Austin was looking for a bilingual clerk to assist in the preparation of deeds and in correspondence with Mexican authorities. When he heard that an immigrant named E. Eccleston had business experience and understood Spanish and French, Austin hired him immediately, no questions asked. Why Williams fled New Orleans using the name of a woman companion—or who the woman was—isn't clear. She was variously reported to be an actress, the wife of a circus owner, a rich widow, and a "high-born Spanish lady" from Cuba. Whoever she was, Williams abandoned her four years later and married a younger woman.

While Stephen Austin rotted in a Mexican jail, Williams hatched a plot to buy some land on the cheap from the corrupt state legislature in Coahuila. A virtual state of civil war existed in Coahuila by now. The government had split into two capitals—the old one in Saltillo, occupied by the Santanistas, and the new capital in Monclova under the flag of the Federalists. The deputies in Monclova had quickly developed a reputation for shady deals and fast bucks.

They had already sold millions of acres of public land to speculators when Williams traveled to Monclova with a petition asking them to sell some more. The request was cloaked under the best of intentions: the money would be used to equip an army to defend the colonies in Texas. The deputies were agreeable. When it was announced that they were selling four hundred square leagues—in faraway northeast Texas, far from Austin's colony—Williams jumped in with an offer to buy. He wanted to close the deal before the public got wind of the bargain. He was eventually able to purchase one hundred square leagues—more than 375,000 acres—for one-fifth the price advertised in Monclova. For this Samuel May Williams would be branded a "Monclova speculator," a term that for many years denoted an unprincipled scoundrel.

The land grab wasn't Williams' only act of legerdemain during that session of the Monclova legislature. He also convinced the deputies to grant him a bank charter, which would allow him to circulate his own bank notes. Texans distrusted banks. Getting his hands on a bank charter after the revolution that was clearly imminent would have been next to impossible, especially for a man with Williams's reputation.

Before leaving Monclova, Williams peddled $85,000 in stock in his new venture. After that he severed his connection with the Austin colony and turned his full attention to a business of his own, which eventually included helping found the city of Galveston.

# 7

DURING WHAT came to be known as the Texas Revolution, Galveston Island was the capital, and nearly the final retreat for General Sam Houston and his ragtag army. Except for a decisive battle across the bay, on the banks of the San Jacinto River, Galveston might have gone down in history as the second Alamo, and Texas might be part of Mexico.

If ever a man seemed destined to lead a rebel army, it was Sam Houston. A man of intrigue and daring, Houston was intemperate, grave, and deeply committed to democratic visions of his own design. He mixed statesmanship with theatrics, and when sweet reason didn't work, he used bullying force. As governor of Tennessee, Houston had been the focus of a marvelous scandal when his bride of a few months suddenly ran home to her parents. Houston offered no public explanation, and threatened to kill any man indelicate enough to stain his wife's honor with speculation. He resigned his office in disgrace, and for years lived among the Cherokees, who knew him as "Big Drunk." Like many other outcasts of his generation, Houston ended up in Texas. He was exactly the sort of man to rally an army of rowdies and misfits, and settlers rushed to join up.

While Houston was putting together an army, Samuel May Williams was in New York selling stock for his proposed bank. When Williams heard that Texas was forming a republic and getting ready to fight, he hurried to Baltimore and worked out a deal to supply arms and equipment. Using his brother's credit, Williams also purchased the 125-ton schooner *Invincible* and dispatched it to Galveston.

The pending war with Mexico did not deter immigration. In the years between 1831 and 1836, the population of Texas grew from about seven thousand to nearly fifty thousand. Many of the colonists came from Europe, especially from Germany, where petty tyrants and feudal laws dominated the political and social systems, and where liberty consisted mainly of the freedom to leave. The European immigrants were mostly educated and cultured, traits that put them at odds with many of the Anglo-American settlers: for example, most Europeans opposed slavery.

They brought with them books, paintings, music and an intellectual curiosity. One of the most interesting families was a group of Prussian aristocrats from Westphalia named Von Roeder. Rosalie Von Roeder Kleberg, who had married a young German lawyer named Robert Kleberg, brought the first piano to Texas.

That the piano arrived at all was a small miracle. The ship carrying the Kleberg and Von Roeder party sank three days before Christmas 1834, in shallow water near Galveston's East Beach. Why the ship sank was a mystery: Robert Kleberg suspected the crew intentionally scuttled it. As the ship foundered, Kleberg and the others threw their goods—including the piano, crates of books, oil paintings, and engravings—over the side. All the passengers and most of their possessions made it safely to shore.

Using the sails, mast, and beam from the wrecked schooner, the Germans constructed a large tent with separate apartments for women and children. There was plenty of deer and fowl on the Island, and the group survived fairly comfortably while Robert Kleberg made his way to the mainland to seek assistance.

Robert Kleberg was both a lawyer and an idealist. He had learned of Texas almost by accident, from a letter describing the generous land grants offered by the government of Mexico. "We were enthusiastic lovers of Republican institutions," Kleberg wrote. "Full of romantic notions and ideas, believing to find in Texas, in preference to all other countries, the blessed land of our sanguine hopes."

What he found was a land in revolt. Leaving his wife and other members of his party on the Island, Kleberg went to San Felipe. He carried letters of introduction to Stephen Austin and Sam Williams, and arranged to charter a sloop to rescue those who had waited in Galveston and bring them up Buffalo Bayou to Harrisburg, now part of the city of Houston. Harrisburg was soon to be the capital of the Republic of Texas. Though Kleberg's small colony of German aristocrats had no intention of settling in Harrisburg, they built cabins and fenced off fields for planting.

By the winter of 1836, Santa Anna and his army of five thousand had pushed across the Rio Grande and were marching toward San Antonio. The Alamo fell on March 6—William Travis, Jim Bowie, Davy Crockett, and all its other defenders were killed.

Three weeks later there was a second massacre in Goliad. If anything, this one was even more heinous than the Alamo: when Colonel J. W. Fannin ordered his men to surrender to the much-larger Mexican army, Santa Anna had Fannin and his men executed. Despite the reverses, Texas declared its independence, drafted a constitution and set up the first government of the Republic of Texas in Harrisburg. David G. Burnet, another empresario, who operated the Galveston Bay & Texas Land Company, was elected president. Everyone in Texas was preparing for war.

Robert Kleberg sent the women, children, and old men of his colony back to Galveston for safety, then he and the other younger men joined the army of General Sam Houston. The Klebergs abandoned their cabin: the piano, the paintings, and everything else was left for the invading Mexican army to loot and burn. Everywhere families were fleeing. Most headed east, across the Sabine River to Louisiana, but some sailed down the bay to Galveston Island, which almost everyone agreed would be the last refuge for the new Republic of Texas.

Santa Anna's army was sweeping unchecked across Texas, while Houston's army was in full retreat. President Burnet fired off a letter to his commander in chief, urging him to stand and fight. "Sir," he wrote, "the enemy are laughing you to scorn. You must fight them. You must retreat no further. . . ."

On paper Houston's army numbered nearly 2,000 but in fact there were less than half that many under arms: many had deserted to save their own families. General Sam was buying time, probing for an advantage to use against the much-larger Mexican army and its egomaniacal commander.

By April 19 the capital in Harrisburg was deserted and so was

almost every other town and settlement in the Republic. President
Burnet had taken his family and staff to Galveston and set up a
new capital.

There was only one building on the Island, the old Mexican customs house. The president and his family—and the members of
Burnet's cabinet and their families—slept on the sand, under borrowed blankets. Fear, panic, and total confusion gripped the Island.
There was an outbreak of fever and the threat of starvation. About
the only food available was a cargo of flour, lard, rice, and biscuits
that the crew of the *Invincible* had looted from a Mexican brig. The
schooner that Sam Williams had dispatched from Baltimore had
already proved invaluable in several encounters with the Mexican
navy. The *Invincible* and two other ships, the *Brutus* and the *Independence*, made up the Texas Navy and constituted the primary
defense of Galveston. Colonel James Morgan commanded a small
volunteer militia, but it was untrained and poorly armed. Morgan
had a single piece of artillery and no way to mount it. Using sand,
their only available material, the militia constructed a fortification
that they called Fort Travis in memory of the commander of the
Alamo.

Burnet and his officers did what they could. The *Invincible*
guarded the approach from West Bay. The *Brutus* anchored to the
east, its armament trained on the harbor entrance. The *Independence* lay off the garrison in the channel. There was no way to
communicate with the army on the mainland and invasion was
expected daily. Burnet declared martial law—among the population
were looters from New Orleans. Every man over the age of sixteen
and under fifty-six was mustered into the militia. The men gathered
around the pile of sand they called a fort, speaking of duty and
honor and vowing to fight to the death. Women and children waited
under canvas awnings, trying to act brave.

Nobody on the Island knew it yet, but the war was over and Texas
had won. The decisive battle had taken place on April 21, on a
marshy peninsula where Buffalo Bayou intersected the San Jacinto
River. Santa Anna had made the strategic mistake of positioning
his army with its back to the water, only about a mile from Houston's camp in a grove of live oaks. The Mexican dictator was so
confident of victory he didn't even bother to post sentries.

For all his pretenses, Santa Anna was almost comically inept as
a commander. He knew so little about the local geography that he

believed the rain-swollen streams his army had crossed were the result of snow melting and running down from nearby mountain ranges. Some of his officers believed that Santa Anna was a raving lunatic: he was certainly addicted to opium. On the afternoon of the attack, Santa Anna was relaxing in his three-room tent, smoking opium and —legend has it—dallying with a mulatto servant girl who would henceforth be known as the Yellow Rose of Texas.

The Battle of San Jacinto lasted just eighteen minutes, though the killing went on for several days. Memories of the Alamo and Goliad boiled over. Deep-seated racial hatreds, long subdued and subjected to the realties of life on the frontier, rushed to the surface. Houston tried to stop the orgy of revenge, riding among his troops shouting "Gentlemen! Gentlemen! Gentlemen!" It was too late. Mexicans fleeing for the woods were run down by the cavalry and slaughtered without mercy. Other Mexicans retreated toward the bayou and stood with their backs to a slough, arms raised in surrender and trembling voices pleading, "Me no Alamo! Me no Goliad!" Rebel soldiers pursued them to the water's edge, then began firing and kept firing until the slough was so filled with dead that it was possible to walk across it.

Sam Houston lost three men in the battle, but Santa Anna lost his entire army—400 dead, 200 wounded, 730 taken prisoner. For days afterward, the fields of San Jacinto were littered with corpses. At night the Mexican prisoners sat huddled against the cold, listening to the howls of wolves feasting on the remains of their comrades and wondering how long it would be before the rest of them were shot.

It was nearly a week before news of victory reached President David Burnet and the refugee government on Galveston Island. A detail led by R. J. Calder had left San Jacinto by skiff the morning after the battle, but locating and reaching Galveston wasn't as easy as it appeared.

None of the men had ever navigated the great bay before. Hungry, dog-tired, probably a little shellshocked from battle, Calder and his three companions fought wind and strong currents until they were close to collapse. They camped one night on a deserted river island where they found a barrel of cornmeal and a flock of chickens. "If memory serves me," Calder wrote, "I think seven well-grown fowl were sacrificed during our stay."

Their skiff leaked badly as they tried to cross the wide part of the bay, and a stiff south wind forced them to turn back. They waded near the shore of the mainland, pulling their skiff and looking for a narrow place to cross. On a shell bank they found a runaway slave who spoke no English but gave them some food and cigars.

A steamer passed near Red Fish Bar, but its crew either didn't hear their shouts for help or chose to ignore them. Just after sunset of their fourth day, they spotted the hazy outline of Galveston. When Calder's detail finally found the president's camp on the morning of the fifth day of their journey, Burnet was furious over the delay and threatened to have them arrested. Later he cooled down and offered them brandy (Calder would later admit that they had already had several brandies, supplied by refugees and military men they had encountered along the way).

In his memoirs Calder describes the frenzy of excitement and the irrational seizure of paranoia that greeted their message of victory. Ships anchored in the bay fired salutes. Men and women and children danced on the beach. A woman who had just given birth to twins insisted on hearing the details of San Jacinto before she agreed to rest. Many refugees refused to believe or accept the news. Calder and the others were probably spies, some concluded. Santa Anna himself taken prisoner? His entire army defeated? It was too much.

"These fellows are deserters and are running away from the army," one man screamed. "They ought to be dealt with as such." Before the man could incite a lynch mob, there was a commotion down the beach and people began to scatter in all directions. Calder saw the Island commandant, Colonel James Morgan, astride his galloping horse, waving his sword and barking orders: "Turn out, men! Turn out or we'll be in hell in five minutes!" A lookout had reported that a thousand Mexican troops were advancing from the west end of the Island. This turned out to be an embarrassing exaggeration. What the jittery lookout had really seen was some laundry flapping in the wind.

When Robert Kleberg, Louis Von Roeder, and the other German immigrants found passage to the Island some days later, they found their families sick with fever and weak from hunger. Kleberg hadn't heard from his wife for more than a month. He had written her a letter from San Jacinto, using pokeberry juice for ink. It had apparently just arrived because Kleberg found her sitting in front of her tent, trying to decipher his pale scratchings.

Her wan and frail appearance overwhelmed him. "This was indeed the saddest picture of those trying and eventful days," he wrote. None of the families on the Island had food or medicine, except the scanty rations they drew from the government. The weather was cold and frequently stormy, and nobody had any idea what might happen next. Mrs. Otto Von Roeder awoke one night to see a huge alligator, its jaws open, a few inches from the heads of her sleeping children.

President Burnet moved his headquarters to the mainland and troops on the Island felt abandoned. Fights broke out among the men. Orders from officers were ignored. The government was virtually bankrupt. There weren't enough supplies to feed the troops and refugees, much less the several hundred Mexican prisoners who arrived at Galveston in early May.

Sam Houston arrived aboard the steamer *Yellowstone*, on his way to New Orleans to receive treatment for an ankle wound. In one of his characteristically dramatic gestures, General Sam had himself carried ashore on his cot and there he addressed his troops, promising that things would get better. He wasn't too convincing. Word passed among the men that Santa Anna and his senior officers were quartered aboard the *Yellowstone*, living like royalty.

A few weeks later Santa Anna was in Washington, D.C., the guest of President Jackson, and then he was allowed to return to Mexico City where he received a hero's welcome. By the time he died in 1867, Santa Anna had been president of Mexico eleven times.

Texans and Mexicans alike spent a hellish summer on the Island. There were no shade trees on the east end where most of them were camped, and the water was brackish and came from holes dug on the bay shore. The only shelters were tents, and by midmorning they were hot enough to bake bread, if anyone had bread to bake. "Such were the swarms of mosquitos," wrote one Mexican officer, "that it would seem the whole species of the world had taken Galveston for a place of rendezvous." Sand crabs gnawed holes in their clothes and were so persistent that some soldiers gave up and treated them as pets. There were storms, too, blocked off by long spells of drought. There are no records of how many died that summer, but the number must have been staggering.

One of those who died was Mrs. Pauline Von Roeder. She was buried near the old Karankawa campgrounds at Three Trees. The enterprising German immigrants had moved to the west end of the Island, far away from the other refugees; the Karankawas had long since abandoned the camp.

The Klebergs and the Von Roeders built a boat and brought lumber from Chocolate Bay to erect a crude frame home. Two Mexican prisoners acted as their servants, gathering oysters, carrying deer and game, packing wood from the beach. Robert Kleberg thought of settling permanently on the Island. He built a much larger boat—nearly forty tons—to ship cattle to and from the mainland, only to learn that the law precluded his owning property on Galveston. A statute passed by the Monclova legislature limited ownership of land on the Island to Mexican-born citizens.

Disappointed, Kleberg returned to the mainland with his family and the two Mexican prisoners. It is interesting to speculate how the course of Texas history might have been altered if the Klebergs had stayed at Galveston and developed a ranch. Instead, Kleberg's son later married the youngest daughter of Richard King, who was in the process of buying 1.5 million acres of ranchland in deep South Texas, near the Rio Grande. Since 1886 the descendents of Robert and Rosalie Von Roeder Kleberg have controlled the King Ranch, the most famous ranch in America.

# 8

IT DIDN'T TAKE long for Samuel May Williams to grab his share of the spoils of war. Williams and his business partner, Thomas McKinney, had furnished nearly $100,000 in goods and services to Sam Houston's army. The Republic of Texas was flat broke: there was no way it could repay this debt directly, but there were many ways the government could express its appreciation. One of them was to turn over Galveston Island to Williams and his associates.

The transaction was suitably complicated, a Byzantine maze of secret deals and moves that traced back to the Monclova legislature. *Monclova!*—the very name rang with corruption. Michel B. Menard, a French-Canadian trader and one of the signers of the Texas Declaration of Independence, came up with the genesis of the plot in 1833. Since the Monclova legislature reserved land grants at Galveston for Mexican-born citizens, Menard got one of his clients, Juan Seguín, to apply for rights to the eastern end of the Island. Seguín, the military commander who buried the ashes of the men killed at the Alamo, was political chief of San Antonio during the Monclova land grab, and agreed to act as a front for his patron, Menard. Seguín transferred the grant—4,600 acres—to Menard, who transferred it to his friend, Thomas McKinney. After the Battle of San Jacinto, Williams, McKinney, Menard, and several others formed an establishment called the Galveston City Company and petitioned the Republic of Texas for confirmation of the Monclova claim. It was granted in December 1836, supposedly in exchange for a payment of $50,000 in cash or merchandise. One of the partners in the Galveston City Company, who was also a land agent for the Republic, acknowledged receipt of a payment that never took place—and the government accepted his acknowledgment. In fact, the entire transaction was carried off without any money changing hands.

One of the surveyors hired by the Galveston City Company was a bright and ambitious young man named Gail Borden, who had also served under Stephen F. Austin. Borden was an eccentric inventor who rode around town on a pet bull, but he was also a man of admirable conscience, interested in matters of public health and morality. Borden was destined to leave a permanent mark on Galveston, one more honorable and far more humanitarian than the legacy of Sam Williams and his associates.

Using the models of Philadelphia and New York, Borden laid out the city in a gridiron pattern. Avenues running parallel to the bay and the Gulf were labeled in alphabetical order, starting with a swampy bayside wagon trail that he called Avenue A and extending to Avenue Q a few blocks from the Gulf beach. Cross streets were numbered, beginning with Eighth Street, which ran along the mud flats at the eastern end of the Island, and extending to Fifty-Fifth Street, at the far western reaches of the Galveston City Company's claim.

In the early years of the city's development, most Galvestonians lived on the bay side of town, south of Avenue J and east of Thirty-Fifth Street. Later the names of some of the avenues were made more elegant. Avenue B, for example, became the Strand, named after London's famed street. Avenue J was renamed Broadway. Until Avenue A was filled in and renamed Front Street, buildings on the Strand backed up to the bay and merchants shipped and received goods out of their back doors. Still later the promoters of the Galveston City Company realized that Borden had been too generous in laying out lots and ordered additional streets cut through. These supplementary streets were given names like Avenue M½ or Avenue P½. For seventy-five years the Galveston City Company controlled growth and municipal planning on the Island, and manipulated city politics in whatever direction seemed most profitable.

Galveston in the late 1830s wasn't something an entrepreneur would care to advertise in a full-color brochure. It was a low, flat, incredibly desolate stretch of sand that flooded with every violent tide and was virtually useless for agriculture. The Island was solitary and monotonous—it reminded one traveler of the marshes and lagoons of the Mississippi—and it was a hotbed of disease and pestilence. The beaches were pristine, firm, and blindingly white; but the harbor was as dreary as a West Texas stock pond, without definition or landmarks.

The first thing travelers saw on entering Galveston Harbor were dozens of small boats and skiffs being rowed madly in their direction, their occupants screaming for news from the outside world and begging copies of old newspapers. Docking facilities were nonexistent. Longboats transported passengers and their belongings from ships to a shallow inlet near the shore, where they waded the final forty yards. For the first two years there were no hotels or boarding houses on the Island. If a traveler wanted to sleep in a bed, he waded back to the ship at night.

Troops still occupied Galveston more than a year after the Battle of San Jacinto, guarding about a hundred Mexican prisoners of war and constantly alert for an invasion from Mexico that was expected but which never materialized. Ornithologist John James Audubon, who led a party of visitors to the Island in 1837, saw only three women, all of them Mexican prisoners. Some of the prisoners had been commandeered by settlers for use as servants and slave laborers, and those who hadn't lived in filthy, windowless huts. The prisoners were a wretched lot, Aububon recalled, half-naked and many with arms and legs shot away. Even so, they weren't much worse off than the citizens.

Immigrants came from all over the world—from Boston, the Carolinas, England, France, Germany, Ireland—and most were as rough and raucous as the colonists who had fought in the Revolution. Though each shipload was cause for celebration, a few city officials took the precaution of mounting cannons in their yards. Business transactions were conducted in saloons, a British diplomat wrote in disgust, and a deal wasn't official until it was "wetted" with a few slugs of "who-shot-john."

Men wore crude frock coats made from blankets, picked their teeth with Bowie knives, and spat tobacco juice on the floor—when there was a floor. Floors were usually sand or mud, depending on the weather. Many of the houses and buildings were dismally crude constructions of sod walls and marsh-grass roofs. To avoid rattlesnakes and alligator attacks, people slept in hammocks. They cooked whatever was available in primitive ovens made of oyster shells baked in mud.

There were plenty of deer on the Island: Audubon reported that his party killed four. There were a few pigs and fowl, too, and some half-wild goats for milk. People gathered oysters from the bay and green turtle eggs from the beach. Cisterns collected rainwater, but most of the drinking water came from holes dug near the bay shore; there was no permanent water system, and none on the drawing board. One early entrepreneur reportedly drilled 144 feet without finding good water.

For some inexplicable reason word spread that Galveston was a wonderful health resort. A traveler from Ohio wrote that invalids who had come to the port to arrange passage to the United States "all revived under the salubrious influence of the climate." When a yellow fever epidemic devastated New Orleans in 1837, the *Houston Telegraph* waxed poetic about Galveston's "balmy and invigorating airs" and predicted that residents of New Orleans would turn the Island into a summer resort. That prediction didn't enjoy a long life. Less than a month later a hurricane laid waste to Galveston, lifting ships out of the bay and tossing them halfway across the Island, leveling nearly every structure including the three-story warehouse of McKinney & Williams.

Two years later Galveston was smitten by its own epidemic of yellow fever. After that, epidemics of the dread disease hit periodically and always with horrible consequences, killing up to 10 percent of the population in a single summer. One of the victims claimed by the yellow fever epidemic of 1844 was Penelope Borden, wife of the eccentric inventor. Stunned by the tragedy, Gail Borden abandoned his other projects—including his self-propelled Terraqueous Machine, which traveled on both land and sea—and applied himself to the task of finding the origin of the disease. It was apparent that the disease was transmitted from person to person: the virus that killed Penelope Borden and hundreds of others in 1844 was known to have been brought to the Island by an afflicted seaman aboard the French frigate *Brillante*. The symptoms were agonizingly familiar—chills and fever, accompanied by pain in the muscles, headaches, and nervousness. After a few days eyes and skin turned canary yellow, then victims began to bleed internally. The final, fatal stage was violent and uncontrollable nausea—the dreaded "black vomit." It was obvious, too, that the disease was seasonal. Epidemics of yellow fever always began with the heat of summer, and ended after the first frost. It didn't occur to Borden —as it would to Walter Reed fifty years later—that the same seasonal characteristic applied to the mosquito population, or that mosquitoes were the true source of the plague. Always the innovator, Borden proposed building an enormous refrigerator to house the entire population of Galveston during the summer months. Historian Joe Frantz writes that Borden actually constucted a giant ice box, utilizing ether to cool the box's interior to a white frost. Fortunately, no one volunteered to be turned into a human Popsicle, and Borden decided to abandon the project and convert the ice box for use with another invention—his meat biscuit.

Although Galveston was on its way to becoming the most advanced and civilized town in Texas, Houston became the first permanent capital of the Republic of Texas. Islanders sniffed that the state was getting what it deserved—a mudhole, populated by thieves. Several travelers, including Aububon, wrote with sinking hearts about their first trip to the capital. Buffalo Bayou had risen about six feet, Audubon recalled, and the neighboring prairies were submerged, wild, and desolate. From the deck of the steamer *Yellowstone*, they saw two girls camped on the banks, under cover of a few clapboards, cooking a scanty meal while vultures nested on nearby prickly pear. The landing in Houston was littered with cargoes of hogsheads and barrels. Drunken Indians yelped and stumbled about in the mud. "These poor beings had come here to enter into a treaty proposed by the whites," Audubon wrote. "The chief of the tribe is an old and corpulent man."

Wading in ankle-deep water, Aububon's party toured the seat of government, which consisted of a capital building, a presidential "mansion," and a cluster of half-finished houses and tents, strung about a prairie that had been cut clean of timber. Food and other merchandise was sold from booths along mud streets. Among other novelties for sale to tourists were the skulls of Mexican soldiers gathered from the battleground at San Jacinto.

There was an abundance of food, much more than on the Island, but prices were outrageously inflated. A dozen eggs cost $1, a bushel of corn $5. Bolts of cotton that would have retailed in the United States for $6 a yard sold on the streets of Houston for $15 to $20. Two-dollar hats were marked up as high as $15 and a $6 pair of boots sold for $18.

Whiskey was almost as cheap as water, and nearly every citizen on the street seemed drunk or set on getting that way. (Islanders joked that the water in Houston tasted so foul that even the rats drank gin.) Speculators swarmed like cockroaches, buying prewar land claims and discharge certificates from soldiers. Soldiers were entitled to 640 acres of land for each six months' service, but most were so hungry and destitute that they were willing to sell their certificates for 10 percent of their true value.

While politicians and speculators were whooping it up in the capital city, Samuel May Williams and his partners kept a tight reign on Galveston. Under the original city charter granted by the Texas Congress, all white male property owners were allowed to vote. That proved far too democratic for the appetites of the Galveston City Company; company officials decided to correct the situation by offering Samuel May Williams as a candidate for the 4th Texas Congress in 1839. As historian Margaret Swett Henson noted in her excellent biography of Williams, the gentleman had a problem of name recognition: too many people recognized him—as an unprincipled land speculator.

To offset this image Williams placed an ad in the paper announcing that the firm of McKinney & Williams would pay 50 cents on the dollar for depreciating Republic of Texas treasury notes; other commission houses were offering 37.5 cents. If this was a cheap trick to buy votes, as many believed it was, it worked: Williams defeated his opponent by a margin of 37 out of the 337 votes cast.

Once the 4th Texas Congress was in session, Williams pushed through a new Galveston city charter, restricting suffrage to white males who owned at least $500 worth of property, thus eliminating half of the electorate in one stroke. That session of Congress, incidently, was the first to be held at the new and permanent capital site at Austin, then a raw village on the Colorado River, just above land owned by McKinney & Williams.

By 1840, Galveston was emerging as a genuine port city. In Europe a militant liberalism had been building since the American Revolution, toppling old regimes and threatening others. Immigrants by the thousands were pouring into ports such as Galveston. Some of the immigrants took a liking to the Island and settled there, on land purchased from the Galveston City Company. Most took one look and headed inland. One regal Galveston immigrant who arrived about that time was a pompous fool named Prince Carl of

Solms-Braunfels. The prince brought along a shipload of serfs and marched them across 170 miles of wilderness to found the German colony of New Braunfels, between Austin and San Antonio. The prince rode ahead of the pack with his retinue of horsemen, including his personal architect, cook, and hunter. Solms-Braunfels passed through Galveston again on his way back to the Fatherland: he had gotten homesick, and left the colonists to fend for themselves.

Galveston's population swelled to 4,000. Crude wharfs were constructed at the foot of 18th, 20th, 21st, and 24th streets (the first one by McKinney & Williams), and something like 225 ships visited the port each year. There was regular steamship service from Galveston to Vera Cruz, Tampico, and Havana—as well as New Orleans—and smaller ships crossed the bay and navigated the rivers and bayous to Houston or other inland villages. There wasn't yet a permanent water supply, but a steamer made daily trips with fresh water from the San Jacinto River. There was talk, too, of building a bridge to the mainland. By now Galveston had not one but two hotels. The Tremont (also owned by McKinney & Williams) was the largest and grandest in the Republic. The Island supported fifteen retail shops, six taverns, an oyster house, three warehouses, two printing establishments, a newspaper, and a number of small artisans' shops. Ice cream was available for three dollars a gallon; schooners brought the ice from the coast of Newfoundland. Gail Borden enventually quit his job with the Galveston City Company and opened a meat-biscuit factory in a two-story building at the corner of the Strand and 25th Street.

But business was brisk at the Galveston City Company. More than six hundred homes flanked the central business district and spread five or six miles to the south and west. The best homes were located near the banks of McKinney's Bayou, which in those days started at the Gulf shore at about 51st Street and snaked halfway across the Island, almost as far north as Broadway. Thomas McKinney, Samuel May Williams, Michel Menard, and other officers of the Galveston City Company had homes near the bayou.

Williams picked for himself a choice twenty-two-acre lot near 35th Street and Avenue O, and ordered a home prefabricated and shipped from Maine. Williams' residence was designed in the Greek Revival style, combined with Louisiana classic. It was a story and a half, with the first floor belted by porches, the attic set with dormers, and the roof crowned with a large cupola and widow's walk. The entire house was elevated on ten brick piers, high above the ground, the better to weather storms. The homes of both Williams and Menard have weathered storms since 1838 and are still standing today: Menard's old residence at 33rd and Avenue N½ is privately owned, but Williams' home is open to the public.

Samuel May Williams took a lot of satisfaction from his station in life, posturing as a leader and servant of the people and seldom overlooking an opportunity to line his own pocket. Though he had no record of military service, he allowed himself to be called "Colonel": almost every gentleman in Texas in those days was called general or colonel or judge, or credited with being the first to do this or establish that. As befit a man of his class, Williams wore white linen suits in the summer and somber black silk suits with velvet waistcoats in cold weather, always touched off with a diamond stick pin and a gold watch.

The affectations of the landed gentry pleased Williams enormously—imported cigars, unlimited quantities of cognac, brandied cherries. A rosewood piano with mother-of-pearl and tortoiseshell keys was shipped from Germany so that his daughters could study music under well-bred nuns. Williams and McKinney owned a race track so close to McKinney's Bayou that Sam Williams could watch the action from his widow's walk. This observation platform served several purposes. In the summer the windows of the cupola were opened to draw warm air from the lower stories, and circulate cool air from ocean breezes. The widow's walk was also equipped with a telescope that enabled Williams to scan the Gulf for approaching ships. As vessels neared the Island, they flashed signals indicating what cargo they carried. Williams deciphered the signals, then rushed downtown to begin trading commodities before rival merchants realized what was happening. The commission house of McKinney & Williams had offices on 24th Street, and was considered one of the wealthiest and most influential establishments in Texas.

The most important piece of legislation Williams introduced in the state legislature Congress—as far as his own interests were concerned—was a bill to authorize banks in the Republic of Texas. He still had his bank charter from Monclova, and a whopping stack of bank notes he had ordered engraved in Philadelphia. In those Jacksonian times people looked on bankers as thieves and con artists, and considered bank notes a poor substitute for toilet paper. How could anyone "create" money with a printing press? It was no surprise, therefore, that Williams' bank bill was handily defeated.

Two years later, however, Williams found an opportunity to at least get his foot in the door. As an emergency measure to relieve the acute shortage of currency in the Republic of Texas, Sam Houston pressured the Texas Congress in 1841 to permit the firm of McKinney & Williams to issue small-denomination notes. The privilege was recinded by a state constitutional convention in 1845 but Williams continued to circulate bank notes anyway. The bank notes—"Williams Paper," they were called derisively—precipitated an antibanking uprising that lasted until Williams' death more than a decade later.

Williams also worked behind the scenes to get trade agreements with European powers. The French immediately agreed. There was a giant celebration at Galveston when a 64-gun frigate and other ships of the French fleet appeared at the harbor entrance in the spring of 1839, exchanging salutes with the Island's shore battery.

The British, however, were more cautious. A representative of the British foreign office visited Galveston and started asking embarrassing questions about slavery. England had made slavery illegal by this time. The policy of the Republic of Texas and the city of Galveston regarding slavery was at best ambivalent. Though there were no plantations on the Island, many wealthy Galvestonians were slaveholders. Williams himself owned twenty blacks. The largest slave market west of New Orleans, in fact, flourished on the Strand, operated by the mayor of Galveston, J. S. Sydnor.

There had been free blacks in Texas since before the revolution, but many citizens worried they would cause unrest among the slave population and pressured politicians to restrict their movement. A law passed by the 4th Texas Congress required free blacks to reaffirm their freedom by acquiring special dispensation from the government. Getting special dispensation was next to impossible.

At the same time, the city of Galveston passed an ordinance requiring all free blacks and mulattoes to register at the office of Mayor Sydnor, the slave auctioneer. There they were required to post a $1,000 bond to ensure that they would not become public charges or disturb the peace. Hardly anyone, black or white, had $1,000 in 1840. Blacks who were legally free were frequently arrested and sold at auction.

Samuel May Williams' private view was that slavery was indispensable to cotton production—just as cotton production was indispensable to his own business—but that's not what he told the man from the British foreign office. There was much talk at the time about the United States annexing Texas, Williams reminded his visitor. Merging the Republic of Texas with the United States was not Williams' idea of good business, a notion with which the British government heartily agreed. One way to stop annexation, Williams pointed out, was for England to recognize Texas as an independent republic, and then lean on Mexico to do likewise. Recognition would have the added benefit of striking a blow against the hated Southern planter, who was counting on Texas statehood to increase the slave vote in Washington.

The British diplomat apparently was convinced by Williams' arguments. In 1842 Great Britian officially recognized the Republic of Texas. In a short time brigs were sailing regularly and directly from Liverpool to the wharves of Galveston, delivering manufactured goods and sailing home to England with their holds loaded with cotton, grain, sugar, and other products of mainland Texas. International trade was a boon to all the merchants in Galveston, but to none more than the firm of McKinney & Williams.

Though McKinney & Williams had been a de facto bank since the relief act of 1841, the firebrands of the antibanking faction repeatedly beat down Williams' efforts to make banking a legitimate and permanent institution. To some degree the public mistrust of banks and bankers reflected an animosity toward Williams personally and against the greedy merchant class on Galveston Island in general.

In 1843, two years before Texas was annexed to the United States and three years before the U.S.-Mexican War, something happened that reenforced in the public mind Williams' reputation for duplicity and self-dealing. Historians disagree on exactly what happened, but it seems likely that Williams was the victim of a double cross arranged as part of Sam Houston's plan to get Texas into the Union.

The political chicanery started when Old Sam (as the hero of the revolution was now called, not always kindly) sent Williams to Mexico as part of a mission to negotiate a permanent peace treaty. Mexico still regarded Texas as a rebellious colony, and had twice attacked San Antonio. Williams had selfish reasons to accept this assignment. He believed that the governments of Great Britain and

France would eventually prevail on Mexico to recognize Texas as an independent republic, and that such recognition would kill plans for Texas to become part of the United States. Williams and his cabal of Galveston merchants were four-square against annexation, and mistakenly assumed that the voters of Texas agreed with their position. Old Sam let Williams believe what he wanted.

Williams and another delegate named George W. Hockley traveled to Mexico in the fall of 1843, but negotiations dragged on until the following winter. Under duress, and fearful that they might be arrested and held captive, Williams and Hockley finally signed a document agreeing to return Texas to Mexican control. They may have believed they were doing what Sam Houston wanted them to do, and they may have been right. Houston was involved in a series of diplomatic maneuvers, and the peace mission to Mexico was a ploy to buy time and to pressure the Congress of the United States to act favorably on annexation. Any document that Williams and Hockley signed was invalid anyway, unless or until it was approved by the Texas Congress.

Nevertheless, when word got out that representatives of the Republic of Texas had entered into secret negotiations to give Texas back to Mexico, people were furious. Sam Houston got a share of the blame—he was heckled and jeered when he came to the Island to speak out for annexation—but Williams paid the biggest price. Following the approval of statehood, Williams twice ran for the U.S. Congress and was twice defeated. Who wanted a congressman who had attempted to give away the Republic? Especially one whose grand scheme included, in the words of the editor of the *Houston Telegraph*, "flood(ing) the country with rag money."

Williams eventually got the bank that he always dreamed of owning, though it didn't last too long and brought him mostly trouble and grief. Openly defying the state constitution, he opened the Commercial & Agricultural Bank in 1848. The first bank in Texas was located in a two-story brick building at the corner of Tremont (23rd) and Market. To his board of directors Williams appointed such Galveston stalwarts as Michel Menard and George Ball, who would later help found Galveston's first legitimate bank.

If there was ever a run on the bank, and there almost certainly would be, Williams needed reassurance that Galveston merchants would redeem Williams Paper at par. Within a year a second bank was established on the Island. Mainland merchants and antibanking crusaders mounted a campaign that lasted nearly a decade, filing repeated lawsuits against the Galveston bankers and demanding that state officials take action. But time was on the side of Samuel May Williams, at least in the short run.

Houston merchants had to acknowledge that some kind of banking system was necessary for Galveston's development as a port. The issue of banking and port development was a double-edged dilemma. After all, the port of Galveston was Houston's outlet to deep water. Almost all of the cotton and grain harvested in the Brazos Valley came down the river to Houston before being shipped to Galveston for export. On the other hand, Houston was Galveston's door to mainland Texas, the place where commerce shifted from water to land. Nearly half of Galveston's business was importing, and Houston was the center of Texas' consumer market. Galvestonians didn't like to think about it, but if Houston ever got its own deep-water port, there wouldn't be much reason for Galveston to exist.

Gail Borden's meat-biscuit business never caught on. In the early 1850s Borden and an associate, Dr. Ashbel Smith—who later founded the University of Texas Medical Branch at Galveston—traveled all over the world touting the biscuit. They provided samples to hospitals and ship captains, to explorers and journalists. They even carried biscuits to the World's Fair in London, where, they hoped, Queen Victoria and the Czar of Russia might be persuaded to nibble. For a while the project seemed promising. The British government ordered 3,600 pounds shipped to its troops fighting in the Crimea—with instructions to Florence Nightingale on how the biscuit could best be used—and another 1,200 pounds were shipped to France. But in the United States a naval surgeon involved in a test found the flavor "absolutely disgusting," and Borden's company was forced to fold with 34,000 pounds of biscuits in its Galveston warehouse. That's when Borden came up with yet another brainstorm—condensed milk. In 1855 he moved from Galveston to New York, and started manufacturing this new product. The rest, as they say, is history.

Thomas McKinney and Samuel May Williams never gave up trying to recover the $100,000 that the government of Texas had owed them since the revolution. In 1851 McKinney petitioned the Texas legislature to reimburse to the firm of McKinney & Williams the amount of $150,000, principal plus interest on their original investment. McKinney arranged for "loans" to members of the legislature who promised to vote his way. Five years later the legislature did agree to make partial payment of $40,000 on the old war debt. But McKinney & Williams cleared only $16,000. The balance of the money went for bribes.

Twenty years later, after both men were dead, Texas finally recognized a scaled-down indebtedness of $16,942. But actual payment wasn't authorized until 1935, almost a hundred years after the debt was incurred. None of Samuel May Williams' heirs ever appeared as claimants.

The Commercial & Agricultural Bank closed its doors in the winter of 1859, less than ten years after its founding. The Texas Supreme Court ruled that its Mexican charter had never been valid in the first place. The first bank in Texas wasn't really a bank at all, it was a house of cards in the hands of a master sharp. Samuel May Williams didn't live to see the collapse of his empire. He had died six months earlier, three weeks short of his sixty-third birthday.

He died a bitter and frustrated old man, emotionally, physically, and financially drained. Today hardly anyone in Galveston remembers his name or what he did. The city of Galveston is tireless, almost shameless, in its devotion to its heroes, but there is no street, no park, no school or building or monument that bears the name Samuel May Williams.

# 9

IN THE DECADE before the Civil War, Galveston became a genuine city, the first in Texas. Merchants began importing ornate iron fronts for their buildings, and the town council constructed sidewalks, installed gaslights, and paved primary streets with shell. For the first time the Strand took on the appearance of a modern eastern city, an affectation that galled Houstonians. The *New York Sun* reported that the streets of Galveston were wide and straight, and that their cleanliness was about on a par with New York—"which is no compliment," the reporter added.

But the Island was not at peace with itself. Tempers ran high, and hypocrisy piled deep. It was a time of Manifest Destiny, of jingoism and muscle-flexing. People talked about "liberating" our neighbors in Cuba and Central America from the "imbecile race," meaning liberate them from themselves. Old patriots like David G. Burnet, first president of the Republic, General Sidney Sherman, and even, for a short time, Sam Houston delivered speeches declaring that it was the right, nay the *duty*, of the United States to expand its influence throughout the Americas. They were not advocating invasion, understand, merely filibustering expeditions. The word came from the French *flibustier*, meaning a citizen who declares a private war on a country with the intent to overrun and occupy: it had a common etymology with freebooter or pirate. One cynical diplomat of the day observed that "the acquistion of Texas has taught these gentlemen how to acquire territory by cheap and facile means."

But this really wasn't about acquiring territory, it was about slavery. "Filibustering" became a euphemism for reopening the slave trade. A powerful bloc of southern politicians, investors, planters and shippers looked on Cuba, Nicaragua, and other Caribbean and Central American republics as potential way stations for the slave trade, and even dreamed of populating the republics with good southern stock, and eventually confering statehood on them. Slave statehood, to be sure.

The point man of this grandiose scheme was a cult hero and self-styled revolutionary named William Walker. When word reached Galveston in the summer of 1856 that Walker and his mercenaries had invaded and conquered Nicaragua, he was accorded instant hero status. Newspapers burbled on about the "Nicaraguan Filibuster" and the "grey-eyed man of destiny," and urged Islanders to emigrate to the Filibuster State. The new steamship line of Garrison & Morgan offered Islanders a discount fare of $35 to Nicaragua. Groups met in church basements and gathered on the courthouse steps to discuss Walker's victory, and wealthy Islanders held a fundraiser in Walker's behalf at the Tremont Hotel.

William Walker was a pious and dangerously deluded man who cultivated his image as carefully as any contemporary television evangelist. In an earlier, unsuccessful attempt to conquer the Mexican state of Sonora, Walker had bestowed on himself the title of colonel. After his invasion of Nicaragua, he promoted himself to generalissimo, and later *el presidente*. Born in Nashville, the eldest son of a banker who had immigrated from Scotland, William Walker was the archetypical southern gentleman and aristocrat. He loved to put on airs. He did not drink or smoke or use profanity, and he considered purity of thought and deed as the first and finest duty of a Christian. William Walker was a practitioner of that unique blend of lunacy and hypocrisy that characterized the antebellum South.

What attracted many of the wealthier Islanders to Walker, however, was his outspoken opinions on race and slavery: he referred to slavery as "the divine institution." In Walker's twisted view God put the black man on earth to "secure liberty and order" for the white race, which in turn was obliged to "bestow comfort and Christianity" on blacks. As proof of this, Walker pointed out that God allowed Africa to "lie idle until the discovery of America gave a chance of utilizing the raw material of slavery." Walker believed that fighting for the institution of slavery was his destiny. Some Texans saw Walker for what he was. "Walker is not a liberator," wrote the editor of the *Quitman Free Press*, "he's a slaver." But many more saw him as man of extraordinary vision.

Even rational men who normally exuded goodwill got swept away in the rhetoric of the times. Hamilton Stuart, editor of the *Galveston Civilian*—who would later join the abolitionist cause and urge Texas to remain part of the Union—argued in 1856 that bringing slave labor from Africa to work the cotton fields of Texas was ordained by Holy Scripture. It was, he said, the only way to save the savage black man. On this, Willard Richardson of the *Galveston Daily News* agreed. England's pathetic attempt to control slave traffic, Richardson wrote, only compounded the cruelty. He cited the report of a slaveship captain who had said that of the nine cargoes of slaves he had run, his "shrinkage" had averaged more than 30 percent. Richardson's point was this: the only solution to such cruelty was to legalize and regulate slave traffic.

Late that summer Walker sent one of his key officers, Colonel S. A. Lockridge, on a recruiting mission to Texas. Lockridge was soon marching companies of volunteers from the mainland to the port of Galveston. Battalions of "Texas Rangers"—not to be confused with latter-day Texas Rangers—were formed in Galveston, San Antonio, Corpus Christi, Austin, and Gonzales. Each man was promised fifty dollars, a Texas saddle, a pistol, and a liberal land grant in Nicaragua. A San Antonio newspaper referred to the recruiting hoopla as "one of the proudest scenes that has ever been witnessed in San Antonio."

In February 1857, these Ranger units rendezvoused in Galveston, where they were guests at a grand reception at the Methodist Church and a gala ball at the Tremont. The principal speaker, Francis R. Lubbock, praised the volunteers for their efforts to strengthen the institution of slavery and secure a base for the slave trade: Lubbock's views on slavery later got him elected to a term as governor. Meanwhile, supplies poured into the port—weapons, ammunition, provisions, even a Ranger hospital unit. Supplies were loaded on troopships that the steamer line of Garrison & Morgan furnished free of charge. As young volunteers in makeshift uniforms marched along the Strand and turned toward the wharves, crowds cheered, bands played, and church society women served home-made pastries and hot coffee.

Service in the jungles and mountains of Nicaragua was not exactly the way it was touted in popular journals. One nineteenth-century writer described the natives as "frijole-eating, tiste-drinking, hammock-lolling, ignorant, ill-governed [louts] without energy for either large virtues or large vices." Money literally grew on trees, the writer claimed (a variety of wild nut was sometimes used as currency), and the jungle was a veritable feast of bananas, mangoes, oranges ("with often 10,000 on a single tree"), papayas, coffee, cacao, sugar, and tobacco. What the Rangers found when they arrived was intolerable heat, insects, disease, and a supply line so depleted that William Walker's army was forced to live off the land.

The much-ballyhooed man of destiny turned out to be an arrogant, racially crazed runt (he weighed less than a hundred pounds) more interested in discipline and shows of decorum than military strategy. Soldiers who swore or drank in his presence, or who demonstrated lapses in chastity, were jailed. Worst of all, Walker seemed to have no respect for his enemy, though the enemy was formidable, fanatical, and well supplied by the British and by Cornelius Vanderbilt, who had sworn a vendetta against Walker when the generalissimo sabotaged Vanderbilt's plan to dredge a canal across the isthmus of Nicaragua. The insurgent army was composed of Nicaraguan patriots, Costa Ricans, Hondurans, Guatemalans, Salvadorans, and Indians, all of them fiercely zealous in defense of their native soil. Colonel Lockridge's Texas Rangers were bonded entirely by self-interest. Instead of a fighting machine Lockridge had recruited a gang of cowards and marauders. One historian wrote later that the term "Texans" became synonymous with the word "plunder." When the Rangers realized that the insurgents weren't going to roll over and play dead, they began deserting in droves.

Within two months of the Rangers' arrival in Nicaragua, word of the unit's disastrous collapse reached Galveston. Newspapers printed lists of the known dead as well as names of deserters, and asked people to donate money and clothing for relief. By May 1857, the bloody fragments of the Ranger unit were arriving back in Galveston, destitute and dazed. There were no hero's welcomes. Texans had had a bellyful of filibustering.

Almost overnight General William Walker became a political burden to Texas politicans. General Sam Houston quickly denounced filibustering as a flagrant violation of American neutrality laws, which it was—and which it had been even when Old Sam was four-square behind it. That same year Walker surrendered to a landing party from a United States warship, deserting his followers. But he hadn't abandoned his dream of ruling the world. Three years after that, on another filibustering expedition to Honduras, Walker was captured and executed. At the age of thirty-seven destiny had finally caught up with him.

Walker's demise didn't end talk of reopening the slave trade, but now the larger issue was secession. Some of the same firebrands who had roused public sentiment in favor of filibustering mounted the courthouse steps and warned that Abraham Lincoln was the true enemy of the Texas, that Lincoln's real purpose in seeking the presidency was to eliminate the institution of slavery. In the national election of 1860 Lincoln didn't get a single vote in Galveston.

Islanders were angry, frightened, and confused. Anarchy seemed to sweep across the Island. Roving gangs of armed thugs dogged immigrants from the North, threatening bodily harm if anyone dared speak up for abolition. A black who attempted an "outrage" on a white woman was dragged with a rope around his neck to a tenpin alley and hanged from a beam, then his head was cut off and his body thrown in the bay.

A self-styled Committee on Public Safety was organized in the marketplace for the purpose of seizing federal property when the break came, as most assumed it would. In the saloons companies of militia were formed with names like the Lone Star Rifle Company and the Lone Star Minutemen. Hardly anyone dared speak out against secession.

A group of mechanics and laborers who had joined together in the aptly named Know-Nothing movement shadowed German immigrants; they were flexed for violence and waiting for a sign that the Germans were involved in "treason." The primary motive of the Know-Nothings was to halt the immigration of Germans, who were likely to be prounion and antislavery and, more important, were likely to take jobs from native-born Americans. Bizarre cliques and fraternal orders popped up all over the Island. The Lone Star Association believed that Texas should stand alone against both the Union and the Confederacy. The Secret Order of the Knights of the Golden Circle also wanted the reinstatement of the Lone Star Republic, at which time they proposed to invade Mexico. Merchants reported a booming business in muskets, bayonets, and almost any item bearing the Lone Star emblem.

Slaves had never been a major factor in Galveston's economy so the issue of Slavery was more emotional than real. According to the 1850 census, there were 678 slaves and 30 free blacks on the Island. Compared to slave owners on the mainland, Islanders generally provided better food, housing, and medical attention for their blacks. Among slaves Galveston was regarded as good duty. Socially minded Islanders dressed their blacks in second hand finery and paraded them down the Strand on holidays. As the clouds of war thickened, however, Islanders began to get rid of their slaves. By 1860 the census showed only 310 blacks in Galveston, 2 of them freedmen.

Free blacks had never had it easy in Texas, and in the antebellum mood of the 1850s their position became untenable. State law prohibited blacks from immigrating to Texas, and required those who were already there to get special legislative permission to stay. Deeds of freedom were meaningless, and blacks were frequently kidnapped off the streets of Galveston and sold. Captain Thomas Chubb, a Galveston shipmaster who would later command the Confederate steamer *Royal Yacht* during the Civil War, hired crews of free blacks in Boston and sold them as slaves when they reached Galveston.

Whatever his status, a black had little standing in a court of law. The testimony of a black was inadmissible in any case involving a white: thus, when a white hauled a black into court for any reason, the black's inability to testify in his own behalf preordained the verdict. Blacks accused of real or alleged crimes were sold into slavery as punishment.

Sometimes slaves were simply stolen from white owners, much as you would steal chickens. Historian Earl Fornell wrote of a gang of slave thieves that operated in Galveston under a blackguard named Kuykendall. Using a massive, dominating, silver-tongued free black as his front man, Kuykendall would arrange for a slave to escape. The big black who worked for Kuykendall would persuade the slave to escape on a horse stolen from his owner, thus compounding the crime of being a mere runaway. Before the unfortunate slave realized what was happening, he was in double trouble. At that point Kuykendall would take him aside and explain just how the cow ate the cabbage—enlightening the unfortunate black to the irony that he was now considerably worse off than when he had merely been a slave. That settled, Kuykendall would sell the black for whatever price the market allowed. As it became more and more apparent that the African slave trade would never be reopened in America, the market allowed plenty.

In 1859 Sam Houston got himself elected governor, but at a great price and against tremendous odds. He was almost seventy, too old to worry about personal political gain, but too crusty to stand by and watch liars and charlatans turn the land that he loved into a bloody battleground. Old Sam had served two terms as president of the Republic and a term as U.S. senator. He regarded himself as the father of Texas politics, and it broke his heart to see what was happening. He had made Texas; he believed that with all his heart. He knew what he had accomplished, and the people knew it, too. His history was their history: he had organized and established the Republic of Texas, had whipped a ragtag army into a fighting force that defeated Santa Anna, had maneuvered annexation with the United States—and every man-jack Texan damn well knew it. Now there was one last battle to fight, the battle to preserve the Union. He knew that he was right, and he prayed that for one final time the people knew it, too.

His opponent in 1859 was a wealthy plantation owner and ardent slaver named H. R. Runnels. Runnels was the candidate of mainstream Democrats, which was usually tantamount to election. To overcome Runnels, Old Sam needed to demagogue as he never had before. So he paid lip service to filibusters and cozied up to the ignorant Know-Nothings. He convinced the Germans he was pro-union, and made a majority of the others believe he supported slavery, or was at least open-minded on the subject.

But, having defeated his proslave rival, Houston realized the full irony: he was almost alone. He hadn't preserved the Union, merely delayed its demise. People were demanding that he call a state convention and put the issues of slavery and secession to a popular vote. He could still cajole, implore, and delay, but he couldn't win. And now he knew it.

When word reached Galveston in January 1861 that South Carolina had seceded from the Union, the town went crazy. A mob stormed the offices of the German-language newspaper *Die Union* and wrecked it. Its publisher, the mild-mannered Ferdinand Flake,

had dared criticize secession. Flake's fellow publisher Willard Richardson, of the *Galveston Daily News*, rather than rising to his defense, urged that the mob turn its reign of terror on other German-
Americans.

When it became apparent that other southern states were about
to following South Carolina, Sam Houston had no choice but to
call a convention and put the question of secession to the voters.
On February 23, 1861, the people of Texas voted 46,129 to 14,697
to secede from the Union; in Galveston the vote was even more
one-sided, 765 to 33. Old Sam and a few others refused to swear
an oath to the Confederacy and were forced out of office.

On April 7, seven days after the opening attack on Fort Sumter,
Old Sam caught a steamboat for Galveston. Sullen and angry about
being forced from office, labeled a traitor in some newspapers, he
intended to speak his mind one more time. City leaders feared that
the old hero's appearance would start a riot.

A committee of four met him at the wharves and urged him to
turn back. Flames shot from the eyes of the old warrior and he
pulled himself straight until he towered over everyone. Then he
said: "If I should go back home, as you suggest, it would go all over
Texas that Sam Houston was scared of making a speech. No, I can't
do it."

With a few friends Houston walked along the Strand, nodding
to the crowd and ignoring jeers and catcalls. The sidewalks were
crowded with men in uniform and armed civilians: the Committee
on Public Safety had seized federal military and naval equipment
and had turned it over to the local militia, which gave the militiamen
a sense of power but no direction on when and where to use it.
There were some threatening gestures, but everyone moved aside
as Houston headed up 20th Street toward the courthouse.

The courthouse door was locked. A friend suggested that he speak
from the balcony of the Tremont, and Old Sam turned back along
Postoffice Street and walked toward the hotel. But the front door
of the Tremont was also locked. Houston found a back stairway
leading to the hotel's wooden balcony overlooking the market. Some
of the street rabble tried to follow. "Let's hang the old scoundrel,"
one man yelled. When the man attempted to lunge, one of Houston's
friends kicked him in the stomach and down the stairs.

Looking down on a mob of thousands, Old Sam composed himself. His deep-set eyes flashed with a sense of power and purpose, then his voice began to rumble and thunder:

"I appeal to you for a frank confession that you have always prospered most when you have listened to my counsels. I am an old man now. I knew you in infancy, took you and dandled you on my knee, nursed you through all your baby ailments, and with great care and solicitude watched and aided your elevation to political and commercial manhood. Will you now reject these last counsels of your political father, and squander your political patrimony in riotous adventure, which I now tell you, and with something of prophetic ken, will land you in fire and rivers of blood?"

There was an uneasy stirring in the crowd. Someone laughed and said he'd gladly drink all the blood that was likely to be spilled. J. S. Sydnor, the mayor and slave auctioneer, told the man to shut up.

"Let me tell you what is coming on the heels of secession," Old Sam continued. "The time will come when your fathers and husbands, your sons and brothers, will be herded together like sheep and cattle at the point of a bayonet; and your mothers and wives and sisters and daughters will ask, 'Where are they?' and an echo will answer, 'Where?'"

The old general hadn't lost his magic. When he was done, even those who had jeered began to nod and some joined, however reluctantly, in the applause. "Three cheers," someone shouted, and part of the crowd responded. A traveler named Thomas North, who had ignored advice from his host to remain in his hotel room, remembered that after the speech Houston moved through the crowd, inquiring after a certain "blustering officer" whose remarks had been particular obnoxious. "Someone bring me that officer," Houston demanded. But the officer's friends had apparently convinced him that it was time to go. So it was. Old Sam allowed himself to be led back to the wharf, where a steamer waited to transport him back to the mainland.

Houston had said what he came to say. He had told them that the path that they were following would lead to death and destruction, to pain, suffering, humiliation, and a mutilation of the public will and spirit. They faced a future so bleak and dismal that few among them could even imagine it. And if they didn't believe him now, they soon would.

# 10

GALVESTONIANS HAVE always been good at throwing a party, and at first that's what the war seemed like. The Island mentality was geared to profit, adventure, and good times, not always in that order. True, there had been a lot of overheated rhetoric and posturing during the argument over secession, but at heart Islanders were not a divisive people.

There was a laissez-faire haplessness in their cultural makeup, a legacy of their pirate heritage. Merchants saw nothing wrong with overcharging for a bag of groceries, but by habit they threw in a free package of lemon drops. Tit for tat, quid pro quo, whatever the traffic allowed. Life was short, cruel, and worth the effort, and compromise and accommodation were easy habits.

Few people believed that war would come to the Island, and if it did, so much the better. War was adventure and good business. Later events—the federal blockade, the capture of the Island by Union troops, its recapture by Confederates during the Battle of Galveston—were passing moments of history, not much different than hurricanes or yellow fever or other endurable side effects of life on a barrier island.

The militia seemed mostly for show, especially in the early weeks of the war. The real action was far away. Companies drilled and paraded and hosted socials, but they fired slogans and taunts, not bullets. Weeks later the Lone Star Rifles and several other volunteer companies sailed for Virginia to join the real war, but other units like the Galveston Rifles and the Galveston Artillery Company were merged with the 1st Regiment of Texas Volunteers and assigned to the forts and batteries around the Island.

Galveston's bayous were natural barriers of defense. McKinney's Bayou extended from the Gulf halfway to the bay, where at high tide it connected with Offatt's Bayou. Even in dry weather and low tide, the two bayous were separated only by a narrow strip of marsh. The Island commandant, General Sidney Sherman, ordered a chain of earthwork fortifications around the city. Gun batteries were mounted at Fort Point on the Bolivar Peninsula, at the foot of 22nd Street on the bay, and at the foot of 15th Street on the Gulf.

Lighthouse equipment was dismantled and packed away so as not to assist the expected federal blockade, and guns and supplies were seized from federal troops stationed along the coast. A federal garrison in San Antonio was ordered evacuated aboard the Union vessel *Star of the West*, but the militia captured the ship before she could sail, and all 450 Union soldiers surrendered without firing a shot. Steamers were confiscated and converted into men-of-war. Commercial vessels were allowed to enter Galveston Harbor, but only those bound for foreign ports were permitted to depart.

The job of keeping watch for approaching ships was given to a quasi-military fraternity that called itself the Worthy and Ancient Order of JOLO. What the letters JOLO signified is lost in history, but the daily log the organization maintained during the first year of the war has been preserved in the archives of Galveston's Rosenberg Library and makes a fascinating study of Island life and attitudes.

Composed of eight ship's captains, detailed to four round-the-clock shifts, the JOLO operated from a watchtower on the roof of the Hendley Building, which fronted the Strand between 20th and 21st streets. It was actually a row of four separate buildings, though it appeared as a single structure, the most imposing one of its time in Galveston. Directly behind the row of buildings, jutting into the bay, was Hendley's Wharf, and next to it another wharf called Kuhn's Wharf.

The Hendley Building had been built six years before the war by Captain Joe Hendley and his uncle, William Hendley, from materials their shipping line brought from Boston. William Hendley— Uncle Billy, he was called—was a crippled eccentric who walked with a stick bent into the same shape as his gnarled leg and amused himself by picking up rusty nails and tufts of cotton along the wharf. Joe Hendley, who like his uncle was a bachelor, became commander of the JOLO. Whatever else the JOLO was about, it was apparently about having some fun. Numerous entries in the log thank various women's groups for dropping by the watchtower with gifts of pies and cakes and who knows what else.

Near the front of the logbook are two faded newspaper clippings that set the mood of the time. One is a story about Lincoln's proclamation to blockade all southern ports. In the weeks that followed there were references to this threatened blockade every several pages, always penned with a hoot and sneer.

*June 20, 1861—8 A.M.: Watch ends with easterly winds. Pleasantly hot day. Thanks to the captain of the yacht* Dart *for bringing late New Orleans papers in advance of the mail. Also the ladies who presented the JOLOs that pie have the eternal gratitude of the whole company. Nothing in sight in the harbor. Lincoln declines presenting himself. Why . . . We know not, but it is evident that he is not a man of his word. . . .*

The other salutational news clip is an essay attempting to find a historical parallel for the "suicide of liberty" being exposed in the North:

*There was something of the sublimity of despair in the fall of Sardanapalus, in the funereal pomp of the Egyptian dynasty, in the decay of Grecian splendor and the decline of Roman grandeur. But historian and poet will look in vain for a single element of greatness in the reckless downward progress of the Northern people.*

The first hint of action came in late May when Captain Hendley spotted a bark on the far horizon. "Bearing east, northeast," he wrote in the log. "About 12 miles distance. Has whole top-sail and appears to be the *Nueces*." Hendley knew that the *Nueces* was expected with a cargo from Boston, and he feared that if local shipping agents spotted it they would order it to turn back. A runner from JOLO headquarters was quickly dispatched to inform General Sherman, who ordered the revenue cutter *Henry Dodge* to capture the bark and bring it to port. A day or two later the *Henry Dodge* seized the brig *Nebraska*, with a cargo of ice from Boston. The *Nueces* and the *Nebraska* were subsequently scuttled near the harbor entrance as part of the fortification against a blockade.

But that was all the excitement the JOLO had to report in its first month on the job. Log entries were dull and spiritless. The weather was hot, and the wind came mostly from the southeast. The *Dart* continued to bring newspapers from New Orleans, the steamer *A. S. Ruthven* made regular runs up the Trinity to the town of Liberty, the *Diana* went back and forth from Houston, and the pilot boats *Sam Houston* and *Royal Yacht*, both armed and ready, cruised the bay like pieces of dolled-up driftwood.

A detachment of engineers arrived to build a fort near the Galveston, Houston & Henderson railroad bridge and run a telegraph line the length of the Island, connecting all fortifications. And still there was no sign of Mr. Lincoln's blockade. One night a JOLO watchman named Captain Charles Fowler was moved to write: "A strange phenomenon observed in early part of night similar to a meteor, a very bright streak from an attitude of 60 or 70 degrees, stretching away in a northwesterly direction." If it hadn't been for an occasional celestial surprise—and the ladies bringing pies and cakes—life on the JOLO watch tower might have unbearable.

In the early-morning hours of July 2 a squall lashed the Island. One of the men thought he spotted a schooner to the northeast, but when the weather cleared, there was nothing in sight. A few hours later, however, there was this entry in the log, written apparently in great haste:

*Wednesday, July 3, 11:30 A.M.—Made a steamer bearing ENE, distance 15 miles, standing to southward and westward. Sent an official dispatch to Col. Sheldon. Continue to watch. A schooner with a Confederate flag passing lighthouse on Bolivar Point to bear NW by N and run for it. Steamer anchors in 5–6 fathoms of water, 2–3 miles from beach. Now can see the U.S. ensign.*

The steamer was soon identified as the USS *South Carolina*, a formidable man-of-war armed with three 42-pounders on each broadside, a swivel gun, and several smaller pieces. The big cruiser, under the command of Captain James Alden, was accompanied by a tender ship, also well armed. In a matter of hours the *South Carolina* sailed into the harbor and began taking prizes. In the first ten days of the blockade she captured a dozen Galveston-based vessels, including the pilot ship *Sam Houston* and the schooner *Dart*, which the federals quickly converted into a warship. From the watchtower on the roof of the Hendley Building, JOLO stalwarts watched astonished and helpless as the *South Carolina* patrolled the entrance to the harbor like a mighty swan with a fleet of duckling prizes in tow.

*July 5, 8 A.M.—Thus ends another day of regret to see our property stolen before our eyes and no chance to retaliate. Old Abe keeping a vigilant watch for our craft.*

The blockade immediately took its toll. The *Diana* continued her runs to Houston, and the *A. S. Ruthven* steamed up and down the Trinity between Liberty and Galveston, but foreign commerce came to a dead halt. Word reached town that two of the prizes, the *Falcon* and the *George Baker*, had been sent to Key West, and a third, the *Sam Houston*, to Pensacola, Florida. Two weeks later the *Sam Houston* was back, armed and loaded with U.S. soldiers. A few merchants began to shut down their businesses, and some people headed for the mainland. Morale plummeted among the military and even the JOLO felt the shock. Ten days after the start of the blockade Captain Jerry Smith failed to report to his post, and his name was promptly stricken from the JOLO roll. The women appeared with a box of cakes and pies, however, and Captain Joe Hendley duly recorded the gratitude of his men.

In the wee morning hours of July 27, JOLO watchmen were jarred from their reverie by shouts from the wharf where the *Diana* had just docked with news of the war. "The streets were alive with many voices announcing the glorious news from Virginia," reads the JOLO log. A few hours later a messenger came by handcar across the railroad bridge with details of a Confederate victory at Manassas, which the federals called Bull Run.

The *Galveston Civilian* published an extra edition with screaming headlines that declared: MANASSAS WON. 10,000 FEDERALS KILLED. CONFEDERATE LOSS 3,000. FEDERALS ROUTED. SIX BATTERIES CAPTURED. The text of the story was more sobering. "The battle was terrible and ended with great slaughter on both sides," it said. In the days that followed, crowds of people waited on the wharves for the arrival of each steamer from the mainland, but no additional details of the battle were forthcoming.

The Island's only communication with the blockade fleet was an occasional visit by the *Royal Yacht*, which traveled under the protection of a white flag to carry messages to and bring mail from the *South Carolina*. Lately, Captain Alden of the *South Carolina* had cut off the mail supply. In a gesture that was probably misinterpreted in town, he decided to release a portion of the mail when he heard the news of Bull Run from the captain of the *Royal Yacht*, Thomas Chubb. An entry in the JOLO log reads: "He was furnished with news of our late glorious victory in Virginia, his anxiety to obtain which doubtless induced him to release a portion of the mails." White flag or not, Chubb was running a serious risk visiting the *South Carolina*. He was wanted by federal authorities for several crimes, including privateering, scuttling his own ships for insurance, and selling black seamen hired in Boston on the Galveston slave market.

For the first month of the blockade no shots were exchanged between the fleet and the shore batteries, but Islanders were getting edgy. On the morning of August 6, the JOLO log reported that the *Dart*, the newly armed federal prize, was "playing cat and mouse" with the South Battery at the foot of 20th Street. Suddenly, the battery opened fire. The *Dart* fired back, then retreated out of harm's way and stayed there.

Two days later the *South Carolina* moved in and began exchanging fire with the South Battery. Who fired first is open to dispute. The JOLO log says that the South Battery opened the fusillade, at which point "the steamer [*South Carolina*] returned fire with alacrity." At long last, the show everyone had waited for was starting. Men, women, and children ran to the beach, too excited to consider the danger, crowding the sand hills to watch.

The show ended in less than half an hour. Most of the *South Carolina's* 44-pound shells burst high in the air, but one struck the beach, blowing a Portuguese civilian to pieces and severely wounding three others. The killing and wounding of noncombatants caused a storm of outrage, not only among Islanders but in the offices of the Island's foreign consuls. Many of the civilians still on the Island were under the protection of the legations of England, France, Spain, Belgium, Holland, Austria, or Prussia, all of whom sent formal protests to the captain of the *South Carolina*.

After that all was quiet for many weeks. The routine consisted of watching and waiting, the boredom occasionally interrupted by news of the war or minor sorties by individuals or small bodies of men. A launch from the *Dart* landed up the coast and stole a sack of potatoes from a Frenchman. A Galvestonian named Nicaragua Smith stole a yawl and surrendered himself to the crew of the *South*

*Carolina*. The schooner *Frolic* hid off the coast, waiting for the ebb tide, then successfully avoided the blockade and brought supplies to the Island. The JOLO log listed the vessels that had run the blockade: three schooners by way of the main channel, and seven light draft coasters which sneaked into the bay through San Luis Pass. A dispatch from Houston reported that General Sam Houston was dead, and all across the Island flags were lowered to half mast. Even the death of the state's greatest hero proved anticlimactic. The next day there was this entry in the log: "It was ascertained that the old General was still alive with fair prospect of recovery, God grant he may." Houston lived another two years.

Rains and squalls battered the Island in late August and early September, and by November the weather was cold and bleak. Under cover of a thick fog, two launches from the USS *Santee* entered the harbor, burned the *Royal Yacht*, and captured its crew, including the unfortunate Captain Thomas Chubb. He was tried and sentenced to death in New Orleans, though later he was freed as part of a prisoner exchange. One night during a driving rain a boatload of U.S. Marines landed on an isolated beach and captured the Hendley Building. "Having early in life learned that discretion is the better part of valor," wrote Captain Hendley, "we didn't dispute their occupation but . . . escaped to the battery." The entry is illegible at that point, but by the next morning the Marines had gone.

The Confederate command had about decided that defense of the Island was useless, not that the CSA (Confederate States of America) had expended any great effort providing it protection. On their own, Islanders had purchased twelve cannons from a foundry in Virginia, but military authorities haughtily ignored the added artillery. Finally, with a show of patronization, they agreed to position the cannons on the bayside, where they would present no threat to the enemy. As if to demonstrate its contempt for the Island, the Confederate command then erected on the Gulf side a battery of dummy wooden cannons—so-called Quaker guns—pointed harmlessly toward the blockade fleet.

In October the commander of the U.S. blockade fleet sent a message demanding the Island's surrender, and agreeing to a four-day truce so that noncombatants could be evacuated. Rather than remove civilians, the Confederates utilized the time to move troops and artillery to the mainland, a clear violation of the truce agreement.

The federals were outraged at the truce violation, and many citizens of the South believed the retreat unconscionable. The *Galveston Daily News* accused the CSA command of being "either imbeciles or neglectful" and the *Vicksburg Whig* said that the retreat was "another evidence of incompetence, imbecility or cowardice." The *Houston Telegraph* published an impassioned plea for the Confederacy to rush 5,000 reenforcements to defend Galveston—after all, Islanders had willingly responded when there was fighting in Virginia and Missouri. The CSA command dismissed the plea: in its estimation, the seaport and its people weren't worth worrying about.

The military retreat wasn't the only example of official stupidity that week. In his order for the evacuation of civilians, Governor Francis R. Lubbock asked Galvestonians to kindly burn their city on the way out. Naturally, the governor's scorched-earth policy was ignored, but Islanders never forgave Lubbock and helped defeat him in the next election.

When U.S. troops arrived to occupy the defenseless Island, they were treated as conquering heroes. The mayor greeted them at Kuhn's Wharf and personally handed over the keys to the Galveston Customs House. While Captain W. B. Renshaw and 150 U.S. Marines marched up 20th Street, women and children hurried beside them, decorating the muzzles of their rifles with flowers. A cheer burst from the crowd as the Marines hoisted the Stars and Stripes above the Customs House. Renshaw called Galveston "a place with strong Union proclivities among the lower and middle class" and indeed Islanders seemed to look on the troops as liberators rather than invaders. Renshaw decided to keep the railroad open to the mainland. Sound military strategy dictated that the bridge be destroyed, but it was the main lifeline and means of subsistence for the Island's civilian population, and Renshaw decided to spare it. The captain would live barely long enough to regret this act of humanity.

The Island was taken without bloodshed—almost. The only violence occurred when a Confederate soldier tried to shoot one of his own officers; he missed and killed Dr. Hurlburt, a popular and prominent citizen. When federal troops discovered that one of the shore batteries that had kept them at bay for weeks was made of wood, they accepted it gracefully and had the Quaker guns mounted as decoration on the hurricane deck. Though some people left the

Island, most decided to accept the occupation and do business as best they could with the occupiers. Extracting money from people temporarily residing on the Island was hardly a novelty for the good people of Galveston.

The men of the Worthy and Ancient Order of the JOLO stayed on, but the unit was only a shadow of its former self. Of the original eight only Captain Hendley and two others remained. The rest either had been drummed out of the order for excessive absences—"I fear they have all played out," wrote Hendley—or had joined the active military. Charles Fowler was commissioned in the Confederate navy, with the rank of commodore, and was taken prisoner the following spring and sent to a prison camp in Boston.

The final entry in the JOLO log is dated Friday, December 27, 1861, and says simply: "Wind light from the SW. Schooner Neptune leaves and returns from Bolivar Channel. Nothing to report." On that note the ancient order vanished into history.

THE UNION lacked troops to properly occupy the city, and by the early part of 1862 Galveston had become a sort of no-man's land. Captain Renshaw set up his garrison in a string of barricaded warehouses that ran between Kuhn's and Hendley's wharves. His troops contented themselves with raising the flag above the Customs House each morning, and retreating behind the barricades each night.

Renshaw and some senior officers of the 42nd Massachusetts Infantry had offices in the Hendley Building, and kept a twenty-four-hour watch from the roof. After dark, Rebel scouting parties moved freely about the Island. The Confederate cavalry usually rode up the Gulf beach a few hours after sunset, concealed behind sand dunes, and rendezvoused at a park at 21st and Avenue N. They always vanished before dawn.

Rarely were there exchanges of gunfire between the opposing armies. There was a notable exception one night in November 1862, when an old, one-armed veteran of the Texas Revolution fired a double-barreled shotgun at a federal sentry. The U.S. garrison opened fire, and so did the gunboats in the harbor, shelling the city for half an hour. Ferdinand Flake, the only newspaperman who remained in the city, wrote that women and children ran screaming in the streets and took refuge in cemeteries. But only one person died in the bombardment.

All things considered, life on the Island during the federal occupation was probably better than conditions in Houston, where most of the citizens of Galveston had taken shelter. Houston merchants used the war as an opportunity to gouge refugees. Hovels that normally rented for five dollars a week now cost ten times that. The *Telegraph* admitted that it "blushed with shame" over the extortion, but acknowledged that currency was in short supply. The newspaper was accepting "corn, bacon, sugar, flour or anything else of value" in payment for subscriptions. The *Galveston Daily News*, one of most ardent advocates of war, also published out of Houston and announced, somewhat reluctantly, that it had decided to accept payment in Confederate bonds, those being the only kind available. Editor Willard Richardson visited the Island and reported that its famous gardens were still well kept, and that a military band entertained three nights a week in the public square.

Things might have gone on that way indefinitely except for a change in command. In November 1862, CSA Brigadier General John Bankhead Magruder took control of the military department of Texas. Magruder was a man of action, a blustery warrior who spoke with a stutter and listened only to his own advice. A true dandy, it was said of Magruder that he could ride all day and dance all night. He was known as Prince John from his days as a lieutenant colonel stationed in Newport, Rhode Island, where he entertained long and lavishly. He wore whiskers and a vigorous handlebar mustache, and designed his own uniforms.

Magruder had fought in the East when CSA troops were winning battle after battle—usually against great odds—and he arrived in Texas full of fire and vinegar. His first priority, Magruder decided, was to retake the port of Galveston. Within a week of his arrival in Texas, Magruder sent a message warning the mayor of Galveston to get his people out of harm's way. Otherwise, the message said, Magruder assumed no responsibility for their safety.

This time the exodus was serious. Women and old men crowded the train station and the wharves, overwhelmed by crying children and piles of household belongings. Merchants and bankers closed their businesses, or moved them to Houston. Hospital supplies were redistributed to army units on the mainland. Flooring was laid across the railroad bridge, and five thousand head of cattle and fifty horses were driven across.

Cotton presses and wharf facilities stopped operation, and churches shut down, their bells silent for the first time in years.

About the only people who didn't desert the island were the families of soldiers, deserters, aliens who claimed exemption from the hostilities, and a few hardheaded individuals like Flake and the nuns of the Ursuline Convent. Though the exodus alerted federal troops that an invasion was imminent, they didn't know when, where, or how.

Magruder planned a joint land-sea operation. In the early hours of New Year's Day 1863, his forces moved into position. Two small steamers, the *Bayou City* and the *Neptune*, had been fitted as gunboats and armored with cotton bales. Laying off Halfmoon Shoals in the dark, waiting for the signal to attack, they looked like two well-loaded cotton boats on a routine voyage.

At the same time, five hundred soldiers armed with siege guns crossed the railroad bridge that Captain Renshaw had declined to destroy. Cannoniers followed, pushing a flatcar of heavy field pieces to within a few hundred yards of where the USS *Harriet Lane* lay at anchor.

Moving quietly through the streets, warning citizens to move out of range, the troops positioned themselves along the Strand, a block from the wharves where the enemy was barricaded. Twenty-two cannons were mounted at the corners of 20th and 21st streets, on either side of the Hendley Building. Magruder's plan was to open fire on the garrison as soon as the moon went down, which would also be the signal for the two cottonclads to engage five Union ships anchored in the harbor.

A few minutes before 5 A.M. Magruder personally fired the first cannon. "Well, boys," he said, "I have done my job as a private. I will now attend to my duties as a general." Somehow, the cottonclads missed the signal. When the first cannonball whistled across the roofs of the warehouses on the wharf, the *Bayou City* and the *Neptune* were still fifteen miles from the Island.

For nearly an hour, the attack appeared to be a debacle for the Confederates. Withering gunfire from the garrison and from the USS *Owasco* and the *Harriet Lane* pinned down Magruder's troops, killing a number of them, plowing up the pavement, and filling the streets with shards of broken window glass. Magruder was about to pull back when his lookout spotted the cottonclads approaching the U.S. fleet.

The *Bayou City* opened fire from a half-mile away, tearing open a hole behind the wheelhouse of the *Harriet Lane*. The pilot of the

*Bayou City* tried to ram the *Harriet Lane*, but in the strong current he misjudged and hit a glancing blow, ripping planking from the side of his own vessel. While the *Bayou City* was turning for another pass, the U.S. gunboat blasted her with a broadside that blew away one side paddle and killed her gun captain and several others, including Lieutenant Sidney A. Sherman, the son of the general who had originally commanded the troops at Galveston. Then the *Harriet Lane* swung about, aimed her eight guns at the *Neptune*, and shot open her hull. The *Neptune* sank near the edge of the channel, but the *Bayou City* managed to ram the *Harriet Lane* a second time, tearing off her wheel and sliding under her gunwale so tightly that the two vessels became locked together.

While the two wounded ships swirled out of control in the tide, Confederate soldiers raked the *Harriet Lane* with rifle and shotgun fire and began boarding her. Yankee sailors retreated below, but the *Harriet Lane's* commander, Captain Jonathan M. Wainwright, remained on deck with some of his officers. The *Harriet Lane* was one of the proudest ships in the United States fleet, a handsome copper-sheathed man-of-war that had seen action in the battle at Fort Sumter, and had been part of the armada that captured New Orleans shortly before the Galveston blockade: Wainwright wasn't about to surrender her without a fight.

His was a vainglorious stand. Wainwright was shot between the eyes by the commander of the *Bayou City*, CSA Major Leon Smith. Every officer aboard the *Harriet Lane* was wounded or killed. As Wainwright fell dead across the skylight, the sailors serving in his command began to appear from below, their arms above their heads.

As soon as the *Harriet Lane* was secure, General Magruder ordered one of his engineers, Major Alfred M. Lea, to board the U.S. vessel, survey the damage, and find a way to extract her from the badly damaged cottonclad *Bayou City*. As Lea came aboard, he happen to notice one of Wainwright's young officers, who lay dying on the quarterdeck. Moving closer, he realized that the Union officer was his own son, Lieutenant Commander Edward Lea, second-in-command of the *Harriet Lane*. The father knelt beside the son, holding him in his arms, blood of his blood, the stains indistinguishable on Confederate gray or Union blue. The lieutenant was still conscious and recognized the man who had stopped to comfort him. "My father is here," he whispered to a shipmate. Then he died.

Most of the other ships in the U.S. fleet had retreated out to sea, but the USS *Westfield* had run aground. While another officer negotiated a truce with CSA forces, Captain Renshaw decided to blow up the *Westfield* rather than surrender it to the enemy. The U.S. commander and some of his men laid a trail of gunpowder leading to the ship's magazine, lighted it, and took to the lifeboats.

But something went wrong. The *Westfield* didn't immediately explode. Renshaw went back to check the fuse, at which point the ship blew to bits, killing Renshaw and fourteen of his men. When word of Renshaw's death reached the fleet, Renshaw's second-in-command ordered it to set sail for New Orleans. The federal troops on Kuhn's Wharf, abandoned though not defeated, had no choice except to surrender. The Confederates had captured six ships, sunk one, run another aground, and taken nearly 400 prisoners. They had lost 143 men, killed or wounded, and one ship, but they had won the Battle of Galveston and secured the Island, for whatever it was worth.

Regardless of the outcome, it seemed like a terrible price. Who could measure the agony of Americans killing Americans, of fathers ordering sons to battle and, in at least one case, of helping the side that caused the sons' deaths? In the face of such tragedy, how do you determine winners and losers?

An emergency hospital was set up at the Ursuline Convent on 25th Street, and Yankees were placed on cots next to Rebels who had fought a war that was essentially about ownership of slaves, a few of whom lay mangled on the same row of cots. Though General Magruder offered his private ambulance to transport the Ursuline nuns to safety, the sisters refused to leave. They were teachers, not nurses, but they did what they could, holding lamps or basins as military doctors amputated limbs or dressed gaping wounds. For days after the battle the sisters comforted the survivors, prayed for the dying, and cleaned away the carnage.

Most of the dead were buried in the cemetery at 43rd and Broadway. Young Sidney Sherman, whose father had helped Texas win its war of independence with Mexico, was put to rest not far from the graves of two Yankees—Lieutenant Commander Edward Lea, who had died in his father's arms, and Captain Jonathan Wainwright, whose grandson and namesake became a famous American general in World War II and hero of the Bataan Death March.

The loss of the *Harriet Lane* and the *Westfield* were serious setbacks for the Union fleet, and welcome assets to the Confederacy. The *Lane* was repaired, then stripped of her guns and sold to a Galveston commission merchant for use as a blockade runner. There wasn't much left to salvage aboard the *Westfield*. Until a snag boat finally removed it in 1906, the ship's engine shaft stood upright under four feet of water, a formidable obstruction to navigation.

Magruder made one additional use of the *Harriet Lane*. For several days after the battle he allowed the American flag to fly from her mast (and from the Customs House as well), hoping to lure into port other American vessels that had not heard of the battle. The ploy worked. A U.S. troop transport, the *Cambria*, appeared at the mouth of the harbor two days after the battle. The *Cambria* was of great political importance, Magruder wrote later, because "the ship contained almost all the Texans out of state who had proved recreant to their duty to the Confederacy and to Texas."

Though the Confederates were unable to capture the *Cambria* herself, they did capture a yawl that her commander sent to scout the Island. It was a victory of sorts for General Magruder. Aboard the yawl was one Nicaragua Smith, the same man who had stolen a skiff the previous summer and deserted to the Yankee fleet. Smith was court-martialed, then hauled off by cart to face public execution. Smith refused a blindfold, says historian David G. McComb, and stood tapping his foot on the coffin lid as the band played firing-squad music.

THE WAR WOULD wind on for another two and a half years, but the Battle of Galveston was the end as far as Islanders were concerned. They felt badly used by both sides, and abandoned by mainlanders. The federal blockade resumed, of course, and Islanders made good use of it, setting up an extremely profitable blockade-running trade.

Magruder fortified the Island with enough artillery to prevent another federal invasion, and spent the rest of the war trying to maintain discipline among his mutinous ranks. Some units hadn't been paid for weeks. Their rations were so vile that on one occasion soldiers marched through the streets carrying a rotting carcass of meat intended for their dinner, and buried it with great ceremony. Some deserted for Mexico. Others stole from merchants, tore down fences and shacks for fuel, and, in one case, lynched a businessman. The lynching took place when soldiers from the 21st Regiment of the Texas Cavalry hauled a saloonkeeper who had shot a member

of the regiment out of his establishment at 27th and the Strand—
an area of joints and brothels called Smokey Row—and hung him
from a wooden sign above the front door of his business.

Soldiers frequently threatened to kill their own officers. Magruder himself was almost blown up when five hundred soldiers with
two artillery pieces surrounded a house where the general and his
officers were being entertained by some of Galveston's ladies—
perhaps the same ones who had brought cakes and pies to the JOLO
in better times. The general appeared at the front door, his six-foot-
four-inch frame looming above the mob. A spokesman shouted that
this was no time for "feasting, fiddling and dancing," not while their
own children begged food in the streets and the nation bled. The
general appeared sympathetic. He promised to look into their complaints, then called out a regiment to disperse them and went back
to the ladies.

While they waited for the war to conclude, Islanders reverted to
their old seafaring and mercantile traditions. The U.S. blockade
fleet was readymade for such maritime pursuits as smuggling, bartering, and trading. By late 1864 the Union had shut down contraband trade at Matamoros on the Mexican border and had closed
all southern ports east of the Mississippi. Galveston was the single
source for cotton in Europe, and despite the blockade it was estimated that three ships left and arrived in the port each week.

The blockade runners hauled cotton to European-turnaround
ports in Havana, Vera Cruz, or Nassau, and returned with trade
goods, munitions, and Enfield rifles. Only about 15 percent of the
runners got caught, a fair risk considering the enormous profits.

One of the boldest of the runners, Captain William Watson, was
in the port of Havana when the *Harriet Lane* arrived on her first
and last blockade-running expedition. Since the converted U.S.
man-of-war was of deep draught and forced to use the main channel, she had been chased all the way; she was fortunate to arrive
at all. An old sea dog like Watson knew that it was folly to use a
ship like the *Harriet Lane* for running.

Watson's own vessel, the *Rob Roy*, was in Havana for repair. She
was one of the flat-bottomed, low-hull schooners much favored by
runners, but she was something more that that. To see her a seaman
would think she was an ordinary trading ship, with low bulwarks
and a tall mast. What couldn't be seen except from below deck was
a unique centerboard apparatus. The centerboard, which Watson

had personally designed, was a type of adjustable keel. It could be raised in shallow water so that a fully loaded vessel drew less than five feet, or lowered in heavy seas so that it drew thirteen.

The *Rob Roy* could turn sharply, and was almost impossible to capsize, but best of all she could cross the shallow bars that guarded harbor entrances—and go places blockade captains only dreamed of going. Watson was standing on the wharf in Havana discussing the merits of his design with a friend when a second friend approached and made him a proposition.

It was simple: a shipper identified only as R.M. wanted Watson and his crew to sail for Galveston with 200 Enfield rifles, 400 Belgian muskets, 400 cavalry swords, ammunition, cavalry currycombs, horse brushes, blankets, clothing, and a few other items. They would return loaded with cotton. R.M. agreed to pay the skipper of the *Rob Roy* $500 in advance, plus $7 for each bale of cotton he landed at a neutral port, plus a percentage of the outgoing cargo. Watson didn't know much about Galveston Bay, but at those prices he could learn.

Since R.M.'s cargo didn't fill the hold, Watson contacted the CSA consul in Havana and offered to carry for free any goods he wanted delivered. The consul sent another four hundred guns, some mail for Galveston's citizens and merchants, and some important dispatches for General Magruder.

After conferring with another shipmaster familiar with Galveston Bay, and getting instructions on how to approach the Island, Watson and his crew of eight slipped out of Havana Harbor just before sunset in August 1863, cleared for Belize and Honduras. Time of day was critical in his business. No vessels were permitted to enter and leave the harbor between sunset and sunrise; if the *Rob Roy* was spotted by U.S. gunboats, she could come to under the guns of Moro Castle and wait until dark to put out to sea. Since the *Rob Roy* sat low in the water, her lookout could spot crusiers long before they spotted her. The most direct course to Galveston was west-northwest, but Watson ordered his ship to stand due west, the course to Honduras.

They sailed west for three days before losing their breeze. Calms were tedious and dangerous for runners. All they could do was lower their sails, wait, and keep a sharp lookout from the masthead. Watson had brought along two hundred fathoms of rope and a heavy grapnel so that he could detect currents during a calm and prevent his ship from drifting off course. After a time a light breeze began to stir, and the *Rob Roy* set sail.

For nearly ten days they crept north, most of the time with their sails down. Watson made it a point to lower sails before daybreak, whether or not there was a wind. This gave his lookout a chance to scan the horizon at first light. If his lookout spotted a sail, the *Rob Roy* kept her own sails furled. Bare masts were hard to spot. "It is very unseamanlike to lay and roll under bare poles," Watson wrote in his memoirs, "but it is a very wise tactic to do the unexpected."

The *Rob Roy* was 120 miles out of Galveston when her lookout spotted trouble. A light breeze had been blowing all night and they were making about two knots, but at daybreak Watson followed his cautious routine, lowering his sails and posting a lookout. As soon as it was light, the lookout spotted a large steamer steering west, right across their path—if they had continued under sail, they would have already collided with it.

Watson knew that if the steamer did catch sight of his ship, she would put about and take them as a prize. He ran to his cabin and gathered the letters and documents, in case he had to throw them overboard—his crew had already gone below to hide their personal money. The dawn was gray and hazy; Watson would have much preferred fog and rain. He brought the *Rob Roy* around so that her bare masts were in a line with the cruiser and therefore more difficult to detect. It apparently worked because the cruiser continued to steam west until it was out of sight.

Over the next few days the wind was calm or very light, and the *Rob Roy* drifted with her sails down, her crew taking soundings to check the current and keeping watch from the masthead. Several times they spotted cruisers in the distance, but the cruisers never spotted them. A steady breeze had finally sprung up from the southeast, and they were whipping along nicely when a crewman called out from the masthead that a sail was in sight.

"It could be the *Sylvia*," Watson told his first mate, Fred the Swede. The Swede was a stoic old salt who had made many runs to Matamoros and Tampico with Watson and the *Rob Roy*. He was a good seaman and Watson trusted his logic and judgment.

"Could be."

"It looks like the *Sylvia*," Watson said, studying the schooner with his glass. "Captain Dave McCluskey sailed out of Havana the same night we did."

"It's the *Sylvia* all right," the Swede told him. "But it's not Captain Dave."

He was right. It was understood that when one blockade runner sighted another at sea, they would steer away from each other: that way, if a cruiser happened along, it could only pursue one of them. But the *Sylvia* had changed course, and was headed straight for the *Rob Roy*.

"Maybe they want to compare longitudes," Watson said. "They did that once before, off the coast of Mexico."

"Maybe the Yankees took her as a prize," the Swede suggested. "And maybe they intend the *Rob Roy* to be next."

"If that be the case," Watson said, "we better haul up at once and keep to windward of her." The *Rob Roy* immediately luffed up her sails and headed east-northeast, a bearing that Watson calculated would take them within a mile of the *Sylvia*. It was still possible that the *Sylvia* had lost her reckoning, and Watson chalked the longitude on a hatch cover and held it up. When they were close enough for the *Sylvia* to read the message, Watson got a good look at her crew. He had never seen any of them before. The Swede was right: this was the crew of a man-of-war.

Watson checked time by the sun. Still early afternoon. He knew the *Sylvia* couldn't overhaul the *Rob Roy*, but if they were caught in a calm—and that had been the afternoon pattern—the *Sylvia* might send a boarding party in a longboat. The Swede remembered the time in Mobile Bay when a federal crew had attempted to board their schooner; they had had to beat them off with handspikes.

Watson decided on a show of force. He couldn't ask his crew to fight, but he could ask them to pretend they were ready to fight. He opened a box of Enfield rifles and passed them around. As the *Rob Roy* passed in front of the *Sylvia's* bow, her crew stood against the rail with rifles and fixed bayonets. The demonstration worked. The *Sylvia* hoisted sail and turned east. Watson followed her until dark, then stood his own ship southeast toward Galveston. By morning the *Rob Roy* lay about thirty miles down the coast from the Island.

Now came the really dangerous part—avoiding the blockade fleet. All that day they sat at anchor, studying the currents and charting the course. Watson wanted to make the final run at night, when there was usually a good breeze. He timed it so they would be within four miles of landfall at daybreak, but the *Rob Roy's* bottom had been fouled by the tedious summer voyage and their speed was reduced.

The day broke hazy, with no land in sight. Watson had been instructed by a captain familiar with the Island to watch for three hillocks on the windward side. Three hours later he sighted them. Nudging his ship as close to the beach as he dared, Watson dropped anchor in nine feet of water. "It was a daring position for a ship on an open coast," he wrote, "but the *Rob Roy* was no ordinary vessel. It was drawing only about four feet of water, and if necessary could be propelled by oars and handled as easily as a ship's long-boat."

A troop of Confederate cavalry appeared on the beach. Watson recognized the soldiers as part of DeBray's Regiment, stationed east of Galveston. The soldiers told him that at last count the blockade fleet consisted of thirteen vessels. Watson decided the best time to run past the fleet was between 3 and 4 A.M.—"the sleepiest time when men on watch are more intent on listening for eight bells than looking for vessels." At sunset he luffed only the lower sails so that nothing would show above the dark loom of the land, and made for the harbor entrance.

Three hours after midnight Watson could hear the distant roar of breakers on the shoal at the eastern edge of the entrance. He anticipated a federal gunboat would be anchored near the shoal. Working close to the shore, away from the gunboat whose dim lines were visible now, Watson held his breath and tried to navigate by the stars. In places there was less than four feet of water. At one point Watson lowered his longboat and began sounding the bottom with a hand lead. When at last they located the main channel and went safely past the gunboat (they could see a second gunboat in the distance), Watson permitted himself a sigh of relief and ordered full sail.

Suddenly, a light flashed on the *Rob Roy's* port bow, and a voice called out: "Schooner ahoy. Heave to or we will sink you right quick."

Watson wasn't sure what to do. He thought he was too far into the harbor for any ship's boat to follow. "Who are you?" he cried.

"Confederate guard boat," came the reply. "What vessel is that?"

"The schooner *Rob Roy*," Watson said. "Out of Havana."

"All right. But heave to quick or you are sunk."

Watson put the helm hard down, forcing the *Rob Roy* into a sweep so wide that she almost ran into the guard boat. Crewmen rushed to push the boats apart, and the Confederate commander told Watson to drop a little astern and anchor until daylight. At first light Watson realized why the guard boat had threatened to sink the *Rob Roy*. It was the surest way to make Watson heave to and avoid certain destruction. Protruding from the surface of the dark waters he saw a pile of iron boilers and machinery: they had nearly run upon the wreckage of the *Westfield*.

There was great excitement as word swept across the Island that a runner had arrived. It had been several months since a ship had made it past the blockade. Watson loaded some gifts into a boat for General Magruder and his officers—tea and coffee, two cheeses, three kits of mackerel, a barrel of potatoes, a box of raisins, and other small articles. He also threw in a case of gin, a half-dozen bottles of brandy, and a dozen bottles of port. Liquor had been declared contraband and there was a penalty for bringing it into port, but Watson told Magruder's aide-de-camp, "This is a small donation for your hospital." The aide replied, "Good. Both the general and I are on the sick list."

As breakfast was being prepared at headquarters, the general himself stalked into the room, singing out in his curious stutter, "I think I smell cah-coffee, sure enough, as the Negroes s-say." Coffee had become one of the great luxuries in Galveston. People roasted and ground corn, beans, peas, and various kinds of seeds, but genuine coffee was so rare that even the general hadn't drunk it in months. "Coffee, sure enough" was the expression used by blacks when they tasted the real thing, and it had become a common expression among the officers and men on the Island.

Watson had heard that Magruder was among the most selfish and tyrannical of men, and was surprised to see the general share the coffee and other food luxuries with the wives and children of his soldiers. From their tattered clothing and shrunken eyes, it was apparent that the families had suffered greatly from the blockade. Watson learned from an officer at headquarters that the *Rob Roy* was the only one of the four ships that left Havana eighteen days ago that escaped capture. He also learned that the *Sylvia* was currently anchored in the Brazos River—with its cargo intact and six

Yankee prisoners. Captain Dave McCluskey had recaptured his ship, and arrived in Texas three days before the *Rob Roy*.

Captain William Watson's return to Havana would be delayed. The Island's main cotton press had broken down and was under repair. Watson didn't mind. It was nearly the end of August, the heart of hurricane season. The days were long, and the wind either blew too hard or not at all, hazardous conditions either way for a runner. The war wasn't going well for the South, but the port of Galveston was doing all right. Blockade running was going to get better before it got worse.

The rampant patriotism of earlier days had vanished. Islanders still read the war news, but it no longer seemed glorious. A reporter revisited the Manassas battlefield and wrote: "In shallow trenches and from broken mounds, petrified limbs stretched out to the sight. Here was a head partially uncovered, with the hair dropping off at the touch of a finger—there was a bunch of ghostly and putrified fingers clenched over the shallow earth of its grave. The stench was almost intolerable even in the morning air. . . ."

By the spring of 1865 everyone in the Confederacy knew the war was lost. On the Island, Confederate soldiers began to ransack stores and private homes. Four hundred armed men tried to desert, but were turned back by guards at the railroad bridge. Islanders took the news of the surrender with mixed emotion. No more war meant no more blockades to run. The party was over, and nobody was sorry to see it end.

# 11

No CITY IN the country recovered from the Civil War quicker than Galveston. In fact, Galveston's rise to prominence as one of the most prosperous and dynamic seaports in America was greatly assisted by the war, which had delayed construction of railroad connections between Houston and the cities and towns of the interior. Southern cities had been shattered by the war, physically annihilated, and spirtually rent with deep class conflict and racial antagonism. In the Texas heartland the planter gentry had been destroyed: most families who had money and station before the war found themselves bankrupt and humiliated in the years that followed. Islanders had not only been spared all that, they had been left with a near monopoly on trade and commerce.

The Island was the undisputed gateway to Texas, and hence to the Midwest: Galveston was 700 miles nearer the producing fields of Kansas and Nebraska, for example, than any Atlantic port, and 360 miles closer than any other Gulf port. Ninety-five percent of all trade goods entering or leaving Texas came through Galveston. By the late 1870s, the port of Galveston ranked third in the world in cotton exports, and continued to rank in the top five until well after the turn of the century. Galveston was one of the country's most prodigious grain exporters, too, and was destined to become the Gulf terminal of two great continental railway systems, the Southern Pacific and the Atchison, Topeka & Santa Fe.

While the citizens of Central and West Texas were still fighting off Comanches, Galveston became the largest, bawdiest, and most important city between New Orleans and San Francisco. In the streets of most Texas cities, armed mobs of bitter, unemployed soldiers rioted or marched against local authorities. You didn't see that on the Island. Galveston's main business street, the Strand, became known as the Wall Street of the Southwest, and its ornate Victorian buildings were the envy of cities all over the country. Five of the largest banks in Texas were located on the Strand, as were eight newspapers. The block between 23rd and 24th streets was known as Insurance Square. The city had six public squares, two parks, two miles of esplanade, street railways drawn by horses, thirteen hotels, three concert halls, and an opera house. Fancy shops sold fine English carpets; French china, wine, and brandy; and German-made rosewood pianos. In 1858 alone Islanders purchased twenty-three grand pianos. Galveston had the first gaslight, the first electric light, the first telephone, the first hospital, the first law firm, the first trade union, the first golf course—name any business or institution or invention and Galveston probably had the first in Texas.

The Strand was without question one of the most interesting streets anywhere. Restaurants like Monsieur Alphonse's specialized in dishes with names like *beefsteak goddam à la mode*, and saloons like the Gem and the Age never closed. Sam's Club and Sample Room was a rendezvous for "mercantile gentlemen," and provided exchange newspapers, free meeting rooms, lunch and whiskey. The street stirred with activity and pulsed with strange sights. A long-haired, wild-eyed drummer who called himself the King of Pain sold patent medicine from his wagon, and strolling show people with trained monkeys and bears performed for coins on street corners. Some of the street characters were nearly mythical. An old pirate called Crazy Ben, who wore an earring and claimed to have been one of Lafitte's corsairs, paid for drinks with gold doubloons. Another man ate glass for tips, and was reported to have consumed a half-dozen lamp chimneys in a single afternoon. There were Mardi Gras parades, some of them costing $10,000 or more, and circus parades; and on New Year's Day there was an annual extravanganza called the Parade of Butchers, in which butchers donned masks and marched in formation from saloon to saloon.

One of the cheaper entertainments was to hurry down to the docks to watch the immigrants disembark—Russians in fur coats,

Scots with bagpipes, Czechs and Poles staggering under the weight of outsized cooking vessels and trunks of memorabilia. Germans who had migrated previously sometimes rushed up the gangplanks searching for unmarried German women. Wedding vows between complete strangers were not uncommon. Immigrants poured in at a rate of 4,000 a year. By 1880 the population of Galveston had tripled from what it was before the war—from 7,300 to 22,240.

A reporter from the *New York Herald* visited the Island in 1874 and dubbed her "the New York of the Gulf." The population represented a Babel of nationalities: one-fourth were English, one-fourth German, one-sixth French, one-sixth Spanish, and the remainder a mixture of all other nations. Some of the immigrants came with money, and immediately settled in to enjoy the languid, luxurious pleasures that Island living offered. They woke with the sun, puttered or strolled in their gardens, and bathed in the Gulf —the women wearing long Mother Hubbards and large sun hats tied securely under their chins. At 7 A.M. the hotels across the Island rang their breakfast bells. After breakfast the men went to their offices on the Strand for a few hours, then played billiards or nine pins until lunch. Lunch was always laid out at the bar of the Tremont. In the late afternoons people gathered on the veranda for mint juleps—with ice, if a ship had chanced to arrive—or a glass of madeira and bitters. After a tea supper the men smoked or talked business, and the women sat on the veranda, listening to a serenade of guitars and violins.

Another reporter wrote that "this is one of the richest cities of its size on the continent." This was no exaggeration. Because of its marketing monopolies, the Island amassed the first real wealth in Texas. Galveston became the second-richest city in the United States: only Providence, Rhode Island, had a higher per capita income. It was said that as many as two dozen millionaires had offices on the Strand. The wholesale firms of P. J. Willis and Leon Blum monopolized dry goods and made fortunes stocking visiting ships and sending goods into the interior. The Sealy brothers, John and George, made big money in banking, and even bigger money monopolizing the Galveston wharves. Colonel William L. Moody and others made theirs by controlling the price of cotton. Harris Kempner was among those who got rich in merchandising, banking, and cotton. This was a new mercantile and landowning class of Texan, happily filling the vacuum left by the demise of the state's planter class. Leon Blum, for example, bought out dozens of bankrupt planters, until he owned a million acres in Texas, including land in every county. The Kempners and the Moodys also bought enormous tracts of land on the mainland.

Concentrated as it was among only a few families—it was estimated that the top twenty-four households were one hundred times richer than the next twenty-four—Galveston's new wealth spawned a new elite. It was better educated and more refined than the profiteers and scoundrels who founded the city, and more genteel than the rough adventurers who populated Houston and other cities in the Texas heartland, or on the frontier. Members of the new elite were unfailingly ambitious, but they also tended to be cautious, and preferred to invest in ventures that depended largely on someone else's capital and labor. Unique among Texas cities, Galveston had twenty-three stock companies, with capital exceeding $12 million.

The new rich put their wealth on display, building three-story Victorian mansions and castles, with turrets, spires, and columns topped with the carved heads of European rulers. Islanders were greatly influenced by Queen Victoria of England, whose reign from 1837 to 1901 closely paralleled the founding, rise to prominence, and final decline of Galveston.

Three families in particular—the Sealys, the Moodys, and the Kempners—dominated the Island, and continued to dominate it for more than a century, conveying social and political sanctions, and asserting the right to identify Galveston's needs and requirements with their own.

THE SEALYS were patricians who took what they wanted and gave a portion of it back as it suited their purpose. The mansion that the George Sealys built on Broadway, Open Gates, was a temple to aristocracy, with first-floor windows topped by soaring arches, and castle towers that opened onto second-floor balconies. The attic, underneath a steep red-tile roof, contained a children's theater. Most of Galveston's great homes were designed by architect Nicholas J. Clayton—who was brought to the Island by Harris Kempner in 1872 to supervise construction of a new Tremont Hotel— but the Sealys hired famed New York architect Stanford White to design Open Gates. Clayton assisted, however, and was permitted to design the Sealys' stables.

The Sealys were descended from Le Sire de Cailli (or Cely), who had accompanied William the Conquerer to England during the Norman invasion of 1066—and from Sir Benedict Sealy, who served the Black Prince and was beheaded at Oxford in 1400. Later generations married into French nobility and settled in Ireland. Robert Sealy, father of the two Galveston financiers, grew up on a large estate near Cork, but in 1818 surrendered his claim to the estate and migrated to Pennsylvania. His oldest son, John Sealy, came to Galveston in 1846.

By the mid-1850s John Sealy and two partners, J. H. Hutchings and George Ball, were running a thriving dry-goods business in Galveston, which soon expanded into a commissions firm called Ball, Hutchings & Company. In the spring of 1857 John's younger brother, George Sealy, also migrated to the Island, and went to work as a clerk for Ball, Hutchings.

George was a real go-getter, a tireless and ambitious young man who had paid his way through school by plowing and by working on a railroad. In Galveston he agreed to work for whatever wages his brother's partners thought fair. When other workers were sick or on vacation, George volunteered to take extra shifts.

Though he opposed secession, George enlisted in the Confederate army and served three years on the Mexican border, without pay. This wasn't as altruistic as it appeared. Throughout the war he used his position in the office of the commanding general of the Western Division of Texas to represent the firm of Ball, Hutchings & Company at Matamoros, Mexico. During the blockade of Confederate ports, Matamoros was the South's main passage to the Gulf, and the firm made a fortune exporting cotton to Europe.

After the war George Sealy convinced the firm's senior partner, George Ball, to expand into the banking business. Ball, it will be remembered, was already familiar with banking, having served as a director of Samuel May William's ill-fated Commercial & Agricultural Bank in the late 1850s.

Two years after the war George Sealy became a full partner in the firm, which was now focusing most of its attention on banking. The Hutchings Sealy National Bank, as it came to be called, was the largest bank in Galveston or anywhere else in Texas. The HSNB could make or break any public project with a nod of its head. It constituted a de facto monopoly until the Moodys and Kempners got into the banking business in the 1870s: for nearly a hundred years after that, three families—the Sealys, the Moodys, and the Kempners—owned all of the banks on the Island.

Over the objections of the city government, the Sealys and their associates forged a monopoly called the Galveston Wharf Company. The city took the company to court, claiming it had no right to take over the entire waterfront, but after a protracted legal battle the company prevailed. John Sealy became president of the port, followed by his brother, followed by his own son, followed by his brother's son. Not until 1945 did someone other than a Sealy run the port of Galveston.

Under Sealy stewardship the port earned the reputation of charging the highest wharfing fees on the Gulf. In Houston and elsewhere in the interior, the Galveston Wharf Company became known as the "Octopus of the Gulf." Its reputation was probably exaggerated—historian David McComb says that company dividends rarely exceeded 6 percent, and never went over 7 percent. Nevertheless, the company's image as a monopolistic monster made it a convenient scrapegoat for all the economic ills of the state. Farmers believed that the Wharf Company was the reason they were barely surviving, and the Grange took up the farmers' battle and provided proof that the grievances were just. While draymen were transferring cotton from rail to ship for 15 cents a bale, a Grange study revealed, the Wharf Company collected forty cents, thus robbing the farmer of twenty-five cents on every bale. The Octopus of the Gulf was near the top of everyone's hate list. Consumers in the interior blamed it for the high cost of imports, and citizens of Galveston, who didn't own stock in the company, charged that the city had granted too many concessions on its waterfront. Ownership of the wharves became the Island's major political issue.

In 1869, in an effort to mollify the voters of Galveston, the Sealys gave the city a larger share of stock, but no concessions were made in response to the chorus of complaints from Houston and the hinterlands. Secure that they were in control of the only true deepwater harbor in the state, the Sealys exacted all the profits their monopoly permitted.

But Galveston Harbor had its shortcomings, as many Houstonians enjoyed pointing out. A twelve-foot bar partially blocked the way between Galveston Bay and the Gulf, and a second bar—the so-called inner bar—had formed between Bolivar Channel and Galveston Harbor proper, probably because of obstructions placed in the harbor during the Civil War. Despite the city's efforts to remove it, this bar shoaled to about nine and a half feet. If the Sealys had consulted a map, they might have realized that a major port on a barrier island didn't make sense in the first place. All the great ports in the United States at the time—Boston, New York, Philadelphia, Baltimore, New Orleans—were sheltered from the open sea. Only Galveston Island was out there by itself, exposed to the fury of nature.

Houston businessmen were already making plans to break the Galveston Wharf Company's monopoly. The Houston Direct Navigation Company was organized for the purpose of putting barges on the bayou to load and unload ocean vessels in mid-channel, thus bypassing the port of Galveston entirely. By the spring of 1868, the Houston Direct Navigation Company had a shipping agreement with a New York steamship company, and was advertising: "through bills of lading from Houston to New York, and from New York to Houston, without touching Galveston, at a saving of 20% to 40% to the shipper." Within five years the navigation company had six passenger steamers, eighteen barges, and five tugs in operation. It was estimated that the company carried 75 percent of the freight and products of the interior, and that it saved the consumers of Texas $1 million a year in Galveston handling charges.

What Houston really had in mind was its own deep-water port. In 1875 a channel was dredged down the bayou to a depth of twelve feet. When a Morgan Line ship successfully steamed down the channel, carrying five hundred tons of steel for Houston's proposed transfer railroad, the editors of the *Houston Telegraph* wrote that the merchants of Houston were at last "free of the extortions of Galveston's *bête noir*, its hideous wharf monopoly."

The wharves weren't the Sealys' only monopoly. Through their private bank they controlled Galveston's gas and electric utilities, and by 1880 they owned the railroads, too. The Island's first railroad, the Galveston, Houston & Henderson (GH&H), went bankrupt in 1867, mainly because Houston politicians refused it right-of-way to connect with the Houston & Texas Central, and hence the cotton-producing Brazos Valley. John Sealy took over the GH&H, and eventually merged it with Jay Gould's Missouri Pacific. Meanwhile, a group of Island merchants led by a good-hearted Swiss immigrant named Henry Rosenberg raised $700,000—an incredible sum for that time—and formed its own railroad, the Gulf, Colorado & Santa

Fe (GC&SF). Within six years it had gone broke, and George Sealy was able to buy controlling interest in the GC&SF for two cents on the dollar.

Sealy had not forgotten the way Houston had bypassed his port with its navigation company, and when the GC&SF expanded in 1873, Sealy made certain that it reached the hinterlands without passing through Houston or even touching the surrounding Harris County. Galveston County subscribed half a million dollars in bonds toward the railroad's construction, and Galveston citizens invested heavily in its stock. By 1881 the line reached all the way to Fort Worth, where it connected with the Atchison, Topeka & Santa Fe (AT&SF). A few years later Sealy merged his line with the AT&SF.

The expanded routes were a mixed blessing to Galveston's new elite. On the one hand, they connected Galveston with Kansas City and St. Louis, opening trade between the Island and the Midwest. On the other, they destroyed the monopoly that Colonel William Moody and other cotton factorers enjoyed, giving farmers and traders an option they hadn't previously enjoyed. As things turned out, it was more profitable to ship cotton and trade goods by rail to places like Dallas and St. Louis than it was to ship them from the port of Galveston. Major cotton-compressing depots popped up all along the line. The railroads had inadvertently become the enemy of Galveston's prosperous cotton-compressing industry. When Colonel Moody realized what had happened, he brought pressure on the city of Galveston to break up the Wharf Company's monopoly. The Sealys were able to resist, but this was the beginning of a feud between the two families that would still be raging long after Colonel Moody and the Sealy brothers were in their graves.

THE MOODYS were never people to put principle over profit. William L. Moody's great-great-grandfather, an English banker and trader named John Moody, migrated to Virginia in 1680, with the intention of getting rich. John Moody was a temperate and God-fearing man—"The drunkard," he wrote in his diary, "is the greatest of all malicious men"—but Moody's principles didn't prevent him from listing among his trade goods "rum . . . sidar (and) beere (ye King's Pure)."

An orphan at age sixteen, William L. Moody worked his way through law school at the University of Virginia, then set out on horseback to make his fortune in Texas. He opened a law practice in the North Texas village of Fairfield in 1852, and married the daughter of a wealthy merchant named Bradley. Unlike many southerners who adopted the rank, Moody was a real colonel and a genuine Civil War hero. Though one newspaper editor later claimed that Moody spent the war shuffling papers in Austin, the record is clear that he served with honor and distinction throughout the South. He was taken prisoner in Tennessee when federal troops captured Fort Donelson, was later released in a prisoner exchange, and thereafter seriously wounded at Vicksburg. He did spend the final two years of the war as a military affairs aide in the State Capitol at Austin. That's where he got promoted to full colonel.

After the war Moody moved to Galveston and established a cotton-factoring business in the old Hendley Building. He had the building remodeled specifically for the business, laying thick translucent glass across the ceiling of the first floor so that cotton graders would have ample light. The second and third floors opened onto a giant atrium, rimmed with offices. Across the domed ceiling was another, even larger skylight. The front of the building was elevated so that drays could unload their cargo directly from the Strand, and the rear doors opened onto Hendley's Wharf and Galveston Bay. On their lunch hour cotton graders used to fish out of the rear windows.

A large and blustery man with eyes like hot coals, Moody knew what he wanted and went after it. Cotton was a rough-and-tumble business just after the war. The only rule was "hard trade," which meant that it was every man for himself. Moody thrived in this atmosphere, but his shrewd sense of the market warned him that things were getting out of hand. Unless traders found a way to cooperate, the forces of supply and demand could ruin everyone. Moody decided to organize an association of agents who bought and sold cotton on commission—so-called cotton factorers. Later he formed one of the Island's central commercial institutions, the Galveston Cotton Exchange. The exchange revolutionized the cotton trade, not only in Texas but in places as far away as St. Louis, Chicago, and even Liverpool. The cotton exchange became as important to Galveston commerce as the wharf company.

The colonel, however, may have had his own selfish uses for the cotton exchange. According to a muckraking journalist of the time, William Brann—who published an outspoken and irreverent newspaper called the *Iconoclast*—Moody used it to cheat cotton farmers.

From his interviews with farmers, Brann cited an example of how Moody worked. Say the market reached 8.5 cents per pound: Moody would hold a large amount of cotton on consignment, but advise his clients to wait for a better price. When the price slumped to 6.5, as Moody knew it would, he would pretend to sell, apologizing to his clients for the unexpected downturn—and at the same time charging them extra storage fees, and interest on money advanced. In fact, Brann claimed, the colonel actually sold the cotton at 8.5, paying hush money to keep the transaction secret.

But that wasn't all. Brann also alleged that the colonel used two sets of scales, one for sellers, another for the buyers. When a farmer brought cotton to one of Moody's warehouses, his hired hand would weigh it and deduct ten pounds per bale "for water." The bales would then sit for a few weeks on the wharf, soaking up Galveston's excessive humidity. Then a second weigher—this one an accommodating state inspector—would weigh the bales again, water and all. The state inspector's figures would be used to calculate what the buyer paid. The difference, which was substantial, went into Moody's pocket.

Colonel Moody was a member of the state legislature in 1874, but he resigned to become the state's financial agent and—again according to Brann—to bilk the state out of hundreds of thousands of dollars. To dispose of its enormous floating debt, the state sent Moody to New York to sell a large block of 8 percent bonds. But instead of selling the bonds through normal channels, Brann charged, Moody formed a syndicate which bought the whole lot at a discount and resold it at par. This windfall profit was supposed to have netted Moody and his associates $500,000. "It seems to me," Brann wrote, "that such a creature [as Moody] would fear to be left alone lest he filch from his own body his own bowels and sell 'em to a sausage factory." None of these allegations ever appeared in the *Galveston Daily News*, of course. They might have been totally false and blatantly libelous, but the colonel never got around to denying them, or suing the editor of the *Iconoclast*.

THE THIRD of the seignorial families that was to shape and dominate Galveston far into the future exercised relatively little influence at first. Harris Kempner, the family patriarch, was a cautious man who for years refused to buy on credit or invest in property on the

Island. Born in a farming community in what is now eastern Poland, Kempner fled to America in 1853 to keep from being drafted into the czar's army, a ploy of the times used to "Christianize" young Jews. For several years he was a rag merchant in New York, rolling his pushcart along the Lower East Side. Before the Civil War he migrated to Texas, settling in the small community of Coldspring in San Jacinto County. Kempner strongly opposed slavery and secession, and refused to own slaves, even though friends warned him that free black labor was a matter of economic survival. He was a practical man, widely trusted for his honesty and steadfastness. During the war wealthy planters in San Jacinto County used him as a surrogate banker, depositing large sums in his trust. Kempner also served a hitch in the Confederate army, duty he found distasteful but necessary.

After the war Kempner moved to Galveston and opened a general mercantile business with a partner named M. Marx. They were an odd couple, Marx and Kempner. Marx had drifted around the West, working in the Montana Territory and in Salt Lake City. He was a genial and affable man, an incurable optimist who believed that Galveston's future was unlimited, and that evil and greed were aberrations unworthy of serious attention. By contrast, Harris Kempner was abrupt, cool, and rigidly businesslike; he believed that Galveston's destiny was doomed by its size, its lack of fresh water, and its seasonal epidemics of yellow fever. Naturally, they made a perfect team.

Kempner was quick to see changes in the market, and Marx understood that Galveston was a place where the market demanded special considerations. Kempner didn't have time for the amenities of life, but Marx knew that many Islanders had time for nothing else. The old Tremont Hotel, where Sam Houston had made his famous speech opposing secession, had burned in 1865, and Marx convinced his partner they should build a new one. A young architect from Memphis named Nicholas Clayton was brought in to design it.

With its rotunda of Corinthian columns, Italian marble floors, and grand staircase, the second Tremont became the finest hotel in the South. Clayton decided to stay in Galveston, and over the next forty years changed the face of the city. He designed many of the great structures on the Strand, including the W. L. Moody Build-

ing, the Marx & Kempner Building, the Hutchings, Sealy Bank
Building, and many spectacular homes. But when Harris Kempner
built his own home, he used a design from a mail-order catalogue.

On one of his frequent buying trips to New York, Kempner met
and married Eliza Seinsheimer from Cincinnati. Eventually, they
had eleven children, eight that lived. They regularly attended synagogue at Temple B'nai Israel, and their mail-order home at 20th
and Avenue M was comfortable, and large enough to include quarters for a coachman, a cook, a maid, and a governess. There weren't
yet any public schools on the Island. The governess taught the
Kempner children to read and write, and while she was at it, she
also taught the children of the black servants, a practice that offended some other members of Galveston's new elite, who believed
that educating blacks was akin to blasphemy.

Harris Kempner was a great believer in charity, and highly critical of men like Colonel Moody, who preached but didn't practice
it. Every Saturday after attending synagogue, Kempner would have
his coachman harness his carriage, and would go from house to
house delivering baskets of food to Jewish refugees. Over the years
he maintained contact with his family in Poland, sending money
to relatives and paying expenses for six nephews who migrated to
Texas. He had an almost fanatical respect for law and democracy,
and frequently lectured his children on the differences between
living in the United States and in his native Poland. Each spring
he hosted a formal dinner for the judges of the Texas Supreme
Court, a ritual that lasted until his death in 1894. "Only in America,"
he told his children, "could a lowly born Pole enjoy such distinguished company."

Kempner was a great believer in the ownership of land, too—
Jews in Poland weren't allowed to own real estate. He purchased
thousands of acres, much of it one-time plantation land that had
been greatly devalued after the emancipation of the slaves. He still
refused to buy commodities, or speculate on cotton, but he did buy
token amounts of local stock—Gulf, Colorado & Santa Fe Railroad
stock for example—because he believed it was his duty as a good
citizen.

Eventually, Harris Kempner relaxed his self-imposed rule against
buying on credit and began borrowing prudent sums to invest in
bank stock. Before long he owned rural banks all over Texas. In

1887 Galveston's Island City Bank was forced into bankruptcy, and its president killed himself. Members of the bank's board persuaded Kempner to take over the bank's reorganization, and then asked him to stay on as its president. Though he had no banking experience, except as an investor—and as a trustee for planters during the war—Kempner found that banking appealed to his practical nature. By the 1890s the firm of H. Kempner had established credit with banks in New York, London, Paris, and Zurich.

Late in life Kempner violated another one of his cardinal rules and indulged in cotton speculation. Advancing a large sum of money for a shipment of cotton from North Texas, he was stunned when the cargo arrived: it wasn't cotton at all, it was *linters*, the fuzz that clings to cottonseed after ginning. He never recovered his money. "Well, Mr. Kempner," a lawyer said to him, "you must think all cotton men are thieves." Harris Kempner thought about this for a minute and said; "No, but I think some skillful thieves have gotten into the cotton business."

# 12

RECONSTRUCTION brought a new black elite to the Island, too, but it never got rich, and it numbered only two. Both were mulatto carpetbaggers whose main activity—at least in the beginning—was to whip up black support for the Radical Republican coalition of Edmund J. Davis.

The first of Galveston's prominent new blacks, George T. Ruby, came to the Island from New Orleans, as an agent for the Freedmen's Bureau in 1866. But his true role was director of the Union League, a secret society whose members went South to educate blacks to vote Radical Republican. "Between the Union League and the Army, the freedmen were dragooned and told that [the Conservative Republicans] intended to reinslave them," wrote historian T. R. Fehrenbach. By forming an alliance with George Ruby—and by rigging the registration process so that only their followers were permitted to vote—the Davis Radicals seized power from the Conservatives in the election of 1869. The Democrats, under Galveston publisher Hamilton Stuart, virtually conceded the election, though many voted for the Conservatives as the lesser of two evils.

The other new black was Norris Wright Cuney, son of a white Brazos Valley planter named Colonel Philip N. Cuney and his slave mistress, Adeline Stuart. When the Radical Republicans were voted out of office in 1874, Ruby returned to New Orleans, but Cuney stayed on in Galveston as president of the Union League, and later as a power in city and state politics, and organizer of the city's (and the state's) first black union.

E. J. Davis wasn't the worst southern governor during Reconstruction, but it is safe to say that during his four-year term (1870–74) he was the most unpopular governor Texas has ever had. The Radicals strongly disliked white Texans, though most of them were white Texans themselves: Davis was a judge in Brownsville before the war. But their ideology went beyond Unionism, to a visceral hatred of anything remotely connected to the Confederacy. Texans were a conquered people, Davis believed, and deserved to be treated as such. He wanted to divide Texas into three parts, and would have if the Democrats hadn't eventually fused with the Conservatives to drive him from power.

While Texas was still under military occupation in the summer of 1869, the Radicals used the army to purge the state of its political officeholders, right down to the county level. Davis' men were appointed in their place. The army and the Freedmen's Bureau not only registered black voters in disproportionate numbers—in a state that was only one-fourth black, they registered 49,779 blacks, as opposed to 59,633 whites—but any white who had volunteered or even supported the Confederacy was refused the right to vote, or the right to serve on a jury, a regulation that virtually destroyed the civil court system. Once Davis was in office, he assumed almost dictatorial powers. The Enabling Act gave the governor absolute control of patronage: he appointed mayors, district attorneys, even city aldermen. The hated State Police, composed of black carpetbaggers, criminals, and psychos, was the governor's private force, and was used as a tool of repression. When Conservative delegates to the state convention in Galveston in 1871 tried to protest the fraudulent nomination of two black Radicals, Davis' State Police cut off the gaslights and drove the convention out on the streets before the nominations could be overturned or questioned.

As a reward for his services to the Radical cause, Ruby was appointed deputy collector of customs for Galveston. Later he was elected to the state senate, where he became an able and honest legislator, supporting not only the rights of blacks, but the economic and social well-being of the entire Island. Having enjoyed a liberal education in his native Maine, Ruby was a strong advocate of public education. At the end of the war there were no public schools on the Island, or anywhere else in Texas. The Freedmen's Bureau established four schools in 1867, using churches and private homes as classrooms. The teachers were mostly people from the North or educated German immigrants, and classes were open to whites and blacks alike, though no whites showed up. But nearly four hundred blacks enrolled, grownups as well as children. Ferdinand Flake's *Die Union* supported these schools, but the reactionary *Galveston Daily News* found them abhorrent. "It will do no black child any good to be taught beside a white child," the newspaper editorialized, "while the attempt would do the white child a good deal of injury because the position is repugnant to its feelings and those of its parents." The *News* took satisfaction in pointing out that George Ruby was married to a blond white woman, to the exclusion of all the fine black women on the Island.

Like his mentor George Ruby, Wright Cuney was far better educated than other Island blacks. He had grown up at Sunnyside Plantation, on the Brazos River bottom in Waller County, one of eight children born to the plantation's chief housekeeper. Adeline Stuart was a shrewd and clever woman who maintained a protracted love affair with her master, Colonel Cuney, through two of his three marriages. None of Adeline's children worked the fields or lived in the slave quarters. Wright learned to play the bass violin from an old slave called Henry the Fiddler, and frequently played for admiring crowds when the colonel took him along on trading trips. In 1853 the colonel left the plantation in the care of an overseer and took Adeline and the children to live with him in Houston. Seven years later he manumitted all of them, and sent Wright and two of his brothers to the Wylie Street Public School for Negroes in Pittsburgh.

During the war Wright Cuney idled around river towns along the Mississippi and worked on the steamboat *Grey Eagle*, which ran between Cincinnati and New Orleans. He became friends with several blacks who would play prominent roles in the radical reconstruction of the South, and at their urging he joined the Union League. At the close of the war he recognized the opportunity Galveston presented, and moved to the Island to help George Ruby and the other Union Leaguers in their quest to sway the black vote to the Radical Republicans. In 1870 Governor Davis rewarded Cuney by appointing him first assistant to the sergeant-at-arms of the state legislature. There Cuney learned parlimentary rules and the skill of political maneuvering. A year later he returned to Galveston as county agent and president of the Union League.

A slender, handsome, dapper man with a fondness for Prince Edward suits and imported cigars, Wright Cuney looked Mediterranean rather than African. Though he frequently had no visible means of support, Cuney and his family lived better than most Islanders, black or white. Many believed that Cuney was a silent partner in the infamous Belle Poole Club, a gin joint and gambling hall notorious for cheating black workers out of their paychecks. Whatever Wright Cuney was, he was a man to be reckoned with. Cuney and George Ruby were the only two blacks on the Island who could walk into the bar at the Tremont without causing trouble. The white elite recognized the black elite and understood that the time would come when the black elite would have its uses.

That time came during a wildcat strike in 1877. Ruby had returned to New Orleans by now, leaving Cuney as the undisputed black leader in Galveston. This was a tense and restless period for labor. Wages were low, and competition for jobs keen. Cuney helped organize a black longshoremen's union in 1876, the first union of any kind for blacks. When black railyard workers staged a wildcat strike a year later, Cuney faced down a mob of more than three hundred and convinced them to return to work—to the gratitude and delight of the white power structure. After that, whenever there was a labor problem involving blacks, the whites called on Cuney. Some blacks accused Cuney of selling out, but the blacks who stood with him always had jobs and a measure of economic security.

In 1883 Cuney got himself elected alderman, just in time to confront a bitter controversy involving public schools. Banker George Ball died in 1884, leaving $50,000 to be used to build the Island's first public high school. Cuney and a second black alderman, J. H. Washington, pressured the school board to open the new school to all races. Cuney did not personally approve of integrated schools —he believed that slavery precluded social equality of the races— but he felt strongly that Ball High School was the only opportunity for blacks to continue their education. At first, the school board agreed, but changed its mind when Ball's heirs bumped the grant another $10,000, provided that the high school admitted only white students.

That same year Cuney solicited Galveston Cotton Exchange Pres-

ident William L. Moody as an ally. In a letter to the colonel, Cuney
pointed out that Galveston commerce was being harmed by a lack
of skilled laborers on the wharves, and that Cuney had three
hundred blacks ready, willing, and able to outwork white longshoremen for two-thirds the salary. Moody wrote back that he
would welcome additional labor on the wharves. When white longshoremen struck Morgan's Wharf in 1883, Cuney undercut the
strike by bringing in black scabs, some from as far away as New
Orleans. Cuney had become more than merely a black man on the
make: he had become a wedge between the white majority's two
economic classes.

A dock strike two years later was one of the bitterest and most
divisive in Galveston history. In the spring of 1885, while business
was poor, white longshoremen voluntarily accepted a reduction in
wages, from 50 cents to 40 cents an hour. The management of
Mallory Lines promised the union that when things got better, the
original wage would be restored. By October the economy had
recovered but the wage hadn't. When a committee of longshoremen
went to the Mallory Lines offices and demanded that the company
live up to its bargain, they were all fired. A strike was called to force
Mallory Lines to rehire the workers and restore the normal wage.
Meanwhile, the steamer *State of Texas* lay unloaded at Mallory's
Wharf. This was a perfect opportunity to use Cuney's blacks.

Cuney agreed that his men would work for Mallory Lines, on one
condition: "I don't want my men used as cat's paws to pull the
chestnuts from the fire," Cuney said, meaning that the black longshoremen would be retained in the future, and would have an equal
chance with whites. By the end of October blacks were unloading
the *State of Texas*, under police protection. At first, there was no
violence. The whites reconsidered, and sent word to management
that they would agree to work for the same wages the blacks were
getting—40 cents an hour for day work, 50 cents for night and
Sunday. Management said thanks, but no thanks. The white longshoremen appealed to their parent union, the Knights of Labor.

In November the Knights of Labor called a general strike, prac-
tically shutting down Galveston commerce. Workers walked off the
job at the Santa Fe Railroad, the cotton presses, the docks, the
harbor shops, the printing offices—nearly two-thousand workers
in all. Despite the efforts of police, strikers stopped trains and
threatened crews. In response to a plea from the Santa Fe, the

sheriff called out the local militia as a posse comitatus. From the railyards to the docks, armed men squared off, rifles and shotguns at the ready. In one of the more ludicrous displays, members of the elite Galveston's Artillery Club arrived with two 12-pound howitzers, to the jeers and catcalls of strikers. The sheriff finally stepped between the posse and the strikers, temporarily restoring order; but tension gripped the Island, and people locked their doors and drew their blinds.

Wright Cuney's daughter Maud remembered that her father came home that afternoon and told his wife to take Maud and her brother Lloyd over to their Uncle Joseph Cuney's house for the night. But Mrs. Cuney flatly refused. "Putting my brother and me to bed," Maud wrote, "she took her vigil at the back window. Friends, a dozen or more, well armed, gathered quietly at dark in our living room and dining room, preparing to stay with father throughout the night." Across the street from the house, hidden among the salt cedars, were black longshoremen, determined to fight if a mob appeared. Other blacks guarded the alley. Some of the men had guitars and other stringed instruments, so that if the police accused them of loitering they could claim they were just there to serenade. "But the night passed safely," Maud recalled. "My baby brother and I could not understand the danger."

In his position as director of the Santa Fe Railroad, George Sealy called the various factions to the negotiating table and offered a compromise. Split the work equally between blacks and whites, Sealy suggested. Let them work alternate weeks, on a basis of two steamers a week. Even though blacks had been promised steady work, Cuney got them to agree to the compromise. The *Galveston News* hailed Alderman Cuney for his "conservative and wise policy," but many blacks saw this as an example of the way Cuney exploited his people for his own gain. However tenuous, the strike was settled. Black longshoremen had gained a permanent place on the docks, and Cuney had made new business and political contacts. In 1889 Cuney was appointed collector of customs, "the most important post ever given to a colored man in the South," wrote the *New York Age*.

LABOR UNREST wasn't the only problem confronting Galveston's white elite in the 1880s. A far more serious problem was Houston's threat to the port of Galveston. On one thing nearly everyone agreed: it was imperative that Galveston secure a true deep-water harbor.

For thousands of years the entrance to the harbor had been hindered by tidal sandbars that formed across the channel, between the Island and Bolivar Peninsula. In Lafitte's time, the bars were twelve or thirteen feet below the surface, no problem for the light, shallow-draught sailing ships of the corsairs. Over the years the bars had continued to silt and expand until, by 1875, the inner bar allowed only eight feet of clearance.

By now sailing ships had been replaced by larger, heavier steamers that required twenty feet and sometimes more. This meant that cargoes arriving or leaving the port had to be lightered—transported across the bar in flat-bottom scows, pushed by tugboats, while the steamship lay at anchor outside the harbor. The method was cumbersome and costly to the shippers, who were finding it more convenient to use the new facilities offered by the Houston Direct Navigation Company. If Galveston was to prosper, and especially if it was to compete with the transcontinental railroads, deep water was essential.

A committee of businessmen that included the Island's three ruling families put the problem in the hands of Captain Charles Fowler, a one-time stalwart in the Worthy and Ancient Order of the JOLO. Fowler, who had become an agent for the Morgan Line after the war, and a member of Galveston's board of aldermen, devised a plan that would use the same current that had created the sandbars to scour them away. By sinking three rows of submerged pilings off the tip of the Island, Fowler hoped to refocus the current, force it to rake across the bars and sweep away the sediment.

The plan did provide a temporary solution, reducing the bars until there was thirteen feet of clearance, but that still wasn't enough. A first-class harbor, according to the classifications of the time, was one that could accommodate a ship drawing twenty-six feet of water at low tide. By that definition there wasn't a first-class port on the Gulf coast. The harbors at Tampa and Pensacola were considered second-class ports, which meant they had assured depths of twenty to twenty-five feet. Any port below twenty feet was considered third class. Mobile and Galveston fell into this category. New Orleans had been a third-class port, but it was solving the problem of deep water by building jetties above the surface rather than submerged, as Fowler's design had produced. Word from New Orleans was that the new harbor would soon be able to accommodate any ship in the world.

Islanders had always insisted that New Orleans was a Mississippi River port, not a Gulf port. Technically, this was true. But it was also true that New Orleans was the port nearest to Galveston, and its main seafaring competitor. The mere thought of a world-class harbor in New Orleans was more than enough to make Galveston businessmen put aside their petty jealousies and intramural squabbles.

Colonel Moody took the lead. In 1881 he called a meeting at the Cotton Exchange, and organized the Committee on Deep Water—more commonly known as the Deep Water Committee or DWC. John and George Sealy and Harris Kempner joined the effort, as did other civic leaders such as Leon Blum, Colonel Walter Gresham, and Charles Fowler. They hired the same engineer who had built the successful jetties in New Orleans, and sent Colonel Gresham to Washington to look for money. That's how New Orleans had been able to afford its jetty project—through federal subsidies.

There was a touch of irony and a dab of hypocrisy in this approach. All of the worthies on the Deep Water Committee were champions of private enterprise, deeply suspicious and scornful of anyone who fed at the public trough. But this was no time for ideology. The engineer estimated that it would cost $7.7 million to guarantee Galveston thirty feet of water. Members of the DWC weren't about to dig that kind of money from their own pockets, but they were willing to pull out all the stops to convince the federal government to fork it over.

The crusade took more than a decade, during which time the new elite did things it had never dreamed of doing. If they were going to get that kind of money from a Republican Congress, George Sealy suggested, they'd better elect a Republican representative. Nearly a quarter of a century after the Civil War, there hadn't been a single Republican elected to Congress from south of the Mason-Dixon line. Everyone in Texas remembered the Radical Republican administration of the despised Edmund Davis.

Nobody hated the party of Lincoln more than Colonel William L. Moody, who was to become an ardent supporter and close friend of Democratic presidential candidate William Jennings Bryan. But these were desperate times. The DWC selected a wealthy sugar merchant named R. B. Hawley, and got him elected on the Republican ticket, a campaign that shocked the Old South but which was fairly consistent with the Island's habit of doing whatever was expedient.

Token Republicanism wasn't the only concession members of the DWC were prepared to make. To offset criticism that the Galveston Wharf Company had been systematically gouging shippers, the Sealys agreed to open their books. An inspection revealed that, rather than paying 100 percent dividends, as some had charged, the figure was usually in the 1.5 to 5 percent range.

Subcommittees were organized to court politicians from as far away as Fort Worth, Denver, and Topeka. The DWC even issued a personal invitation to President Grover Cleveland—a Democrat— to visit the Island and try the fishing. Despite the fact that Galveston had sent a Republican to Congress, Cleveland accepted the invitation, and ended up supporting the deep-water project.

And still it was a long, hard pull, stymied at every turn by congressional representatives from rival cities. Nobody had forgotten the Octopus of the Gulf. A federal grant of $1.5 million was finally appropriated, thanks more to Colonel Gresham's lobbying than to Hawley's influence in Congress. The first attempt to build jetties failed, but by 1890 things were falling into place. Looking again at the problem, engineers decided to construct two parallel jetties, one extending from the tip of the Island and the other from the tip of Bolivar Peninsula. They built a railroad trestle over the water and hauled five-ton sandstone blocks to form a trapezoidal wall. Where the wall broke above the waterline, they capped it with ten-ton granite squares until it stood five feet above the surface.

Dredges worked along the channel, removing silt and the wreckage of old ships. The Wharf Company spent $2 million of its own money improving wharves and docks, digging deep slips, and laying railway tracks along the whole waterfront, with branches to each wharf and pier. By 1896 there were two miles of stone-capped piers, and the water depth ranged from twenty-seven feet on the outer bar to nearly forty feet along the channel in front of town. That same year the Galveston Artillery Company hauled its cannons to the beach and fired a 100-gun salute, welcoming the British steamer *Algoa*, the largest cargo ship in the world.

It had taken a Herculean effort, and a massive amount of pride-swallowing, but the project was a huge success. Within a year Galveston was the second leading cotton port in the world, surpassed only by Liverpool. "It is doubtful," wrote one historian, "if any port in the world ever attained such prominence in such a short time."

Long after the problem of deep water had been solved, the Deep Water Committee continued to function. It was too powerful—and too useful—to let die.

# 13

THERE WAS an idyllic quality about Galveston in the last quarter of the nineteenth century, a sort of Toy Town mystique that suggested that life was a party that went on forever. It had grown into a distinctly cosmopolitan city, tropical in appearance like New Orleans, but smaller and less southern. From the time of Jean Lafitte, Galveston had absorbed its laissez-faire culture, and some of its population, from the old French-speaking port. In true New Orleans style, Galvestonians tolerated, even appreciated, wickedness. They lived according to their own rules, their own values, their own interpretations of morality.

But there were important differences between the two cities. However unique its heritage and tradition, New Orleans was part of the mainland. Galveston was first and always an Island, a place apart. The birthright of every Islander was blessed isolation, a condition to be ardently defended, but one that extracted a price. The isolation did strange things to the psyche, fostering a conceit that Galveston was not part of the whole, that it could deny the obvious and escape the universal. At the same time, there was a claustrophobic perception of limits. Crowded together as they were, Islanders understood that there was little room for error, and that tolerating that which would be intolerable in other circumstances was a precondition of existence.

Though the fabric of Galveston society was a blend of nearly every thread in the world, Islanders found it fashionable to thumb their noses at outsiders. When it was necessary to mention Houston at all, they called it Mudville. The story went that an Islander attempting to cross one of Houston's boggy streets observed a sign that read NO BOTTOM! There had been a time, to be sure, when pedestrians attempting to negotiate the Strand sank ankle-deep in sand, but by the 1890s the Strand had elevated sidewalks and was paved with wooden blocks—an impressive civic improvement, except during times of high tides when the Strand's pavement had an annoying tendency to float away.

Many Island homes stood on stilts and looked as fragile as grasshoppers ready to scatter. But this was the age of Nicholas Clayton, too, and the churches, cathedrals, and synagogues were oversized and wonderfully ostentatious. Even the warehouses had a touch of Victorian Gothic so that they looked like crypts rather than simple storage places. The famed architect was a compulsive Christianizer: his doodles were sketches of church windows, altars, and steeples. His first day on the Island, Clayton headed directly for St. Mary's Cathedral, stopping along the way to purchase a ceramic Madonna and Child from a pawn shop on Market Street. As though it were his primary duty, Clayton checked in with the local bishop, and in the course of their conversation convinced the bishop that what the cathedral needed was a central tower to balance the two towers at the front of the basilica. After the hurricane of 1876, the church agreed and Clayton was allowed to build his tower. He crowned it with a statue of Mary, Star of the Sea, positioned to look out over the Island and protect it.

There was an ongoing battle among the new elite to see who could build the grandest mansion, and the winner was Colonel Walter Gresham, lawyer and lobbyist for the Deep Water Committee. The mammoth structure that Clayton designed for Gresham and his wife at the corner of 14th and Broadway was a gray sandstone and granite fortress, with four four-story turrets, topped with the winged horses of Assyria, a trio of tiled cones, and numerous chimneys and balconies. In today's dollars it would have cost about $5 million.

Most of Galveston's elite lived on Broadway. One notable exception was Colonel William L. Moody, who lived at 23rd and Avenue M, in a pre–Civil War mansion. But Broadway was the place to be and be seen, a street of elegant homes set along a wide esplanade planted with oaks, oleanders, and palms imported from the West

Indies. Streetcar tracks ran along the esplanade, between these borders of tropical foliage, and at night people sat on their galleries or gathered on street corners and watched the so-called "pretty cars" strung with multicolored electric lights and filled with young people singing and laughing.

Mardi Gras parades and balls got more elaborate every year. The wealthiest Islanders retained Parisian designers, who made yearly trips from France to outfit their Galveston clientele. Exclusive gowns and costumes were tailored to annual themes—the Crusades, Peter the Great, Beelzebub and the Devils. Horse-drawn wagons decorated at enormous expense paraded the city streets, as did krewes with names like the Knights of Momus and the Knights of Myth.

The Grand Opera House, with its marble foyer, grand staircase, and parquet floors was an exquisite work in miniature. Any number of American cities had "opera houses" in the late 1800s, but most were nothing grander than vaudeville houses where song-and-dance teams, acrobats, and animal acts entertained. Over the years Galveston's various opera houses had hosted some of the great performers of the world—Sarah Bernhardt in *Tosca* and *Camille;* Edwin Booth in *Othello* and *Julius Caesar;* the great prima donna Adelina Patti, covered from head to foot with diamonds, singing arias from Verdi's *La Traviata.* The new Grand Opera House, completed in 1894, was modeled after the opera houses in the great capitals of Europe, and was in its time one of the splendid theaters in the country. The auditorium was constructed without square corners, to prevent echoes and assure perfect acoustics. Its 1,600 plush seats were arranged in a gentle curve, stepped downward toward the stage, which was equipped to accommodate any type of production—including live-animal chariot races for performances of *Ben Hur.* Though it wasn't discussed in its day, some of the Grand Opera House's best seats were in the topmost section, which was reserved for "coloreds," who entered and left through a special door that opened onto the alley.

The four-story building that contained the Opera House also contained shops, cafés, and the Hotel Grand. It was located on Postoffice Street, between 20th and 21st, at the intersection of every streetcar line in town. In the same block was Toujouse's bar, and nearby were two of the Island's best restaurants, Nick Balish's and Ritter's. Charles Ritter was said to be the first chef in the South to filet fish, and his tenderloin trout was famous. Shops along the Strand stayed open late and sold French perfume, Cuban cigars, and imported English wool that was far too heavy for the Galveston climate.

In their compromise with the peculiarities of Island living, Galvestonians learned to tolerate degrees of squalor. The sweet, heavy smell of oleander and the exotic fragrances of green bananas and South American oranges swirled with the scent of fish, decaying weeds, and open sewers. Originally, the Galveston sewer system had consisted of pigs that ran wild and ate all forms of human waste, including excrement. Things had improved, but not much. Until the 1890s, when water and sewer service became generally available, citizens still stored the products of their outhouses in barrels, which were collected by night in horse-drawn carts and dumped into the Gulf.

The nationalities mingled, formed partnerships, and made marriages. The British patronized the Aziola Club (for men only) downtown. The Germans, who made up nearly one-third of the population, commissioned Nicholas Clayton to design a dance pavilion called the Garten Verein (Garden Club), at Avenue O and 27th Street. Clayton constructed the building as an octagon, with pilasters, flamboyant vergeboard, expansive windows, two balustrades, and a cupola. In a sort of whimsical, how-dare-the-man fashion, the mix worked astonishingly well.

The pavilion flew the flags of all nations, and was surrounded by a landscaped park with a bowling green, tennis courts, and a small zoo. On summer evenings young people danced and kindled romances, and red-faced German waiters served platters of cold meat, lemonade, and steins of beer. Wednesday night concerts at the Garten Verein became an Island tradition. Club regulations were enforced with German thoroughness: membership was limited and maintained at exactly five hundred, and women were forbidden to smoke or use rouge or lipstick.

Gambling and prostitution flourished on Postoffice Street, a few blocks from the Opera House and the Strand—and continued to flourish until halfway through the twentieth century. The scum of the Gulf Coast congregated between 28th and 29th streets, in a pesthole called Fat Alley; it was not uncommon for police to find the unidentified bodies of murder and drug victims there. The most exclusive whorehouse was located not on Postoffice Street but immediately behind the Artillery Club, the most snobbish and formal club on the Island. Members of the Artillery Club observed strict protocol, never appearing at the clubhouse in shirtsleeves. Women were prohibited, except at dances or the annual cotillion, when their daughters made their debuts into society.

When Miss Bettie Brown entertained at Ashton Villa, her footman rolled a red carpet down the front walk so that the skirts of ladies alighting from their carriages would not be soiled. Miss Bettie was one of the Island's wealthiest and most independent women. She lived with her parents—her father James M. Brown, was a merchant and civic leader—in a pre–Civil War Italianate mansion at the corner of 24th and Broadway. Miss Bettie enjoyed shocking the grand dames of Island society. She smoked cigarettes, and an occasional pipe, and went unchaporoned to garden parties, wearing the jewel-crusted $5,000 coat that she had once worn to a garden party at the castle of Emperor Franz Josef in Austria. She had traveled extensively in Europe (she kept an apartment in Paris) and studied art in Vienna with the court painter. Her idea of sport was racing down Broadway in her own fancy carriage, pulled by magnificent teams of matching stallions—a black team for day, a white team for evening. Though many of the Island's most eligible bachelors courted Miss Bettie and drank champagne from her slipper, she never married. Some believed that she was a lesbian, but there is no historical evidence this was true. What she was was remarkably homely. She had thin lips, a prominent chin, and a nose upon which a family of eagles could have roosted—positioned, disconcertingly, atop a fantastic hour-glass figure. Miss Bettie once painted a self-portrait, using her sister as a model. As she grew older Miss Bettie spent her days mostly in the privacy of the Gold Room at Ashton Villa, painting, playing the piano, collecting treasures. She died in 1920, but her ghost is said to haunt the villa (which is now a museum) to this day.

One of the Island's morning rituals was Rabbi Henry Cohen scurrying down Tremont Street in the direction of John Sealy Hospital or pumping his bicycle toward the city jail. Though the rabbi approached every act as if it were a matter of life and death, he always found time to stop and talk, and maybe pass out meal tickets or listen to someone's tale of woe. A man of wit and infinite generosity, the rabbi was always good for a touch—his raised frame house at 1920 Broadway was a habitual sanctuary for the less fortunate.

He was a chipmunk of a man, barely five feet tall, but he had the presence of a cyclone and the constitution of a dockworker. The rabbi did not suffer fools or scoundrels easily. Once he charged into a Galveston whorehouse and rescued a young woman who was being held against her will. He threw a blanket around her naked body, marched up the street with one arm around the woman and the other balancing his bicycle, and shouldered his way through the door of Levy's Department Store. "Outfit her from head to foot," he commanded. Then he took her home to Mrs. Cohen and helped find her a job. He found jobs and solved family problems for Jews and Christians alike. Cohen taught Christology (which he had learned at his university in London) to a young man who wanted to enter the Episcopal ministry but couldn't afford the studies. On request, he administered Christian burials for destitute hookers.

Since most of the members of his congregation of Temple B'nai Israel were businessmen who depended on brisk Saturday trade, Cohen held services on Friday night—Sabbath Eve—usually to overflow crowds, and much to the distress of the chief rabbi in London. Cohen had left his native London as a young man for adventure in Africa, working the diamond mines and defending his settlement against Zulu warriors. He had served as a rabbi in Jamaica, and later in Mississippi, and had come to Galveston in 1884 and decided to stay. Though he was a scholar with considerable linguistic talent and training—he collected colloquialisms, which he recorded on the cuffs of his shirt—Cohen stuttered when he spoke in public. Young women in his congregation giggled and whispered "Kick it out!" when he spoke at temple. Leo N. Levi, president of the congregation, said: "He'll get over it, and if he doesn't, we'll get used to it." They got used to it.

Down at Pier 20 the small handcrafted boats that made up the Mosquito Fleet were backed to the docks, their bleached nets tangled on spindly masts. Entire families, mostly Portuguese, Greek, or Italian, lived aboard the boats, fishing, bartering, raising families. Shrimp and oysters were spread out for sale on straw mats, along with firewood, produce, and pots of honey that had been brought back from trips up the bayou.

Towering above the tiny shrimpers, square-riggers and steamships from nearly every port in the world delivered or took on cargo. Though Galveston's wharf charges were among the highest on the

Gulf coast, business had never been better. On a typical day the port would service four or five steamships from, say, Bremen, Manchester, and Marseilles, and maybe a half-dozen or so schooners and barks from places like New York, Boston, and New Orleans. This was still one of the world's busiest cotton ports: 21,000 bales had just been shipped to France, and another 53,000 to other foreign ports. Foreign exports in the fiscal year 1899–1900 totaled $86 million.

Mule-drawn streetcars provided regular service to the beach, at five cents a ticket. Because of the warm, predictable currents, and the gentle slope of the continental shelf, the Gulf was normally as calm as a bathtub. The apex of beachside luxury was the portable, horse-drawn bathhouses that were pulled in and out of shallow water so that bathers didn't have to get sand on their feet. But nude bathing was also popular, a nightly occurrence, in fact. According to newspaper reports, the sport of bathing in the buff attracted mixed groups of up to two hundred people, though city ordinances restricted it to the hours between 10 P.M. and 4 A.M. Sections of beach were reserved on Sunday for baptisms, one area for whites, another for blacks.

For the first time, the beach was thought of as a tourist attraction, not that everyone agreed that tourism was what Galveston needed or wanted. On weekends special trains brought day-trippers from Houston. Islanders complained that Houstonians came to town with a dirty shirt on their back and a five-dollar bill in their pocket, and never bothered to change either one.

The Galveston Pavilion, a two-story ornamental beachside structure at 21st Street and Avenue Q, was the first building in Texas to have electric lights. Another of Nicholas Clayton's designs, the pavilion was supported by four enormous steel arches, opening onto an unobstructed dance floor that measured 16,000 square feet. In 1883, while fire engines spun out in the deep sand, the pavilion burned to the ground. It was replaced by the three-story, two-hundred-room Beach Hotel, also designed by Clayton and financed by public subscription. Colonel Moody opposed the project, but the Kempners made a hefty donation. The Beach Hotel was an instant showplace, attracting visitors from as far away as Chicago and Denver. With its high-ceilinged verandas and open galleries that took advantage of Gulf breezes, the hotel had a self-conscious grandeur that might have pleased the czar of Russia. It was painted mauve, with green trimmed eaves, and its octagonal dome was adorned in large red and white stripes. In front a fountain bubbled fresh water, a luxury that astonished oldtimers, to whom fresh water was still a luxury.

In the afternoon, when the breeze from the Gulf began to caress the Island, gentlemen in tall silk hats left the floor of the Cotton Exchange and strolled down to Toujouse's bar to discuss the issues of the day. The cotton futures market in Liverpool was booming again. In New York the Irish were meeting to show sympathy for the Boers, and in Berlin Lord Kitchener was telling reporters that the Boers would be subdued within the year. There was revolution in Colombia, and plans for a canal in Nicaragua. The czar had issued another manifesto, and in a meeting in Minsk that went largely unreported, a small group calling itself the Russian Social Democratic Workers' Party called for the overthrow of the Romanov rulers. But on the Island, spirits could not have been higher. Everyone seemed to be making money and spending it. Longshoremen black and white earned better than $6 a day. All worsted blue serge suits in new spring styles went for $8.75. The purchase of a $1 bottle of Wine of Cardui promised to cure female troubles. One dollar would also buy a roundtrip ticket on one of the three daily trains to Houston.

Two BLOCKS east and five blocks south of Ashton Villa, in a cramped apartment above a saloon, Louisa Rollfing lived a life very different from the rich and self-indulgent Miss Bettie Brown. A frail young woman who had immigrated from Fuhr Island, one of the North Sea islands off the coast of Germany, Louisa shared the apartment with her husband, her three children, her saloonkeeper brother, and her brother's bartender. A seamstress by profession, she cooked and cleaned up after not only her family but the customers of the downstairs bar. These were the days of the free barroom lunch, and she was expected to have a kettle of fish chowder ready by ten o'clock every morning.

Late at night after she had finished the supper dishes, put the children to bed, and done the mending, she sat alone at the top of the stairs, listening to her husband entertain the drunks on his zither, thinking about another island so far away it seemed like a dream. She remembered that Wilhelm, the future Kaiser, and other young nobles used to come to her island to pick gooseberries and rummage around the ancient graves of a tribe of giant warriors. Her father discovered the *Hünengrabers* (giant graves) while digging for potatoes. There were flint battle-axes, stone knives, and urns of ashes, buried no telling how many centuries ago. Later her people found other giant graves across the island, some with stone weapons, some with bronze. Who were these giants' forebears? Louisa never knew, but they changed her life. Her father became superintendent of the *Hünengrabers* and sold tickets, and the proceeds helped pay her way to Galveston. In her cramped apartment above a saloon twenty years later, Louisa Rollfing remembered those happier, simpler times and wondered what her life would have been had she stayed at home.

On the other hand, Louisa and her husband August were lucky to find the apartment—half the houses on the Island had burned during the Great Fire of 1885. It started on Friday, November 13, the evening before Louisa's wedding day. She was sewing her wedding dress when she heard the fire whistle and saw flames in the direction of the business district. The fire began at a foundry near 17th and the Strand, and a stiff north wind swept it from rooftop to rooftop. She remembered looking at the night sky, sequined now with red and gold, and seeing a flock of seabirds drifting silently among the dancing sparks.

Flames raged out of control, cutting a four-block-wide swath across the center of the Island—from the Strand, over Broadway, past Avenue O, nearly to the beach. Homeowners raced ahead to save what they could. August Rollfing was carrying his bride's sewing machine to the buggy when he realized that the second floor of their building was burning. Louisa escaped just before the ceiling caved in, the tail of her coat on fire. In the street, people stumbled about, dazed and bewildered. A neighbor woman wandered around carrying a single possession, a bowl of water on which orange blossoms floated.

Galveston's first professional fire department was barely a month old and no match for the conflagration. The pressure of its newly installed saltwater system proved insufficient, and bits of shell clogged the nozzles of the firehouse. By the time it burned itself out, the fire had consumed forty-two blocks, destroying 568 buildings and homes, including the mansions of Leon Blum and Morris Lasker. Louisa Rollfing lost her home, her furniture, even her trousseau. "You can not imagine how sad it was," she wrote. Amazingly, no one died. Churches and synagogues opened their doors to the homeless, as did the Beach Hotel, but it was months before the city recovered.

# 14

In the spring of 1900, as Islanders looked with great expectations to a new century, William Jennings Bryan came to Galveston to campaign for the presidency, and also to hunt and fish with his old friend Colonel Moody at the colonel's private preserve on the mainland, Lake Surprise. Bryan had just turned forty, and his political career was still on the upswing. His "Cross of Gold" speech had taken the 1896 Democratic convention by storm and won him the party's presidential nomination. He campaigned on the issue of free silver, but lost to McKinley. Now he was running again, and he needed Moody's support—and indeed the support of Galveston, which had surprised the rest of Texas by going for McKinley in the last election. Hardly anyone knew it at the time, but the main reason Bryan was able to campaign for as long as he did was the behind-the-scenes financial support of Colonel Moody.

Though the *Galveston Daily News* had supported McKinley, it covered Bryan's visit in adoring detail, running the report across most of page one. Bryan and his family were met at the train station by Colonel Moody, and driven in his carriage to Moody's massive red-brick mansion, where they were guests. Bryan was interested to learn that Colonel Moody's property had once been the site for one of the most unique experimental programs in the American West. Before the Civil War, the colonel explained, camels were shipped from Egypt to Galveston and placed in corrals in what was now the colonel's front yard. The idea was to use camels rather than horses or mules to cross the desert to California. The experiment caught the eye of early-day Galveston investors, but it ultimately failed.

Bryan spent an hour with his host at the Moody Bank, then accompanied the colonel on his usual midmorning visit to the Cotton Exchange. This must have been a challenge for an orator like Bryan. Most of the gentlemen at the exchange supported United States imperialism, especially the Spanish-American War, and claimed to be "gold-standard men." Bryan, on the other hand, railed against foreign adventure and preached a doctrine of free and unlimited coinage of silver. As Bryan expounded on his various theories, he did so with arresting eloquence—even his offhand remarks assumed the mantle of oration. "Behold the change that has taken place. Behold the influence, behold the power higher than the highest consideration of justice and good faith, more influential than plain duty. . . ." This to a question about an obscure trade bill on the floor of Congress.

There was a reception that afternoon in the rotunda of the Tremont Hotel, and another reception that night, hosted by Colonel Moody and his two sons, W. L. "Will" Moody, Jr., and Frank Moody. From the hotel a band led a parade down 22nd Street to flag-draped Harmony Hall, where Bryan spoke to a standing-room-only audience of 2,000 for two hours. Among the dignitaries on the speaker's platform were Ike Kempner (oldest son of Harris Kempner, who had died suddenly in 1894), Morris Lasker, and, of course, Colonel Moody and his sons. During the speech Bryan deviated from his usual message of "Bi-Metallism" in order to chastise Islanders for voting Republican in the last presidential election. Bryan must have known that the vote was heavily influenced by his friend Colonel Moody as part of the Deep Water Committee's larger strategy to gain federal funds. Nevertheless, as Bryan noted sharply, Galveston was the only district in Texas to support McKinley in 1896. And it happened again in November 1900.

This was the age of enlightenment in Texas. The children of the rich and powerful were sent off to military academies, or eastern prep schools, and after graduation they went abroad to travel and finish off their educations. It was said of the son of one prominent Island family: "He learned to drink liquor at Harvard and learned to carry it at the Sorbonne." The sons of George Sealy were mostly Princeton men—Bob Sealy was so dedicated to his alma mater that for fifty years, almost until his death, he didn't miss a Princeton Reunion or a Princeton-Yale footall game. Ike Kempner, or I.H., as he preferred to be called on formal occasions, studied law at Washington and Lee under the great constitutional scholar John Randolph Tucker, and was preparing for a long trip abroad when word reached him that his father had died.

Ike Kempner was just twenty-one. Nevertheless, as the oldest son he saw it as his duty to return to Galveston and assume his role as head of the family. By sacrificing his own European adventure, Ike made certain his siblings wouldn't have to. His three younger brothers, Dan, Lee, and Stanley, each graduated from the University of Virginia and then studied for a year in France and Germany. Their mother, Eliza Kempner, a remarkable woman in her own right, supervised the education of the four daughters: all received college educations, but usually closer to home. In those days it wasn't considered proper for a young woman to travel without a chaperone. Brother Ike, as he was known within the family, became the surrogate father for his seven brothers and sisters, while raising five children of his own. As each male Kempner finished his education and travels, Brother Ike asked what area of the family business interested him. Lee Kempner, for example, said he'd like to start at the family bank, Texas Bank & Trust. "Fine," Brother Ike said. "You go down there tomorrow morning at seven-thirty and sweep out."

Ike Kempner always remembered something his father had told him. "If at twenty you are not socialistic, you have no heart. If at forty you are *still* socialistic, you have no mind." Harris Kempner had escaped Europe one jump ahead of the czar's army, and now, a generation later, his children read books by Cooper, Hawthorne, and Cervantes, and followed the journals of radicals, social Darwinists, and muckrakers like Lincoln Steffens and Ida Tarbell. Steffens' book *The Shame of the Cities* exposed the corruption of municipal government in America, and became a textbook for young progressives like Ike Kempner.

In the three and a half decades since the Civil War, Galveston had grown rapidly, and so had the egalitarian nature of local politics. Among Galveston's elite, politics was considered coarse and vulgar. It was enough to control the banks and dominate commerce; the actual job of governing was left to the plebeians. But things were getting out of hand. Mayor Ashley W. Fly, an irascible, hard-drinking rogue, ran city hall as though it were a clubhouse for his drinking buddies. Fly wore six-guns, and frequently threatened to use them, especially when he had had a few drinks, which was almost always. He once broke up a wharf strike by drawing a line across the dock and asking anyone in favor of a strike to please step across, adding in the same breath that "I'll shoot the first son of a bitch who tries."

Fly was a good politician but a rotten administrator. Hardly anything got done at city hall, and if it did, it was probably a mistake. The city's books were a mess, and its debt was staggering. Since nobody could figure out who owed what, many wealthy citizens— and almost all the politicians—took this as an excuse to ignore their taxes.

The irregularities charged against Fly's administration weren't so much a case of fraud and corruption as they were plain old incompetence and procrastination. In the judgment of I. H. Kempner and the other elitists in the reform movement, the fate of the city could no longer be trusted to this cabal of lower-class ruffians. How to get them out of office was the problem. Offering himself as a compromise candidate in the 1899 election, Kempner got elected city treasurer. So far so good. Kempner's head was full of radical notions, and he waited for an opportunity to make his move.

Following his own family tradition, W. L. Moody, Jr., graduated from the Virginia Military Academy, then traveled and studied for a year in Germany. In 1886, on his twenty-first birthday, young Moody became a junior partner in the cotton firm of W. L. Moody & Company. Three years after that he persuaded his father to permit him to purchase a private bank and merge it with the National Bank of Texas, of which the colonel was president. The newly named Moody Bank then opened a branch office in New York, with W. L. Moody, Jr., in charge. In effect the younger Moody now controlled the family banking interest, leaving his father to concentrate on cotton. The Moodys took no part in local politics, with the major exception of Colonel Moody's continuing membership in the DWC.

As had been the case for more than a quarter of a century, the Deep Water Committee was a consolidation of the Island's wealth, power, and influence. Its original mandate had been to widen and deepen the ship channel, and it had done that and continued to do it. By 1900 the DWC had re-formed itself into an ad hoc committee dedicated to promoting commerce and perpetuating its own self-interest. The committee was chaired by George Sealy, whose family controlled the Galveston Wharf Company. All fifteen members of the DWC either held stock in the Wharf Company or engaged in business located on Wharf Company property.

Members of the DWC and their associates directed the Island's eight banks, controlled 62 percent of the corporate capital, and owned 75 percent of the real estate. In the fiscal year 1899–1900, the port of Galveston generated $86 million in business, and total business for the Island was almost $220 million. But what seemed to be a healthy, highly competitive business environment was in fact a lock. The owners made deals among themselves, excluding outsiders and limiting expansion. The boards of the various companies were frequently interlocking, and composed of the usual suspects—George and John Sealy, R. Waverly Smith, P. J. Willis, Colonel W. L. Moody, Leon Blum, Bertrand Adoue, Morris Lasker, and I. H. Kempner. These financial dynasties were perpetuated by the fact that many of the families had intermarried. George Sealy, Sr., married the daughter of P. J. Willis; Waverly Smith married the daughter of John Sealy, Sr.; Ike Kempner married the grand-daughter of Leon Blum; and, later, one of Kempner's daughters married an Adoue.

The largest enterprise on the Island was Texas Star Flour Mill, owned by Morris Lasker. As industrialists went, Morris Lasker was fairly progressive. A Jew from East Prussia, Lasker had studied the classics, and thought of himself as a liberal and an intellectual. His Texas Star Flour Mill was the first industry in Texas to install an eight-hour workday, for which Lasker was labeled "a traitor to his class." But he was also a director (along with Sealy, Blum, and Adoue) of the infamous Galveston Cotton Mill, which recruited women and children from the mainland and worked them six days a week, thirteen hours a day. The Galveston Cotton Mill was one of the first—and last—serious attempts to establish an industrial base on the Island, and its failure illustrated the shortsighted approach to management that foredoomed the Island economy even as it was running full throttle.

The mill was a hopeless anachronism. It was constructed in 1899, a good ten years after cotton processing in Texas started its decline.

The mill employed 550 women and 150 children, and paid them 90 cents for their thirteen-hour day. They worked in hot, poorly ventilated, poorly lighted rooms—one light bulb for every four looms—under brutish foremen who slapped them around and docked them five to fifteen cents a day for mistakes. Many tried to quit and return to their homes on the mainland, but few could afford a ticket off the Island. They appealed to city aldermen, who were sympathetic but unwilling to buck the power structure. Company officials claimed that a sixty-six-hour work week was standard for the industry, and pointed out that, after all, the workers had gotten off Christmas Day. When the women and children decided to strike, mill owners did what management almost always did in those days—brought in strikebreakers. In the end, everyone on the Island lost.

But this was a time of entrepreneurism, too, and Island living seemed to bring out native ingenuity. Albert Lasker, Morris' son, was as daring and resourceful as any robber baron. In 1892, at the age of twelve, Albert published his own newspaper, the weekly *Galveston Free Press*, which took note of coming events at the Opera House and the Garten Verein, and offered biting social comments on local politics: "alleys all over the city are festering with filth, and yet the health department tells people the city is clean." From this small enterprise young Albert made $15 a week, more than most adults, and more than twice the salary of the women and children at his father's cotton mill. At sixteen Albert became a full-time reporter for the *Galveston Daily News*, at a salary of $40 a week. One of his jobs was collecting the daily quotations from the Cotton Exchange. This was before the time of syndicated wire services like the Associated Press, and Lasker got the idea of starting his own syndicate. By 1896 he was wiring daily quotations to newspapers in St. Louis, Chicago, and New York.

One day Lasker got a tip that the celebrated labor leader Eugene V. Debs had come secretly to the Island to take part in the annual convention of the Brotherhood of Locomotive Firemen. The struggle of organized labor was big news in Galveston, which had been a hotbed of union activity since before the Civil War. Debs, who was later the Socialist Party's candidate for president five times, had just served a jail sentence for organizing a railway strike, and since his release nobody had been able to find or interview him.

Jean Lafitte

Attack of the Confederates upon the Federal gunboat flotilla, Battle of Galveston, 1863

The Strand, or
Main Street,
Galveston
(Harper's Weekly,
1866)

Galveston after the Great Fire of 1885

Bird's-eye view of
Galveston, 1890s

The Strand , east from
Twenty-second street

Residence of J.C. Trube

Medical Department of
the University of Texas
("Old Red"), ca.1894

The Cotton Exchange, which was
demolished in 1941. To its left, the
News Building, which still stands
behind a thick concrete facade

The offices of H. M.
Trueheart & Co.

The Beach Hotel

The second
Tremont Hotel,
the finest hotel
of its time
west of the
Mississippi

The lobby of the
Tremont Hotel

The Gartenverein and the Ursuline Academy

Boulevard and seawall

Some homes
of the
Galveston
elite

The "Bullpit" at the
Cotton Exchange

Murdoch's Bath House

An advertisement for W. L. Moody & Co.

Colonel W. L. Moody, 1828-1920

An advertisement for the Mallory Line

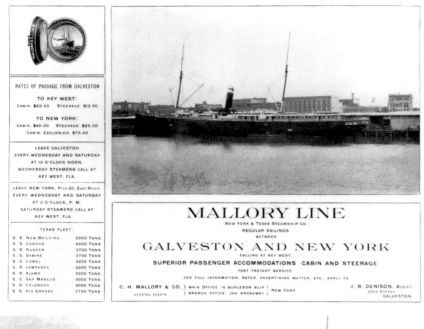

Wharf scene at Galveston

The Hotel Grand (note the arched entrance to the Grand
Opera House)

Broadway and Thirteenth. Sacred Heart's ruins (right) and the Walter Gresham mansion

Demolished docks. Ships were swept miles away and run aground

Earth scraped clean. Looking toward the beach from Twelfth and First

Grade Raising, showing the old and new grades, ca. 1906, Avenue P and Twenty-eighth street

The International Bathing Girl Revue, June 1928

The Hotel Galvez, After the construction of the seawall

Edward Protz and Mary Moody Northen (Houston Chronicle)

The Moody Mansion, now a popular tourist attraction

"Old Red" in recent times

Shearn Moody, Jr.,
in the 1970s
(Gittings©)

Dickens on the Strand festival, the first week of December
(Galveston Historical Foundation)

Splash Day, a Galveston tradition

Lasker found Debs holed up in a rooming house on the edge of town. Wearing a uniform borrowed from Western Union, Lasker rang the bell and handed Debs a telegram that read:

I AM NOT A MESSENGER BOY. I AM A YOUNG NEWSPAPER REPORTER. YOU HAVE TO GIVE A FIRST INTERVIEW TO SOMEBODY. WHY DON'T YOU GIVE IT TO ME? IT WILL START ME ON MY CAREER.

Impressed and amused, Debs consented to a long interview, which was picked up by newspapers all over the country. On the strength of the scoop, the *New York Sun* offered Lasker a job. But he turned it down. He was making more money in Galveston.

In his spare time, Lasker organized a boxing club and began promoting fights. For most of the nineteenth century, prizefighting was legal in Texas, as was dogfighting, bullfighting, and bearbaiting. But in 1891 the law was changed to make boxing a felony, punishable by prison terms of two to five years. Islanders got around the law by billing matches as "exhibitions" and "scientific demonstrations," sponsored by private clubs—using public facilities, by the way. Lasker found a streetcar conductor who could box, and nicknamed him the "Dixie Champ." By local standards, the man was a fairly good heavyweight, able to put away most of the pugs in one or two rounds. But the seventeen-year-old Lasker had his eye on bigger things. He contacted a nationally known heavyweight from Philadelphia named Joe Choynski and offered him five hundred dollars to take on the Dixie Champ.

On the day that Choynski arrived in Galveston, hundreds of fight fans crowded the train station to get a glimpse of the famous boxer. According to John Gunther, Albert Lasker's biographer, "The Dixie Champ took one look at Choynski, who had hands like hams and was a real professional to boot, and promptly fled town on the same train that had brought Choynski in." Lasker had invested most of his savings in this fight. He had promoted it, sold tickets, rented Harmony Hall. What to do? That's when he remembered a black dockworker that people called Li'l Artha' Johnson. Li'l Artha' could fight. He had proved it in an improvisational match on the wharf, when he cold-cocked a tough known as the "Deaf Bully." Albert found Li'l Artha' and offered him twenty-five dollars to crawl in the ring with Choynski.

The young man's full name was Arthur John Johnson, and he

lived with his five brothers and sisters in a shack at 808 Broadway, in an area known as the Flats. His father, Henry, a former slave, was the janitor at Galveston's Central High School, the first black high school in Texas. His mother, Tina, who was nineteen years younger than her husband, was a cleaning woman. Tina was too young to remember slavery, and her children were the first generation of American blacks born since emancipation. Li'l Artha', the third-born, quit school after the sixth grade and helped his father sweep floors. Later he worked as a stable hand and as a stevedore, picking up extra change fighting other black dockworkers in makeshift matches on the waterfront. Sometimes he worked as a sweep-up boy at the Galveston Athletic Club.

Albert Lasker had watched Li'l Artha' spar with the Dixie Champ; the kid wasn't bad. His only real ring experience—and this was a white man's joke—was taking part in exhibitions known as battle royals. These were free-for-alls in which eight or more black fighters were thrown in the ring together and urged to maim one another. Sometimes the blacks were blindfolded, and sometimes their wrists or ankles were tied together. Occasionally, they were stripped naked. Li'l Artha' had once appeared in a Sambo mask. White Galvestonians screamed approval—"Get going, black boy . . . kill him, kill that black sonabitch! . . . That's right, Sambo!"—and threw pennies and nickels into the ring. There were no rules, and the last one standing took the money.

The exact date of the Choynski-Johnson fight is in doubt—since the fight was technically illegal, it wasn't covered by the local newspaper. Historian and biographer Randy Roberts believes it was February 25, 1901, but it may have been a year, two years, or even three years earlier. Anyway, it was a cold, wet night, and Harmony Hall was packed to the rafters. This wasn't a sport, it was a social event: it rivaled—or maybe exceeded—the visit of William Jennings Bryan. Some of the same illustrious citizens who had been on the platform with Bryan sat at ringside, including I. H. Kempner, who attended in the company of George Sealy, Sr., a federal judge, and the district attorney. Before the main event there was a battle royal featuring two one-legged black boys who hopped around the ring like pogo sticks. Underfed and poorly trained, Li'l Artha' Johnson made a fight of it for five rounds and then quit. At that exact moment, five Texas Rangers raided the arena and hauled away both boxers, though not the promoter, and certainly not the well-connected spectators.

Even though the grand jury refused to indict, authorities held the two boxers in jail for twenty-four days. They were treated well, however, and sparred daily for the amusement of their jailers. In his book *Papa Jack*, Randy Roberts claims that Li'l Artha' really learned to box during these jailhouse sparring sessions with the old pro, Joe Choynski. A short time later Johnson left Galveston for a career in the prize ring. In 1903 he won the world's black heavyweight title. And five years after that, in Sydney, Australia, he defeated Britain's Tommy Burns in fourteen rounds to become the first black ever to win the heavyweight championship of the world. Arthur John Johnson—or Jack Johnson, as he was better known—never returned to Galveston, not that he would have been welcome. When Islanders read about Johnson's famous affinity for white women, they let it be known that the champion was *persona non grata* in his hometown.

Albert Lasker left the Island about the same time as Jack Johnson, also never to return. The young entrepreneur had seen Galveston from the inside, had met its ruling families, and had been appalled by their propensity for caution. They seemed arrested in their own orbit, trapped like flies in amber. Though he was still a teenager, Lasker moved to Chicago and took a job with an advertising agency, Lord & Thomas. Later he became the sole proprietor of the agency, and Lord & Thomas grew to be the largest, richest, and most famous advertising agency in the world. When he died in 1952, Albert Lasker's estate was worth more than $11 million, a figure that failed to reflect the millions he had given to individuals and charities.

THERE MUST have been times when the mystique of Island living overwhelmed the senses. This place could have been just south of Eden. Wildlife around Galveston Bay wasn't merely abundant, it was spectacular. All that was required for a successful oyster roast, for example, was a fire and someone willing to row out to a reef and fill up a barrel—oysters, plump and snug in their shells, littered reefs like stones in a boulder field. Ducks and geese were so dense that when startled they darkened the sun. A hunter told of killing thirty-two mallards with one shot. Joseph Cline, a Galveston meteorologist, wrote this passage after flushing birds from marsh grass:

*As they were flying away from me, I sent two shots into the animated cloud. Ducks began to fall all around me. It literally rained ducks. I picked up as many as I could and started back toward the horses, leaving as many more crippled or dead upon the ground. . . . I am certain that such numbers of brilliantly plumaged birds will never be seen again in the air at one time.*

And yet maintaining the mystique also required a certain capacity for deception. Part of the price of being a seaport in the 1800s was the certainty that killer storms and periodic epidemics of yellow fever would extract awesome tolls. It was difficult—though not impossible—to talk about tropical paradises when the smell of black vomit hung over the Island, and the clang of church bells mourning the dead barely overrode the moans of those yet to die. In the deadly days of summer, when the yellow-fever epidemic was claiming up to twenty lives a day, the bitter irony came crashing home. And still there was a reluctance on the part of the government and the business community to acknowledge the obvious. Quarantines, of course, were bad for business. For years medical experts on the Island claimed that quarantines weren't effective—when in fact quarantines were the only remedy that *was* effective. When an epidemic hit Galveston in 1870, Houston sent its militia out with shotguns and bludgeons to stop trains from Galveston, with orders to tear up the tracks if necessary. Islanders yelled that Houston was using the quarantine for its own profit, but six years later Galveston did the same thing to New Orleans, halting trade because an epidemic had swept the Crescent City.

The ultimate irony, however, was the boldness with which Island leaders used yellow fever to court a new industry. According to historian David G. McComb, this is how the University of Texas Medical Branch came to be located in Galveston: In 1880 when the University of Texas was looking for a place to establish its medical school, four cities were in competition—Galveston, Houston, Austin, and Tyler. Galveston had the size and wealth to support such a facility, not to mention a $50,000 grant from the estate of John Sealy, Sr., to build a teaching hospital. Opponents argued that Galveston was vulnerable to hurricanes and yellow fever. Quite right, responded Dr. Ashbel Smith, which is exactly why the Island is such a perfect location. "Students need practical as well as theoretical experience," argued Smith, who was president of the Texas Medical Association at the time. The legislature agreed, and in 1891 the new medical school opened. For a hundred years now it has been among the Island's major employers.

Islanders had a cavalier attitude about hurricanes, regarding them at worst as inconvenienes and at best as cheap thrills. Most adults had lived through their share of hurricanes. There were three big blows in 1871, washing one schooner and three sloops up 19th Street and partially destroying St. Patrick's Church. But when damage was assessed at the end of the season, only four lives had been lost. Tides from the 1875 storm measured thirteen feet above normal and covered the entire Island. That same storm struck with lethal fury just down the coast, sweeping away three-quarters of the port town of Indianola and killing 176 people. But Indianola was on the mainland, not the bay. What happened there in 1875 seemed to prove what Islanders had maintained all along—that only when a storm surge hit a solid object like the mainland was there likely to be major damage. If a similar storm hit Galveston, Islanders assumed that the bay would absorb the shock.

Eleven years later they apparently were proven correct. A storm in 1886 completely destroyed Indianola; those who survived moved away, and the town was never rebuilt. Meanwhile, in Galveston the storm blew off a few roofs, flattened some fences, and as usual, washed away the Strand's wooden paving blocks. Afterward, there was some discussion about building a seawall, but no one took it seriously. On the contrary, Islanders assumed that Galveston had stood up against the worst that nature had to offer.

# 15

FRIDAY, SEPTEMBER 7, 1900, started out oppressively hot, then turned into one of those seemingly perfect days when the wind swings around and blows out of the north and the heat of summer starts to retreat. Frayed strings of clouds stitched a satin blue sky, promising the relief of rain. Long swells broke on the beach, and young sports who should have been tending to business on the Strand took off early to frolic in the breakers. This was a day for getting out, for experiencing life.

Isaac Cline saw the surf, too, but wasn't amused. Cline, the chief of the U.S. Weather Bureau's Galveston Station, had been plotting a storm that had started days earlier in the Cape Verde Basin, off the western coast of Africa. Swept along by the easterly trades, the storm had blown just north of Cuba on Tuesday. By Thursday it had passed through the Straits of Florida and was traveling across the Gulf of Mexico in a northwesterly direction, headed toward the Texas coast. On its present course it would likely make landfall well to the east of Galveston, which would put the Island on the comparatively safe left side of the storm's vortex. Cline dutifully hoisted storm-warning flags on the pole above the Levy Building, where the Weather Bureau was located.

Later in the day Cline walked along East Beach, feeling uneasy and trying to put things into logical order. He was a practical man, a scientist, and a physician, and he had a low tolerance for inexactitude. Something didn't add up. The barometer was falling

slowly, as one might expect, and the wind was blowing out of the
north at a brisk fifteen to seventeen miles per hour. And yet the tide
was four and a half feet above normal and rising; it had already
inundated the Flats on the Island's east end. That was what worried
Cline. The tide was rising even though the wind was blowing directly
*against* it. Normally, a north or offshore wind meant a low tide—
on such occasions, Islanders joked that you could walk halfway to
Cuba. The phenomenon of high water with opposing winds was an
uncommon occurrence, but Cline knew its name: it was called a
storm tide.

Cline had been with the Weather Bureau for eighteen years,
eleven of them in Galveston, and in all that time the only severe
hurricane to hit the Gulf Coast was the one in 1893 that drowned
2,000 people on the Louisiana, Mississippi, and Alabama coasts.
The 1886 hurricane that wiped out Indianola was a trifle by comparison. In 1900 there was little information available on the habits
of tropical storms, but Cline knew that under the right conditions
they were capable of devastation beyond belief. The sixteen-foot
storm tide that swept over the Ganges delta and blasted Calcutta
in 1864, for example, drowned 40,000 people. All that afternoon
Isaac Cline and his brother Joseph, who was also a meteorologist
with the Weather Bureau, distributed information about the storm's
movement and warned people to move away from the beach.

Rain started just after midnight and fell steadily all night. At one
in the morning Joseph Cline finished up at the bureau and went
home to bed. Joseph lived four blocks from the beach, in Isaac's
two-story frame house at 25th and Avenue Q. It was a sturdy house,
constructed to withstand any storm in memory, and it was raised
on pilings well above the high-water mark of the 1875 hurricane.
Nevertheless, Joseph slept fitfully until four, when some "sense of
impending disaster" awakened him. He went to the south window
and looked out. In the few hours that he had slept, the backyard
of the Cline home had become part of the Gulf of Mexico. "I shook
my brother awake and told him that the worst had begun," Joseph
Cline said. Joseph hurried back to the Levy Building to file a report
over the bureau's national circuit, and Isaac Cline harnessed his
horse to a two-wheeled cart and drove along the beach from one
end of town to the other, warning people of the approaching storm.

By nine o'clock rain was running calf-deep down the street in
front of Louisa Rollfing's house, a few blocks from the beach. People

in her neighborhood were enjoying the downpour. Children and even a few housewives removed their shoes and stockings and waded amid pieces of driftwood and clumps of seaweed. On the beach, waves crashing against the streetcar trestle shot into the air high as telephone poles. Everyone was having fun until someone came up from the beach and told them that the bathhouses were breaking to pieces. "Then it wasn't fun anymore," Louisa recalled. Her husband, August, was working with a paint crew downtown, and she sent her eldest son by streetcar to tell August to come home immediately. Her son reported back later with this message: "Papa says, 'You must be crazy,' he will come home for his dinner." Water was already coming in over the doorsill. Louisa began packing.

TWO COMPETING forces were tearing at the Island. Far out at sea the storm was piling up walls of water and pushing them toward shore, and on the mainland a north wind was pushing in the opposite direction. The tide had forced itself steadily into the harbor, raising bay waters six feet, and the north wind drove angry brown waves against and over the wharves and railroad tracks. By one in the afternoon the wagon bridge and the three railroad bridges across the bay were all submerged. If anyone had thoughts of escaping to the mainland, it was too late.

Rabbi Henry Cohen was returning from temple when he noticed a long exodus of people moving up Broadway from the east end, carrying odd pieces of household goods and armloads of clothing. Broadway was the Island's highest point, a sort of continental divide, 8.7 feet above sea level: from there the Island tapered down to the bay and the Gulf, where the distinction between sea and land was measured in inches. But there was no record of a flood tide seriously threatening Broadway. Though the rain was pounding down and the sky was dark as twilight, the rabbi observed among the refugees something resembling a holiday mood. Children ran ahead, sliding on the mud slicks. The rabbi found spare umbrellas and blankets and passed them out, and Mrs. Cohen gave apples to the children.

Mollie Cohen finally persuaded her husband to come inside and put on some dry clothes. The electricity was off, and they sat down to lunch by candlelight. "We had a storm like this in '86," she told the children as they ate. "My father's store on Market Street was flooded." At that moment a gust of wind shook the house, causing plaster to shower from the ceiling. "It's just a little blow," she tried to assure them. Presently, the rabbi went to the door and looked out. He couldn't see the boulevard through the dark curtain of rain, but he could see water lapping over the first step of his front porch. "It looks as if the water has reached Broadway this time," he said, gathering the children and steering them away from the door. "Come in the parlor, Mollie, and let's have some music."

August Rollfing had finally realized the seriousness of the situation and sent a wagon from Malloy's Livery Stable to fetch his family and take them to the home of his mother on the west end. "It was a terrible trip," Louisa Rollfing recalled. "There were electric wires down everywhere and we had to go slow. The rain was icy cold and hurt our faces like glass splinters, and little 'Lanta pressed her face hard against my breast and cried all along the way." By the time they reached 40th and Avenue H, their horse was up to his neck in water. They were only a block from their destination, but when they tried to turn down 40th, a man shouted for them to stop. "You can't get through," he said. "There's a deep hole ahead." Louisa made a desperate decision: their only hope was to try and reach her sister-in-law's home at 36th and Broadway.

The tower that Nicholas Clayton had built above St. Mary's Cathedral began to lurch and sway—and the statue of Mary, Star of the Sea, placed there to protect, now threatened to crash through the ceiling and crush the people who had taken refuge beneath. The lower apartments of the rectory had already flooded, forcing Father James Kirwin and other priests and members of the household staff to move to the second floor. The cathedral and the rectory seemed about to disintegrate. Windows exploded, shooting shards of glass across the room. Cornice work tore lose and rambled down the seashell pavement like concrete tumbleweeds. Father Kirwin observed, "Slates from roofs were flying more thickly than hail and more deadly than Mauser bullets." Ironically, slate shingles had been a safety precaution mandated by city ordinances after the great fire of 1885. Now they were cutting people in half.

Through broken windows priests witnessed the tableaux of death, conscious, perhaps, that there was something almost biblical in the strength and random cruelty of the storm. A family of four, desperately trying to reach the cathedral, appeared for an instant, then vanished in the darkness. A panicking horse galloped through the surging waters of 21st Street, on a rendezvous with death. At that exact moment the wind ripped an enormous beam from a building and launched it, end over end, as casually as an Olympian might toss a baton, killing the horse in his tracks. Above the fury they could hear shotgunlike explosions as the iron bands and clasps that anchored the two-ton tower bell began to break free. A second tower at the front of the cathedral groaned, then its iron crosses toppled and crashed through the roof. Moments later the tower itself gave way and pitched forward into the racing brown torrent that used to be 21st Street. The bishop touched Father Kirwin's arm and told him; "Prepare these priests for death."

A German servant girl working in the home of W. L. Moody, Jr., was sent outside on an errand, and returned to report that the water standing in the yard tasted salty. Salty? How could that be? Then Moody began to understand, and ordered his servants to evacuate his wife and children to the home of his father, a block west on 23rd Street. The unthinkable had happened—the entire Island was covered by water. The Gulf and the bay had converged, and for the time being, Galveston was no longer an island, but merely part of the ocean floor, its houses and buildings protruding like toys in a bathtub.

By three-thirty Isaac Cline had recognized the scale of the disaster and drafted a final message to the chief of the Weather Bureau in Washington, D.C., advising him that great loss of life was imminent and the need for relief was urgent. Joseph Cline waded through waist-deep water to deliver the message to Western Union, only to discover that all the telegraph wires were down. He was able to get a telephone message through to the Western Union office in Houston, but he had no sooner delivered his report than the line went dead. Now Galveston was completely cut off from the outside world, alone with the fury of the gale and the rage of the tide.

Having done his duty, Isaac Cline left the bureau in the hands of assistants and waded nearly two miles to his home, thinking of his pregnant wife and three young daughters. Because of complications with the pregnancy, he had been unable to move his wife to a more secure place in the center of town. The wind wasn't yet constant—Cline estimated the gusts at between sixty and a hundred miles per hour—and by waiting for the lulls between gusts he was able to make headway. He had never seen anything like this: nobody on the Island had. Entire roofs were sailing through the air like discarded pages of newspaper. Timber and pieces of brick rocketed out of nowhere, splitting the paling and weatherboarding of houses. Nothing was where it had been that morning. Homes were gone. Streets had disappeared. Waves had washed wreckage against the pilings of his own home, creating a dam and backing up water to a depth of twenty feet: Cline's house was now in the center of a small lake.

Issac Cline found his family and about fifty neighbors huddled together on the second floor, frightened but apparently well. Joe Cline, who had made one last attempt to warn people to seek shelter in the city's center, arrived a few minutes later, badly shaken. "I tried to tell them that the worst was yet to come," he said. "I saw a family trying to reach the Catholic Convent, but they never made it. I saw people killed by flying debris and people drowned." Isaac began to realize that they were witnessing a sort of cataclysmic chain reaction. As buildings nearest the beach were wrecked, the wreckage was collected by winds and waves and driven against other buildings, which in turn collapsed and joined the grinding, swelling, insatiable mass. The storm was creating a battering ram of debris, mowing down everything in its path, scraping the earth clean. Soon it would be their turn.

THE STORM was intensifying with each minute. At five the ane-mometer at the weather station recorded a two-minute gust at 102 miles per hour. Fifteen minutes later the wind carried the instrument away. By six the tide was swelling at an incredible rate of 2.5 feet an hour, and the wind was shifting around to the northeast. At about seven-thirty, in a single enormous swell, the tide rose four feet in four seconds. The center of the hurricane apparently passed west of the Island between 8 and 9 P.M. By then the velocity of the wind was estimated at 120 miles per hour. The tide on the side of the Island nearest the Gulf was at least 15 feet, and breakers 25 feet or higher crashed over the beachline.

Every church, hospital, business building, or home still standing became a shelter for the homeless. Sailors tied boats to the fence in front of the Sealy mansion at 24th and Broadway, and pulled people out of the storm surge and onto the porch: more than four hundred found shelter at Open Gates that night. In a frantic effort to do what they could, against a force nobody could comprehend, workmen braced walls with beams, and nailed shut doors and windows. Holes were drilled in floors, inviting floodwaters to enter, in hopes that the water would help anchor houses and keep them from floating off. From one end of the Island to the other—in their instinctive struggle to survive for even one more minute—people committed astonishing, desperate, heroic, and sometimes foolish acts.

A nurse on duty at a home near the beach wrapped the body of a stillborn infant in a blanket, administered a sleeping potion to the helpless, pain-racked mother, and then, as the house began to disintegrate, calmly made preparation for her own escape. She put on a man's bathing suit, cut off her hair with scissors, and plunged into the sea. From eight in the evening until two in the morning, she clung to a piece of driftwood, finally washing ashore on the mainland. Naked, bleeding, and shivering in the cold rain, she found a shaggy dog and snuggled up against him until daylight.

The highest structure on the Island, the 220-foot tower above St. Patrick's Church, crashed unceremoniously into the street. But the storm was so loud nobody heard it. By seven in the evening the church was rubble. More than a thousand refugees took shelter at the Ursuline Convent and Academy, including several hundred blacks. When the north wall collapsed, the blacks began to sing and pray. "They shouted and sang in true camp-meeting style," wrote Father Kirwin, "until the nerves of the other refugees were shattered and a panic seemed imminent. Mother Superioress Joseph rang the chapel bell and caused a hush of the pandemonium. When quiet had been restored the mother addressed the negroes and told them that this was no time nor place for such scenes."

On the beach three miles west of town, the sisters of St. Mary's Orphanage herded their ninety-three children from room to room as the storm worsened. Their final refuge was the second-floor girls' dormitory. A caretaker brought a coil of clothesline from a store room, and the sisters wrapped the ropes around their own waists and then around the children's. A short time later the roof caved in, and all the nuns and all of the children except three were crushed or washed to their deaths.

When the front section of YMCA secretary Judson Palmer's house on Avenue P½ washed away, Palmer, his family, and fourteen others crowded into an upstairs bedroom and began to pray. Palmer's young son, Lee, prayed for the safety of his dog, Youno, and asked Jesus to "give us a pleasant day tomorrow to play." One room after another collapsed and disappeared, until all that remained was a room at the north end, part of the roof and the bathroom. As water continued to rise, Palmer and his wife and child climbed onto the edge of the bathtub. When the water reached their chins, the boy put his arms around his father's neck and asked if everything was all right. Palmer never got a chance to reply. At that moment the final section of the house gave way, hurling everyone into the roiling current. For three hours Palmer drifted on a floating shed. Eventually, he was rescued, but he never saw his wife or little Lee again. Of the fourteen neighbors who had taken refuge in the Palmer home, only one survived.

Far down the west end of the Island, Henry R. Decie, his wife, and baby boy took shelter in the home of a neighbor. The Decies were resting on the end of a bed, the baby between them, when the water began to rise "four or five feet in one bound." At that same moment a wave slammed into the side of the house and took it off its blocks. "My wife threw her arms around my neck," Decie recalled, "and kissed me and said, 'Goodbye, we are gone.' " The house shook violently, dislodging a beam that came crashing down. Decie tried to scoop his son into his arms, but the heavy timber caught the child and killed him instantly. "Another wave came," Decie said, "and swept the overhanging house off my head. I looked around and my wife was gone. Catching a piece of scantling, I held on to it and was carried thirty miles across the bay, landing near the mouth of Cow Bayou."

Though the front and rear porches of Isaac Cline's home had been smashed to sticks, the fifty refugees inside told themselves that the house was secure. Joseph Cline remembered feeling strangely calm. He kept thinking of an uncle who, alone of all those aboard a sinking ship, saved himself by hanging onto a plank and riding it five miles to shore. Around him, people were singing or praying or crying—or wandering about aimlessly, looking for some place that might give them an advantage when the end came. "I knew the house was about to collapse," Joseph Cline said, "and I told my relatives and friends to get on top of the drift and float with it."

The storm had been pounding against a quarter-mile-long section of streetcar trestle, built out over the Gulf. Suddenly, the trestle pulled loose from its mooring—rails, ties, crosspieces, and all. The storm surge and the 120-mile-per-hour winds carried a 200-foot trestle section like a scythe out of hell directly toward Isaac Cline's home. A fraction of a second before the collision, Cline felt his house move off its foundation. Then it began to topple and break apart. Cline tried to wrap his arms around his wife and six-year-old daughter, but the impact threw them into a chimney and swept the three of them beneath the wreckage, to the bottom of the water. Cline lost sight of his daughter. A dresser pinned him against a mantel, and his wife was trapped nearby, her clothing tangled among the wreckage. It's over, Cline thought. Surrendering to the inevitable, he told himself: "I have done all that could have been done in this disaster, the world will know that I did my duty to the last, it is useless to fight for life, I will let the water enter my lungs and pass on. . . ." Then he lost consciousness.

Joseph Cline had been standing near a window on the windward side. When the house began to capsize, he grabbed the hands of Isaac's other two daughters, smashed the window glass and storm shutters with his back, and let the momentum carry the three of them through the window. The building settled on its side, rocked a bit, and then rose to the surface of the floodwaters. Joe Cline and his nieces were alone on the top side of a flotilla of wreckage, momentarily safe and drifting with the tide. Rain was driving down, and pieces of timber went by like swarms of giant insects. A dim moon shone through broken clouds, making it possible for Joseph to see a short distance. Heaving masses of debris, like the one that served as their rescue ship, stretched for blocks. Cline and the two youngsters were the only humans in sight.

In a night of catastrophic losses it was impossible to separate coincidence from miracles, but there was an abundance of each. Isaac Cline regained consciousness to find himself hanging between two timbers: the wave action against the timbers had apparently pressed the water out of his lungs. There was a flash of lightning and Cline saw his youngest girl, alive and floating on the wreckage a few feet away. A short time later another flash revealed his brother and his other two daughters, still riding their raft of debris. "I took my baby and swam toward them," Isaac Cline recalled. "Strange as it may seem these children displayed no sign of fear, as we in the shadow of death did not realize what fear meant. Our only thought was how to win in this disaster."

For four hours they drifted through endless darkness and despair. Over the downpour and the wail of wind, they heard houses being crushed, and the screams of the dying. Isaac and Joseph Cline turned their backs to the wind, placing the children in front to protect them from flying debris. To shield their own own backsides, they gathered planks from the floating wreckage and propped them up like chairbacks. "The wind-driven debris was showering us constantly," Isaac Cline wrote. "Sometimes the blows were so strong that we would be knocked into the surging waters, but we would fight our way back to the children and continue the struggle to survive."

Periodic flashes of lightning added to the surreal specter, and revealed the terrible carnage—and sometimes the approach of new danger. At one point they saw a weather-battered hulk that had once been a house, streaming in their direction, one side upreared at a forty-five-degree angle. The hulk towered six or eight feet above them, and was bearing down like a derelict freighter, crushing everything in its path. Joseph Cline retained sufficient presence of mind to leap just as the monster reached them, gaining a grip on the hulk's top edge. His weight was enough to drag it lower in the water, and with his brother's help he pulled the upper side down. They climbed on top with the children, just as the drift upon which they had been floating went to pieces under their feet.

For a time their new makeshift raft was swept out to sea, but then the wind became southerly, indicating that the storm's center was bending northward and heading inland. Gradually, they could see the lights of shore. They were drifting toward a steady point of light, and as they got closer, they realized that it was a house on solid ground. Battered and exhausted, they climbed through an upstairs window, into a room where a group of refugees were huddled. This house, they learned later, sat at the corner of 28th and Avenue P, only five blocks from where Isaac Cline's home once sat. Their journey through hell had delivered them close to the place where they started.

By midnight the storm had passed over the Island, and the tide was falling rapidly. In the backyard of the Kempner home at 16th and Avenue I, the water dropped from more than eight feet to less than six feet in the time it took Ike Kempner to swim from his back porch to the stable and back. Kempner had gone in search of his coachman, who had been sent to release two carriage horses. When the coachman failed to return, Kempner tied a rope to his belt and went looking for him. As it turned out, the coachman and horses were safe: they had found a high, dry spot on the porch of a neighbor. "After that, I needed a stiff drink," Kempner recalled. Since the flood was obviously receding, Kempner and his friend Safford Wheeler started on foot to inform their neighbors. "In our dripping clothes and shoes, we were cordially received at four or five residences. In each, we were promptly tendered refreshments, and after imbibing several we found the 'spiritual courage' to continue spreading the good news."

In high fettle, Kempner and Wheeler began to wade in chest-deep water in the direction of the Tremont Hotel, their mission being to toast the renewal of life with whoever was there. Unfortunately, they found the hotel doors locked. They rang the bell but got no response. Undeterred, the two millionaires gathered paving blocks they found floating along Tremont Street, and used them to smash hotel windows. They were so engaged when a security officer from the hotel appeared and placed them under arrest.

August Rollfing was frantic. At the peak of the storm he had stood on the counter of a store with eighty strangers, holding a small boy he had never seen before on his shoulders and praying that his own family had somehow survived. When the water began to recede, Rollfing ran toward the west end neighborhood where his mother lived. He was relieved to see her house still standing—it was the only one on the block that was—but when he got inside and asked about Louisa and his children, his mother just shook her head. "They are not here, my boy," she told him. "I haven't seen them." She begged August to wait until daylight, but he bolted out the door and disappeared into the rain.

His throat dry and his chest burning, August raced along 23rd Street in the direction of Broadway, thinking that his family might have taken shelter at his sister Julia's house. A faint moon broke through the clouds, and August saw some sort of gigantic shadow stretching across Avenue N, blocking his path. It looked like a levee, or a small mountain range, and it stretched from east to west, as far as he could see. August was nearly to the base of the shadow when he realized that what he was looking at was a monstrous wall of wreckage. It was taller than a two-story building, and six to eight blocks wide. It started at the Flats on the far east end of the Island and ran all the way to 45th Street. In its relentless, grinding fashion the battering ram that Isaac Cline described had rumbled across 1,500 acres of the Island, finally playing itself out against a breakwater of its own creation.

August Rollfing stood looking up at this grotesque monument to death, trying to comprehend. "It seemed endless," he said. "House upon house, all broken to pieces, furniture, sewing machines, pianos, cats, dogs . . . and what was underneath? How many people had gone down with their houses? And behind the wall of debris, nothing! Absolutely nothing! The ground was as clear as if it had been swept, not even a little stick of wood. For blocks and blocks, nothing, and then that terrible pile of debris . . . and what was in and under it."

By the time August Rollfing reached his sister's home, the rain had almost stopped and a fresh breeze was whipping straight out of the south. In a few hours it would be light. Julia's home was still standing, more or less. There was a twenty-foot hole in one wall where the kitchen had broken loose, and the house had been lifted off its brick pillars on two sides so that it leaned like a house in a child's drawing. When August saw that his wife and children were safe and well, he collapsed in a heap on the stairway.

# 16

SUNDAY MORNING was a scene out of hell, played against a brilliant blue sky and a drowsy sea. At low tide the Gulf seemed as peaceful as a sleeping teenager, spent and unaware of its night of murderous violence. Small groups of people began to appear in the streets, tentative at first, as though they didn't want to disturb anything. Bruised and stunned, wet and chilled to the bone, they stumbled about, trying to assimilate the scope of this tragedy.

Those who had stoves and chimneys standing did what they could to cook breakfast. Others looked for dry wood. The entire Island was water-logged and covered with an inch-thick layer of foul-smelling slime. Still others dared to survey the damage. It was worse than anyone imagined—far worse. In the blackest hour no one had conjured up a vision like the one that spread before the survivors this Sunday morning. One-third of the Island was scraped clean, and the other two-thirds battered almost beyond recognition. In the Sunday morning stillness people climbed on top of the debris and looked around. They heard faint cries from people buried alive. At first, their impulse was to attempt rescues, digging with their bare hands or whatever tool they could find, but it was hopeless. No human effort could alter the inevitable or limit the final suffering of those who were trapped and waiting to die.

A more urgent concern was aiding the injured and homeless. There wasn't a building on the Island that escaped damage. More than 3,600 houses were totally destroyed, as were hundreds of buildings and institutions. Like an avenging angel on a special mission, the storm had been coldly selective in its choice of targets. Sacred Heart Catholic Church was in ruins, while just across 14th Street the mansion of Walter Gresham had escaped with only damage from the high water. The fourth floor of the Moody Building was gone, sheared away as though by a giant knife. St. Mary's Cathedral was nearly destroyed, but miraculously the tower that Nicholas Clayton built survived, and Mary, Star of the Sea, continued to stand watch. The east wall of the Opera House had collapsed, and the interior was coated with slime the consistency of axle grease. Except for a few scattered bricks, there was no trace of St. Mary's Orphanage. Railroad tracks were buried or twisted into hideous forms, trees uprooted, telephone poles flattened, streets and sidewalks buckled or washed away, wires ripped loose, gas and electric lines ruptured, sewers plugged with vegetable, animal, and human remains. Huge oceangoing ships had torn loose from their ropes and cables and had been swept across the bay and deposited on the mainland. The British steamship *Taunton* was carried from its anchorage at the mouth of the ship channel to a thirty-foot bank at Cedar Point, twenty-two miles from deep water. Household items, clothing, trade goods, machinery, almost every material possession that wasn't stored higher than fifteen feet was saturated with salt water and scum, and either ruined or badly damaged. Weeks and even months later, bicycles that seemed no worse for the experience suddenly fell apart, rusted from the inside.

There were so many bodies that after a while the senses numbed, and the corpses seemed to be merely some sort of demented design. They were heaped together in the streets, strewn across vacant lots, sticking from mounds of wreckage, floating in shallow pools of water, scattered along the beach, bobbing in the filthy backwash of the bay. Most were naked, mutilated, and dashed beyond recognition. They hung like macabre ornaments from trees, trestles, and telephone poles. One observer counted forty-three bodies dangling from the framework of a partially demolished railroad bridge. The horror and the unspeakable suffering of the victims' final moments were often preserved in ghastly frescoes of death. The body of twelve-year-old Scott McCloskey, son of a sea captain, was found with his left arm shattered, his right arm still wrapped protectively around the body of his younger brother. A woman, her long blond hair entangled in barbed wire, reached back in death as though to disengage it. Miles down the beach from the orphans' home, the bodies of a nun and nine children, still tied together with clothesline, lay half-buried in sand and seaweed.

For days survivors continued to search among the ruins, hoping to find some trace of loved ones. Most of the dead were so badly battered they couldn't be identified. Father Kirwin, who had waited out the storm in St. Mary's Cathedral, told of seeing a man going from corpse to corpse, looking into their mouths, hoping to recognize his wife's bridgework. Twenty days after the storm Isaac Cline found the body of his wife, under the wreckage that had carried the rest of her family to safety. He knew it was she because of her diamond engagement ring.

Late Sunday morning Mayor Walter Jones called an emergency meeting at the Tremont Hotel. Most of the city's leading citizens were there—Ike Kempner, John Sealy, Rabbi Henry Cohen, members of the Deep Water Committee. Not a single department of city government was functioning, so the mayor appointed these men to an ad hoc Central Relief Committee, with the power to do whatever they believed necessary. Looters were already roaming the Island, stripping the dead and ransacking shops, banks, and warehouses. The mayor declared martial law, and local militiamen were ordered to shoot looters on sight. By one account as many as seventy-five "ghouls" were summarily gunned down.

The Central Relief Committee in effect assumed the monumental job of governing the Island for the duration of the emergency. There was no communication with the mainland, except by boat. The three railroad bridges and the wagon bridge had been destroyed. The only city-owned craft afloat that could navigate the shallow waters of the bay was a twenty-foot steam launch, and even that was badly battered. Nevertheless, a crew and messengers volunteered. After a perilous journey across the bay, they scrambled ashore at Texas City, ten miles to the north, and made their way overland, across a flooded prairie littered with debris and corpses. At a railroad they found a handcar and pumped along the tracks for fifteen miles until they met a train that took them to Houston. The journey took sixteen hours.

The committee decided that every able-bodied man would be required to work on cleanup squads. Everything had to be rationed—food, medicine, water, transportation. Commissaries were set up in each of Galveston's twelve wards, dispensing supplies to those with no money. Hotels and restaurants accommodated all who applied, with or without money, and shop owners handed out canned goods as long as their supplies lasted. Galveston got its water from artesian wells eighteen miles from the city, and though the thirty-six-inch main under the bay survived the storm, the pumping station did not. Most residences still retained cisterns from the old days, but only a few were positioned high enough to escape contamination. It was almost a week before the pumping station was repaired, and in the meantime supplies of water came from these few cisterns, and from water barrels shipped from the mainland.

The homeless took refuge anywhere they could—in the train station, at city hall, in commercial buildings, in warehouses, in hotels and private homes. Saloons, gambling halls, and whorehouses were either closed or turned into temporary shelters. Churches that were still standing welcomed worshipers from those that were not: four Protestant denominations worshiped in Rabbi Cohen's temple. Most Islanders willingly opened their homes and shared what they had. But when the relief committee asked W. L. Moody, Jr., to take in a group of orphans, he refused. "We had no place for them," his daughter Mary explained later. "We had no water, no food. We couldn't take care of orphans. It would have been impossible." Will Moody, Jr., and his family had waited out the worst of the storm in his father's mansion. The colonel and his wife were in New York at the time—it was Moody company policy that Will Junior and his father couldn't both be off the Island at the same time. Moody did permit the relief committee to use his father's yacht, but only after his wife and daughter had been ferried safely to the mainland.

At first, the number of dead was estimated to be no more than five hundred, and some members of the relief committee insisted on the legal formality of a coroner's inquest. By Monday morning, however, that suggestion was dismissed as ludicrous. The death count was running into the thousands. Funeral homes and improvised morgues were already overflowing with corpses uncomfortably close to putrefaction. Work crews attempting to load bodies on carts reported that the corpses were falling to pieces. The only solution, it became apparent, was immediate and wholesale burial at sea. All day Monday and Tuesday carts and wagons full of corpses plodded along the ravaged streets of Galveston, in the direction of the wharves, arms and legs protruding under tarpaulins. The job of loading the bodies onto barges and taking them to sea was so abhorrent that recruits had to be rounded up at bayonet point and plied with whiskey. "An armed guard brought fifty negroes to the barges and went on with them," wrote Father Kirwin, who had helped supply whiskey to the white volunteers. "The barges were taken out into the Gulf and remained there all night, until it was light enough for the negroes to fasten the weights and throw the bodies overboard. When the barges returned those negroes were ashen in color."

Two days later Father Kirwin's face was similarly ashen. A member of his congregation came to the cathedral and told the priest: "My mother-in-law is back." "That's impossible!" said Father Kirwin, reminding the man that they had dumped his mother-in-law's weighted body eighteen miles out to sea. But she *was* back, as were the bodies of hundreds of others: they had washed up on the beach overnight. The committee had to rethink its strategy. Since it was no longer possible to haul decaying bodies through the streets, the committee decided to burn corpses on the spot. The bodies, and the mountain of debris created by the storm's battering ram, were burned in sections. From one end of the Island to the other, funeral pyres burned night and day: at night you could see their glow from the mainland. No one alive during that terrible time would ever forget the sight, or the smell.

In her report to the Red Cross, a volunteer named Fanny B. Ward recorded a conversation with a custodian of one of the bonfires.

"This here fire's been going on more than a month," the fireman told Miss Ward. "To my knowledge, upwards of sixty bodies have been burned in it—to say nothing of dogs, cats, hens, and three cows."

"What is in there now?" she asked.

"Well, it takes a corpse several days to burn all up. I reckon there's a couple of dozen of them—just bones, you know—down near the bottom. Yesterday we put seven on top of this pile, and by now they are only what you might call baked. Today we have been working over there (pointing to other fires a quarter of a mile way) where we found a lot of them, eleven under one house. We have put only two in here today. Found them just now, right in that puddle."

"Could you tell me who they are?"

"Lord no," he said. "We don't look at them any more than we have to, else we'd been dead ourselves before today. One of these was a colored man. They are all pretty black now, but you can tell them by the kinky hair. He had on nothing but an undershirt and one shoe. The other was a woman; young, I reckon. At any rate, she was tall and slim and had lots of long brown hair. She wore a blue silk skirt and there was a rope tied around her waist, as if somebody had tried to save her."

With a long pole the fireman poked an air hole near the center of the smoulder heap, and Fanny Ward stepped back from the unearthly smell and took a new position windward. Sparks showered the ground, leaving bits of bone and singed hair. She stooped and picked up a curling yellow lock, tears in her eyes as she wondered what mother's hand had lately caressed it.

"That's nothing," remarked the fireman. "The other day we found part of a brass chandelier, and wound all around it was a perfect mop of long, silky hair—with a piece of skin, big as your two hands, at the end of it. Some woman got tangled up that way in the flood and just naturally scalped."

No one would ever know for certain how many Islanders died, but the most reliable estimate was somewhere between six and seven thousand. Since the population of the city in 1900 was 37,700, that meant that in the hours between Saturday afternoon and Sunday morning one out of every six citizens of Galveston perished. Thousands more were killed on the mainland. The storm was recorded as the worst disaster in the history of the United States. An article a month later in the *National Geographic* described Galveston as "a scene of suffering and devastation hardly paralleled in the history of the world."

One reason the death count was so inexact was the massive migration that followed the storm. In the immediate aftermath people were paying huge sums for boat passage to the mainland. Once rail service was restored, railroads gave victims free transportation anywhere in the United States, and hundreds of families took advantage of it. Many never returned. So great was their suffering and grief —so terrible the memory of that night—that they didn't even bother to go back for their possessions, or to look for or bury their dead.

Many predicted that the city would never be rebuilt, or if it was rebuilt, it would be relocated on the mainland. But Joseph Cline reminded skeptics that Galveston was the only city on the Gulf west of New Orleans. "Commerce always takes precedence over life," Cline said. He was right. Within eleven days one of the railroad bridges across the bay had been repaired, and rail service restored. There was talk of a new causeway, ten feet higher than before. Repairs and extensions to the wharves were pushed forward. Saloons, gambling joints, and whorehouses reopened. The streets hadn't yet been been cleared of the dead, but already the electric trolley was running again. Cotton arrived by rail and barge, was processed, and then loaded aboard oceangoing ships. On October 14, 30,300 bales cleared port.

When Will Moody, Jr., told the colonel that people were leaving the Island and that business was bound to suffer, the colonel uttered one of the best-known and most cynical remarks in Galveston lore. "Good," he declared. "Remember, we both love to hunt and fish. The fewer people on the Island, the better the hunting and fishing will be for us."

The colonel was speaking metaphorically. The Island would recover—there was no doubt about that—and in the meantime it was a buyer's market. Property values had dropped drastically. Indeed, prospects for hunting and fishing hadn't been this good since Samuel May Williams and other founders of the original Galveston City Company began dividing up the Island in 1838. The colonel returned from New York convinced that the eastern press had greatly exaggerated the damage done by the storm—he'd even brought a stack of newspapers to show his son—but when he saw with his own eyes that the devastation was even worse than reported, the Moody Family made plans accordingly. Two weeks after the hurricane, Will Moody, Jr., purchased a thirty-room mansion at 2618 Broadway, for ten cents on the dollar.

# 17

THE MOODYS weren't the only ones who saw opportunity in disaster. This was the moment I. H. Kempner and his reformers had been waiting for. City government was bankrupt and tottering on anarchy. Walter Jones, a former police chief who had defeated the irrepressible Ashley Fly in the race for mayor in 1899, was well meaning but ineffectual, and hadn't been able to collect taxes or balance a budget much better than his predecessor. City bonds were quoted at their lowest level in history, and money was in such short supply that the city was using heavily discounted scrip to pay its bills.

Even before the storm nothing worked right—the sewer system, the public health service, rodent control, every function of every agency was a daily roll of the dice. Trolley tracks zigzagged across the Island in no discernible pattern: some districts didn't have tracks, and some had more than they could possibly use. There were constant rumors of fraud and corruption in city government, some of them instigated by the young reformers in pursuit of their own agenda.

The crisis created by the hurricane was the perfect excuse for a political power play—if Galveston had been Nicaragua, what Kempner and his friends accomplished might have been described as a bloodless coup. The instruments of insurrection were in place. Kempner was already city treasurer, and minister of finance for the Central Relief Committee. Kempner, John Sealy, Morris Lasker, and Bertrand Adoue provided a link between the Central Relief Committee and the Deep Water Committee. By simply withholding taxes, members of the DWC created the illusion that the Jones administration was being irresponsible and probably dishonest in handling the public purse. Whatever the DWC had in mind, the *Galveston Daily News* could be counted on for support. When Mayor Jones accused the DWC of using the hurricane to bring down the duly elected government, the newspaper charged that the mayor was appealing to "class differences."

The truth, of course, was the exact opposite. It was the DWC, the Central Relief Committee, and the progressives from Kempner's reform movement who were suggesting that Islanders were incapable of self-government. The DWC put forward a plan that would replace the twelve democratically elected aldermen with a five-member commission appointed by the governor. Though this approach was blatantly undemocratic—and probably unconstitutional—there was a precedent. Following a yellow-fever epidemic in 1878, the city of Memphis, Tennessee, surrendered its charter to the state legislature, which then appointed a commission to manage the affairs of the city. Ostensibly temporary, the Memphis commission continued in office for many years, and became a paragon of good government.

In November 1900 the DWC made its move. At a state convention in Fort Worth, called to address the needs of Galveston, members of the DWC made a surprise announcement, revealing for the first time their plan for a new city government. It worked like this: First, the state legislature would nullify the old city charter and adopt a new one already drafted by a DWC subcommittee. Then the governor would appoint a mayor-president and four commissioners. Each commissioner would oversee an area of city government— finance and revenue, police and fire, waterworks and sewerage, streets and public improvements. The plan would also exempt the city from state taxes for two years, refinance its bonded debt at a lower rate, and give the commission taxing authority to finance major projects to safeguard the city against future storms. Since the hurricane of 1886, there had been talk of building a breakwater or maybe even a seawall. Now it was time to stop talking and start acting.

The new legislative session didn't start until January 1901. In the meantime, members of the DWC formed a new political party called the City Club, whose mission it was to sell the public (and the state legislature) on the advantages of a commission form of government, then get its candidates appointed to office. I. H. Kempner coined the term "Galveston spirit," which came to mean an unquestioning solidarity with the goals of the City Club. Those who opposed the plan and called it undemocratic were branded as knaves or fools. Pamphlets spoke of an antiquated system of bagmen and ward heelers, as though Galveston were a suburb of Chicago, where such evils really did exist. Kempner had read all the right books and should have known better, but for whatever reason, he fell easily into the elitist trap. He wrote that plans for a new government were "opposed chiefly by those to whom politics has become a revenue bearing profession." As for the voter's rights to referendum and recall, Kempner termed such institutions "an insidious brew of political poison."

Despite heavy lobbying by the DWC, the state legislature wouldn't buy the plan as proposed. To make it more palatable, a compromise was negotiated and approved. Under this plan the governor would appoint a president and two members of the commission, and the other two would be elected by popular vote. When the bill became law in September 1901, Governor Joseph Sayers appointed Judge William T. Austin as mayor-president, Valery Austin as commissioner of streets and public improvements, and I. H. Kempner as commissioner of finance and revenue. Two other commissioners were chosen by election. Not surprisingly, the plan was eventually declared unconstitutional, and had to be scrapped in favor of a plan in which all five commissioners were elected by popular vote. It didn't matter: the City Club's candidates swept the subsequent election.

Though the effort to bring it about was heavy-handed in the extreme, the new government proved popular and remarkably efficient. Moreover, its success sparked a municipal revolution across the country: the national progressive movement to which I. H. Kempner subscribed had found a touchstone in Kempner's hometown. It was argued later that Galveston's government would have collapsed with or without the storm, but in the face of similar disasters in San Francisco and Chicago, similarly incompetent municipal governments managed to survive. What happened in Galveston happened because young progressives like Kempner were basically smart, honest, and altruistic, and because they were in the right place at the right time.

Still, the domino effect was startling. Taking note of Galveston's success, the city of Houston adopted a similar charter in 1903, followed in short order by Dallas, Fort Worth, Denison, El Paso, and other Texas cities. In 1907 the city of Des Moines copied the Galveston model, and by 1910 Kansas City, Boston, Tacoma, and sixty-four additional American cities had adopted governments by commission. Galveston continued to be managed by its board of commissioners until 1960.

Meeting in makeshift offices in a building at 20th and Market, the commission set about the task of rehabilitating the stricken city. One of its first acts was to appoint a three-man team of engineers to explore ways to protect the Island from future storms. The age of technology was dawning across the Americas: the locks at Sault Ste. Marie were considered one of the world's wonders, and there was talk in Washington of digging a canal across the Isthmus of Panama or maybe Nicaragua. Engineers were regarded as the heroes of the new millennium, and Galveston's board of commissioners voted to put its problem in the hands of three of the best known—Colonel Henry M. Robert, Alfred Noble, and H. C. Ripley. Robert, who had recently retired from the Army Corps of Engineers (and was famous for having drafted *Robert's Rules of Order*), knew Galveston well. He had been instrumental in deepening the harbor, and had recommended constructing a dike between Pelican Island and the mainland, to redirect the current and prevent sedimentary deposits from clogging the channel. He had also recommended building a breakwater along the beach, a recommendation that, had it been approved, might have saved thousands of lives in the 1900 storm. But it had been rejected, beaten back by the argument that such a construction would obscure the view and play hell with the tourist trade.

Alfred Noble had built bridges across the Mississippi, constructed the breakwater across the lakefront at Chicago, and helped build the locks at Sault Ste. Marie. Ripley had served with the Corps of Engineers in Galveston—he had designed the wagon bridge across the bay—and was considered an expert on Island pecularities like tides, winds, currents, and the workings of storm tides on sand and subsoil. This latter field of expertise was especially vital since the 1900 storm had drastically rearranged the Island's topography.

In January 1902, the engineers published a report that stunned even the most progressive thinkers. It made two general recommendations, both of them spectacular. First, the city should build a seawall seventeen feet tall and three miles long. Then it should raise the entire elevation of the Island between eight and fifteen feet. The board of commissioners quickly agreed, and adopted the recommendations as their own. "Never before in history has a city taken such means—at least on such a scale—to protect itself," wrote the *New York Press*. Other cities had built breakwaters to check the ravages of the sea. Holland had built great dikes to keep out the Zuider Zee. But the idea of jacking up an entire island, filling it in with sand, and then lining its beach with a seventeen-foot wall was a concept almost too large to grasp.

So was the estimated cost: $3.5 million. The city was broke, and its credit was abysmal. The new commission had inherited a bankrupt government and had been forced to default on $17,500 worth of 1881 forty-year bonds. If that wasn't bad enough, the national media was painting a picture of an Island population in the throes of despair and irreparable malaise. The chairman of the New York Bondholder's Committee contended that "Galveston is not in her right mind yet, and is not qualified to judge what is best for her future credit or prosperity." The *New York Herald Tribune* wrote, "Unable to meet the interest of its bonded indebtedness, the city of Galveston has defaulted and thereby acknowledged itself bankrupt." Things weren't quite as bad as the media made out. Islanders were able to negotiate a plan that lowered the interest rate of its indebtedness from 5 percent to 2.5 for five years. But the default made it impossible for the city to sell additional bonds in the near future.

Until now most of the outside money that had sustained Galveston through its emergency had come from private charities. Clara Barton and the Red Cross had appealed nationwide for donations, and William Randolph Hearst had used his chain of newspapers for the same purpose. Various groups held fund-raisers—a bazaar at New York's Waldorf-Astoria netted $50,000. In all more than $1.2 million had been collected. But the sort of money necessary to finance a seawall and grade elevation had to come from bigger fish. That meant the state. It also meant finding an entity other than the city that was willing and able to peddle bonds for the projects. What was required was the sort of entrepreneurship that made Galveston infamous.

In 1902 Ike Kempner spent a great deal of time on the road, lobbying state legislators, trying to solicit tax relief for Galveston. This wasn't easy. Galveston's longtime reputation as the Octopus of the Gulf tended to offset sympathy for its current condition. Part of his job included wining and dining members of the Democratic Executive Committee, who were mostly from rural districts and hence not as likely as big-city representatives to be automatically anti-Galveston. At a party in Dallas, Kempner recalled, these gentlemen were "quite responsive to frequent servings of champagne." In his cups late in the evening one of the hayseeds was reminded of the time he happened across two girls sitting on a riverbank with fishing poles in their hands: "I ask 'em if they was having any luck," the legislator began his story. "They said no, that they'd been there all day and hadn't caught no fish or no men either. Well, I told 'em, the reason probably is that you are sitting on your bait."

By enduring evenings such as this, the wily Kempner was able to bring a majority of the lawmakers around to his way of thinking. That same year the legislature passed a bill allowing the city of Galveston to keep its state taxes for two years. The city could also retain all state ad valorem taxes collected in Galveston County for a period of fifteen years—later amended to forty years. Kempner came up with another idea: what if Galveston County agreed to build the seawall? There was nothing wrong with the county's credit. Since 80 percent of the county population (and 85 percent of its tax base) was simultaneously a part of the city, getting county approval was easy enough. Ultimately, it was agreed that the county would issue and sell $1.5 million in bonds to construct the seawall. Once the seawall was completed and the city had time to recover, the city would assume responsibility for the $2 million needed to raise the Island's elevation.

Selling the seawall bonds proved difficult, since they carried a low interest rate of 4 percent. Most bond houses declined. It became necessary, therefore, for the people of Galveston to underwrite the bonds. In response to an editorial in the *News*, most of Galveston's wealthiest families pledged their purchases. I. H. Kempner stepped forward with a $50,000 subscription, but his pledge carried an interesting condition: equal subscriptions had to be made by eight other individuals or firms. The names of the eight were not made public, but daily lists of pledges published in the newspaper made speculation inevitable and shamelessly appealing. The Hutchings and the Sealys certainly did their part. The banking firm of Hutchings, Sealy & Company put up $50,000, followed by similiar $50,000 pledges from John Sealy and his brother-in-law, R. Waverly Smith. The firm of Adoue & Lobit pledged $50,000, as did the Gulf, Colorado & Santa Fe Railroad, the Guaranty Trust Company, and an unnamed firm on the Strand. That made seven. Houston businessman John Kirby pledged $50,000, but Kirby wasn't among the names on Kempner's list. Neither was Galveston businessman J. E. Wallis, who handed in a $50,000 check, as opposed to a mere subscription. But the eighth designated name continued to hold out, prompting the *News* to report that the other seven "have been hanging fire for many weeks" and may be ready to renege. Meanwhile, dozens of smaller pledges were forthcoming—$30,000 from the Galveston Brewing Company, $10,000 from the Galveston Bagging Mill, $10,000 from the Order of the Elk, $10,000 from the citizens of Beaumont, $4,000 from employees of the Customs House, $4,500 from local firemen—there was even a $1,200 pledge from the survivors of St. Mary's Orphanage. More than a million dollars was pledged—and still the eighth name had not responded. No one dared say the name aloud, but everyone knew that it was Moody. Though Kempner refused publicly to pull down his condition, he and the other subscribers made good on their $50,000 pledges anyway. The Moody Bank eventually subscribed for a nominal amount, but only after the bonds were almost gone.

The Denver construction company of J. M. O'Rourke built the seawall in sixty-foot sections, using massive and sophisticated equipment and techniques never seen before in Texas. Giant four-foot-square blocks of granite and carloads of gravel came by rail from Granite Mountain west of Austin. Forty-two-foot pilings were shipped from the forests of East Texas. Four-horse wagons delivered the materials to the Little Susie line at 15th and Avenue N, and from there they were hauled on specially constructed tracks to the excavation along the beach where the wall would eventually sit. Steam-powered pile drivers that looked like oil derricks hammered the pilings down into the clay stratum, and work crews covered the pilings with foot-thick planking that became the base for the wall.

Once the materials started arriving in steady supply, four pile drivers worked simultaneously. Following the pile drivers, carpenters hammered together caissons or forms; following the carpenters, "mixing plants" mounted on rails filled each form with concrete, reinforced with steel rods. Since it took seven days for the concrete to set, crews built alternate sections, and linked them with tongue-in-groove joints.

At its base the wall was sixteen feet thick, tapering to a width of five feet at its top. The seventeen-foot-high wall presented a concave face to the sea, driving the force of the waves upward and back over onto themselves. To protect the toe of the wall from the constant pounding of the sea, a twenty-seven-foot apron of riprap—giant granite boulders—was laid in front, extending out into the Gulf at high tide. The first piling was hammered into place in October 1902. A year and four months later, the initial three-mile section was completed.

The wall started at the south jetty on the east end of the Island, followed 6th Street to Broadway, then angled to the beach. From there it ran straight up to 39th Street. In the meantime, the federal government authorized extending the wall from 39th to 53rd, so that it would protect the army installations at Fort Crockett. This mile-long section was completed in October 1905. Over the years the county continued to extend the wall until by 1960 it was 10.4 miles long and girded one-third of the Gulf coastline.

Building the seawall was child's play compared to the task of raising the grade. To bring the city to a level that would protect it from the ravages of the sea, every house, every building, every church and school over an area of five hundred blocks had to be raised on jackscrews and filled under with sand. Streets had to be torn apart and repaved. Streetcar tracks, water pipes, gas lines, trees, and even cemeteries had to be elevated. The grade would vary across the Island, from seventeen feet at the beach to ten feet or less at Broadway: the average was about thirteen. The technology of jacking up large buildings had been used successfully during Chicago's grade elevation: Alfred Noble had worked on that project.

A more troubling question was where to find the 11 million cubic yards of sand estimated to be necessary for the fill. The board of engineers wanted to take it from the Gulf. "Nature is continually taking sand from the Gulf and putting it upon the land," H. C. Ripley reminded the commissioners. But others argued that removing millions of yards of sand from the Gulf would alter the gentle slope of the beach, which was the main reason that Galveston had survived many past storms. A local engineer pointed out that Ripley and the other high-priced engineers had already been proved wrong on one count—the riprap had not prevented erosion in front of the seawall. On the contrary, erosion had already cut from 100 to 150 feet of beach from 16th Street to 6th Street. If Ripley and the others were wrong about the effects of taking sand from the Gulf, it could endanger the seawall and even the Island itself.

P. C. Goedhart, an engineer from Düsseldorf, Germany, came up with a solution that pleased everyone. Why not take the sand from the ship channel, which required periodic dredging anyway? That way Galvestonians could raise their Island and deepen their ship channel in the same process. Goedhart proposed using giant self-loading dredges, and delivering the fill by way of a canal that he would dig across the city. Dikes would be built, dividing the city into quarter-mile squares, and the city would be raised a section at a time. As houses were jacked up, the dredges would move along the canal and discharge the liquid sand through pipes. The sand would settle and become a permanent part of the Island, and the water would run back into the canal and return to the bay. Goedhart estimated that his firm could move 11 million cubic yards of fill from the bay, at a cost of no more than 20 cents per cubic yard. That was 9 cents cheaper than the only competing bid, so Goedhart and his partner John Bates got the contract.

The city agreed to pay the cost of moving houses from the right of way of the canal, and back again after the canal was filled in. It would also pay taxes on the property for three years, and pay rent on the property where houses were parked in the meantime. All the property owner had to do was loan the city the use of his lot and permit the city to move his house to another lot while the grade-raising project was underway. The *News* cited the actual case of a man who owned twelve lots on the south side of Avenue P½, along the canal's route. The property would be raised from its current grade of 5.3 feet to 12.2 feet, thus requiring a fill of almost seven feet. That would take 17,144 cubic yards of material, which meant that the actual cost of raising the man's property to grade would be $3,171. But the owner would pay nothing, not even his normal taxes. On the other hand, owners of property *not* in the canal's path would have to pay for the raising of their houses, as well as their taxes: the city would pay for the fill. Amazingly, the entire project was carried off without a single condemnation suit, demonstrating the spirit with which Islanders approached a feat that amounted to pulling themselves up by their own bootstraps.

The project took six of the strangest years in Galveston history. Goedhart brought five seagoing dredges with him from Germany —six, actually, but one, the *Texas*, was lost at sea on the way over. Using the dredge *Holm*, workmen dug a canal parallel to the seawall, from the jetty to 21st, then along P½ to 33rd, where there was a turning basin. There was a second turning basin at 14th and Avenue N½. Islanders got used to seeing the dredges chugging along the canal, and listening to the unrelenting din of heavy machinery and the curses from workers who seemed to be constantly frustrated by their monumental task. Though the canal was two hundred feet wide and twenty feet deep, it wasn't always wide enough or deep enough to accommodate the monster-size dredges. The *Leviathan* was so huge it had to be handled by tugboats. The canal kept filling with quicksand, forcing the dredges to reduce their loads until the silt could be removed. Sometimes incoming dredges squared off against outgoing dredges until someone agreed to back off. When the *Nereus* was rammed by the *Holm* and sank at 7th and Avenue K, people bought picnic lunches and waited to see what the engineers would do next.

Despite inconveniences, Islanders adjusted, and even enjoyed the ordeal. Schoolboys made sport out of racing in front of the cannonlike pipes spewing mud and silt. In the heat of summer afternoons, children crawled under the stilts of raised houses and played or read in the damp shade. People learned to live with mud. Every tree and plant, every shrub and flower, was either buried or uprooted, and most of them died before they could be replanted in topsoil brought from the mainland. The canal became part of the scenery, something that seemed to have been there forever. The city looked like a river town during a big rise, and people walked wherever they had to go, across narrow planks or trestles, some of them eight or ten feet above ground. Old habits were changed, old routes altered. It became acceptable practice for people to take shortcuts through the homes of strangers. Vehicles were allowed only in those parts of the city where the work was finished, or not yet begun. But there were constant traffic problems anyway, especially at the drawbridges that spanned the canal. The Tremont

Street drawbridge closed at nine in the evening, and people who lingered too late at the beach were forced to use the ferry operated by the bridge's night tender, "Admiral" Billy Irwin.

Five years into the project, Goedhart and his partner split up—they had lost $200,000—and the North American Dredging Company took over the contract and pumped sand from Offatt's Bayou. By 1911 more than 2,100 structures had been raised, and more than 16 million cubic yards of fill spread across the Island. It took 700 jackscrews to lift the newly restored 3,000-ton St. Patrick's Church a mere five feet, but they did it without interrupting services.

Already Galveston was bigger, busier, richer, and more full of itself than it was before the storm. The newly completed Galveston Causeway arched seventeen feet above the bay, and handled five railroads, an interurban, a county highway for cars, and a thirty-inch water main. The Galveston-Houston Electric Railway, as the interurban was called, ran every hour from 6 A.M. until 11 P.M. and cost two dollars roundtrip. Travel time between the Island and downtown Houston was about an hour and fifteen minutes, which made it the fastest interurban in the United States in the 1920s. The city streetcar system was completely electrified; they had finally retired the last mule. The dredging operation that raised the Island deepened the ship channel to thirty feet. By 1905 Galveston was handling more exports than Baltimore or Boston. Only New York and New Orleans handled more, and in 1912—when Galveston shipped out 4 million bales of cotton—New Orleans slipped to third.

If anything, Island life was more idyllic and more vibrant than it had been in the 1880s. The Moodys built Galveston's first skyscraper, an eleven-story building to house their new insurance company. The Opera House opened again in 1902 and in the seasons that followed hosted Al Jolson, Sarah Bernhardt's farewell tour, and an ensemble from the Imperial opera houses of St. Petersburg and Moscow, featuring the world's most famous ballerina, Anna Pavlova. The Tremont Hotel restored its flood-damaged dining room. On Christmas Day 1907 it offered suckling pig with baked apples, *filet de bouef pique aux champignons*, roast canvasback duck, and Spanish mackerel *au beurre* Montpelier. Workers finished pouring the promenade atop the seawall. It was wide enough for people to walk six abreast, and it ran from 6th Street all the way to 53rd, making it the longest continual sidewalk anywhere. The strip of land that bordered the wall was paved into a six-lane road called

Seawall Boulevard, which immediately became one of the most impressive marine drives in the world. Pleasure piers were built out over the Gulf—Murdoch's Bath House was the best known of them—and on the beach below, establishments like Brownie's Casino and Resort Pavilion offered gambling and entertainment night and day, weather permitting.

The old Beach Hotel was long gone—its site was buried where 23rd Street intersected the seawall—but a group of businessmen announced plans for a new hotel called the Galvez, at 20th and Seawall Boulevard. The group included Ike and Dan Kempner, Bertrand Adoue, John Sealy, and H. S. Cooper of the Galveston Electric Company: as usual, the Moodys declined to invest in anything that smacked of aesthetics.

The Galvez became one of Galveston's great landmarks, one that endures to this day. Its waiters were imported from New York, its silver service was custom-designed, and its menu was unexcelled anywhere in Texas. Almost any night of the week an orchestra played in its ballroom. On its south lawn, honeymooners from all over the country sat on wooden swings, watching the tropical moon, listening to the roar of the Gulf, and wondering, perhaps, what would happen when another severe hurricane hit the Island.

The answer to that question came in 1915. The storm hit with such fury that it lifted a three-masted schooner out of the water and tossed it over the top of the seawall, and hurled four-ton blocks of granite riprap across the boulevard. The storm blew out windows, flooded downtown streets, and demolished nearly all the buildings beyond 53rd Street. On the Island eight died, compared with more than three hundred on the mainland and Bolivar. But the seawall did its job. In the ballroom of the Galvez Hotel people drank champagne and danced the night away.

# 18

EVEN IN A place as confining as the Island, the Kempners seldom crossed paths with the Moodys, and the Moodys never had cocktails with the Sealys. The Moodys were hard-shell Baptists, strongly opposed to drinking, smoking, gambling, and almost any type of socializing. With the exception of the Deep Water Committee and the Cotton Exchange, which were strictly business, the Moodys belonged to no clubs or organizations, and took no part in civic affairs. They even refused to join the Galveston Chamber of Commerce, preferring to operate their own private chamber of commerce.

The Kempners and the Sealys were never close friends, but at least they were compatible. Members of both families sat on the boards of the Galveston Wharf Company and the Santa Fe Railroad, and were patrons of the City Party, which dominated Island politics almost until World War II. The newspapers were full of social items chronicling events in the lives of the two families, gushing over announcements that Lee Kempner, say, or Robert Sealy was king of the Mardi Gras, or that Cecile Kempner or Caroline Sealy was making her debut at the Artillery Club Ball, or that John Sealy, Jr., was vacationing again in Paris (he seemed to spend more time in Paris than he did in Galveston), or that Ike Kempner and his wife Henrietta were spending their summer in St. Moritz, and planning to be in London for the Derby at Epsom Downs. Colonel Moody rarely went abroad, and when he did, it was usually to the Holy Lands.

Though the Kempners and the Sealys didn't always agree on ideology—the Sealys were far more conservative—both tended to be pragmatic about Island politics. It was through the influence of George Sealy, Sr., that Ike Kempner got appointed to the original board of commissioners. In 1901, when Sealy died suddenly aboard a train en route to New York—on a mission to convince bond-holders to lower the interest rate on Galveston bonds—Ike Kempner was at his side. You hardly ever saw the name Moody on the society page or in the political column. Politically, socially, spiritually, the Kempners and the Sealys were about as far removed from the Moodys as they could be and still be on the same Island.

It must have come as a shock, therefore, when one morning in 1904 W. L. Moody, Jr., walked two blocks down the Strand, from his own office to the offices of H. Kempner, and announced that he wanted to talk business and form a partnership. The business Moody wanted to discuss was a firm called the American National Insurance Company, or ANICO. The company had been founded a few months earlier in Houston, but it was undercapitalized and its owners were willing to relinquish control to the right investors. They were particularly interested in moving their headquarters to Galveston. Through some sort of mix-up one of the ANICO partners had approached I. H. Kempner and another had approached W. L. Moody, Jr. On the morning of his visit Moody came straight to the point: "There's no reason for us to bid against one another. I suggest a joint venture." Kempner agreed, and a most improbable partnership was formed, using the Moody Building as its headquarters.

At the turn of the century almost all of the insurance companies doing business in Texas were controlled by eastern interests. But once the ANICO deal was done, Kempner lobbied the state legislature, just as he had done after the 1900 storm, and new insurance regulations highly favorable to Texas-owned firms were approved. In this climate ANICO became an immediate success. Then in 1908, four years into the partnership, something unexpected rocked the firm. Returning from a ten-day trip, Kempner learned that in his absence the state insurance commissioner, Tom Love, had visited ANICO and issued a proclamation. The commissioner had insisted that the partners come up with more capital, Moody told him, and that they devote more of their time to the company. "I'm not prepared to give more time," Moody said, "unless, of course, your family is willing to sell your interest in ANICO to my family. I presume that you feel the same way." So there it was: in order to comply with Commissioner Love's directive, one partner had to buy out the other. As Kempner admitted later, he should have anticipated "trickery and deception." Probably because they were such decent people, the Kempners harbored a noble but naive belief in the decency of others. Just as their father had once bought a load of lint thinking it was cotton, Ike Kempner and his brothers agreed to sell their family's share of ANICO to the Moodys in 1908.

Two years later Kempner happened to run into Tom Love, who was by then assistant secretary of the United States Treasury. Love mentioned that he had always wondered why the Kempners sold their part of ANICO, since it was such an obviously thriving company. It was such a thriving company, Love added, that he had advised Moody that the partners should increase their capital investment, which was no more than good business practice. Kempner was shocked. Hadn't Love demanded that one partner sell to the other? No, Love told him, he had only recommended that ANICO hire an executive who could devote full time to the rapidly growing company. So Moody had lied. And the gullible Kempner had given away a half-interest in one of the most valuable corporations in the country. "A typical instance," Kempner wrote in his memoirs, "where an associate's cupidity and duplicity triumphed over my own stupidity."

At the time ANICO was acquired, Colonel Moody was still alive, though he was pushing eighty and little more than a figurehead at the firm of W. L. Moody & Company. The firm still occupied its old building at 22nd and the Strand—the cotton company had the ground floor, and ANICO had its offices on the second floor. Once elegant, the building had pretty well gone to seed in the quarter century since it was built. The fourth floor, which had been sheared away by the 1900 storm, was never replaced: they just covered the hole with a new roof and reduced the structure to three stories, which gave the Nicholas Clayton design a squatty, semiretarded look. This was one of the last remaining buildings on the Strand without electricity, or fans, to provide relief from the unrelenting heat of summer. It was said that the colonel didn't believe in electricity, and certainly fans would have been a luxury almost beyond his comprehension. The colonel and his wife, the former Pherabe Elizabeth Bradley—who came from a prominent family of planters in Freestone County in northeast Texas—lived an incredibly spartan life in their crumbling pre–Civil War mansion. At breakfast they sometimes shared a single egg. Mrs. Moody owned a car, but it gave her no pleasure. In fact, it strained her sense of propriety. "If I drive it, I have to buy gasoline," she told her son on one occasion. "But if I don't drive it, the tires will rot." A story passed along by generations of Bradleys in Freestone County revealed that the colonel and his wife never exchanged gifts, even at Christmas. Libby Moody Bradley, a niece who had gone to live with the Moodys after her parents died, told of coming downstairs on Christmas morning and finding—nothing. Not even a tree.

Even in his dotage, the colonel was always the first one in the building each morning. He sat at the desk nearest the door, his fierce Old Testament eyes penetrating into every corner of the room, his beard clipped as always, his hair completely gray by now. His son, Will Junior, spent most of his time at the private family bank, W. L. Moody & Son Bankers, Unincorporated, but the colonel maintained his vigil at the company headquarters on the Strand every day until closing time. Pauline Wortham, who joined the firm in 1908, recalled that the colonel would station himself at the desk by the door and check when his employees came and went. "We didn't have any clocks to punch," she said, "but as you came in, old Colonel Moody had his watch out. He didn't say a word, but he looked at his watch, and if you were late, you knew it." When anyone applied for a job, the colonel gave them his personal aptitude test. He asked them to recite the Lord's Prayer, asked them to spell the word Tuesday, and asked them to explain an eighth of a dollar and a thirty-second of a dollar. The colonel spent most of his day talking with old cronies in the cotton business, trying to figure new angles. The cotton-factoring business was diminishing on the Island: many of the factoring operations had moved to the interior of the state, closer to the fields. The Moodys also had new competition from the Sealys, who had constructed a factoring cooperative called the Galveston Cotton Concentration Company on West Broadway.

In 1909, the colonel came up with a scheme to promote Galveston's cotton business. He proposed an annual event called the Cotton Carnival, loosely modeled on the traditional Mardi Gras celebration, which had been suspended indefinitely after the 1900 storm. The difference between Mardi Gras—which had been celebrated on the Island as a prelude to Lent since before the Civil War—and the Cotton Carnival was one of dynamics. The purpose of Mardi Gras was fun. The purpose of the festival that Colonel Moody proposed was business. It was designed for the express purpose of attracting planters and cotton industry big shots to the Island. It was Moody's belief, and his fervent desire, that the carnival would demonstrate the advantages of the Island to these cotton capitalists, and thus reinvigorate Galveston's depressed cotton market. In a rare public appearance, before the Galveston Business League, the colonel offered to put up $1,000 of his own money, and challenged others to match it. "If Galveston doesn't readily and cheerfully contribute $10,000," he said, "the question should be asked, 'Are you fit to have a carnival?' "

Members of the league were not immediately receptive to the Cotton Carnival idea. For one thing, the league had been sponsoring its own attraction, the Neptune Festival ("six days of pleasure, six nights of mirth"). Members worried that the Cotton Carnival would cut into their action, which was designed to promote tourism rather than cotton factoring. For another, hardly anyone trusted the colonel: maybe his motives were genuinely altruistic, but they never had been before. Moody appeared hurt that anyone would doubt his selflessness, and assured everyone that he had come forward out of a sense "of patriotism and regard for the city."

In the weeks that followed, Moody formed a secret booster's club called the KKK—Kotton Karnival Kids. The colonel surely must have realized that particular set of initials had been identified since the Civil War with the Ku Klux Klan, one of the most hateful organizations in American history. The Cotton Carnival never amounted to much. In 1914 Islanders buried it and revived the traditional Mardi Gras. The KKK took that opportunity to rename itself the MMM—Mystic Merry Makers—and Colonel Moody retreated once again to the private darkness of his own world.

If anything, W. L. Moody, Jr., was more tight-fisted and ruthless than his father. He was a man with a will—and a heart—of iron. According to family lore, Moody used to keep a stuffed parrot on a perch in his bank office. When someone would come in and ask to borrow money, he would say, "Excuse me, I have to talk to my partner." He would whisper into the parrot's ear, then put his own ear close to the parrot's mouth and pretend to listen. Then he would treat the loan applicant to a tiny smile and shake his head, slowly and deliberately—no way, my friend!

He was prompt and punctual to the point of madness, and lived

by an unshakable routine. He once left the governor of Texas standing at the dock because the governor was a few minutes late for a
fishing trip aboard Moody's yacht, the *Anico*. Every day at exactly
noon, Will Moody, Jr., ate lunch. Every afternoon at exactly four,
he took his mother for a drive. On the exact same day in June, year
in and year out, he left the Island for his vacation retreat in Virginia.
On a fixed day in August, he visited his ranch on the mainland. His
abhorrence of alcohol and tobacco came not from religious
convictions—unlike his father, he had none—but because he considered them wastes of time.

By the turn of the century the Moodys had established a reputation as the repo men of the Gulf coast. W. L. Moody, Jr., preferred
to do business whenever possible through foreclosure, and he appeared to actually enjoy watching people squirm. He took particular
pleasure in his mansion on Broadway, not just because he had
bought it for ten cents on the dollar, but because he had bought it
from the widow of Richard S. Willis, who with his brother P. J.
Willis had operated one of the oldest and most successful merchandising firms on the Island, until the last decade of the nineteenth century. In Moody's mind, perhaps, Willis' ultimate failure
seemed to be a prerequisite to his own sucess. In some ironic way
the mansion was as graceless and unforgiving as its new owner.
Despite its massive, fortresslike facade, the house generally failed
to impress. The late architectural critic Howard Barnstone wrote:
"With all its pretension, the Willis-Moody House ends up as the
least inventive and the least beguiling of the great Galveston
houses."

When the colonel died in 1922 at the age of ninety-two, W. L.
Moody, Jr., was in absolute control. The colonel sired six children,
but four died young, leaving only Will Junior and his younger
brother Frank as heirs to the family fortune. The fortune was considerable, thanks almost entirely to the energy and willfullness of
Will Junior. While the cotton business slipped, he steadily increased
the firm's banking interests, adding the City National Bank (later
called the Moody National Bank). This was a unique institution, in
that it bragged of never borrowing a dollar nor discounting a note.
Will Junior boasted, too, that while his brother Frank was off gambling and chasing girls, he had stayed home and made Colonel
Moody's first million. Frank was a playboy who spent much of his
time in Cuba. When his own position in the firm was secure, Will

Junior blackmailed the colonel, threatening to resign and start a competing company unless the colonel banished Frank from the family business.

Two years after the colonel died, Will Junior began to expand the firm in ways that would have been unthinkable during the colonel's lifetime. First, he built the eleven-story ANICO Building as the new headquarters for his burgeoning empire. It had electricity, and fans, and was the Island's first skyscraper. ANICO was on its way to becoming the largest, most prosperous insurance company in the South. In 1923 he purchased the *Galveston Daily News*, which was the state's oldest active newspaper (the *Dallas Morning News*, which made the same claim, was actually an offshoot of the paper in Galveston). Dan Kempner owned the competing *Galveston Tribune*, but in 1926 Moody bought the *Tribune*, too, and for the next three and a half decades the Moody family enjoyed a press monopoly on the Island.

About that same time Moody began buying and building hotels all over the country. First, he built the Jean Lafitte Hotel in downtown Galveston, then the Buccaneer on Seawall Boulevard. He added a number of smaller hotels and tourist courts—the Coronado, the Miramar Courts, and others. Still later he purchased the Galvez from the Kempners, the Sealys, and other original investors. By the 1930s Moody owned one of the largest hotel chains in the nation, stretching from the Rocky Mountains to Washington, D.C.

Something else happened in the early part of the twentieth century that affected Galveston—and Texas—far into the future. Oil in unimaginable quantities was discovered. Until then there had been hardly any oil in the state: total production in 1891, for example, amounted to $1,650. By 1900 the state was producing $900,000 a year, and producers across the country were beginning to take notice. A wildcatter named Patillo Higgins leased a thousand acres along an inconspicuous hill called Spindletop, near Beaumont, but ran out of money before he completed drilling. Looking for investors, Higgins first contacted John D. Rockefeller at Standard Oil, but Rockefeller wasn't interested. Finally, he found a backer named Joseph Cullinan, a Pennsylvanian who had set up a refinery in North Texas, at Corsicana, and who had experience in raising seed money for drilling operations. Cullinan had heard of the Moodys of Galveston and decided to visit the Island and offer them a chance to invest.

The story of that meeting is one of the Island's enduring legends. During the negotiations, the story goes, Cullinan happened to mention that he had recently paid $10,000 for a painting by a well-known New England artist. The look that passed between Colonel Moody and his son would have fried a ship's anchor—*ten grand for a single picture!* The Moodys decided that anyone that gullible wasn't worth additional conversation, and they dismissed Cullinan as quickly as possible. Cullinan and Higgins eventually hooked up with a gambler and speculator named John W. "Bet-a-Million" Gates, who had hung around Texas in the late 1890s trying to peddle barbed wire, and in his dealings had acquired ownership of the Kansas City & Southern Railroad. Gates' railroad connections were an invaluable asset for a field as isolated as Spindletop, and he agreed to take 46 percent of the action. On January 10, 1901, Spindletop blew in with such force that it shattered the derrick and spit drills and equipment hundreds of feet in the air. The raging spout of oil measured a steady 160 feet—it was nine days (and a loss of half a million barrels) before they got it capped and controlled. So prodigious was the strike that at the time it was estimated that Spindletop could supply one-sixth of the world's oil. The company in which the Moodys declined to invest became known as Texaco.

The Kempners and the Sealys had more luck in the oil boom, but not much. The Kempners drilled a ten-acre tract near Spindletop, and struck a gusher capable of producing 10,000 gallons a day. But there was a catch. Their field wasn't adjacent to any pipeline or railroad siding. They were forced to sell their petroleum as it came out of the mouth of the well, and producers like Bet-a-Million Gates bought it at three cents a barrel. When the well played out, so did the Kempners' interest in the oil business. John Sealy, Jr., organized his own oil company and named it after his mother-in-law—Magnolia. But he sold out to Standard Oil of New York before the company reached anywhere near its potential.

As World War I began in Europe, Galveston seemed to be entering a period of industrial expansion, on a path to that elusive tax base its leaders had always craved but refused to court. For a time Texaco, Magnolia, and several other petroleum companies maintained facilities on the Island, until it became cheaper and more convenient to relocate on the mainland. Flour and rice mills, a packing plant, a shrimp cannery, and a company that processed spices and roasted coffee moved to Galveston, as did the Southern Beverage Company, which produced soft drinks and brewed Southern Select beer. The Moodys, the Sealys, and the Kempners continued to invest in low-risk ventures like banks and insurance companies, and declined to loan money to Island merchants. There were now six insurance companies on the Island, including the First Texas Prudential Life, which the Kempners founded after their misfortune with ANICO, and American Fire & Marine, owned by John and George Sealy and Hutchings, Sealy. The Kempners also purchased a railroad in North Texas and a sugar plantation on the mainland, but none of these helped the Island's economy.

The opening of the Panama Canal in 1914 was a boost for Galveston, at least in the beginning. The Island's proximity to the canal made it the natural port for rail lines shipping goods to the Orient or South America. The Wharf Company billed it as "the last port for ships headed south to the canal or the first port for ships headed north." Galveston was 827 miles closer to the Panama Canal than New York, 2,390 miles closer than San Francisco. It was the closest, and most economical, port for such cities as Denver, Chicago, and Kansas City. The port of New Orleans had the natural advantage of the Mississippi River, but since the Interstate Commerce Commission took this water competition into consideration when it figured rail rates, it was still cheaper for midwestern cities to ship goods by way of Galveston.

But the same year that the Panama Canal opened, something else happened that overshadowed Galveston's eternal optimism: an oceangoing schooner, the *William C. Mays*, made it up the Houston Ship Channel and unloaded a cargo of pipe. Since 1896, when Congress approved a plan to dig a channel up Buffalo Bayou, Houston had been preparing for a deep-water port. On the subject of deep water, the traditional tension between Houston and Galveston had gotten out of hand. Delegates from the two cities challenged each other before the Interstate Commerce Commission in Washington, D.C., and the Texas Railroad Commission in Austin, as well as in hotel lobbies and barrooms. During a National Rivers and Harbors Congress in Washington in 1901, an official of the Galveston Chamber of Commerce bloodied the nose of his Houston counterpart, who in turn smashed the Galveston gentleman over the head with his cane. Most Islanders treated the Houston Ship Channel as a joke, a sort of oxymoron. When the schooner *William C. Mays* made its historic voyage up the channel on September 26,

1914, the *Galveston Daily News* marveled that the ship was able to turn around and get back out to sea. Because of the war—and the reluctance of shippers to send their vessels up the poorly charted waters of the bay—the port of Galveston effectively maintained its monopoly for the time being.

The Kempners helped the Sealys maintain control of the wharves because they needed the Sealys' support for their own agenda. They were activists, constantly devising what they considered to be cures for the Island's malaise—building a bridge to Pelican Island, filling in mud flats, extending the seawall, advocating new parks and playgrounds. The Moodys recognized no malaise, and liked Galveston just the way it was. To the Moodys, the Kempners and the Sealys were arrogant fools. To the Kempners, the Moodys were cretins who exhibited, as I. H. Kempner wrote, "the smugness and the self-conceit of those whose wealth so far exceeds their civic pride."

Ike Kempner incurred the wrath of the Moodys and many other wealthy families in 1907 when he fought against an ordinance that would require blacks to sit at the rear of streetcars. Not only did he oppose the ordinance, Kempner made certain that the names of those who signed petitions favoring it were published and distributed across the Island. In the space of a few weeks about one-third of the Island's maids, coachmen, and cooks quit in protest. But the ordinance was passed anyway, and remained in force for more than fifty years.

In response to this fight against bigotry, a reorganized Ku Klux Klan handed out pamphlets attacking "that rich Jew Kempner." The Kempners were not always on the side of the angels. The family took a lot of heat for exploiting cheap convict labor at its sugar mill on the mainland. The use of convict labor wasn't all that uncommon in the early part of the century, but for a family that championed reform—and prided itself in its practice of noblesse oblige—the publicity was embarrassing.

From 1900 until World War II, the Moodys battled the Kempners and the Sealys for control of Island politics. When I. H. Kempner was elected mayor in 1917, his seat on the board of commissioners was handed over to George Sealy, Jr., the first and only time a Sealy lowered himself to serve in an elective office. The Moody-backed Independent Party charged that the Kempner-Sealy machine was "the puppet of the Wharf Company," which was probably true. The Wharf Company employed the largest number of men in Galveston, most of them black, and most of them in the pocket of the City Party—the party of John "Boss" Sealy.

But I. H. Kempner was an able politician, and he managed to seize on another issue and make it the focus of his term in office. The issue, strangely enough, was prostitution. In cities across the country there was a general movement to shut down red-light districts. Between 1912 and 1917 districts were closed in Atlanta, Baltimore, Chicago, Cleveland, Denver, Little Rock, Minneapolis, New York, and twenty other major cities. Just the opposite happened in Galveston. Since the 1880s there had been a clearly defined red-light district on the Island: it ran down Postoffice Street, between 25th and 29th. Galveston was one of the few cities in America where a red-light district was not only permitted, but viewed as a natural urban development. Like most other businessmen, Mayor Ike Kempner argued that the segregated district was the only way to control vice and the incidence of disease.

With the start of World War I, however, the antivice crusaders found some unexpected allies. Armed with a proclamation from the War Department in Washington, the commander of the troops at Fort Crockett demanded that the city of Galveston move immediately to halt prostitution. At the same time, Secretary of War Newton D. Baker enlisted the support of women's organizations, including the Texas Equal Suffrage Association. For Ike Kempner this was hitting close to home. The president of the Galveston chapter of the suffrage association, Mrs. E. D. Harris, was also a friend of Hennie Kempner. Under pressure from the suffrage association, Galveston cops began arresting hookers, madams, and pimps in the district and charging them with vagrancy, white slavery, disorderly conduct, and liquor violations. Only rarely was the charge prostitution, in which case the defendant was usually fined one dollar and costs. Most of those arrested were blacks, and the police department's blatantly racial policy put even more heat on Kempner.

The hyprocrisy of this situation finally became intolerable. Kempner took a train to Washington, ostensibly to lobby the administration to build a shipyard on Pelican Island, but also hoping to persuade the War Department to lighten up on its antiprostitution demands. An old friend, Admiral Benson, took Kempner to see Assistant Secretary of the Navy Franklin D. Roosevelt, who promised to consider the shipyard, but couldn't help with the problem of the red-light district. Back in Galveston, Kempner tried to work out a compromise with the military. About this same time an embarrassing incident added to his political troubles. Dr. H. C. Hall, chief of the state bureau of venereal disease in Austin, slipped into Galveston unannounced, on a mission to expose what he regarded as city corruption. As a result of Hall's secret visit, five city cops stood before the commission trying to explain why they willingly told the doctor where he might find women of lewd character. Fortunately for the commission, the war ended a short time later. Thereafter, Galveston's red-light district flourished unhindered and with new vigor, at least until the next world war.

But Kempner paid a political price for bucking the bluenoses. When he ran for reelection in 1919, Moody-backed reformers defeated him.

# 19

UNIVERSAL DISASTERS had a way of skipping across the Island, and careening off without doing much damage. Galveston had its own types of calamity, of course, but periodic flood tides, hurricanes, and epidemics of yellow fever seemed to temper the population, make it more resistant to traditional hardship. As adversity tested Islanders' imaginations, it seemed to correspondingly sharpen their wits. In the Civil War, for example, the Island was occupied by two different armies, and got off with nothing worse than a bloody nose. And on the upside a lot of Islanders got rich running the federal blockade. As terrible as it was, the 1900 storm united Islanders like nothing else in their history. World War I came and went almost unnoticed. It caused some inconvenience to residents of the red-light district, and the port experienced the general havoc that war plays with commercial shipping. But all things considered, the revolution in Mexico, which caused major shipments to be rerouted to Cuba, probably hurt Galveston's economy more than the war in Europe. When the Armistice was signed in 1918, business returned, better than ever.

Most cities in Texas—indeed, most cities in the United States—suffered a depression in 1921, but Galveston enjoyed full employment, and in fact broke all previous records for grain exports that year. On October 23, 1929, when investors on the New York Stock Exchange were losing $50 million a minute and jumping from tall buildings, nothing extraordinary occurred in Galveston. What became known to the rest of the world as the Great Depression was scarcely more than a dip in the road to Islanders. There were no food riots in Galveston, no massive demonstrations. Since there were hardly any factories to lay off workers, unemployment was something Islanders only read about. Port business was stable: throughout the Depression, Galveston remained one of the world's top exporters of cotton and grain. Military commands at Fort Crockett and the Coast Guard station at Bolivar Point got by with no reduction of manpower or payroll. The Works Progress Administration (WPA) set up a workshop at the old Alamo School on Broadway, but it closed for lack of attendance.

Not a single Galveston bank closed because of the Depression. Quiet the contrary. Because of the demand for cotton in Europe, millions of dollars from banks in Switzerland, Germany, England, France, and other European countries traveled the Atlantic and were deposited in the banks of Galveston. The Moodys' insurance company, American National, actually *grew* by 104.8 percent during the Depression. ANICO's success was constructed not on huge policies written on the wealthy, but with what was known as "industrial insurance"—oldtime nickel-and-dime policies, in which premiums were collected door-to-door from working people. ANICO's rates were far higher than the rates of most other insurers, but the trick was catering to the downtrodden and unsophisticated class that most other insurers ignored. When times were the hardest, ANICO's assets nearly doubled: $6 million in 1930 ballooned to $11.5 million in 1935. When economic relief arrived in 1940, the company's assets skyrocketed to $89 million.

There was one other reason, however, that the Great Depression went almost unnoticed in Galveston, and it was the biggest reason of all: the rackets. Gambling and prostitution had always thrived in Galveston—particularly so in times of economic hardship—but the national crisis that really jump-started Galveston's economy and kept it at full throttle for years was Prohibition. In its fifteen-year run, from 1919 to 1933, Prohibition altered the city's power structure and changed its character. Galveston was like Chicago in that there was already a good supply of gangsters, impatient for lawmakers to think up new crimes to which they could address their unique talents. Prohibition was a jackpot waiting to pay up. Gangs of rumrunners and bootleggers—recruited from the larger population of thugs, hustlers, adventurers, and hangers-on—hurried to get in on the action.

Starting in the spring of 1919, schooners from Cuba, Jamaica, and the Bahamas began running booze to the Island, up to 20,000 cases at a time. The ships dropped anchor thirty-five miles out at sea, at a rendezvous point southwest of Galveston called Rum Row, and the booze was off-loaded into small powerboats or flat-bottomed launches for delivery to spots along the miles of deserted beach. The boats usually beached in shallow water, and work crews waded out and carried the goods to shore. Each case was wrapped in a burlap sack, and two sacks were tied together for easy handling. Sometimes the goods were delivered to remote piers at Offatt's Bayou, or to one of the coves near San Luis Pass. On rare occasions it was even unloaded at one of the out-of-the way piers at the port, the same as coffee, bananas, and other legal delicacies. From there it was either stored in warehouses to await transportation, or immediately loaded onto trucks and freighted off the Island. Galveston became a main supplier of bootleg liquor for Dallas, Houston, Denver, St. Louis, Omaha, and other thirsty cities in the Southwest and Midwest. The gross income from illegal liquor must have rivaled the money that flowed into Galveston's economy from legal imports, with the important difference that the city didn't share directly in the profits of the rumrunners.

Eventually, two rival gangs divided up the Island, using Broadway as a line of demarcation. The Beach Gang, so called because it landed most of its goods on West Beach, occupied the south half of the Island. It was led by an oldtime mobster named Ollie J. Quinn, and his partner, Dutch Voight. A rotund, unfailingly pleasant man, Quinn was an Island icon. On Sundays he faithfully attended services at the First Baptist Church, always placing a hundred-dollar bill in the collection plate. In secular circles, however, Quinn was the acknowledged kingpin of Galveston vice. He ran a joint at 21st and Postoffice called the Deluxe Club, and leased slot machines and other gambling equipment through his Modern Vending Company. Quinn and Voight ran a dependable, relaxed, downhome operation, known for its tolerance to competition and its commitment to peace among outlaws.

The other major smuggling outfit, the Downtown Gang, was distinguished by its reputation for having considerably more guts than brains. The Downtown Gang was headed by a dandy named Johnny Jack Nounes, a legendary high roller who wore a diamond stickpin and carried a roll of hundred-dollar bills as thick as a cucumber. Johnny Jack was famous for his generosity. He gave toys to kids at Christmas, and once spent $40,000 on a party at the Pennsylvania Hotel in New York, where silent film stars Nancy Carroll and Clara Bow are said to have bathed in expensive champagne. He was equally famous for his careless approach to business. He sometimes hijacked truckloads of booze belonging to rival smugglers, and once stiffed a group of Cubans by paying for their boatload of rum with soap coupons.

One of Johnny Jack's partners was a Sicilian immigrant named Francesco Raffaele Nitti. According to Alan Waldman, a former Galveston journalist, Nitti ripped off $24,000 belonging to Johnny Jack Nounes and Dutch Voight, and split for Chicago, where he made a name for himself as Frank "The Enforcer" Nitti, executioner and right-hand man of Al Capone. Nounes and Voight eventually got their money back, Waldman says. They spotted Nitti drinking at a Houston speakeasy one night and spirited him back to the Island, where they controlled the odds. At a joint on Seawall Boulevard, over a plate of spaghetti and hard talk, the two Island hoods showed the Chicago mobster the error of his ways. Nitti was allowed to catch a train back to Chicago the following morning, but only after forking over $24,000, plus interest.

Johnny Jack liked to play it close. His gang was so brazen that it once unloaded a shipment on the jetties only two hundred yards from the Coast Guard station. He owned the fastest boat on the Gulf, a gasoline launch called the *Cherokee*, and one of his favorite sports was outrunning Coast Guard vessels. For years Johnny Jack played cat and mouse with a case-hardened federal agent named Al Scharff. Nobody knew the rackets better than Scharff—he had been a smuggler, a gambler, and a counterfeiter before joining U.S. Customs. Three times Scharff arrested Nounes and seized the *Cherokee*, and three times the dapper mobster beat the rap and bought back his speed boat at public auction. Finally, Scharff recruited a Houston hoodlum named Frankovich, and put him to work as a snitch. Frankovich was well known to the Galveston underworld— he had helped hijack both the Beach Gang and the Downtown Gang, and with the exception of one near-fatal beating at the hands of Johnny Jack Nounes, had escaped unscathed. Under threats from

Scharff, Frankovich wormed his way into Galveston's network of racketeers, gaining confidences until he found something of use to Scharff. After several months he tipped off the federal agent that the Downtown Gang was about to off-load 4,200 cases of liquor from a British schooner. Scharff didn't attempt to stop the off-loading, but when the *Cherokee* tied up near Offatt's Bayou, agents grabbed the boat, its load, and Johnny Jack Nounes.

Standing before Judge Joseph C. Hutcheson, Jr., a few months later, Johnny Jack was his usual arrogant self. When the judge fined him $5,000, the flamboyant smuggler smiled and said, "Hell, Judge, I've got that much in my right-hand pocket!" Judge Hutcheson was impressed. "Then look in your left hand pocket," the judge said, "and see if you can find two years in the federal penitentiary at Leavenworth." With Johnny Jack on ice for a while, Al Scharff faced one more task to make the bust complete. When the *Cherokee* came up for auction again, Scharff made sure that U.S. Customs was the high bidder.

Though rumrunning was the Island's big game in the 1920s, Prohibition spun off any number of related cottage industries. Speakeasies lined Market Street, and cops drank side by side with paying patrons. Whorehouses sold liquor or wine at an inflated fifty cents a glass. Almost every café, newsstand, and barbershop along Seawall Boulevard sold bootleg hooch. There were a fair number of home-brewers and distillers, too, passing off their products as genuine articles. At Jimmy's Bar on 39th Street, saloonkeeper Fatty Owens confided that burnt sugar or caramel would add just the right color to local rotgut. A couple of young hustlers, Freddie Musey and Otis Skains, stumbled across a formula for creating booze out of spirits of cologne. Their distillery was in a building at 21st and Church, and when the stuff had aged for a few hours, they bottled it under the very best labels—Martell Cognac, Bacardi Rum, Ambassador Scotch, Gilbey's Gin. If customers knew the difference, they didn't think to complain.

This sort of petty crime was tolerated by the big gangs because it profited everyone to help maintain the peace. Just about the only time local authorities paid attention to the racketeers was after a gang killing or a shootout in public. Besides, almost all the small operators also worked for the gangs. Fatty Owens, the saloonkeeper, was also a gunsel for Johnny Jack Nounes. Hauled into court on murder charges after a gangland shootout in front of Kid Backenstoe's cigar stand on 23rd Street, Owens protested his innocence by explaining: "I don't even like to kill a bird." Otis Skains sometimes made trips to Jamaica, arranging shipments for the Downtown Gang, and worked with off-loading crews (for fifty dollars a night) when shipments arrived. Freddie Musey was connected to the Downtown Gang through his older brother, George Musey, the number-three man in the organization. Musey, a cold-eyed immigrant from Syria, was regarded as one of the racket's coming stars.

Two other promising newcomers in the early days of Prohibition were Rosario (Rose) Maceo and his younger brother, Salvatore (Sam) Maceo. Born in Palermo, Sicily, the Maceos migrated to Louisiana with their family around the turn of the century, and moved to Galveston in 1910. The Maceo brothers were barbers. Sam worked in the shop at the Galvez Hotel, and Rose operated a single barber chair in a corner of a seafood canteen at Murdoch's Pier. Rose passed out glasses of "Dago Red" wine to his customers, and sold bottles of liquor concealed in hollowed-out loaves of French bread.

In those days Murdoch's Pier was a hangout for members of the Beach Gang. A lifeguard named Jasper Amato was a key man in the gang's smuggling routine. His fishing hut on West Beach became a favorite landing spot. Each time a shipload was expected, Amato positioned himself on the top floor of the Moody-owned Buccaneer Hotel, scanning the Gulf through binoculars to make sure there were no patrol boats around. When the coast was clear, Amato instructed the hotel's chief engineer to flash a light on the roof. The light was a signal for the boats to land their cargoes.

Just before Christmas one year, Dutch Voight asked Rose Maceo if he was interested in making a quick $1,500. The Beach Gang needed a place to stash 1,500 bottles of liquor, some place the feds would never think of looking, and it occured to the mobster that the space under Rose's raised beach cottage would be nearly perfect. The gang would move the stuff off the Island in two days, three days tops, but in the meantime Voight was willing to pay $1 a bottle for a hiding place. Rose was cutting hair for 25 cents, and making a little on the side peddling loaves of bootleg hooch. He was desperately afraid of being deported, but this was the kind of stake he needed. Rose was so nervous he didn't sleep for two nights. When they finally moved the goods on the third night, and Dutch Voight came with the payoff, Rose told him in broken English: "I donna wanta da money. You buy another loada da booze, put my $1,500 in, and let me go with you." Voight talked to his partner, Ollie Quinn, and they decided to include Rose Maceo in their next deal.

Quinn liked the Maceo brothers. Rose was mean, tough, and calculating. Sam was smooth and diplomatic. When Quinn and Dutch Voight opened the Island's first big-time nightclub in 1926, the Maceos were included in the partnership. The Hollywood Dinner Club was built from ground up, at 61st and Avenue S, on the western edge of the city, beyond the seawall. Instantly, it was the swankiest night spot on the Gulf coast—Spanish architecture, crystal chandeliers, rattan furniture, a dance floor bigger than the ballroom at the Galvez. And air conditioning! The Hollywood was the first air-conditioned night club in the country. Sam Maceo gave instructions that the temperature be maintained at 69 degrees, on the theory that drinkers who were cool didn't feel the booze, and drinkers who didn't feel the booze were lousy performers at the crap tables.

The casino had thirty crap tables, in addition to roulette, blackjack, and slot machines of all denominations. None of the gambling places downtown and along Seawall Boulevard went out of their way to hide what they were doing, although they didn't advertise either. But Sam Maceo was the consummate showman. He made certain that high rollers all over Texas heard about the Hollywood Dinner Club. A pair of searchlights out front made the place impossible to miss. For opening night Sam booked Guy Lombardo and his Royal Canadians, one of the biggest names in the business. The club drew 20,000 customers during Lombardo's three-week engagement. In the months that followed, Sam brought in only the biggest names—Ray Noble's band, with Glenn Miller playing first trombone, Sophie Tucker, Joe E. Lewis, the Ritz Brothers. Rhumba contests, offering first prizes of $1,000, lured some of the best dancers in the country. A young hoofer named Fred Astaire was the Hollywood Dinner Club's resident instructor for a while. The country's first remote radio broadcast originated at the Hollywood, featuring Ben Bernie and All the Boys. Stations all over the Midwest picked it up. Phil Harris and a number of other stars got national attention by way of the radio hookup. A young musician from Beaumont sat in one night when the regular trumpet player was drunk and got regular work with the band. His name was Harry James.

The opening of the Hollywood was a landmark event, not just in

Texas but nationwide. Nobody had ever offered the public gambling, gourmet food, and top-name entertainment all under one roof. (Remember, this was 1926, years before there was a Strip in Las Vegas.)

In the late 1920s and early 1930s such top mobsters as Johnny Jack Nounes, George Musey, Dutch Voight, and Big Jim Clark either went to prison or were forced to flee the Island and become fugitives. The Maceos bought out—or squeezed out—Ollie Quinn. Soon a new and far more dynamic syndicate took control. For the next thirty years, the rackets would be directed by the Maceo family.

ROSE WAS the muscle, and the brains, of the family. He didn't speak much English, but everyone understood him clearly. Dutch Voight once knocked a revolver out of Rose's hand to keep him from gunning down a relative. Rose's first wife, and her lover, were mysteriously murdered: the crime was never solved, but Rose's second wife was wise enough to remain faithful. Sam Maceo, on the other hand, was smooth as velvet. He was gregarious and well-mannered, and wore suits custom-tailored in New York. He didn't gamble, seldom took a drink, and knew how to cultivate celebrities and make them comfortable. Everyone liked Sam. There were two other brothers, Vincent and Frank, and a number of cousins and inlaws, but Rose and Sam were the unquestioned dons. They were the perfect complement: the enforcer and the diplomat.

The Maceos opened a second big-name dinner club and casino called the Grotto. It was situated on a pier off Seawall Boulevard, at the foot of 21st Street. The Grotto was damaged by a hurricane in 1932 and reopened later the same year as the Sui Jen (pronounced Swee Rin), with a Chinese menu and a bandstand shaped like a pagoda.

The downtown district, which had once been the exclusive province of Ollie J. Quinn, now became the exclusive province of the Maceos. Other gambling joints were permitted to operate, as long as their owners understood that they existed at the pleasure of Papa Rose and Big Sam, as they came to be called. This live-and-let-live policy had served Ollie Quinn for years, and now it served the Maceos as well. The Maceos formed a new business called the Gulf Vending Company, replacing the old Modern Vending outfit that Quinn had operated. Soon every barbershop, drugstore, washateria, café, and bar in Galveston County had slot machines, pinball ma-

chines and tip books, furnished by Gulf Vending. "They didn't ask
if you wanted their slots," said Mike Gaido, whose family owned a
seafood restaurant on Seawall Boulevard. "They just asked how
many." But everyone made money. One café owner estimated that
his six slots turned more profit than his food service. Otis Skains'
little joint on 24th Street, the Alamo, counted on $600 a week from
its five machines.

The syndicate headquarters of the Maceo family was the Turf
Athletic Club, a three-story building on 23rd between Market and
Postoffice. On the ground floor was the bookmaking parlor, where
bettors could wager on baseball or buy a ticket on any horse in any
race in the country. Race results were broadcast live on the club's
public address system. The second floor was secured by a private
elevator and an electronic buzzer system that was highly sophisticated for its time. The floor was divided into two sections: a bar
and nightclub called the Studio Lounge, decorated in Art Deco
fashion, with murals, black lights, and mirrors trimmed in zebra
skin; and a second bar and restaurant called the Western Room.
The top floor was actually an athletic club, with a boxing ring,
weightlifting equipment, pool tables, and a steam room.

In the months and years that followed, the Maceos expanded
their empire until it included dozens of casinos, nightclubs, and
betting parlors, not only on the Island but in such small mainland
towns as Texas City, Kemah, La Marque, and Dickinson. Motorists
driving south on the highway from Houston spoke of crossing the
Maceo-Dickinson Line. With their unabashed attitude toward sin
and corruption, the Maceos brought prominence, notoriety, and an
enduring nickname to the Island. For the next three decades it was
known as the Free State of Galveston.

# 20

THE MACEOS changed the rules in Galveston. The underworld become the overworld. Activities that had been merely tolerated became part of the mainstream economy. Professional criminals became respected businessmen—and friends, not to say patrons, of the police commissioner. The Maceos weren't exactly welcome at the Artillery Club, but in time the Island's elite gave them legitimacy by doing business with them and by patronizing their nightclubs and casinos.

Ike Kempner once rented the Hollywood Club for a debutante party. After a visit to the Turf Club he wrote to his daughter Cecile, who was living in New York: "Nowhere this side of Hollywood has there been more lavish or lurid decor. It is on the whole in good taste—but I imagine it would be rather trying to live with it night after night." The commission form of government was the perfect tool for organized crime: for $25,000 the Maceos could buy an entire slate of candidates. Nevertheless, Kempner blithely defended the system and didn't ask a lot of questions.

Papa Rose Maceo was a preferred customer at the Moodys' City National Bank. He borrowed up to a half-million dollars at a time. On his signature alone Maceo could borrow $100,000 for a load of bootleg liquor. He usually repaid the money within two weeks, at 25 percent interest. Big Sam Maceo went to his broker's office every Monday morning and bought a $25,000 municipal bond: in those days municipal bonds were a foolproof method of laundering money. The Moodys and the Maceos used the same lawyer, a master of the loophole named Louis J. Dibrell. When the city was looking for investors to build its Pleasure Pier at the foot of 25th Street, the Moodys and the Maceos both came forward to do their civic duties. Sam Maceo was at the top of every charity's fund-raising list. He was also one of the founders of the Galveston Beach Association, and sponsored an annual Christmas party for underprivileged children.

Had they chosen to, the Island's ruling families could have shut down the Maceos with a few phone calls. But they didn't. Maybe they didn't notice, or maybe they didn't care. An article in the *Chicago Journal* in 1930 suggested as much: "Galveston generally seems to be a community satisfied to live withdrawn in the smugness and fallacies of its selfappraisal and conceit." But there was something else about the Maceos, something near and dear to the hearts of Galveston's upper class. The brothers from Sicily had a primary instinct for laissez faire, and they always took care of business first. The Maceos had their own private police patrol, a group of hoods known as Rose's Night Riders, whose job it was to protect slot machines and maintain law and order in the gambling joints. Crime was down, at least statistically. There was no unemployment. Everyone was making money. The banking and insurance businesses had never been better. The Moodys' hotels were full, even in the winter. Without the Maceos, it seemed, the Island might dry up and blow away.

Ike Kempner was more interested in Washington politics than in what was happening on the Island. Though the Great Depression had largely bypassed Galveston, it had almost devastated the Kempner family's interests on the mainland, particularly Imperial Sugar, their flagship operation in Sugarland. This in turn had threatened the solvency of the Kempners' United States National Bank. Ike Kempner spent a great deal of time in Washington, lobbying Congress in support of legislation favorable to banking and sugar, and trying to defeat the Hawley-Smoot tariff bill, which he later blamed for laying the economic groundwork that brought Hitler and Mussolini to power.

The Sealys had their own problems, mainly how to fight off the Moodys' unrelenting efforts to gain control of the Galveston Wharf Company. In 1921 a Moody-controlled administration attempted to sell the city's share of the Wharf Company, a move that could

have thrown control of the company to the Moodys. With the Kempners' help, the Sealys beat off this attempt. The administration did
manage, however, to have the Wharf Company's properties reap-
praised, a ploy that increased its taxable assets by an astonishing
$1.8 million. In 1924 company officials claimed they were being
taxed in excess of 94 percent. John Sealy the Younger, who had
taken over the presidency of the company when his uncle George
died, was sometimes referred to as "Boss" Sealy, a title far more
dynamic than his record as an executive indicated. Though city
commissioners were alleging that Sealy was defrauding the tax-
payers, a more accurate charge would have been neglect, or maybe
even stupidity.

The Sealys hadn't modernized the wharves since before World
War I. The company lost contracts because of the arrogance and
inefficiency of its management, and because when there was a truly
tough problem that needed the president's attention, John Sealy
was usually off on one of his extended European vacations. Though
the company was partially owned by the city, it granted special
rates to the Galveston Cotton Concentration Company, a Sealy subsidiary, while stubbornly refusing to provide free mooring space
for naval vessels that would have otherwise purchased their stores
from Island merchants. Worst of all was the perception that John
Sealy was lining his pockets with money that properly belonged to
the city. When the public demanded that John Sealy reveal his
annual income, he refused—on the novel grounds that no one re-
spects a man who talks about his own wealth or accomplishments.

John Sealy died in January 1926, in the American Hospital at
Neuilly, France, following an attack of influenza contracted in Na-
ples, Italy. His position as head of the Wharf Company was filled
by his nephew, George Sealy, Jr., a chip off the old block. George
Junior was also chief executive officer of the Cotton Concentration,
and the world's foremost authority on the cross-pollination of oleanders. His mother, Magnolia Willis Sealy, had planted oleanders all
over the Island in the 1920s, and had made this poisonous shrub
Galveston's official flower. When the family built the Cotton Concentration complex on West Broadway, George Junior included an
oleander nursery that covered fourteen city blocks. Much as his
uncle had loved Paris, George Junior loved his nursery: together
with the company's horticultural superintendent, Edward F. Barr,
Sealy developed sixty varieties of oleander, each named for a

wealthy Galvestonian or a distinguished visitor to the Island. Some critics believed that Sealy spent so much time with his plants that he forgot about the Wharf Company.

But he remembered enough to make at least one blatantly self-serving deal. In the late 1920s, again with help from the Kempners, the Sealys devised a plan whereby the assets of the Wharf Company were made available to the Cotton Concentration. This gave the Sealys a tremendous advantage over their chief cotton-industry competitor, the W. L. Moody Cotton Company.

W. L. Moody, Jr., slashed back with a series of articles in his newspaper, the *Daily News*, accusing the Wharf Company of a wide range of offenses. If anyone wondered why new corporations were not moving to the Island, the *Daily News* offered this answer: the Wharf Company didn't want them to. Nothing happened in Galveston without prior approval of the Wharf Company, the newspaper charged. The Wharf Company didn't fear competition, it *controlled* competition. Articles described the subtle ways the Wharf Company put the squeeze on manufacturers—rail cars not delivered on schedule, new imports denied, storage sheds curiously unavailable. The series ran for eighteen days and concluded with a page-one editorial, disguised as a news story, declaring that "Galveston has been a fief of the Galveston Wharf Company since 1869" and demanding that the company be held accountable before "the bar of public opinion for its laggard and selfish administration." The Sealys weathered this blast, just as they always had.

But Galveston was no longer viewed as just a port town. In 1930, in fact, Houston temporarily replaced Galveston as the top cotton port. Galveston regained its traditional status a year later, but it was only a matter of time until Galveston slipped for good. The port of Houston was growing at a phenomenal rate: Houston had accomplished in sixteen years what it took Galveston eighty years to accomplish.

Meanwhile, the Island was changing in subtle and not so subtle ways. Its traditional flow of immigrants was reduced to a trickle, and its European-style culture was on the wane. About the only people migrating to the Island in the late 1920s were the mostly uneducated and predominantly rural families from small communities along the coast. Nobody craved opera anymore: the Grand Opera House was sold to Atillio Martini, who reopened it as a movie house and vaudeville theater.

Liberal—or maybe it was libertarian—politics continued to prevail: in 1928 Galveston was the only city in Texas to support Al
Smith, a liberal Democratic and an avowed wet. Anti-Prohibition
sentiment was so strong that when the sheriff accidentally seized
a truckload of liquor, Galveston County turned the evidence over
to the federal government for prosecution.

With the influx of lower-middle-class outsiders from the mainland, the city's residential areas expanded to the southwest. At the
same time a ritzy new area known as Cedar Lawn curved off of
45th Street, attracting the Island's newest generation of millionaires, including William L. Moody III.

Blacks were being urged to move west of Fort Crockett, an area
largely uninhabited, or to a proposed ghetto north of Broadway,
which had been the heart of the warehousing district when cotton
was king.

GALVESTON'S neighorhoods had been integrated since before the
turn of the century, in the sense that black families frequently lived
in the same block with whites. Galveston remained among the most
tolerant of cities, but there were undercurrents of racial tension,
too. Whites didn't socialize with blacks, of course, and the separation by color of religious and educational institutions was official
policy. Blacks were expected to sit at the rear of buses and streetcars, and the only beach open to blacks was a two-block stretch
between 27th and 29th. But enforcement of Jim Crow laws was
benign and sometimes nonexistent, unless a white registered a complaint. Black kids hung out at the Penny Arcade on the Boulevard
at 23rd and played along the seawall without incident. Black leaders
accepted whatever the white power structure handed down, and
warned their people to beware of radicals preaching dangerous
ideas like social equality. The black editor of the *City Times* wrote
that his people had a loving spirit for whites: "The colored people
of Galveston are not trying to run the city in her commercial, financial, labor, or political progress, but instead are honestly doing
their humble part to help keep things going right."

And things went right—or at least peacefully—until 1928 when
a black schoolteacher named John H. Clouser stood before the city
commission and demanded that the signs in Menard Park that read
FOR WHITE PEOPLE ONLY be removed. Black people paid taxes, too,
Clouser reminded the commissioners, and had a right to walk

through the park and listen to city band concerts. The city was spending $26,000 a year for the recreation of whites, but not a penny for blacks. "Our children live in alleys," Clouser said. "There's no place for them to play."

Islanders, black and white alike, were shocked at Clouser's audaciousness. Not since the days of Wright Cuney had a black stood up to the white power structure. The nearest thing the black community had to a champion was an old man named Henry Noble, who operated a black newspaper and urged blacks to boycott streetcars. In earlier times Noble had sponsored an annual Juneteenth celebration at Cottonjammer's Park at 37th and Avenue S. Cottonjammer's Park was a black recreation center owned by the black screwman's union—the so-called cottonjammers—but as the cotton industry diminished, so did the union. The park was sold, eventually, and after that there was no place on the Island where black children could gather and play. But nobody bothered to protest until John Clouser stepped forward.

The protest frightened Island blacks, but it didn't surprise them. Everyone in the community knew that John Clouser had been doing things his own way since he was a small boy. He was raised in a tidy but crowded house at 35th and Avenue M½ by his mother and a niece. The two of them worked for slave wages to support the family, fourteen hours every day except Sunday—on Sunday they worked ten hours—at a combined salary of $6 a week. To make ends meet they baked cakes and pies, which six-year-old John sold on the docks. A few years later the enterprising young Clouser traded for a donkey named Billy and expanded his business, buying charcoal and watermelons from the Mosquito Fleet shrimpers, who brought them from Double Bayou in Chambers County, and reselling them door-to-door. By the time he was eleven, Clouser was making $30 a week, more than most adults. As a student at Central, the Island's black high school, Clouser was influenced by Henry Noble, and shocked his principal and the school board by making a speech blasting the city's Jim Crow ordinances.

In those days the only qualifications to teach were a high-school diploma and the ability to pass a teacher's examination, so when he graduated from Central in 1918, Clouser took a teaching job on the mainland. In 1923 he returned to the Island and took a job at the West District School. Despite a school board policy prohibiting teachers from taking part in politics, Clouser regularly made his views known.

The commission paid attention as Clouser made his case against the offensive sign at Menard Park, then voted to have the sign removed. Moreover, they designated a square block, bordered by Avenues P and Q and 41st and 42nd streets, as a playground for black children. This was a magnificent, though short-lived, victory for Galveston's blacks. Unfortunately, it created a backlash among a group of white racists. White vigilantes burned crosses at the site of the proposed park, and held a series of indignation meetings. Eventually, they forced a referendum vote, the first in Galveston's history. By a two-to-one margin the commission was overturned, and the site became a park for white children instead. To placate the blacks the commission voted to turn a second site on what had been the old Lasker homestead into Wright Cuney Park for blacks. Most blacks accepted the compromise, but not John Clouser, who waited a chance to strike back at the power structure.

THE ISLAND was changing, too, in its perception of itself as a tourist mecca. Visitors no longer asked about the port or the cotton-factoring facilities, but about the surf and the casinos. Galveston was on its way to becoming a year-round resort. The Moodys built two new beachfront hotels, the Miramar Courts—"an apartment camp"—and the four-hundred-room Buccaneer. They also built the ten-story Jean Lafitte Hotel, which replaced the old Tremont as Galveston's downtown social center: after fifty-two years of service, the Tremont Hotel was allowed to close in 1927.

Now that the Hollywood Club had broken the barrier, there were gambling joints on all four corners of the 61st Street and Avenue S intersection. Supper clubs with names like the Roseland and the Kit-Kat Garden spread across town. Bathhouses and amusement piers ran for five miles along the seawall, which was being advertised as "Galveston's counterpart to the famous Boardwalk of Atlantic City." Murdoch's Pier was expanded to three floors, and included a gambling casino, a bathhouse, and Gaido's restaurant. Across the Boulevard was the Crystal Palace, a multifaceted emporium that offered gambling, a dance pavilion, a restaurant, a bathhouse, a penny arcade, and an indoor saltwater pool billed as the largest of its type in the South. The Grotto, which later became the Sui Jen—and still later became the Balinese Room—extended out over the Gulf at the foot of 21st Street. A block west of the Grotto, at the foot of 22nd, was a dance pavilion called the Garden of Tokio, where marathon dancers worked for cash prizes. On the Boulevard at 25th the city put up a sixty-foot-high sign spelling out, in 3,000 electric light bulbs, GALVESTON, THE TREASURE ISLAND OF AMERICA.

The Galveston Beach Association hired a professional showman named Bill Roe to promote the Island's wide-open image and manage its annual bathing-girl revue. Under Roe's inspired leadership the beach area became a perpetual carnival, with a roller-coaster, a Ferris wheel, the Kentucky Derby merry-go-round, and a game of chance called Corno that paid out in hard cash. The bathing-girl revue eventually became the International Pageant of Pulchritude, which in turn evolved into the Miss Universe contest. In 1929 contestants came from Russia, Rumania, Turkey, France, Hungary, England, Austria, Luxembourg, Spain, Cuba, and Brazil. Despite a protest from Bishop Christopher Byrne that the pageant was indecent, the crowd was estimated at 150,000, triple the population of the Island.

Prohibition was coming to an end, but the Free State of Galveston was just awakening to opportunity. In the decades that followed, Postoffice Street became synonymous with red-light district. Every schoolboy in Texas knew intimate details about Postoffice Street, or claimed he did. Every big city in Texas had prostitution in the 1930s, and some of it was fairly open, but only in Galveston did the district have identifiable, official boundaries, and tacit police protection. The district started at 25th and ran west along Postoffice to 29th. Over the years generations of young men from the mainland crossed over the causeway, drove east along Broadway, and turned left when they spotted the bronze statue of Lady Victory atop the Texas Heroes Monument.

In earlier times this strip on Postoffice had been a neighborhood of pricey two-story homes with narrow, ornamental front porches, carved railings, and ubiquitous green shutters, a street once remarked on for its "European sameness." Over the years the aristocracy had moved farther west and south of Broadway, and the property had been handed down and finally collected in stacks of unliquidated estates owned by the widows of railroad executives, firemen, and butchers. The managers were usually real-estate agents or law firms, professionals not disposed to maintenance but committed to the highest possible rent. The fancy railings were broken now and the salt air had eaten away most of the paint. Once there had been trees, but the single remaining tree was an ancient pecan on the north side of the street, in front of a two-story mansion that had faded to the color of dead grass.

By day the street was mostly deserted, except for an occasional delivery truck or a streetcar that didn't stop. But it came alive after dark. Prostitutes dressed for the evening appeared in lighted doorways, or leaned against the sills of open windows, calling to the passing parade of seamen, dockworkers, soldiers, medical students, and conventioneers. Businessmen, trying to look nonchalant and appear as though they were just pricing the real estate, ducked furtively behind latticework screens that had been positioned in front of the houses for precisely that reason. Some houses had steep flights of steps, in various stages of disrepair, and doors with tiny stained-glass windows and peepholes. Black maids answered the doors and led customers to shabby parlors where they were permitted to buy watered-down whiskey for themselves, and colored water for the girls. They were urged to feed quarters into the music box, and permitted a dance or two before being led upstairs. If the guests behaved, they were allowed to hang around afterward to dance and drink. Standard price in the late 1920s was $3—$5 for sailors. Interestingly enough, those prices prevailed into the 1950s.

Scattered among the houses were small cafés, barbershops, and soft-drink stands. As a professional courtesy, there were no speakeasies or organized gambling in the district, although there were plenty of both a block away on Market Street. In the alleys between the numbered streets were tiny one-room shacks inhabited largely by blacks. On the opposite corner from a house patronized mostly by Mexicans was the power plant of the Galveston Electric Company. Across 29th Street, at the edge of the railroad yards, was a mysterious green-shaded two-story structure known as the "Brick House," owned by a madam and practitioner of the occult named Ardis. Several of the madams owned their houses and practiced their trade like hard-eyed capitalists. One madam left the district, purchased a medium-sized hotel for $50,000, and ran it as a respectable business. Another who called herself Queen Laura lived regally, with a coach and footman for business trips.

In 1929 there were fifty-five houses of prostitution in the district, with an average of six whores per house—this according to a University of Texas graduate student named Granville Price who did a survey and wrote a remarkable thesis on the subject. Counting other prostitutes spread along the beach area, and in residential flats and down-the-island nightclubs, Price estimated a total of nearly 900 prostitutes for an Island population of about 50,000. That was a ratio of 1:55. By way of comparison, London had a ratio of hookers to citizens of 1:960, Berlin 1:580, Paris 1:481, Chicago 1:430, Tokyo 1:250, and Shanghai 1:130.

At one time the city attempted to register and inspect the girls, but the officer in charge was discovered accepting bribes in 1921. After that the city left it up to the individual houses to take precautions against disease. Apparently, the system worked well. Residents of the district looked after their own: hookers who remained within the boundaries never worried about paying for protection. Considering the number of people who passed through, there were few muggings. An oldtime newspaperman recalls that seamen would get off ships with $2,000 in their pockets, go down to the district, and give their money to a madam for safekeeping. When they were ready to leave, the money was waiting. The madam might charge them fifty cents for a ten-cent beer, but she wouldn't dream of robbing them. Apparently, the district also served as an outlet for sexual frustrations: according to another former reporter, there was an eight-year stretch in which the city didn't record a single rape.

The only law against prostitution that was enforced in the district was a city ordinance prohibiting miscegenation. Reports of sex between blacks and whites drove the cops crazy. When six white girls opened a house in a black section, police ran them out of town. Cops had no quarrel with perversion, though some claimed that it had greatly increased in the district since World War I. They blamed this on American soldiers coming in contact with the prostitutes of Europe. A madam named Janet opened the district's only "French house," spreading the word that she would cater to the "pervert trade." Janet's was one of the most popular and highest-priced houses on the Island. Business was so good that Janet treated her star hooker, Stella, to an all-expenses-paid trip to the 1929 World Series.

Another madam named Mary Russell recruited college girls from the mainland to work the summer vacation trade. Some fresh-faced coeds plied the oldest profession as a way to pay their fall tuition, and some, like the daughter of a prominent Houstonian, did it just for kicks. Mary Russell's house was a favorite hangout of some of Galveston's wealthiest citizens, including John Sealy, Jr. Sealy, who never married, would take over the entire house and throw parties that lasted two or three days.

The district was part of the 5th Ward, which voted almost as a block for three-term mayor J. E. Pearce, who in turn defended prostitution as an essential social balance for the community. "Every city that has tried to repress prostitution has found that it's impossible," said Pearce, who had the backing of the Kempner-Sealy machine. "In the segregated district, they do the least harm to the population of the city, and the police know where they are, in case something happens." Most businessmen agreed: like gambling and drinking, prostitution was considered a natural part of Island culture.

Even the clergy accepted it. Bishop Christopher Byrne said: "We segregate mental and physical diseases, let us do the same for moral sickness, for soul sickness." This was an astonishing declaration from a man who had almost single-handedly crippled Galveston's major beach attraction, the Pageant of Pulchritude, by rallying Galveston's Catholic women in a futile attempt to have the pageant abolished. The bishop not only opposed bathing revues, he opposed community bathing itself. "Through exhibitions such as the annual revue," he said, "the public bathing places on the beach have developed into places where young men and old men ogle women's unclothed bodies and where men and women jiggle thighs together rather than swim."

# 21

IN THE STRANGE swirl of permissiveness that replaced the Island's traditional genteel culture, nothing was stranger than the spiritual metamorphosis of W. L. Moody, Jr. Approaching his sixty-fifth birthday in 1930, Moody became almost a caricature of his time, an object of curiosity and even sympathy. He was a deceptively frail man, with a fringe of white hair and a snow white mustache: if he had worn a monocle and a top hat, he would have looked exactly like the little man on the Monopoly board. People called him Old Man Moody, or just the Old Man, but the vestments of age seemed to suit him. The sourness of youth was gone now, replaced with the mellowed texture of mature, well-reasoned cupidity. Though he was still an ardent prohibitionist and ultraconservative, the Old Man found it easy to compromise with the hedonistic attitudes of Galveston in the 1930s. There was a time when he would have looked on such frivolity as the International Pageant of Pulchritude as the work of the devil, but now he supported it. Indeed, judging from the coverage the pageant received in the *Daily News*, he regarded it as in a class with the Oberammergau passion play.

Two incidents in the 1930s profoundly shocked the Old Man and changed his life. Both involved his sons, William L. Moody III and Shearn Moody. Old Man Moody and his wife, Libbie Shearn Moody, also had two daughters—Mary, who was the oldest of the four children, and Libbie, who was the youngest—but the Old Man looked to his two sons to carry on the family empire. His namesake,

Will Moody III, seemed at first to be everything his bloodline suggested. Bright and ambitious, he dropped out of high school at
seventeen to work at his father's bank. By the time he was nineteen
he was the youngest bank president in the country. In another two
years he was vice president of the Moody family's insurance company, the hotel company, and the publishing company.

But Will III sought his own identity in the business world, and
he began to gamble and make what the Old Man regarded as hasty
and reckless business decisions. The lavish $100,000 home that he
built on Cedar Lawn Circle was a statement of the son's independence, and though the Old Man financed it, he didn't like it. He
didn't like it, either, that his son spent time with Sam Maceo, and
sometimes borrowed large sums of money from the mobster. Maceo, who was leading a move to upgrade the Island's tourist facilities, convinced young Moody to build a new luxury hotel on the
east end of the Island, separate from his family's chain of hotels.
The Jack Tar Motel had the best furnishings and the latest technology, including air conditioning. The Old Man took this as a slap
in the face: until now no Moody hotel had ever had air conditioning.

Will III sometimes dealt in foreign currency, which the Old Man
thought was foolhardy. When a new silent movie house opened on
Market Street, young Moody agreed to finance the organ, disre-
garding the Old Man's advice that movies were a fad and that organs
belonged in church. The son mocked not only his father but his
grandfather, too, when he decided to invest heavily in oil, gas, and
mineral properties. This time the son was wildly successful. From
1925 until 1929—in partnership with a high roller named O. D.
Seagraves—young Moody made millions from oil and gas deals.
Then he lost it all, and more, in the stock market crash of 1929.
The Old Man granted his son a bailout loan, but it wasn't enough.
In 1933 Will Moody III was forced to declare bankruptcy, something
no Moody before him had ever done.

W. L. Moody, Jr.'s humiliation was beyond description. "A Moody
man always pays his debts" had been one of the Old Man's set-in-
stone creeds, and now his oldest son and namesake owed a staggering $8.5 million. The Old Man studied the situation, then moved
with the terrible swiftness of an avenging angel, repossessing his
son's house on Cedar Lawn Circle and banishing him from the
Island. When Will III's ranch was auctioned off on the steps of the

Kimbell County Courthouse, W. L. Moody, Jr., bought it. He allowed his son to live there, but placed the ranch in trust so that Will III would have no control. With one brief exception William L. Moody III ceased to be a factor in the Moody business empire after that.

When Will Moody III hit rock bottom, his younger brother Shearn became the heir apparent. More than any of the other children, Shearn had a way of manipulating the Old Man. He was a strapping, swaggering ex-athlete, who prized his manhood and liked to bully underlings. He had won gold medals on his wrestling team at the Lawrenceville School in New Jersey, and at Moody company picnics Shearn would challenge all comers to wrestling contests. It was considered bad luck to refuse his challenge and worse luck to beat him. Shearn bought the Galveston Sandcrabs, one of the oldest baseball teams in the Texas League, and changed the name to the Buccaneers, after the Moody-owned Buccaneer Hotel. Then he built the largest baseball park in Texas, which he called Moody Stadium.

In the 1930s no young man in Galveston was richer, or more handsome, or more virile than Shearn Moody. His wife was one of the Island's real beauties, a former model and show girl from Parsons, Kansas, named Frances Russell. The Old Man didn't approve of Frances, who had children from a previous marriage, and insisted that she sign a prenuptial agreement disavowing any claim to the Moody fortune. Other members of the family treated her as cooly as they might treat a shopgirl. It was no secret that Shearn flirted with other women, including his cousin Alice Bradley, who had come from Fairfield to work as a secretary at ANICO. "Once a year," recalled a relative, "Shearn and Aunt Alice took a train trip to Mexico. No one ever claimed they were lovers—he made her pay her own way—but everyone assumed *something* was going on between them." According to family lore, Shearn only gave Alice Bradley one gift in all the years they traveled together. It was a gold cigarette case, which she secretly sold.

Some say that Shearn was the meanest, toughest, and tightest Moody of them all. He was a blunt man with the energy and the personality of a fire hose. As publisher of the *Daily News*, Moody used the news columns to punish his enemies and reward his friends. The eighteen-part series roasting the Wharf Company was his idea. Even the Old Man was occasionally surprised by the intensity of his son's hatred. When Will Junior, in a burst of softheartedness, gave two hundred dollars to the Galveston Chamber of Commerce, Shearn burst into his father's office and screamed, "How dare you give money to our enemies!"

For years the City Party of the Kempners and the Sealys had been vulnerable to charges of "bossism," but Shearn Moody was so egregious in the way he hammered home Moody causes that a new, equally sinister term was coined—"Moodyism." Because a high percentage of the black men in Galveston worked for the Wharf Company, the City Party controlled the black vote. But in the 1931 city election, the Moodys gained an unexpected ally when the black activist John Clouser joined their Independent Party. Clouser was still outraged at the way the board of commissioners had caved in on Menard Park, how they had thrown a bone to the black community, and how cravenly the black community had gobbled it up. He had learned that black leaders supported a hidden agenda that would have denied any kind of park to their people—until or unless the black population supported the City Party in the 1931 elections. That's when Clouser decided to cross over to the opposition.

What curious bedfellows John Clouser and W. L. Moody, Jr., made. But Clouser explained later: "Old Man Moody was never a man to give hardly anybody anything, especially black people, except a job. This meant more to us than a handout. Because I was always opposed to a handout. Handouts can handicap you more than just everyday working on the job and doing for yourself." Jobs were an issue blacks understood, and Clouser believed that the Island was in danger of losing shipping to the new deep-water port of Houston.

Stumping the county in a horse-drawn wagon, Clouser told black audiences, "The port is the bread and butter of our people, especially the parents of our schoolchildren. It's losing money because of years of mismanagement." Supporters of the Wharf Company ridiculed Clouser's concerns, and laughed at the notion of "a ship going up a ditch." But Clouser reminded his people: "Ships *are* going up that ditch! They're dredging it while we're standing here talking. You're gonna have to hitch a ride to Houston to get a day's work. Get involved! Stand up like men! Save your jobs!"

The City Party prevailed in the election, as usual, thanks largely to the black vote. Many blacks resented Clouser and feared that he might cost them their jobs, or even create race riots. Bigots who had led the series of indignation meetings three years earlier when

Clouser was fighting to get a playground accused him of trying to promote "mingling of the races." After the election a group of civic leaders—black, not white—went to the school board and asked that Clouser be fired. The board wasn't prepared to go that far, but when the list of teachers was published before the 1931–32 school term, Clouser's name was not included. Clouser went to the superintendent and asked why. He was told: "You have offended some of the rich people of this community. Teachers are not supposed to do that." The following January, Clouser was informed by a member of the school board that if he kept quiet and asked for reinstatement, his application would be viewed favorably. By the spring of 1932 Clouser had his job back.

There was a classic clash between bossism and Moodyism in the campaign of 1935. The Sealys managed to link the Moodys to New Deal politics, spreading the word that if the New Deal ticket won, blacks would immediately be disenfranchised. To counter this the Moodys imported a black politician named DePriest from Chicago, hoping to sway Galveston's blacks away from the City Party. The strategy backfired, however, when DePriest, the son of slave parents, said something about "social equality." The Sealys jumped on this remark, accusing the Moodys of advocating social equality. The Moodys, of course, denied this, and claimed that Mr. DePriest had come to town entirely on his own, without any encouragement from them. George Sealy wrote a letter, published in the *Houston Press*, claiming, "Our Negro population had no part whatever in bringing this Chicago Negro here, who has been an advocate of social equality." The letter placed the blame squarely on the Moodys. Rather than using his own newspaper to respond, Shearn Moody pressured a black editor, James M. Burr, to take responsibility for bringing DePriest to Galveston. In an editorial in the black-owned *Sentinel*, Burr wrote: "The editor of this paper claims to be a Negro 'a yard wide and all wool . . . fast black and can't fade.' He admits that he had much to do with bringing DePriest here and offers no apologies for doing so. But he would not have brought DePriest—nor anyone else—to Galveston nor to any other place, north or south, to preach social equality, for the editor does not himself believe in that 'rot.' "

At the peak of the Depression, the Moodys were making money hand over fist, much of it from repossessions. Shearn Moody filled his home on Cedar Lawn Circle with linens, silver, and china that had once belonged to creditors. Conrad Hilton, who managed the

Moody hotel chain in the early 1930s, once described Shearn Moody as the kind of man who liked the Depression. "People are desperate for money," Shearn had told Hilton. "It's the time to drive a good bargain."

Hilton considered this fair warning: he had come to the Moodys in exactly that situation—desperate for money. He had fallen into the Moodys' clutches when he was forced to put up his Hilton Hotels, Inc. stock as security for a $300,000 loan from the American National Insurance Company. When he defaulted on the debt, the Moodys naturally foreclosed. But they also offered Hilton a prop-osition. They agreed to merge the Hilton hotels with the sorely mismanaged Moody hotels, and form a new entity called the Na-tional Hotel Company. Hilton would be one-third owner, and acting general manager, at a salary of $18,000 a year. Despite some mis-givings, Conrad Hilton accepted, and the deal was sealed with just a handshake.

In the beginning Shearn Moody expressed very little interest in the operations of the hotel company. But Hilton instinctively mis-trusted the younger Moody. He couldn't forget the remark Shearn had made about the Depression—or the passion with which Shearn regarded his enemies. Shearn absolutely doted on his enemies: he was addicted to them. When Hilton asked Shearn why it was that nine out of ten men who did business with him ended up as enemies, Shearn replied coldly: "Because that's the way I like it. I'd like it even better if it was ninety-nine out of a hundred." With all this in mind, Hilton returned to the Old Man's office—this time in private—and asked that the terms of the deal be put in writing. "If we disagree some place down the line," he told the Old Man, "then we partition the hotels on the same basis we organized. Two-thirds and one-third." The Old Man said that was acceptable, that he would have the papers drawn up and mailed to Hilton.

In Birmingham a few weeks later, on an inspection tour of the hotel chain, Hilton got his first hint of trouble. When Hilton sug-gested to the manager of the Thomas Jefferson Hotel that he have the lobby desk painted, the manager asked: "Are you authorizing me to hire a painter?"

"Certainly," Hilton said.

"And pay for the paint?"

"What's the matter with you? Certainly we'll pay for the paint."

"Shearn Moody won't like it," the manager said. "One time I

decided to hang a picture of Thomas Jefferson in the lobby. When the bill came, Shearn Moody had written across it, 'You have just bought yourself a portrait.' When I got my next paycheck, I found out that I had."

Hilton was running short of patience. This was a different kind of painting, he explained to the manager. "Just get the lobby desk repainted," he said, "and send me the bill." When the bill came, Shearn Moody had written across it, "I can get paint for thirty cents a can less in Galveston. Next time it will come out of your salary."

And that's how it went in the weeks that followed. Hilton would order a dozen towels, and Moody would fire back a letter stating that they could have made do with ten. Hilton would submit an invoice for kitchen supplies, and Moody would complain that he could have got the stuff for half-price. He considered things like soap and toilet paper luxuries anyway, and threatened to fire maids who dispensed them too liberally. Nothing was too petty to attract Shearn Moody's attention.

On a fishing trip aboard the yacht *Anico*, Hilton pulled the Old Man aside and told him, as tactfully as possible, that Shearn was trying to undermine Hilton's authority as manager of the hotel chain.

"Shearn does want his pound of flesh," the Old Man admitted, shaking his head in wonder. "But he's a smart boy, Connie. And I've got to stick by my son."

As much as he admired Old Man Moody's honesty and loyalty, Conrad Hilton couldn't shake the feeling that Shearn was going to stab him in the back. It had been weeks now and the contract still hadn't been signed. The more that Hilton thought about it—and the more he saw how adroitly Shearn Moody dominated his father—the more he realized that a handshake was no protection. Now he confronted the Old Man face-to-face, demanding that their agreement be formalized in a contract.

"Shearn doesn't want you to have it," Moody said flatly.

"But *you* promised it to me," Hilton reminded him.

For a minute Moody looked squarely at Hilton, then his eyes seemed to soften and his lips drew tight. "Yup, b'gad, I did," he admitted. The contract was drawn and signed a day later.

But the contract didn't solve the basic problem, which was how to run the hotel chain. Because of Shearn's arrogance and high-handedness, the chain was in financial trouble, especially Hilton's old hotels in Dallas and Abilene. Hilton began to realize that his disagreement with Shearn was so fundamental that mediating a workable compromise was as unrealistic as trying to teach a snake to tap dance. There were times when Hilton had to laugh to keep from crying, like the incident with the starving artist at the Stephen F. Austin Hotel in Austin. The artist had been working for room and board, painting hallways and lavatories. He was too proud to accept charity, so Hilton offered him $35 to paint an original portrait of Stephen F. Austin, the father of Texas and namesake of the hotel. Naturally, Shearn refused to pay. The manager wrote a memo to Shearn, pointing out that the guests had been very enthusiastic about the painting, and in fact felt that the artist had "created a very fine Austin." Back came Shearn's terse reply: "Your artist didn't create Austin. His father did. Your mistake."

In 1932, after months of trying to hold things together, Hilton decided to force a showdown. The next time Shearn returned a legitimate small bill unpaid, Hilton sent it back to him with this penciled notation: "As general manager of this company I order you to pay this bill." Shearn refused, and lawsuits followed.

The Moodys filed their suit in Galveston, of course, seeking to freeze Hilton out entirely. When Hilton reminded them of their agreement, Shearn offered his own interpretation of the contract: "No durn good. You just get out of National Hotels." Hilton countersued in his own town, Dallas, asking that the court force the Moodys to return his hotels, plus a $110,000 loan for his time. It wasn't a fair fight, of course. The Moodys had the money to outlast Hilton, unless he could figure out some angle.

Hilton was desperate to get back in the hotel business. The newspapers were full of stories about the repeal of the Eighteenth Amendment, and Hilton knew that the end of Prohibition and the return of legalized booze would be a boon to hotel owners. When he heard that the Moodys were about to abandon the El Paso Hilton rather than pay $30,000 back rent—Shearn refused to "send good money after bad"—Hilton saw his chance. But this was the peak of the Depression, hardly a good time to borrow money. President Roosevelt had just closed the banks, and the holder of the mortgage on the El Paso Hilton gave Hilton just six weeks to come up with $30,000.

Suddenly, Hilton's luck turned. First, E. P. Greenwood, president of the Great Southern Life Insurance Company of Dallas, agreed to loan him $30,000. So now Hilton had his hotel in El Paso, but no money. Then Dallas banker Bob Thornton invited Hilton to take a $110,000 gamble, to pay double or nothing on his outstanding $55,000 loan at Thornton's bank. Thornton had taken an oil lease as settlement on a loan, but banking rules wouldn't let him keep it. He proposed that Hilton take it off his hands, and even offered to loan him the money. Though Hilton had never made a penny from oil deals, he knew that this was a gamble he had to take. Over the next three years the oil run paid off his entire debt. Hilton even managed to buy back his old hotel in Abilene when the Moodys decided to drop it.

In 1934 Hilton settled with the Moodys, who gave back his hotels in Lubbock, Dallas, and Plainview, and even agreed to loan him $95,000. The Old Man shook Hilton's hand and told him, "No hard feelings, Connie." But Shearn remained standoffish. "Finally, he offered to sell me a $100 advertising signboard in his baseball park for $175," Hilton recalled. "When I accepted, he gave me his hand."

Avariciousness finally caught up with Shearn Moody. On a bitterly cold day in Chicago in February 1936, Moody caught pneumonia and died at the age of forty. He had left his overcoat in Galveston, and was too cheap, or too macho, to buy another one. His death devastated the Moody family. The widow, Frances Russell Moody, had never felt welcome in Galveston, and with the Old Man's permission she placed his two grandsons, Bobby and Shearn, Jr., in boarding schools and moved to New York.

Old Man Moody's sorrow may have run deeper than anyone realized; his sense of loneliness seemed nearly unbearable. His youngest daughter, Libbie, had married a young congressman, Clark W. Thompson, and was living in Washington, D.C. His oldest child, Mary, had married a failed medical student named Clyde Northen, and lived just west of the family mansion, in a small house that her father had given them as a wedding present. After Shearn died, the Old Man required that Mary and her husband have dinner at his table every night. After dinner, Clyde Northen would return home, and Mary would stay with her father until he fell asleep. Frequently, she would stay all night.

The Old Man tried bringing Will III back from exile, appointing him to his old post of vice president of the family empire, but the wounds were too deep, and the strain too great. Little by little the Old Man relieved his son of duties, until all that remained was his title and a $15,000 salary. Finally, in 1951 W.L. Junior fired his son and again banished him from the Island. They never spoke again.

WHILE OLD Man Moody was settling his problems with Conrad Hilton, he faced trouble on another front. He learned that Sam Maceo was building a luxury apartment complex at 23rd and Avenue Q. Big Sam was constantly complaining about Galveston's poor hotel accommodations, moaning and bitching that the big oilmen and high rollers from Houston were avoiding the Island because they didn't want to spend the night in some overpriced claptrap hotel that kept running out of toilet paper and soap. W. L. Moody, Jr., was naturally sensitive to such criticism.

Even though construction on the Maceo project was already underway, Old Man Moody called Rose Maceo to his office—he always did business with Rose, not his wisecracking younger brother. "You will note that I have stayed out of the gambling business," Moody told Papa Rose. "I expect you to stay out of the hotel business." The following morning a construction crew began dismantling the project.

A series of gangland killings rocked the Island in the 1930s, causing Galveston's ruling families to wonder if the Maceos were keeping their end of the traditional bargain. Gambling and prostitution were supposed to be good, clean fun, and until now they had been. With their network of Night Riders and their friends at city hall and the *Daily News*, the Maceos had always managed to keep the peace. For example, when the Syrian thug George Musey caught an informer and buried him near Goose Creek—head first in quick lime—the Maceos quickly put a lid on what could have been a civic embarrassment. Not long after that Musey was sent to the penitentiary for six years. On two different occasions the Night Riders intercepted hired killers sent to rub out Federal Agent Al Scharff. The would-be hit men were disarmed and escorted off the Island —with the explanation that "one Al Scharff alive is less trouble than the fifty who would replace him if he was murdered."

Things started to get out of hand in 1933 when a young aviator named Lee Hausinger robbed Frank Fertitta, a member of the Maceo family. Two hours later Hausinger died on the operating table at the John Sealy Hospital, a bullet in his heart. As he slipped away,

Hausinger gasped out a final word—"Rose." Rose Maceo was arrested and indicted, but a Galveston jury acquitted him.

About that same time George Musey got out of the joint and came back to Galveston, looking for new action. Prohibition had ended, but gambling, prostitution, and liquor by the drink were still illegal in Texas, and therefore attractive opportunities for anyone willing to take on the Maceos. According to one report, members of Al Capone's Chicago mob came sniffing around, but went home again convinced that the Maceos had the Island locked up. George Musey was not so wise, however. He opened a successful pinball-machine operation right in the middle of Maceo territory. A few months later, as George and his boys were having a drink at the Alamo Club on 24th, a waiter informed Musey that he was wanted at the back door. Musey walked out the back door and into a barrage of .45 bullets. Police charged Windy Goss, a Maceo employee, with the shooting, but Goss was acquitted.

There were a number of other slayings, but the most sensational—and the most tragic—happened on Christmas Eve 1938. The victim was Harry Phillips, a young engineer who worked for the Galveston Ice and Cold Storage Company. Phillips and some friends were drinking at a bar on Seawall Boulevard, minding their own business, when two Maceo thugs came up looking for trouble. According to historian David McComb, a man named Mike Calandra said to Phillips, "That's my chair, Buddy. Do you mind?" Phillips apologized and surrendered the chair, at which point Calandra hit Phillips in the face with his fist. As a friend of Phillips' grabbed Calandra, another Maceo hood named Leo Lera pulled out a .45 with a hair trigger and fired four times. Three of the shots hit the ceiling, but the fourth struck Phillips below the left ear, and went out the top of his skull.

This was a ticklish situation. Calandra and Lera were Maceo boys, but Galveston cops couldn't ignore the cold-blooded murder of an innocent man in a public place. Vic Maceo, a cousin of Sam and Rose Maceo, intervened, offering to deliver the two hoods to police headquarters before things got ugly. Things did get ugly, however. In the days that followed, witnesses were threatened and ordered to get out of town. People reported sudden memory losses. Lera's girlfriend admitted that she was seated at the bar a few feet from the killing, but couldn't say who did the shooting. "I was reaching for a pickle from a dish at the bar when I heard a noise that sounded like a firecracker," she said. "I looked down and saw this boy lying on the floor. Then I left, because I didn't think it was any place for a lady."

The murder of Harry Phillips sparked one of the few local antivice crusades in memory, but it didn't last long or achieve much. There were a few church sermons attacking the underworld—though not the Maceos by name—and politicians like Herbert Y. Cartwright, who wanted to be mayor, denounced the murder as "a challenge to the good people of Galveston." George Sealy and Lee Kempner held an unofficial meeting with members of the board of commissioners, and a short time later Police Chief Tony Messina resigned. Lera was eventually tried, convicted, and executed in the electric chair. Most people believed that the police chief and the gunsel were sacrificed for the larger cause. At any rate, once they were gone, the antivice crusade faded and business continued as usual.

The social event of 1938 was the visit of President Franklin D. Roosevelt. Every Islander, Democrat and Republican alike, went out of his way to welcome FDR. I. H. Kempner turned the Galvez Hotel into a temporary White House and the media capital of the United States. W. L. Moody, Jr., invited the president on a fishing trip aboard the *Anico*. George Sealy named an oleander after him. No doubt Sam Maceo would have invited FDR to one of his clubs had he been in town. Unfortunately, Sam was in New York, facing federal narcotics charges.

The allegations came as a shock to most Islanders. Sam seldom took a drink, and nobody had ever known him to use drugs or even mention the subject. Drugs weren't all that popular or profitable in the 1930s. With millions coming in from his clubs and slot machines, why would he bother with drugs? Apparently, the drugs had been planted in Sam's car by a local prostitute in an attempt to frame him. Sam was eventually acquitted, thanks to Galveston lawyer Louis Dibrell and some high-priced New York legal talent. The mystery of who tried to frame Sam Maceo was never solved, but most people believed that it was Old Man Moody.

# 22

ISLANDERS SURVIVED World War II without missing a beat. While German U-boats prowled the Gulf, new casinos and clubs opened on Seawall Boulevard, old Italians sat around the Turf Club cursing the Immigration Service and playing the stock market, and the small garrison at Fort Crockett enriched itself in the Island's unique culture, as soldiers had done for years. The fort's coastal batteries were obsolete by the time the war started, but the army used the facilities for training and recreation, and later as a camp for prisoners of war. There is a story, never confirmed, that German submariners landed on the beach one night, enjoyed an evening in Galveston's bars and cathouses, and returned to the war undetected.

In 1942 the Maceos renovated the Sui Jen and renamed it the Balinese Room. It replaced the Hollywood Club—which was wrecked by axe-wielding Texas Rangers in the late 1930s—as the swankiest and most famous nightspot on the Texas coast. The décor was South Seas, with a lot of fishnets, clamshells, and fabric-covered walls hand-painted to look like tropical beaches. The food was supposed to be good, though Ike Kempner complained that it was overrated. Again, Sam Maceo hired the top names in the entertainment business: Peggy Lee, Freddy Martin, Ray Noble, Shep Fields, Jimmy Dorsey, Phil Harris. The Balinese attracted exactly the sort of high rollers from the mainland that Sam Maceo had always wanted. Houston oilmen like Diamond Jim West, Glenn McCarthy, and Jack Josey were regulars, and spectators became accustomed

to watching big-stakes players win (or lose) a hundred grand with
a single roll of the dice.

Without being too obvious about it, the Maceos attempted to
screen customers. Working-class Islanders were welcome in the
bars and dining rooms of Maceo-run clubs, but were not allowed
to gamble. Galveston's upper class was treated with great deference,
of course, but Sam Maceo quietly discouraged them from gambling,
too. Win or lose, Sam believed it was bad business to have locals
in the casinos. No Kempner was ever seen rolling the dice or pulling
the lever of a slot machine. That was because Sam Maceo had
quietly asked the Kempners (though not the Moodys, apparently)
to stay out of the casinos. But the Kempners enjoyed the other
amenities fairly regularly. "Crowded as usual, but with very few
people we know," I. H. Kempner wrote after an evening at the
Balinese Room. "They have two orchestras, so there is no lull in
the music. One of the orchestras is a Mexican or Cuban Rhumba
band, and when they play it is difficult to hold a conversation."

Strictly speaking, the Balinese was a private club. So were most
of the other joints across the state by the 1940s: this was a way to
get around Texas liquor laws, which prohibited serving mixed
drinks. Membership in most clubs required a modest donation, or
sometimes just a dropped name or a friendly smile. In the case of
the Balinese Room, club privileges were part of the security system.
The B-Room was laid out along a two-hundred-foot pier at the end
of 21st Street, and it terminated in a T-head, well out over the Gulf
of Mexico.

The T-head was where the gambling took place. To get there
from the street, a visitor had to negotiate a guard station, where
membership cards were checked or issued, walk through a door
and past the bar, pass through another door and cross the dining
room, then walk down a long hallway, past the kitchen, where a
Chinese cook was usually fishing through a trapdoor in the floor.
From there the visitor went through the last in a series of six heavy
glass doors, and into the casino. The Maceos were usually tipped
in advance when a raid was planned. If not, the guard up front
sounded an alarm. On this signal the slot machines were folded
into the walls like Murphy beds, and the green felt-covered crap
tables were converted into backgammon and bridge tables. On the
occasion of one raid, the band leader announced, "And now the
Balinese Room takes great pride in presenting, in person, the Texas

Rangers!"—at which point the band struck up "The Eyes of Texas." Frank L. Biaggne, who was sheriff of Galveston County from 1933 to 1957, once explained to a state investigative committee in Austin that he had never raided the Balinese because it was a private club and he wasn't a member.

Biaggne was what law enforcement was all about in the Free State of Galveston. A big man with a clown's smile, Biaggne claimed he had never seen a marble machine or slot machine pay off in Galveston County, much less a dice game in progress. When Rangers confiscated dice tables from the Little Club and the Del Mar, they couldn't find Biaggne to take custody of them. "I was by the Little Club about 11:00 or 11:30 and nothing was going on," the sheriff declared innocently. "I didn't know the Little Club had a dice game. And I'm surprised at them out at the Del Mar." But if Frank Biaggne was a poor lawman, he was at least a great politician. He never missed a funeral, whether he knew the dearly departed or not. On Sunday morning he would manage to be seen at nearly every church in town, usually without having to set foot inside or hear a sermon. He never paid for anything. At picnics and barbecues he'd fill a sack and take some home. Though he was frequently seen knocking down free drinks and shooting dice at the Turf Club, he told the chairman of the state investigative committee: "I don't gamble, your honor. I'm not a drinking man, and I don't know the taste of tobacco. Maybe I'm too good to be a peace officer." Everyone assumed Biaggne was on the Maceo syndicate's payroll, but nobody ever proved it. Rarely did any Galveston lawman get caught taking bribes, though it was inconceivable that an illegal multimillion-dollar business could have existed all those years without a system of payoffs.

Some people believed the Maceos had some sort of hot line directly to the governor's office in Austin. In those days the Rangers were the governor's private police force, and no Ranger captain would make a move on the Maceos without the governor's permission. But raids were few and far between, and even when there was a call for action, the Maceos knew about it hours in advance.

Different governors, of course, had different attitudes toward the Free State of Galveston. In the mid-thirties, when James V. Allred was governor, the Rangers wrecked and shutdown both the Hollywood and the Turf Club. The Turf reopened, but several hundred slot machines had to be replaced. Ten years passed before the Rangers made another run on the Maceo syndicate, this time knocking off the Balinese Room, chopping up furniture and smashing slot machines with sledgehammers. The B-Room reopened a few weeks later, with new equipment. The real target of these raids was the gambling paraphernalia. Lawmen could close down a gambling house with the simple expediency of a temporary restraining order, but they couldn't keep it closed. On the other hand, the law permitted them to destroy gambling equipment on sight, without a hearing or court order or any other legal inconvenience. On the occasions when they were unleashed, the Rangers were extremely adept at converting slot machines into paperweights.

In 1949 the Maceos encountered the wrath of a fire-and-brimstone preacher, the Reverend Harry Burch, whose protest against "those nickel-gulping monsters" aroused not only his congregation but nearly the entire citizenry of the little unincorporated town of La Marque. Every small town on Galveston Bay was saturated with dice tables, slot machines, tip books, every illegal item in the syndicate's storehouse. Slots and marble machines—the nickel-gulping monsters of which Reverend Burch spoke so eloquently—were as ubiquitous as street signs. Petrochemical workers, housewives, and students encountered them wherever they went, in drugstores, cafés, dry cleaners, grocery stores, even on sidewalks, mounted on roller skates so that they could be wheeled inside at the end of the business day. "These things are against the kids!" Reverend Burch roared as he filed charges in a justice of the peace court in La Marque. "We won't have them here!" Three syndicate men drove to the mainland and tried to reason with Burch, but the preacher would have none of it. They offered cash contributions to him or his church, or both, but he refused. "All I want," he told the mobsters, "is those machines moved—every one of them." Finally, Sam Maceo made a personal trip to La Marque and had a long talk with Burch. Nobody ever knew what was said, but afterward Sam ordered his men to get the machines out of La Marque and keep them out.

One reason vice and corruption had such a long and successful run in Galveston was Big Sam Maceo's sense of public relations. Do Sam a favor, he'd return it in spades. During one of the early Depression years his employees agreed to take a salary cut, which Sam more than paid back with an end-of-the-year bonus. When anybody needed anything, Sam was their man. He sent orphans to college and kept widows from being evicted. Once a year he paid the expenses for Monsignor O'Connell, rector of St. Mary's Cathedral, to visit his mother in Ireland. He gave generously to the building fund at the First Methodist Church, and headed a committee to fight pollution in Galveston Bay.

In the summer, when the doldrums hit the Island and it seemed as though nothing would ever stir again, Sam staged free concerts on the beach, featuring such stars as Frankie Lane and Phil Harris. When the Mardi Gras committee was looking for a headliner, Sam delivered Edgar Bergen and Charlie McCarthy. When a French cargo ship loaded with ammonium nitrate exploded at the port of Texas City, creating a massive chain reaction that killed 512 and caused more than $200 million in property damage, Sam Maceo called a few celebrity friends and asked them to come to Galveston to help raise relief money for the victims. Among those who showed up were Frank Sinatra, Jack Benny, Gene Autry, Phil Silvers, Victor Borge, Jane Russell, Kay Kyser, George Burns and Gracie Allen.

Sam and Phil Harris became close friends. The bandleader-singer-comedian was a character witness at Sam's narcotics trial in New York. When Harris married Alice Faye in 1940, Sam Maceo's Galvez Hotel penthouse was their wedding chapel, and the reception was held at the Studio Lounge, on the second floor of the Turf Athletic Club. A year later Sam divorced his first wife, Jessica— after first transferring ownership of his share of the syndicate to his partners, so as to avoid the state's community property laws. Not long after that he married a young dancer named Edna Sedgewich. Sam was in his forties by now, and so full of life that he bet Phil Harris that he and Edna would have twins—which they did, both of them boys. A year later a daughter was born. The annual birthday party for Sam Maceo's three children became an Island tradition.

While Big Sam basked in the limelight, his brother Rose greatly preferred the shadows. Rose lived quietly at 2412 Avenue O with his second wife and his son Rosario, Jr. Worried that his son might be kidnapped, or that he himself might be assassinated, Rose employed a squad of bodyguards—including one combat veteran who acknowledged that he had killed a lot of decent foreigners during the war and now found killing the enemies of Rose Maceo refreshingly American. There was at least one assassination attempt, in 1950, but no one got hurt. After that Rose surrounded the grounds of his home with floodlights, which burned all night, every night, for the remainder of his life.

The war was ending, and so was the political grip of the Sealys and the Kempners. In 1941, for the first time this century, the City Party failed to offer a candidate for office. George Sealy, Jr., died of pneumonia in New York in 1944, leaving most of his fortune and power to the Sealy-Smith Foundation, whose interest was mainly in perpetuating the John Sealy Hospital and the medical school. What remained of the family fortune was by now dispersed among third- and fourth-generation Sealys, many of whom had moved off the Island. During the campaign of 1947 a thirty-two-year-old tennis hustler named Herbert Y. Cartwright handed out thousands of cards with his trademark phrase, "Thanks a million," and scored an upset victory over the incumbent mayor.

Cartwright belonged to no party, but he had the backing of W. L. Moody, Jr., who needed a demagogue to rail against the Galveston Wharf Company. Cartwright delivered, not that it required any special skill: by this time discrediting the Wharf Company was an exercise in redundancy. Voters had already approved $8.7 million in bonds to purchase the Wharf Company, though the Sealy interests maintained control until the bonds were redeemed. After the 1947 election Old Man Moody bought the final block of $2.5 million in bonds at par, which gave the city the surplus that it needed to pay off its debt to the Sealys. This maneuver no doubt gave Moody enormous personal satisfaction: it was the culmination of a fight that had been going on since shortly after the Civil War. He may have believed that the city would eventually default and that he would ultimately gain control of the wharves. If so, he was wrong. But whatever his motive, this was one of Old Man Moody's greatest gifts to Galveston. For the first time in more than a century, the city owned its own waterfront.

Though the demise of the Wharf Company as a private entity was inevitable—and attributable mostly to W. L. Moody, Jr.'s dogged determination—Herbie "Thanks a Million" Cartwright took most of the credit. "I knocked the Sealys and Kempners down pretty good when I took that wharf company away from them," he told an interviewer. "They warned me that the Sealys and Kempners would come back to get me, that the Old Man wouldn't live forever, and damned if they weren't right."

Cartwright had a talent for hype, and he managed to stretch it into five terms as mayor. Like all the mayors before him, Cartwright was BOI—Born on the Island—and knew the Island psyche and how to touch all the right buttons. As a student at Ball High School in the thirties, he had grown up on bootleg hooch and late evenings at Mother Harvey's whorehouse, and he considered it both a duty and a privilege to keep the Free State of Galveston free, and wide open. "If God couldn't stop prostitution," he said, "why should I?"

Cartwright had criticized the Maceo syndicate in an earlier campaign, but had apparently reconsidered his position. "I now believe," he said, "that anyone who is twenty-one years of age has a right to make up his own mind." Regarding the rackets, Cartwright made only one promise: he was going to by God see to it that mainland gangsters stayed the hell off the Island—meaning that he favored a closed shop for the Maceos. This attitude probably reflected a consensus in the late forties and early fifties. Galveston wasn't the only place in Texas where you could gamble, but it was the only place you didn't have to know where to look. Islanders didn't merely tolerate their wide-open image, they celebrated it. Journalist and historian Paul Burka, who was BOI, remembers that when he was in junior high in the mid-fifties, Tuesdays in the fall were eagerly awaited, because kids whose fathers worked for the Maceos would bring football betting cards to school. So-called Yellow Sheets listed the point spreads for the weekend games.

"Young runners guarded the cards as if they were dirty pictures," Burka wrote in *Texas Monthly*. "Just to acquire one cost 50 cents. If you wanted to bet on the games, that was another dollar, and if you bet on the minimum three games (your best chance of winning), they tried to goad you into betting on more, thus lowering your odds. It sounds pretty sleazy, I admit, but at least I learned at an early age what many men don't discover until they are 35 or 40: I am not very good at betting on football."

Herbie Cartwright's nitty-gritty style of boosterism did a lot for Galveston. He was always on stage, and always good for a laugh. When General Jimmy Doolittle and his Raiders had a gala reunion at the Galvez, recalling their magnificent raid over Tokyo during the war, Cartwright and his publicist pal Christie Mitchell arranged a mock air attack on the hotel—causing a traffic gridlock that took hours to unsnarl. Herbie willingly drank and partied with Houston oilmen—he once drove Jack Josey all the way to New Orleans to collect a bet—and when visiting firemen felt the need for companionship, Herb supplied the girls. His friendship with the infamous madam Mary Russell was the main reason Lipton Tea decided to build a plant at the port of Galveston, or so Cartwright suggested during an interview with journalist Alan Waldman.

A Lipton's executive was scouting locations for a plant when Cartwright discovered that he had a weakness for young, Christian women of manners and breeding. His Honor the Mayor made several trips to the man's headquarters in New York, accompanied by just such women—Mary Russell knew where to find them. After several visits the gentleman from Lipton was hooked, but there was still the matter of signing the contract. On the Sunday morning that the deal was to be finalized in Galveston, the executive was in his suite at the Galvez with a stunningly beautiful nineteen-year-old Dallas hooker whose manners were so impeccable she could have had tea with the queen. Mary Russell had taken her to Nathan's and personally helped her select $2,000 worth of new clothes. When Cartwright arrived at the hotel that morning with the contract, Lipton's representative signed hurriedly, then excused himself. He said that his lady friend would be back any minute. "She will only be gone long enough to teach her Sunday School class," he explained.

# 23

NOBODY REALIZED it back in 1950, but the rackets had enabled Galveston to remain an important place well beyond her time. But her time was up. Instead of growing like nearly every other city in Texas, Galveston was holding at 65,000, or declining. She was no longer the most important seaport in Texas, or even the second or third. Pestholes like Texas City and Freeport had passed her by. Fort Crockett closed for good after the war: for the first time in her history Galveston was no longer the home of a military base, with the exception of the Coast Guard station at Bolivar Point. Even her red-light district seemed passé: exorbitant rent forced some madams to close, and the houses that remained open were becoming more and more tawdry. Business got so bad that the houses had to stay open twenty-four hours a day to show a profit, and the girls fought among themselves and engaged in shouting matches to lure hapless passersby.

The gambling houses were beginning to feel the pinch, too, and some of them were folding. Many of the top dealers, pit bosses, and croupiers were migrating to Las Vegas, and so were big names in entertainment, and the big-money players. Gamblers complained of cheating—a charge never heard in the days of the Maceos—and at least one club manager admitted that business was so slow he could no longer run a straight game. Things got so bad that the Turf started offering a 25-cent special. For a quarter, a sport could bet a horse, play a hand of blackjack, or wager on any game in the house. Once the fastest action in Texas, the Turf was making a marginal profit skimming lunch money from medical students, secretaries, and clerks.

In 1951 Gulf Properties, the Maceos' holding company, declared that profits were down for the third year in a row and began laying off people. At one time Gulf Properties had employed 2,500 people, roughly 10 percent of the adult population, but when it began to go south, so did everything else. Every merchant on the Island felt the ripple effect. Nathan's could no longer count on selling designer dresses to prosperous madams, much less to the wives and mistresses of oil millionaires, who were likely to ignore the Island and head straight for Las Vegas or Reno. The clothing store of E. S. Levy & Company had been an Island institution since 1890, but when Harry Levy tried to borrow money to expand after World War II, every bank in town turned him down—that is to say the Moodys, Sealys, and Kempners turned him down, because those three families still controlled all the banks. There *was* one other unofficial bank: the Turf Athletic Club. It had been known as the "Weekend Bank" of Galveston since the 1930s. Businessmen sometimes cashed checks for tens of thousands of dollars at the Turf. But no more.

The men who had made Galveston great, or at least interesting, were old, dead, or dying—or under investigation. In 1951 the Internal Revenue Service filed income-tax-evasion charges against Maceo family members. About that same time the "Little Kefauver Committee" began investigating organized crime in Texas. By then Big Sam and Papa Rose were too sick to testify, but four other members of the Maceo family were subpoenaed and sat tight-lipped while lawyers for the committee rummaged through their books and made their business public. Most Islanders were surprised to learn how profitable the rackets had been: the Maceos had been averaging between $3 and $4 million a year. At least that's what showed up on the books. But the syndicate's accountant, Sam "Books" Serio, told the committee of numerous omissions. In the summer of 1947, for example, Rose took twelve bundles of cash out of a secret safe at the Turf Club and split it in half. "There's $600,000 here," he told his brother Sam. "Three hundred grand for you, and three hundred grand for me." And none for the IRS. Among the quainter revelations was that Sam had neglected to pay taxes on the $49,000 wager he had collected the night Harry Truman defeated Thomas Dewey.

Sam Maceo died of cancer in 1951, aged fifty-seven. "The angels in heaven will welcome this good man," Monsignor O'Connell said in his eulogy. Rose was hospitalized with heart disease and clinical depression, and died in 1953 at the age of sixty-six. When word of his death reached the Turf Athletic Club, the boys at the crap tables just kept on playing. According to one of Rose's nephews, his uncle was no sooner in the ground than Sheriff Frank Biaggne came around demanding a payoff to allow the clubs to remain open. Whatever arrangement Rose had had with the sheriff apparently went with him to the grave.

W. L. Moody, Jr., finally died in 1954, at eighty-nine. In its obituary *Time* magazine called him one of the ten wealthiest men in the country. I. H. Kempner lived on into the 1960s, but he had long since relinquished power to his son, Harris L. "Bush" Kempner. Kempner genuinely mourned the passing of the Maceos, whom he referred to as "an element that has always been liberal."

The postwar boom brought about an enormous expansion in the petrochemical industry on the mainland, which in turn dramatically altered the demographics of Galveston County. Bayside towns like Texas City, La Marque, Dickinson, and Kemah were no threat to replace Galveston as the county seat, but together they made up a majority of the electorate. The war had changed other things, too, mostly for the good, but sometimes in pious and unforgiving ways. Young men who had gone overseas to fight a godless enemy returned home consumed with visions of their own righteousness, a call to action ringing in their ears, and epiphanies of reformation dancing before their eyes. It was morning in America, a time to be strong, a time to do right. Crusading county attorneys like Will Wilson in Dallas were elected on reform tickets and seemed bent on saving Texas from itself.

Early in 1953 a young state legislator from Galveston made headlines when he dared to speak out against the Island's crime syndicate. This came about almost by accident. Bill Kugle didn't think of himself as a reformer. The ex-paratrooper graduated from the University of Texas law school in 1950 and came to Galveston because it was the only place he could find a job. "I wasn't a prude," Kugle recalls, "but the corruption in Galveston was absolutely unbelievable. I once sat in the back office of a lawyer friend and heard the police commissioner, Walter Johnston, brag that he was on the payroll of 46 whorehouses." Kugle had tried to get the police commissioner indicted, but his attempts got nowhere. And still, when Kugle ran unopposed for the state legislature in 1952, corruption wasn't an issue.

But something else had happened: a runaway grand jury had indicted twenty-two members of the syndicate, including Vincent Maceo, Joe T. Maceo, Frank Maceo, Sam Maceo, Sam Serio, and the terminally ill Rose Maceo. The county attorney was mortified at the thought of having to try such powerful and dangerous men, and offered only token objections as the syndicate's lawyer, Louis J. Dibrell, sought delay after delay. Ultimately, all charges were dismissed, many of them by District Judge Charles G. Dibrell, father of the syndicate's mouthpiece.

Kugle had been in the legislature only a couple of weeks when the charges were dropped. He was sitting around the Capitol coffee shop one night, talking to two colleagues, Barefoot Sanders and Don Kennard, when he happened to mention that the situation in Galveston was "an insult to every law-abiding citizen of Texas." Ralph Dodd, a reporter for the *Houston Press*, overheard the remark, and asked Kugle if he would mind being quoted. Kugle wouldn't mind. By today's standards the next day's headline sounds fairly innocuous—GALVESTON OFFICIAL RAPS GAMBLING—but this was the first time in more than a quarter of a century that any elected official had even hinted that gambling was something less than divinely mandated.

On the Island the reaction to Kugle's comment ranged from wonderment to outrage. Kugle started getting calls from people he knew, saying things like "The boss over at the Turf is real sorry about this misunderstanding, and he just hopes that nobody in your family will get hurt." Several callers made vague references to sums of money that might be available. The most blatant offer came from one of Kugle's fellow Galveston legislators, the late Representative Harold Seay, who first telephoned that he represented a group that wanted to give Kugle "a cash retainer" for future service, and later came by Kugle's house with a sack of money. "I think there was $30,000 in the bag," Kugle recalls. "Now I was hungry as hell back then. I think I was making about $6,000 a year. But it was apparent that Seay was trying to compromise me and I turned it down."

At first, Kugle didn't know what to do or whom to tell; then he decided to tell his old law-school friend, Jim Simpson. Simpson, a former FBI agent, practiced law across the bay in Texas City and shared Kugle's distaste for the Maceo syndicate. As it turned out, Simpson already knew about the bribe attempt: he had found out from a local FBI agent and was waiting to see if Kugle would accept. Simpson and Kugle talked about how to proceed. They didn't have the evidence to nail Seay, but they knew there would be other bribe attempts. Another friend, Jim Bradner, who owned a Galveston radio station, arranged to plant a bugging device in a wastebasket in Kugle's office.

Not long after that a procurer named Sam Amelio called and asked for an appointment. Kugle could guess what the appointment was about: Amelio owned five whorehouses. Amelio had no sooner sat down across the desk from Kugle than he started calculating the payoff. "Let'sa see, five houses timesa three hundred dollars a house"—Ameilo pursed his lips, then continued—"that'sa fifteen gees." Kugle studied the balding, low-rent thug coolly, then asked, "How much do you pay the police commissioner?" Amelio didn't hestitate to respond. "We-a gonna pay you the same as we paya Walter Johnston," he assured the lawyer.

Kugle took the tape to the grand jury, and this time it listened. Amelio, of course, had no idea his conversation had been recorded. When he was subpoenaed and asked to explain the accusation that he had attempted to bribe a state legislator, he denied that he had ever met Kugle. The grand jury indicted him for perjury. Though there wasn't sufficient evidence to indict Walter Johnston too, the tape was certain to be played at the trial, which would at least prove what people had been saying for years, that the police commissioner was on the take.

Again, the county attorney stalled and delayed trying the case. Then less than a week before the trial was scheduled to begin, Amelio's body was found at the bottom of the stairs of one of his whorehouses. Police discovered $2,500 in traveler's checks on Amelio's body, suggesting he was about to take a trip. Amelio's death was ruled accidental, though a baseball-size knot on the back of his head suggested otherwise. When Kugle heard what had happened, his blood ran cold. An informant had told him only the day before: "Walter Johnston will never let Amelio testify."

Bill Kugle was a rugged and fearless man, but for the next two years he slept with a shotgun beneath his bed. He worried particularly about his two young daughters, and made it a point to never start his car or open his mailbox if they were around. In 1954 Kugle ran for reelection, but the Moody-owned *Daily News* ripped into him, and thugs followed him around and jeered his speeches. After one particular speech in which Kugle had hammered home his message that the Constitution was the bedrock of a free society, an old man pulled him aside and said, "Sonny, these people don't care no more about the Constitution than a tomcat does about a marriage license." Though he carried the mainland, Kugle lost every box in Galveston, and with it the race. His political career finished, Kugle packed up his family and moved off the Island for good.

In that same election Jim Simpson ran for county attorney on a pledge to clean up Galveston County. Simpson was the first candidate since before Prohibition who actually campaigned on a promise to bust up the rackets. Bill Kugle spoke his mind, but in reality there wasn't that much a state legislator could do: the rackets were *already* against the law. On the other hand, the county attorney (the office is now called district attorney) could put racketeers in jail. Like his friend Kugle, Simpson was no Pollyanna, just a citizen tired of seeing the law abused.

"Things were wide open, in absolute defiance of the law," he said. "You saw gambling joints a hundred yards from schoolhouses. What made it so vicious was its immediate accessibility to working people, who could ill afford to lose a paycheck. When you rip open the fabric of society like that, there is no hope at all for honest government. I didn't blame the Maceos. They were doing what came naturally. I blamed the Moodys and the Sealys and the Kempners, the people who owned the newspapers and the banks. They could have stopped it years ago."

The 1954 election became a plebiscite on whether or not the Free State of Galveston would continue to exist. Simpson lost by eight votes. But the writing was on the wall. Simpson was only thirty, and he was already planning to run again in 1956. The 1954 election was also something of a last hurrah for Frank Biaggne. The sheriff won, but his margin was only a hundred votes; two years later Biaggne was turned out of an office he had held for more than two decades. In 1955 Herbie Cartwright was voted out, though the issue in that race wasn't the Free State of Galveston. His opponent, a Galveston radio station owner named George Roy Clough, promised that "gambling and prostitution will keep Galveston an isle of enchantment as long as there are people around to spend money on them, and as long as I'm around to see it." As fate would have it, Clough wouldn't be around all that long.

After his daughter was born, Jim Simpson changed his mind about running again for county attorney: he needed the financial security of his law practice, and he didn't particularly relish a political battle with the Galveston mafia. Still, Simpson remained determined to bring down the syndicate. He saw his opportunity in 1956, when Will Wilson was elected attorney general of Texas. As a crime-busting county attorney, Wilson had cleaned up Dallas, and had used his credentials as a reformer to get himself elected to the Texas Supreme Court, and then to the office of the attorney general. In the back of Wilson's mind was the notion that a similar crime-busting demonstration as attorney general could spring him into the governor's chair. Wilson hadn't even been sworn in when a letter from Jim Simpson arrived suggesting a method by which these ambitions might be accomplished.

What the former FBI agent proposed was a deceptively simple scheme to bust the rackets in Galveston County. While the attorney general has no prosecutorial powers, Simpson reminded Wilson, he does have the power of the civil injunction, which in some ways is even more effective. It works like this: First, law officers collect evidence that the Turf Club, say, has a dice game in progress. This evidence is presented in the form of sworn affidavits to the court, which issues a temporary restraining order requiring the Turf to stop its gambling activities. Within ten days the court is required to have a hearing, at which time the court can either dissolve the restraining order or, if the evidence warrants, issue a temporary injunction. All of this can be done without a jury trial. If the owner of the club violates the injunction, he can be sent to jail for three days. But here is where the scheme has real bite: the attorney general can stack five or six injunctions together, each carrying a three-day jail sentence. As soon as the club owner is free and returns to his evil ways, the process can be repeated. "Ultimately, it will break the back of the syndicate," Simpson told the attorney general. "Ultimately, they will give up."

But there was one additional component to Simpson's plan. He wanted to hire unknowns to do the undercover work, and he wanted to train them himself. Simpson didn't trust the Texas Rangers. He had heard stories that the Maceo syndicate had a hot line directly to the governor's office. True or not, the syndicate had an uncanny way of anticipating raids. "Will Wilson was a good man, totally honest," Simpson said, "but he was fundamentally naive. I had a different view. I'd been an FBI agent in Chicago, and I understood corruption." The attorney general agreed to do it Simpson's way, and gave the Texas City lawyer a free hand to develop evidence.

At the time, Simpson was the lawyer for the Oil, Chemical, and Atomic Workers International Union, and he recruited two young oil-company workers that he knew through union activities. Carroll Yaws, thirty-seven, and Jimmy Givens, thirty-three, were intelligent, honest, and dedicated to Simpson's crusade for ridding the county of organized crime. Simpson gave them a quick course in collecting evidence and keeping records, then sent them out to infiltrate bars, whorehouses, and gambling joints.

A job that in other circumstances might have been fun was in fact dangerous, demanding, and physically exhausting. Their workday started about 8 P.M. and lasted until 2 A.M. and sometimes later. In one two-month period, Yaws and Givens put in thirty nights of undercover work, and still carried their regular work loads at the oil company. Each night they mapped out an itinerary, hitting all the places in a particular geographical area. On their busiest nights they visited as many as seventeen places, sometimes staying only a couple of minutes, sometimes a couple of hours. Neither man was much of a drinker, so there was the problem of ordering and pouring out dozens of glasses of whiskey without attracting attention.

Since the primary target of the investigation was the Maceo syndicate, Yaws and Givens quickly became known at the Turf Athletic Club's Western Room. "The Western Room was the key to the Balinese Room," Yaws recalled. "We became acquainted with the receptionist, and one night I happened to mention that we'd like to take our wives to dinner at the Balinese. It was my birthday, and it was the Givenses' wedding anniversary. It really was." The receptionist telephoned the B-Room and made reservations. Soon the two undercover agents and their wives were in the heart of the Maceo empire. "The service was excellent and the food was fine," Yaws recalled. In his notebook he wrote that the casino had five dice tables, four of which were operating, three roulette tables, two blackjack tables, half a dozen slot machines, and room for 150 players. Simpson had drilled them to play as many games and machines as they could, and to keep playing until they got a payoff. Yaws fed twenty quarters into a slot machine before it paid back two. "That's a pretty rough return on your money, or I should say the state's money," Yaws said. Meals, drinks, and gambling for the two couples at the B-Room ran to $62. In two months Yaws and Givens went through $3,000.

The quickest way to get inside a gambling joint was to flash money, and the two undercover men carried clips of cash, with the big bills on the outside so they could peel off a hundred dollars to pay for a drink. In most cases this tactic would prompt the bartender to ask if they cared to visit the back room. One night in Kemah this tactic almost caused them to blow their cover and could have cost them their lives. "You guys wanta try a really big game?" the bartender asked, and the next thing Yaws and Givens knew, they were in their car following the bartender to some waterfront casino, down some dark road. They were already moving before they realized that the leather notebook detailing their investigation was in the glove compartment, which they had no way to lock. At the gambling house a tough-looking guard led them inside while a black attendant parked their car. At that point all they could do was try to act like high rollers and pray that nobody looked inside the glove compartment. "We made our bets in a hurry and left as quick as we could," Yaws recalled. "My old heart boomed every time the telephone rang or someone came in the door. But nothing happened and we got out without questions."

Aside from the danger and the grueling hours, living a double life was at times embarrassingly difficult. Yaws and Givens were known among friends and associates as straight arrows, Christian gentlemen who seldom took a drink or frequented nightclubs. It would have been unthinkable for either of them to spend time in a Maceo hangout. Givens was president of the Young Democrats of Galveston County, and at a meeting one night attracted comment when a minister noticed him lighting a cigarette with a book of matches from the Balinese Room. A plant worker who had got up at 4 A.M. to go fish accidentally ran into Givens and Yaws going over their notes at an all-night coffee shop. Plant workers in those days were lucky to make $100 a week, but people noticed that Givens and Yaws sometimes carried what appeared to be fat rolls of hundred-dollar bills. One or the other was always rushing off for some kind of clandestine appointment. One night Givens excused himself from a neighbor's dinner party early on the pretext that he faced an especially hard day at the plant and needed a good night's sleep. Unfortunately, the neighbor's eight-year-old son happened to notice Givens slipping into a car with another man. What was going on here?

Throughout the investigation, Jim Simpson insisted on absolute secrecy. Except for Simpson and his two novice investigators, nobody knew what places had been targeted, or what evidence had been collected. Nobody else except Will Wilson even knew that there was an undercover operation in progress—not the Texas Rangers or the governor or the assistant attorney generals.

Finally, Simpson was ready to make his case. It was June 1957, and Givens and Yaws had been working undercover for nearly seven months. They had collected evidence against more than sixty gambling joints, whorehouses, and liquor-by-the-drink establishments. It was time to plan the raid, and Simpson knew in his heart that meant trouble, because he was going to have to take other law-enforcement people into his confidence. Simpson felt certain that somebody was going to betray him, but there was nothing he could do about it.

At a meeting in Austin, Simpson laid out the evidence and discussed strategy with the top men in Texas law enforcement—Homer Garrison, the chief of the Texas Rangers, Attorney General Will Wilson and his assistants, and representatives from the governor's office. Since the primary target was the Galveston mafia, they decided to send the first wave of raiders against the Balinese Room, the Turf Athletic Club, Cedar Oaks, and a few other big-time violators. They could mop up the lesser places later. Ostensibly, the purpose of the raid was to gather evidence, which would be used to secure temporary injunctions, which would in turn force the racketeers to shut down. But a secondary purpose was to garner publicity for Will Wilson's future political career.

D-Day was set for June 5. That afternoon two assistant attorneys general drove to the Island and obtained search warrants from a district judge who could be trusted in keep their plans secret. Just after dark, undercover agents from the Department of Public Safety began to position themselves inside the clubs that were to be raided. Meanwhile, in Houston, the main body of the task force was broken into five squads, each with several Rangers, a larger group of DPS troopers, and an assistant attorney general. Half an hour before midnight—or that was the plan, at least—Ranger chief Homer Garrison would personally lead his caravan down the Gulf highway to Galveston.

Jim Simpson was so deep in thought that he only half-heard the ring of the phone at task-force headquarters. He had been expecting it. Homer Garrison answered, mumbled something into the receiver, and hung up. "Boys," said the chief Ranger, "Somebody tipped them off. They didn't open tonight and all the gambling paraphernalia has mysteriously vanished." Simpson looked at Will Wilson, who didn't seem to understand, or to remember Simpson's warning that they would be betrayed. The attorney general and his men drove back to Austin that night, discussing among themselves what to do next. Someone pointed out that the raids were mostly for show anyway and suggested that they just file their cases based on the evidence collect by Givens and Yaws. Reluctantly, Wilson agreed. He didn't have much choice.

On Monday, June 10, eleven assistant attorneys general appeared at the courthouse in Galveston and began filing petitions asking for temporary restraining orders against fifty-two places. This tactic apparently caught Islanders by surprise, and word spread along Market Street that the raid that never happened was happening anyway—that the attorney general's crusaders were here to shut down the Island. Reporters walking the streets were beset by politicians and club owners wanting to know which places had been targeted. Behind the locked doors of the Turf Club, Joe Maceo and other family members met with lawyers, trying to save what they could. But they were too late.

A half-dozen Texas Rangers came along to assist the attorney general's men, which was fortunate because local law enforcement officials didn't raise a finger to help. Paul Hopkins, who had replaced Frank Biaggne as sheriff, at least didn't interfere, but members of the Galveston Police Department did whatever they could to slow or stymie the process. It didn't matter. A panel of judges granted the injunctions in every case. The list of people and places enjoined against future operations crossed the spectrum of the Galveston underworld—JoJo and Dottie Welsh's bawdyhouse at 2709½ Market Street, Dorothy Tyler's 409 Club on 24th, the Balinese Room,

Cedar Oaks, the Western Room, the Metropole, Omar Khayam, the Rod and Gun Club, Mary Russell, Vic A. Maceo, Anthony Fertitta —the list ran on for pages and covered sixty-two cases.

Armed with search warrants, Jim Simpson, along with the assistant attorneys general and a squad of Rangers, visited every place on the list, smashing slot machines where they found them, and seizing books and records. Simpson knew there would be no machines or gaming devices at the Balinese Room or the Turf Club, but an informant had told him where else to look: stashed behind the draperies inside the old Hollywood Club—abandoned for twenty years—they found nearly 2,000 gaming tables, roulette wheels, and slot machines. Another 350 slot machines and 150 marble machines, along with other gambling devices, were discovered in an underground bunker at old Fort Travis on Bolivar Peninsula. Simpson could have worn out the state's entire supply of Rangers smashing up all those machines, but he had a better idea. A Houston newspaperman told Simpson that if he could find a way to "dramatize" the disposal of all this contraband, *Life* magazine would send a reporter and a photographer to cover it.

Simpson studied the proposal and came up with an idea that seemed perfect. He would load the machines aboard a barge and dump them in the bay. But not just anywhere in the bay. He knew exactly where. One of the Island's enduring landmarks is the wreckage of the concrete ship *Selma*, which went down between Pelican Island and the entrance to the ship channel in 1920. The remains still protruded above the water, and would make a fitting and symbolic backdrop for deep-sixing the last of the machines from the Free State of Galveston.

There were several problems with Simpson's theatrics. He had assumed that the machines would sink as soon as they were shoved off the barge. Who could have guessed that the damn things would *float?* But that's what they did. From the Bolivar Roads halfway to the port of Houston, slot machines bobbed in the current like steel jellyfish with fruit eyes. Mayor Clough, who had stood by indignantly while Simpson closed down every joint on the Island, took this opportunity to accuse Simpson of endangering navigation, and threatened to have him arrested. The Corps of Engineers also called Simpson to account for his actions, and several shrimp-boat owners threatened to sue. Worst of all, *Life* never showed.

But Simpson had won. This was the end of the Free State of

Galveston. More than a hundred gaming indictments were handed down against scores of business people, and the major clubs and whorehouses closed their doors for good. There was still some gambling and prostitution, of course, just as there is in any city in America, but the rackets were no longer an industry. Most of the old Maceo gang drifted off to Las Vegas. Some went to Houston, and a few even found straight jobs on the Island.

The town of Galveston didn't die exactly, but things were never the same. On the other hand, doctors and merchants who hadn't been paid in months began to receive checks a month after the secretaries and clerks stopped losing their quarters at the Turf, and the family trade began to return to the Island. "The year they shut down gambling, we had a dozen high chairs," recalled restaurateur Mike Gaido. "A year later that figure was four dozen."

As for Will Wilson, he kept his hand in Galveston's affairs by overseeing the multimillion-dollar Moody Foundation that the Old Man had established before his death, but he never did get elected governor. During the Nixon administration, Wilson resurfaced as an assistant United States attorney general and used his knowledge of former client Houston developer Frank Sharp to instigate an investigation that resulted in a purge of the Texas Democratic Party. At this writing Bill Kugle is a successful lawyer in the East Texas town of Athens, and Jim Simpson and his daughter have a thriving law practice in Texas City.

# 24

WHEN W. L. Moody, Jr., died in 1954, leaving his oldest daughter in charge, he deliberately placed the Moody empire in the hands of a woman who had never had a day of formal schooling. The Old Man didn't believe in education for women, and whatever Mary Elizabeth Moody picked up along the way came from her father or from nannies or servants. She was sixty-two when her father died, a childless widow who had never made a bed, cooked a meal, signed a check, or had sex. At least that's what she told friends. Though she was married to Edwin Clyde Northen for nearly forty years, Mary Moody claimed to have remained a virgin.

Old Man Moody liked Clyde Northen, and in fact handpicked him as a son-in-law. Northen was a quiet, studious man who grew oleanders as a hobby and enjoyed hunting and fishing. He came from solid Anglo-American stock: his ancestors were among the first English settlers in the New World, landing on the banks of the James River in 1635, and a branch of the family migrated to East Texas before the Civil War. Clyde Northen was born in 1873, which meant that he was just twelve years younger than W. L. Moody, Jr., his future father-in-law. Northen came to Galveston in 1904 to attend medical school, but was forced to drop out because of chronic eye problems. He was working as night clerk at the Tremont Hotel when W. L. Moody, Jr., befriended him and helped him start his own small insurance company. Later Northen joined Old Man Moody's company, American National Insurance Company

(ANICO). The Old Man probably wasn't thinking about grandchildren when he arranged for Northen to marry his daughter. Clyde Northen was forty-two and Mary Moody was twenty-one.

Moody built a home for his daughter and son-in-law on Broadway, just west of his own mansion. After the humiliating downfall of his namesake, W. L. Moody III, and the premature and crushing death of his other son, Shearn, Old Man Moody developed an almost pathetic dependency on his daughter Mary. They ate together every night, and when he traveled, Mary traveled with him. They spent the summers together at their vacation retreat at Mountain Lake, Virginia, and in the autumn they went to his hunting lodge at Lake Surprise. During these interludes Mary's husband usually remained in Galveston, looking after the family business. Clyde Northen was listed as vice president of the Moody banks, hotels, insurance, and publishing companies, but the titles were mainly for show. W. L. Moody, Jr., remained in absolute control until his death.

In 1942, when the Old Man was seventy-seven and still in excellent health, he created the Moody Foundation, which was the first step of his master plan to place the bulk of his fortune out of reach of both the tax collectors and his own heirs. Under Texas community property law, half of the fortune belonged to his wife, Libbie Shearn Moody. She died about a year after the foundation was formed, but on her deathbed she signed a will creating a second tax shelter, the Libbie Shearn Moody Trust, which provided an income for her children and grandchildren. Though the corpus of her part of the estate remained in the trust, her heirs would receive annual dividends from its interest: over the years this has paid each of them from several hundred thousand to more than a million dollars a year.

The crown jewel of the Moody fortune—its cash cow—was the giant insurance company, ANICO, which had become one of the ten largest insurance companies in America. But the key to the treasure was the Moody Foundation. The Old Man fixed it so that after his death, 35 percent of the stock in ANICO went to the Moody Foundation, and another 35 percent went to the Libbie Shearn Moody Trust. He additionally provided that the stock controlled by the Libbie Shearn Moody Trust would be voted by the trust department of the Moody National Bank. Whoever controlled the Moody Foundation also controlled the bank, and therefore controlled ANICO, not to mention the newspapers, hotels, ranches, and other property Will Junior had accumulated. Originally, the foundation had two trustees—Mary Moody Northen and the Old Man's attorney, Louis J. Dibrell—but within a year the lawyer resigned, and Mary found herself sitting alone at the head of an empire with assets of nearly $2 billion.

It is interesting to speculate why the Old Man left all that power in the hands of a daughter whose vision of the world was limited to what she had seen from her upstairs window. Mary Moody Northen was hardly CEO material. She wasn't dimwitted exactly, but she had the coarse manners of one who had lived isolated from society. She had never even been inside the Moody Building, or visited the ANICO offices. "Until my father died," she admitted, "I had never been farther than Houston by myself." In some ways Mary Moody Northen was her father's alter ego: she refused to fly on airplanes, and regarded air conditioning as a silly fad. In her later years she became absent-minded, and sometimes went weeks without bathing or changing her underwear. Money was something so abstract that she could barely fathom its concept: she once turned a New Orleans hotel room upside down looking for a lost strand of pearls that had cost her $1.89. She owned expensive jewelry, of course, but it never occurred to her to have it insured, even though she was chairman of one of the largest insurance companies in the country. "Mary never gave gifts," her friend June Harris remembered. "But one Christmas she surprised me with a jar of strawberry jam. I looked on the back of the bottle and it said: Compliments of the Bank of the Southwest. Mary didn't like strawberry jam." When the Old Man was drawing up his will, he never expected Mary Moody Northen to oversee the daily operation of the Moody empire. He had a handpicked staff for that. She wasn't expected to be the brains, only the guardian, of the family fortune.

But what was the Old Man really thinking? Not about charity, obviously. During the final twelve years of Old Man Moody's life— from 1942 to 1954, when he personally directed the foundation— its single contribution was a $242,000 grant to a cerebral palsy home. The family version held that he placed his fortune out of reach so that future generations of Moodys could appreciate the value of making it the hard way. The popular view was less kind. W. L. Junior just couldn't stand the thought of sharing with anyone: like a pharaoh, he wanted to rest eternally in the womb of his treasure.

Of the estimated $440 million in the estate, only about $1 million went to the family. Mary got $250,000, some ANICO stock and the family mansion. The youngest daughter, Libbie, got $200,000. W. L. III was cut off with a token $1. Shearn Moody's family had been given the shaft years earlier, though nobody knew it until W.L. Junior's will was probated. The Old Man had cunningly bilked Frances Russell Moody and her two sons, Shearn Junior and Bobby, out of a large share of their inheritance by transferring some worthless stock and bad debts to Shearn Senior's estate.

But maybe there was another reason that W.L. Junior placed his fortune so near and yet so far from all the Moodys who followed. Maybe the Old Man was so full of piss and vinegar that he just wanted to play a little postmortum king of the mountain. Put it up for grabs. See them scramble and fight. Last Moody standing gets it all. This was exactly the sort of challenge that might have appealed to the Old Man. Just as his own father's legacy had been a disdain for fair play, and a conviction that laws were to be used rather than followed, W. L. Moody, Jr., seemed to have left his heirs the means and the motive to cut each other to ribbons.

Not surprisingly, the lawsuits and legal maneuvers started as soon as the will was probated, and continue into the 1990s, leaving an unending trail of bitterness, vindictiveness, greed, malice, and disastrously bad judgment. In the months just after the Old Man's death, his daughter, Libbie Moody Thompson, and her two children sued the estate and settled out of court for $8.5 million. W. L. Moody III and his daughter sued and settled for $3.6 million. Lawyers for Frances Russell Moody and her sons negotiated a $2 million settlement. Most of it went to the boys, Shearn Junior and Bobby, who had grown up in boarding schools and military academies after their father's death.

In the meantime Frances Russell Moody had married a wealthy British industrialist, Augustus J. Newman, and had become an international socialite. She maintained her Galveston home on Cedar Lawn Circle, but spent most of her time in New York, London, Monte Carlo, and Palm Beach. Frances loathed the Moody family, especially her sister-in-law, Libbie Moody Thompson, who at the time of her mother's funeral had told Frances: "We don't need you here. You're not a part of this family."

Just about the only direct descendant who didn't challenge the will—outside of Mary Moody Northen—was W. L. "Billy" Moody

IV, whose father had disgraced the family name by going bankrupt. Billy Moody grew up on the Moody Ranch in Kimbell County, but his mother died when he was two. More than any of the others Billy was close to his grandfather. The Old Man took him hunting and fishing, and wrote him long letters full of advice when Billy was stationed in the South Pacific in World War II. Respect others, the Old Man told Billy. Don't be greedy. Do as I say, not as I do.

In the mid-fifties Mary Moody Northen appointed her three nephews, Shearn Junior, Bobby, and their cousin Billy, to serve with her on the Moody Foundation board. There wasn't much to the job, really. They met at regular intervals and decided which church, university, or military academy got a Moody grant. Until the tax reform act of 1969 forced the board to be more generous, the Moody Foundation was among the least magnanimous of the big foundations. Billy Moody took the job of handing out his grandfather's money in stride, but Shearn and Bobby resented the fact that all they got to do with the money was give it to someone else. Shearn, in particular, seemed to regard the millions of foundation dollars as his birthright.

Shearn and Bobby—as well as some of the other Moody heirs— thought that the stock issued as dividends by ANICO should be distributed by the Libbie Shearn Moody Trust as income. *Their* income. Billy Moody and Aunt Mary believed that the stock should be treated as capital and retained in the trust, eventually to wind up in the Moody Foundation. The foundation board found itself divided two to two over this issue. Some of the dissident family members who wanted the stock dividends distributed as income began buying stock in the Moody National Bank. To forestall this apparent effort to gain control of the Libbie Shearn Moody Trust, the Moody Foundation bought 51 percent of the stock in the bank, thus getting control of 70 percent of the ANICO stock and putting an end to the notion that stock dividends should be treated as income. But the compromise came at a bitter price. From that time on, the four Moodys split two to two on nearly every vote, with Shearn and Bobby always paired against Billy and Aunt Mary.

In the late fifties Texas Attorney General Will Wilson intervened in the family squabble, threatening to break the impasse by appointing five outsiders to the foundation board. By law, the attorney general has a duty to oversee charitable foundations in Texas, and the power to reshape them if they are not true to their charter.

Their majority in jeopardy, the Moodys negotiated a compromise, agreeing to accept three outsiders. But there was a clinker in the equation. Billy IV, the family maverick, sided with the three outsiders, thus creating an outsiders' majority that thwarted the ambitions of his cousins. From that time, the backstabbing and recriminations started and got increasingly dirty.

SHEARN MOODY, JR., wasn't at all like his father, with the exception that he was obsessed with getting his hands on the family fortune. Shearn was a complex young man, part dilettante and part businessman. He enjoyed posturing as an Islander too wealthy to care, but there was something frenetic in his posturing. He worked hard to gain his reputation as the Island's leading eccentric.

Making friends was an art that Shearn never mastered. As a substitute, he surrounded himself with a coterie of hangers-on, lackeys, and aides. One aide was employed mainly to follow Shearn around with a suitcase full of money. Shearn called this satchel his "grand army," claiming that it was a habit he had picked up from his grandfather. The Old Man had told him, "Use your money the way you would use an army, deploying only what is necessary and maintaining plenty in reserve." One of the aide's daily chores was to stop by the bank and pick up $2,000 in fresh, crisp bills.

Shearn enjoyed bragging that he came from "old money," but frequently acted like a man who had just won a lottery. On an impulse he might take a round-the-world trip, indulging his whims by purchasing items his grandfather would never have dreamed of owning—huge quantities of exotic perfumes, rare tapestries, polar-bear skins. "My polar-bear stage," he called one period in his life.

He compared himself to a stage director choreographing his own life, and he seemed to be continually going through phases and stages. On a round-the-world trip in the early sixties, Shearn experienced what he called "my penguin stage." Killing time with his coterie in southern Chile, awaiting the start of Carnival in Rio de Janeiro, Shearn decided to go penguin hunting. He thought a few of the winsome creatures would look good around the swimming pool at his ranch in Galveston. Shearn and his pals bagged nine penguins in the Strait of Magellan, but a U.S. Coast Guard crew caught up with the party and made Shearn return the birds.

Shearn's ranch was a bayside compound on the west end of the Island, a virtual fortress with electronic gates and doors, and bulletproof glass. A slide connected Shearn's pink upstairs bedroom to the pool. Poolside was a hangout for Shearn's coterie, what one visitor called "all those round-bottomed, curly-haired young men." Shearn conducted business—such as it was—seated in his bubble bath, talking on the telephone for hours at a time.

During the 1960s the ranch was infamous for its wild parties. Billy Furr, a friend of Bobby Moody, remembered that when he walked through the front door on one occasion he was greeted by a naked woman who asked him to sign the guestbook. "Then I looked around the room," Furr said, "and realized there were several dozen naked men and women standing around. Somebody told me they were the cast of the San Francisco Ballet. I never found out if that was true or not, but I'd never seen anything like it in the state of Texas."

Shearn had a special relationship with his mother. Frances Moody Newman spent most of her time jet-setting: though she had never made it in Galveston society, Frances was a star on the international circuit. Nevertheless, she maintained her home on Cedar Lawn Circle. One of her great pleasures in life was spoiling Shearn. When Shearn was a toddler, Frances dressed him in girl's clothes, curled his hair, and fed him bonbons. "Shearn never had a chance," said a family friend. "His brother Bobby was virile and athletic. You'd see him on the diving board, showing off. Shearn learned that the only way he could get attention was by doing or saying something outrageous." In contrast to Bobby, Shearn seldom dated. Frances fretted that he was too shy to meet girls, and was constantly on the prowl for a suitable mate for Shearn.

In 1959 Frances flew to the Island from New York, accompanied by a young and extremely attractive Englishwoman, Annabelle Cawthorne. Annabelle was the daughter of Sir Terence Cawthorne, a distinguished British eye-ear-nose-and-throat specialist, and had grown up among the beautiful people of Europe. "Frances and her husband were friends of my mother and father," she recalled. "Frances was this very glamorous socialite, and I was just 23 and greatly impressed. I happened to be in New York vacationing with my parents, and on an impulse Frances invited me to fly to Galveston." At first, Annabelle wasn't sure why Frances had invited her to Galveston, but she gradually realized Frances was hoping she would marry Shearn.

The Island seemed depressingly dead and sleazy, Annabelle

remembered. The central business district had deteriorated into a handful of seedy stores surrounded by blocks of vacant buildings and weed-choked lots. The Strand had become a skid row, with winos sleeping in abandoned buildings, and streetwalkers seducing drunken seamen in dark alleys. The Grand Opera House was now an X-rated-movie theater. There was still some small-scale gambling. After-hours joints like Jesse Lopez' Rio Grande Club rocked throughout the night.

In a sad and bloodless way the Galveston of the 1960s was more decadent than the Galveston of the Maceo era. Young people Shearn Moody's age had grown up never knowing anything except the Free State, and now that it was gone they seemed unable to adjust to reality. When they went away to school to places like Austin or Dallas, they were stunned to discover liquor curfews, and dismayed that card games and prostitutes were difficult to find.

"We didn't study Galveston history," said Louis "Chicken" Pauls, Jr., whose family had migrated from Denmark in the 1870s and made a fortune in the Galveston cotton trade. "We had never heard of the Wall Street of the Southwest or all that stuff." Chicken Pauls —the nickname came from his grandmother who referred to him affectionately as "Pollo"—was one of Bobby Moody's running mates, and like the other kids who grew up in the Free State, took sin and corruption for granted. You saw among these young men an unfailing cynicism. Steve Greenberg, a Galveston realtor and a city councilman in the 1980s, remembered that he never had to pay for anything at the Club Rio, because he was Henry Greenberg's grandson. Henry Greenberg was a legendary trial lawyer during the Maceo era. It was said that he once convinced a jury that a client was innocent, even though the jury had watched while the defendant shot and killed a man on the witness stand. Steve never knew if the story about his grandfather was true, but others believed it, and the believing made Steve's life something that it wouldn't have been otherwise.

Annabelle Cawthome dated Shearn Moody a few times, but nothing came of it. "I don't believe he was really interested in women," she said. Frances Moody Newman made sure that Annabelle was introduced to all the right people, meaning the Sealys, the Hutchings, and the Kempners. Annabelle ended up marrying Robert Burton, a fourth-generation Sealy. But she divorced him a few years later and married Jesse Lopez, a Mexican-born gambler and club owner who had once worked for the Maceos. This was the sort of wild and wicked romance that Islanders loved, a low-born son of a wetback marrying the daughter of an English lord. It was a story that made fun of the ruling families. "What this Island really needs," went the joke of the day, "is three good funerals."

Still seeking his identity, Shearn Moody took another trip around the world. He was approaching thirty by now, and his cousin, Billy Moody IV, remembered that when Shearn returned to the Island he seemed dejected and depressed. "I asked him what was wrong," Billy Moody said, "and he told me that now that he had been every-where and done everything, there was nothing left for him in life." Billy Moody suggested that Shearn start a business, preferably something off the Island, away from the Moody dynasty, away from his coterie of hangers-on and sycophants.

The suggestion must have appealed to Shearn. In 1963 he decided to charter a life insurance company in the state of Alabama, where the rules governing the industry were more relaxed than they were in Texas. Brother Bobby also founded an insurance company during this period of time, capitalizing the firm by assigning it his interest in the Libbie Shearn Moody Trust. But Shearn's venture was a sort of breakthrough for him, something deeply symbolic: insurance was the bedrock of the Moody empire, and Shearn Moody, Jr., had sworn to himself that someday the empire would be his. He called his new enterprise the Empire Life Insurance Company of America, and predicted that it would one day outrank his grandfather's company, American National.

Though Shearn and Bobby had a common interest—getting control of the Moody fortune—there wasn't a great deal of broth-erly love lost in their relationship. Even as children there had been something vicious in their sibling rivalry, something that portended an eternal struggle for dominance. After their father died, the boys were spoiled by their grandfather and their aunt. Mary Moody Northen used to tell the story about the time at Mardi Gras when Bobby upstaged his older brother. Shearn was fitted out as a little prince, in a crown and a long robe that trailed behind him. "I don't care if he is the prince," Bobby proclaimed. "I'm going to come out first." On the night of Mardi Gras, just as he promised, Bobby shoved ahead of Shearn and came out first.

Over the years Bobby continued to come out first. As grown men, their relationship was cordial, even friendly, but as Shearn told an interviewer for *Finance* magazine in 1966, Bobby "has a tendency of wanting to run everything, but, frankly, I think he's wrong half the time." No doubt Bobby felt the same way about Shearn. Shearn was probably the more intelligent of the two, but Bobby had a better mind for business. "Careful, calculating, and competent"—that's how one acquaintance described Bobby Moody.

Shearn chartered his company with assets of only $256,000, small change in the insurance business. He got around minimum requirements for capitalization by assigning Empire Life 40 percent of his interest in the Libbie Shearn Moody Trust; Bobby had assigned his company 100 percent of his interest. Though a 40 percent share of the trust amounted to only $150,000 a year in 1963, Shearn convinced the Alabama insurance commissioner that his share's true value, measured over his projected lifetime, was $14.4 million. For the next eight years, that was the amount that Empire carried on its books. Shearn began to buy up insurance companies all over the country. By 1968 Empire had expanded to sixteen states, and Shearn was being hailed by the media as a boy wonder of finance.

That same year Shearn convinced the other trustees of the Moody Foundation to let him buy his grandfather's private bank, W. L. Moody & Son, Bankers, Unincorporated. Considering the acrimony that divided the board—Billy Moody and the three outsiders still commanded the majority—this transaction came as something of a surprise. But all the trustees wanted something from the foundation, and were willing to compromise. Billy wanted a ranch. Mary Moody Northen wanted a resort in Virginia. Bobby Moody wanted . . . well, nobody was sure what Bobby wanted, only that he would let them know in due time.

This was a period of great turbulence within the Moody empire. Rumors circulated that Attorney General Crawford Martin was angling to tip the balance of power by appointing more outsiders to the Moody Foundation board, including his friend and mentor, former Texas Governor John Connally. Shearn was convinced that Martin and Connally were conspiring to gain control of the Moody fortune. Inside the board room of American National Insurance Company, loans were being rubber-stamped, transferring millions of dollars to shady characters in St. Louis and Las Vegas. In one four-year period ANICO loaned $31.7 million to mob-connected gambling interests, who apparently kicked back part of the money to ANICO executives. According to a report issued by a Texas legislative committee in 1971, the Galveston-based insurance giant had replaced the Teamster's Union Pension Fund as the major source of revenue for the mob in Las Vegas.

Simultaneously, Shearn was making his own plans for a takeover. He hired a lobbyist named Jimmy Day to ram a bill through the Texas legislature that would siphon off millions of dollars from the Moody Foundation, and divert it to Shearn and Bobby. The bill might have passed except at the last minute Mary Moody Northen sided with other board members to crush it.

When Shearn learned that his beloved Aunt Mary had personally intervened to thwart his will, he was crestfallen. Though they had had their little differences, Shearn had always believed that in a pinch Aunt Mary would be there for him. He was her boy, the child she had never had. They were a lot alike: a little eccentric, a little too wrapped up in their own fantasies. They were night owls, both of them, and they would sit up until dawn talking about art or opera. Aunt Mary lectured Shearn about his salty language, and scolded him for his hedonistic lifestyle, but she was always forgiving in the end. Mary was in her late seventies by now, a little wobbly, a little spacey. Shearn would sometimes find hundred of thousands of dollars in uncashed ANICO checks stashed under Aunt Mary's bed, and inside her clothes hamper. When there were documents that needed her signature, she was sometimes agreeable and malleable, but just as often obstinate. More than once she had forced Shearn to the limit of his patience. More than once he had considered ways to work around her. Now that she had joined forces with the conspirators, it seemed more urgent than ever that he find alternative solutions to his problem.

It is hard to pinpoint the exact date that Shearn Moody, Jr., made the transformation from eccentric to sleazeball, but it was probably the spring of 1969, when he hired Roy Cohn, Senator Joseph McCarthy's old lawyer. No longer able to control his Aunt Mary, and having seen his efforts to influence the legislature end in failure, Shearn turned to the courts. Cohn's job was to find a way to snatch the foundation from the outsiders.

Roy Cohn was a brilliant attorney—nervy, vicious, and absolutely unencumbered by scruples. A generation of American television viewers had been repelled by the image of the mad McCarthy scowling and nodding as the greasy Cohn whispered advice in his ear during the Army-McCarthy Hearings. But what repelled most people fascinated and reassured Shearn, who began to refer to Cohn as "my Doberman." Though they were cut from different cloth, Shearn Moody and Roy Cohn had much in common, starting with their distrust of established authority. They believed that the legislative and judicial systems were totally corrupt, and controlled by dangerous conspirators, and they shared a passion for right-wing crusades and shady dealings. Like Shearn, Cohn was reported to be homosexual, an accusation that Cohn denied right up until he died of AIDS in 1986. Cohn and some of his associates used to satisfy their sexual appetites by "adopting" young men from orphan homes and taking them for extended orgies aboard their yachts, or stashing them indefinitely on private islands in the West Indies.

Moody and Cohn understood each other's lust for money and power. Though Shearn was virtually addicted to litigation, he loathed all attorneys and deeply resented having to pay their fees. He referred to lawyers as camels and rode them unmercifully, then dropped them and got another. This attitude presented no problem for the duplicitous Cohn, however. Cohn asked for and got a hefty retainer, plus an additional $1,000 a day as his trial fee. Cohn encouraged Shearn to believe that the client controlled the situation, but Cohn knew who was in charge—he was, and everyone knew it except Shearn. When there was a complicated brief to write, Cohn had Shearn pay for an around-the-world ticket on a Pan Am flight out of New York, and secluded himself for days in the first-class section to work on Shearn's problem.

On a yacht trip from New York to Galveston, Roy Cohn and Shearn Moody plotted a strategy to gain control of the Moody fortune. The centerpiece of the plot was ANICO's dealings with the Mafia, which had not yet been made public. Shearn had hired a private detective named Norman Revie, a former agent for an American National subsidiary, to snoop on company officials, and on other members of the Moody family. Digging through the archives of courthouses across the country, Revie filled two filing cabinets with documents. Using this information, Cohn drafted a $610 million suit against several ANICO directors, accusing them of fraud and self-dealing. To avoid any appearance of conflict of interest, the attorney kept Shearn's name off the record, using a Moody cousin, David Myrick, as a surrogate plaintiff. But Cohn needed a clincher, something dramatic that would place ANICO in the harshest light and rally public opinion to their side. An ideal vehicle presented itself in Austin, where a legislative committee was hearing testimony on American National's activities. Cohn, who had perfected his smear techniques as Joe McCarthy's mouthpiece, made arrangements to testify. Before a packed house Roy Cohn worked himself into full indignation, then denounced ANICO as "the bank for the mob." As he expected, the story was gobbled up by newspapers and magazines nationwide.

But the strategy failed. A subsequent investigation by Texas Attorney General Martin disclosed that Myrick was a "front man," that Shearn was behind the scheme, and that he made the charges in an attempt to inflame public opinion and compel the ANICO directors and the outside trustees of the foundation to resign. All of this was true, of course, though maybe beside the point. There was no question that ANICO had served as a bank for the mob—as a final report from the investigative committee would affirm—but for whatever reason, Martin chose to dismiss the charges against ANICO's directors. All Shearn got out of the Myrick suit was a huge legal bill.

The failure didn't squelch his ambitions, however. In a second law suit, in 1970—this one targeted at the directors of the Moody Foundation—victory was achieved, not only for Shearn but also, inadvertently, for Bobby Moody. Victory came in the form of a judicial ruling declaring that former Attorney General Will Wilson's original board-packing deal in the fifties was illegal. Control of the foundation was returned to Mary Moody Northen, who, after much deliberation, reappointed Shearn and Bobby but not Billy IV. It isn't clear why Aunt Mary turned her back on Billy—except maybe to avoid another stalemate—but it is clear that this was a turn of events ardently desired by both Shearn and Bobby.

In the decade that followed, things went smoothly at the Moody Foundation. Each of the three Moodys on the board had private agendas, and they got along by going along.

# 25

As always, the contrast of styles and methods of the Moodys and the Kempners made interesting gossip, and reminded Islanders that class breeds class. Nowhere was this more apparent than in the manner in which members of these two ruling families shared their hereditary wealth. The Kempners squabbled over money, of course, but they did it privately, without animosity or recriminations. The family patriarch, Harris Kempner, had been an unusually decent man who put principle above profit, and who taught his children that charity and community service were their own rewards. The Kempners didn't have nearly as much money as the Moodys, but they gave more generously, and without calling attention to themselves. During the Depression, Jewish widows learned that if things got really bad they could see Lee Kempner at the United States National Bank and he would quietly arrange for them to receive monthly allowances. In various forms this tradition continues into the 1990s.

When Harris Kempner died unexpectedly in 1894, he left no will. Under the state's community-property law, his widow, Elizabeth Seinsheimer Kempner, continued to control her half of the estate, and his half as well. The eldest son, Ike, became the titular head of the household, but all four brothers—and eventually their four sisters, too—shared in conducting and developing the family business. They shared almost everything, including a sense of humor, and a finely honed rapport encoded with glances and phrases that nobody except the family understood. On a vacation to Glacier National Park, for example, Lee Kempner, always the peacemaker, jumped into the middle of a family quarrel and got the others to agree not to disagree for the duration of the trip. After that the phrase "Glacier Park" meant cool it, back off, put a lid on it.

Every Friday night for sixty years the entire Kempner clan gathered for dinner at Granny Kempner's home at 17th and Broadway. On Saturday night they ate at Brother Ike's house. As the father figure, Ike Kempner extended himself to maintain tradition. He insisted, for example, that all the younger Kempners attend temple, at least until their fourteenth birthday, at which time they were permitted to make up their own minds.

In 1920 Eliza Kempner decided to divide the estate equally among her eight children, and the H. Kempner Trust was formed, with the eight siblings sitting as its board of trustees. Brother Ike's dining room became their boardroom, literally. Differences of opinion were settled by majority rule. One of Ike's sisters, Sara Kempner Weston, always opened and closed the meetings with a few brief remarks. Sara was famous for her martinis, and for never appearing in public without white gloves. Down through the years, the eight never divided the family wealth, except to distribute profits from the many enterprises—including eight railroads, banks in a dozen small towns, several irrigation projects, a shopping center, and their own crown jewel, Imperial Sugar.

Though it was the Kempner men who got most of the attention, the house of Kempner was equally famous for its tough, forceful, strong-willed women. In the aftermath of the 1900 storm Eliza Kempner took off her own white gloves and worked in the mud and stench as a Red Cross volunteer. Her daughter, Gladys Kempner, led the family to buy back the old Kempner home at 16th and Avenue I, arguing that it would be more honorable to tear it down than permit it to deteriorate as other family homes had done. Jean (Mrs. Dan) Kempner helped found the first Texas chapter of the League of Women Voters back in the 1920s.

There was a saying on the Island to the effect that while it wasn't always easy to be a Kempner, it was even tougher to marry one. Ruth Levy Kempner, who was married to I.H.'s son Harris (there is a Harris in nearly every branch of the family), once noted, "Either you end up being more of a Kempner than the Kempners or you find that they make you feel inferior and you resent them and fight them." Ruth chose to be more of a Kempner than the Kempners. Two of the most influential people on the Island in the 1950s were Mary Moody Northen and Ruth Levy Kempner, but for totally different reasons.

The daughter of one of Galveston's oldest Jewish families, Ruth Levy was an early feminist. Her father was an attorney, a teacher of forensic medicine at the medical school, and one of the founders of the Family Service Bureau and the Galveston chapter of the Salvation Army. Her mother was also a civic activist, and her uncle Adrian Levy had been mayor of Galveston. "I was brought up to believe that's what you did," she explained. "That it was a responsibility to do whatever you could for people, not politically but in civic affairs." Ruth's mother dreamed of sending her daughter to Wellesley, but because of the Depression the family could only afford to send her to the University of Texas. Ruth was secretly relieved. "I would have had to study Latin," she recalled. "The only reason I got through Latin in high school was because I had the longest eyelashes in the class and knew how to bat them at the teacher." She graduated from the university with honors, majoring in history and minoring in government at a time when proper young ladies daring enough to demand a college education were at least expected to limit their studies to home economics or education. She ended up back on the Island teaching third grade, for which she had no training. "But by God I taught them to read," she remembered.

Ruth Levy had known Harris Kempner all of her life. They started dating during Mardi Gras, 1939, and married a few months later. Harris Kempner, who was called Bush because of his prodigious head of hair, was a Harvard graduate, a yachtsman, and a gentleman of impeccable manners. Among the third generation, Bush Kempner was the heir apparent to his father's unofficial title as family spokesman. He ran the family's cotton business—his brother Herb took charge of Imperial Sugar, and his Uncle Lee continued to preside over the bank—and took the lead in civic and cultural activities. Yet he was essentially a quiet, introspective man. His wife Ruth was considerably more outgoing and aggressive.

Saturday night dinners at Brother Ike's table were lively, stimulating, and even rowdy occasions. There was frequently an out-of-town guest, usually someone famous like the great lawyer Clarence Darrow or noted socialist Norman Thomas. Conversation was open—no holds barred—and the younger Kempners contested each other to see who could speak out and hold his own. Ruth Levy Kempner more than held her own. There must have been some touchy moments when Brother Ike got off on one of his favorite subjects, the commission form of government, because Ruth seldom missed an opportunity to criticize it or point out that the results had been four decades of cops on the take and street commissioners demanding kickbacks.

During World War II, while Bush Kempner was stationed in Washington, D.C., as an officer in naval procurement, Ruth worked for the Democratic Women's Committee, analyzing precinct lists and studying grass-roots politics. This was heady work for a woman from Galveston. Libbie Moody Thompson was also part of the Washington scene during those years, but she limited her political activities to having tea with the wives of other congressional members, and hosting parties for Sam Rayburn.

Washington's social whirl bored Ruth Kempner. She was more interested in power, and came to believe that it was her mission to make the world a better place. She was interviewed by Dean Acheson for a job in the State Department, but lost it to a woman whose background included working with the League of Women Voters. "I was impressed with this," she recalled, "and decided that the first thing I was going to do when I came back to Galveston was join the League of Women Voters, which I did. I think I joined before I even got unpacked."

The Kempners thought they had lost Ruth during the Texas City disaster in April 1947. The first hint of what was about to happen occurred about eight-thirty, as children were walking to school and merchants were opening up shop. Without warning an enormous plume of orange smoke belched above the mainland, followed by a blast that rattled windows and cracked ceiling plaster all over the bay area. A ship loaded with hundred-pound sacks of highly volatile ammonium nitrate fertilizer had caught fire and exploded in the heart of one the largest petrochemical complexes in the United States.

A second explosion a short time later disintegrated a French cargo ship, the SS *Grandchamp*, scattering sections of decking and great pieces of twisted steel thousands of feet in every direction and igniting secondary fires along the docks and among the oil storage tanks. An airplane circling overhead fell like a shot duck, and a fifteen-foot tidal wave surged across the harbor, carrying barges and ships onto dry land.

As head of the Red Cross disaster committee, Ruth Kempner rushed to the mainland soon after the first explosion. By the time she reached Texas City, the entire port was in flames. Devastation was beyond belief. Bodies were scattered everywhere, most of them so mutilated that they barely resembled human remains. Buildings and storage tanks burned out of control, and layers of black smoke billowed hundreds of feet in the air. In the harbor, tugboat crews worked frantically to move other ships out of harm's way. Men in asbestos suits waded into the fiery wreckage of the Monsanto chemical plant, looking for anyone still alive. Texas City no longer had a fire department: all twenty-five of its members had been killed in the second explosion. So had an unknown number of seamen, dockworkers, and spectators, who had rushed to the area after the first blast. Red Cross workers were trained to deal with hurricanes, but this was a situation beyond their experience.

"I was on the docks all day," Ruth Kempner recalled. "I tore up a perfectly good petticoat to make tourniquets, and did what I could to administer first aid. I didn't have time to call home, and Harris thought I'd been killed in one of the secondary explosions."

That night word spread that another ship, the *High Flyer*, was about to explode. Ruth and a friend saw a boy carrying a banana and a flashlight, crying and wandering in a daze. He had gotten separated from his father, the boy told them. Using the flashlight to find their way in the darkness, they sought shelter in a ditch and waited until they believed it was safe, then started out across a prairie in the direction of Galveston. They were safely away from the port when the *High Flyer* blew, showering the night sky with a chemical rainbow and spitting its four-ton turbine four thousand feet across the bay.

Ruth took the boy home with her that night. In the morning another Red Cross worker called, asking about the lost boy. "They asked his name and I told them," Ruth said. "And they said, 'my God, you've got one happy mother here.' You cannot imagine the horror of that night."

CONTRARY TO the popular image of ivy-covered cottages financed by GI loans and Mom Cleaver in the kitchen baking cookies from scratch, social change was sweeping the country in the 1950s. The

United States Supreme Court demolished the doctrine of separate-but-equal in 1954, in the historic case of *Brown* vs. *Board of Education of Topeka*, and in Galveston that same year a petition circulated calling for immediate integration of the public schools. Islanders ignored the petition. A year later another petition circulated, this one backed by the NAACP. Islanders ignored it, too. Islanders had always viewed themselves as extraordinarily tolerant, and felt no urgency to prove this to outsiders. It was true that no other city in Texas enjoyed as much racial or ethnic harmony as Galveston, not even San Antonio, to which she was often compared. There were no Jewish ghettoes in Galveston, not even self-imposed ghettoes like the ones you saw in Dallas. "I never even heard the word 'kike' until I went away to college," said Harris "Shrub" Kempner, Jr., Bush and Ruth Kempner's son.

Unfortunately, most of Galveston's celebrated racial and ethnic harmony came at the expense of the black community. Separation of the races wasn't a matter of right and wrong, Islanders told each other: it was just the way things had worked out. Call it the cruel reality of economics. In the 1940s some city officials had predicted that the time would come when a majority of Galveston's blacks would live in the old warehouse district north of Broadway and west of 21st. When the federal government decided to build housing projects in this area after World War II, the prediction become a self-fulfilling prophecy. The old warehouse district became known as the Jungle and was the Island's first and only ghetto.

Island blacks were house renters, not homebuyers. Banks and other lending institutions wouldn't even discuss home loans for blacks. This didn't reflect a policy of overt redlining, merely the reality that blacks did not earn enough to justify loans. Since most blacks lived in the projects—and since the projects were almost exclusively black—the school board was able to rationalize sending them to separate, black schools. In this atmosphere there was hardly any pressure to revoke Jim Crow ordinances, or integate public accommodations. The few small victories won by Galveston's blacks were almost accidental. They won the right to use the municipal golf course by the simple expediency of driving out to the course one morning and teeing off: after they had played a couple of holes, someone came out to collect green fees, and with no additional formality the course was integrated. But such bold displays were rare.

In general, Islanders told themselves, integration wouldn't work. Blacks simply weren't ready. Galveston was hardly unique in this respect. When President John F. Kennedy heard that Freedom Riders were trying to integrate whites-only waiting rooms in southern bus terminals, his reaction was to tell an assistant who handled "Negro problems" to "Get your goddamn friends off those buses!" Liberal northern congressmen up for reelection in 1962 begged Kennedy to lay off the civil-rights rhetoric. "Most white people have resigned themselves to the fact of integration," Representative Martha Griffiths of Michigan wrote to Kennedy's congressional liaison, Larry O'Brien, "but the suburbs of Detroit believe it will be years before it applies to their exact area. . . . In case the counsel of those seated less close to the fire than I am prevails, however, and I lose this election, would you mind asking the president if I can have the next Supreme Court vacancy, where I can legislate in safety far from the prejudices of the precincts?"

It should come as no surprise, therefore, that even progressive Islanders like Harris and Ruth Kempner cautioned patience. It wasn't as though nothing was being done. The school board had appointed a biracial study committee, under the chairmanship of a respected white attorney named Griffith D. Lambdin and including black leader T. D. Armstrong. Other cities in Texas had formed similar study groups, invariably with the intent of circumventing the law of the land. But Lambdin made it clear that his committee wasn't there to circumvent the law but to accommodate it. The committee began by addressing the usual, unfailingly irrational fears of the white community—that integration would cause rapes in the hallways and the girl's rest rooms, that blacks weren't intelligent enough to compete with whites, and so on.

"We simply took every argument that we had ever heard and analyzed it," Lambdin recalled. "And we took into account the concept that Galveston has always been a seaport town and is more liberally inclined in matters of race, religion, and whatever than most communities. We felt we could successfully be a leader in Texas in this operation." One by one, the committee took aim at the arguments and shot them down. To the suggestion that blacks are not intellectually equal to whites, for example, the committee gathered army test scores from World War II that showed that black soldiers from across the country had IQs superior to Arkansas high-school graduates. Such statistics were strong antidotes against race baiters. Nobody wanted a school system merely equal to the one in the state of Arkansas.

In its final report the committee exceeded all expectations, recommending immediate city-wide desegregation of all classes in all schools, first grade through the twelfth. One committeeman resigned rather than sign the report, but otherwise the recommendation was unanimous. As Lambdin anticipated, the report created ripples all across Texas. Leading citizens of other cities, including Stanley Marcus of Neiman-Marcus in Dallas, sent for copies. When a member of the Galveston school board read the report, he told Lambdin, "I have no argument with you, Mr. Lambdin, in connection with this report, but did you have to get it *printed*?" A school official cornered Lambdin at the Turf Club and whined, "What are you trying to do, ruin our schools?"

Lambdin knew that the school board would never agree to integrate all twelve grades in a single year. "But we wanted to make it tough on them," he said. "So that we would have a meaningful desegregation program immediately instituted—so that there wouldn't be twelve years pass [sic] on a one-year step progression of desegregation." For all of the committee's good work, however, the school board still found excuses to delay. In 1957 the NAACP tried to force the issue by filing suit. More delays. By 1960, three years after the Lambdin Committee's report, not a single black student had been admitted to a white school in Galveston.

Despite all the forces at work both for and against the breaking down of racial barriers—the NAACP, the courts, the school board, the Lambdin Committee, the Kempners and other Galveston liberals, the White Citizens Council and other hate groups—integration was a cause whose time had come. In February 1960, students in Greensboro, North Carolina, sat down on the stools at a segregated lunch counter and refused to move. It was an act that attracted nationwide publicity and inspired other sit-ins, including one that ended in violence in Houston where one black boy was stabbed and a man tied to a tree with "KKK" carved on his chest. The story was downplayed by the Galveston media, but it created a stir among Island blacks.

Kelton Sams, a senior at Galveston's black Central High, heard reports of the victorious sit-ins in Greensboro—though not about the deadly one in Houston (not that the thought of trouble would have dissuaded him)—and wondered what would happen if he staged his own sit-in at Woolworth's or one of the other segregated lunch counters in downtown Galveston.

The sixteen-year-old Sams was an average student with average grades, a street kid who had never been more than 250 miles from the Island in his life. He hardly seemed the type to lead a movement. Kelton grew up in the projects, in a tumble-down unit on 43rd and Avenue H called Palm Terrace, and he hung out in Wright Cuney Park, where the lesson of life was fight or run. His mother was a domestic, and his grandmother and aunt ran a beer joint and gambling house in a room downstairs. "There were slot machines on every wall," he remembered. "Even upstairs in our living room." After hours, in another building, they gambled and shot craps all night. "I was comfortable in that environment," Kelton said. But it was hard duty. A talented athlete, Kelton had to give up football to take a job on the docks as a longshoreman. He refused to shine shoes or sell newspapers. "People thought I was lazy and trifling," he said. "But I thought shining shoes and selling papers was undignified."

Kelton Sams followed newspaper accounts of civil-rights activities—the bus boycott in Montgomery, Alabama, and the menacing presence of Black Muslims in New York—but had never considered himself as activist until the fall of 1959, when Congressman Clark Thompson came to speak at Central High School. This was just before the November elections, and voting machines were already being set up along the school hallways. Congressman Thompson, who was married to Old Man Moody's youngest daughter, Libbie, was answering cream-puff questions calculated to demonstrate his importance to the Galveston electorate in a risk-free manner when the impudent young Sams pulled out his notebook and said: "Congressman, can you explain why you have chosen to vote consistently with the states of Alabama and Mississippi, and why your civil-rights voting record does not reflect the words that you are sharing with us this evening?" The teachers at Central were shocked that a mere student would dare question the voting record of a member of Congress, and word got around town that Kelton Sams was a hothead and a troublemaker.

Among those who took more than a passing interest in this incident was John Clouser, who had also dared to speak up when he was a student at Central thirty-two years earlier. Clouser had remained a teacher since his reinstatement following the 1931 city election. Since 1946 he had also been state treasurer of the NAACP. As a member of its executive committee, Clouser had instigated numerous lawsuits and fought numerous battles on behalf of his people. Following the confrontation with Congressman Thompson, Clouser asked Kelton Sams to organize a youth chapter of the NAACP, which Sams did. Later Clouser took credit for recruiting Sams and the other kids who took part in the Galveston lunch-counter sit-ins, but that's not the way Sams remembers it.

To make the sit-ins a success, Sams believed at the time, he needed to recruit the best and the brightest from Central's student body. First he approached students in the high school's accelerated classes—Sams hadn't qualified to study in such elite company— but they turned him down, contending that the plan was too risky. He did find a few supporters among less-gifted students, and at a sock hop on Thursday, March 10, he put out the word that tomorrow would be the day. He picked Friday because it was a school holiday. "I didn't sleep well that night," he recalled. "I didn't know if anybody would be with me."

Early Friday morning Sams telephoned the only lawyer he knew, or rather the only white lawyer he had ever heard of. He phoned Griffith Lambdin and said: "My name is Kelton Sims and I'm about to be arrested. Will you get me out?" Lambdin was mystified by the call. The caller was obviously young and black. True, Lambdin had chaired the committee that recommended integration in the public schools, but the attorney sensed that this was something more threatening, something he wasn't prepared to handle. His clients were among the most conservative in Galveston—major insurance companies, a railroad, a bank, and a savings and loan association.

"Mr. Sams, I don't know what you are talking about," Lambdin replied. "But consulting me to get anyone out of jail is really unwise because I have never handled a criminal case in my life."

Nevertheless, Kelton Sams outlined his plans to stage a sit-in at Woolworth's. Lambdin was amazed at the caller's audacity. Visions of riots and bloodshed flashed through his imagination. As soon as Sams hung up, Lambdin telephoned Harris Kempner and several other civic leaders who were likely to sympathize with the black cause. Lambdin thought he could buy some time, but Kelton Sims was already on his way downtown.

At 9 A.M. Sams was waiting on the street corner around the block from Woolworth's. A handful of students showed up, and he led them to the store's lunch counter and sat down. Some of the students didn't sit, but stood around telling Kelton he was going to jail. Reporters showed up, and so did the police. Then a remarkable thing happened. Instead of arresting Kelton, the police positioned themselves around the perimeter of the store and kept order. This encouraged other students to take seats. Too frightened (and too broke) to actually order anything, Kelton Sams had nevertheless done what no black in Galveston had ever done before—dared sit at a segregated lunch counter.

From Woolworth's the blacks marched to other downtown lunch counters, their number growing, chanting, "We'll take a seat and sit for a week." When managers at Kress and McCrory's heard what was happening, they closed their counters. The manager at Walgreen's went so far as to remove the seats. But there was no rioting, no bloodshed, no violence whatsoever.

For the moment Kelton Sams felt ten feet tall. But later, when he heard his voice on radio news reports, butchering the language in his spitfire ghetto fashion, Kelton was horrified. "I'd never heard my voice," he recalled. "I sounded inarticulate and grammatically inept. I went straight to a bookstore and starting scanning books for something to say. After that I started keeping a notebook of new words, and practicing putting them together into sentences."

Sams' next target was the Dairy Queen stand on Broadway, next to the Moody mansion. Blacks had been able to make purchases from the outside serving window, but it was Sams' intention to walk in, take a seat, and order. Then it dawned on him that he might actually be served, in which case he would also be expected to pay. The black students didn't have a dime among them. Sams went to T. D. Armstrong, who, along with John Clouser, was recognized as a leader of the black community, and borrowed enough money to buy a round of milk shakes.

Meanwhile, a group of white leaders that included Griffith Lambdin, Harris and Ruth Kempner, and radio station owner James Bradner arranged to meet with white merchants, hoping to convince them to voluntarily integrate lunch counters before the sit-ins got ugly. The first priority, everyone agreed, was to avoid any publicity. In a series of three meetings they reached a compromise.

"Look," Lambdin told the merchants. "You people are cutting your own throats. Nearly one-third of our citizens are black. You sell them tablets and Kleenex and toothpaste. They might also like to come in and drink a Coke and have a hamburger. So you are economically injuring yourself."

"We'd lose our white customers," one merchant said.

Another argued that if he bent to the will of the kids taking part in the sit-ins, then large numbers of blacks would troupe down to his store, smart-alecking and causing trouble and rubbing it in how they'd brought him to his knees.

Harris Kempner assured the merchants this wouldn't happen.

Finally, George Clampett, a partner with Grady Dickinson at the Star Drugstore on 23rd, stood up and cleared his throat. "I was born in the South, and my parents were born in the South," he began. *Oh, my lord*, Lambdin thought. But Clampett continued: "You know, Grady and I got together and discussed this business about losing business, causing trouble, and we finally got around to the ultimate question—what is right? What is right?" There was a moment of silence, then Ruth Kempner started clapping and so did everyone else.

Clampett's stand swept away the final vestiges of resistance. From that moment on, Galveston's lunch counters were integrated. When Lambdin asked Clampett a month later if he'd lost any white customers, the druggist said that one woman had sworn she would never set foot in his store again. But as it turned out, the Star Drugstore was the only store in town that sold her favorite perfume, and after examining the depth of her convictions, the woman resumed her patronage.

But Kelton Sams wasn't finished. The experience had left him disenchanted with the adult leadership of Galveston. Nobody had invited him to the series of meetings; nobody had consulted him about the compromise. Both black and white civic leaders cautioned Sams to go slow, but the young black had already decided that his next target would be the city's beaches—in particular, Stewart Beach, the most convenient and popular. This idea bordered on insurrection. It was one thing to quietly slip up to the lunch counter at Walgreen's and order a cheeseburger, and another thing entirely to parade a pack of young blacks along the public beaches at the peak of tourist season. This tactic struck at the heart of the Island's economy. What's more, it could result in bloodshed. Likely as not, the tourists on the beach were from small towns in East Texas, where it was still common to hear folks brag about having "the blackest land and the whitest people," and where lynching was recently a way of life.

When Griffith Lambdin learned that Sams planned to take his fellow students to Stewart Beach, he wrote a letter to the Kempners and others suggesting that events were moving too fast. "Immediate desegregation at Stewart Beach is extremely improbable," he wrote, adding that the economic factors that favored the students in the lunch-counter situation would be working against them at Stewart Beach. "We advise them not to attempt such a great stride," he wrote. When it became apparent that Kelton Sams would ignore Lambdin's advise, black leader T. D. Armstrong called the students together and told them: "You got to keep cool. We hear that a bunch of rednecks are coming down from East Texas, saying they're gonna clean out Stewart Beach. Leave your knives at home. Go on to the beach, but act like decent self-respecting citizens, so that there will be no blame attached to you." Sams and the others said they would think about it.

At a city council meeting that same week, a council member cautioned the black students that trouble at Stewart Beach could endanger the city's outstanding debenture bonds.

"Do you know what debenture bonds are?" the councilman asked Sams.

"Yes," Sams replied, though he had no idea.

"Well," the councilman said, "then you understand how you are imperiling the city."

A few days later Sams and a small group of blacks took a swim at Stewart Beach. There were no riots, or imperiled debenture bonds, or harsh words. In fact, hardly anyone noticed. Kelton Sams went on to become president of the student body at Texas Southern University, where he majored in economics and graduated with honors. Later he became a minister in the United Church of Christ, and a black political leader in Texas.

WHILE GALVESTON's blacks were pressing for integration, Ruth Kempner and the League of Women Voters were in full revolt against the old, corrupt commission form of government that had served the Maceo syndicate so well. "The commission government promoted toadyism," Ruth charged. "The voters elected the commissioner of streets or whatever, and he appointed everyone under him. He controlled who got his streets done, who got to use city equipment, which people got paid to do nothing. Even the honest commissioners were guilty of toadyism."

A study sponsored by the league in 1958 advocated rewriting the city charter and changing to a modern city-manager structure. The plan called for radically altering the established power structure and was of course strongly opposed by incumbent politicians, men's civic clubs, the Chamber of Commerce, the *Daily News*, and nearly the entire business community.

There was even a division of opinion inside the Kempner household. I. H. Kempner—known to his children and grandchildren as Muggins—was of course the godfather of the form of government that Ruth Kempner was determined to bring down. On the subject of the new government they agreed to disagree, but the tension was always present.

"Muggins," she said at one point, "the next couple of years are going to be hard on all of us."

"Just remember one thing," the old man reminded her. "No government is any better than the people you elect to run it."

While working with precinct lists in Washington in World War II, Ruth had learned where to find the voters, and how to determine what was on their minds; this was a lesson she never forgot. In dozens of public forums and in thousands of telephone calls and mail-outs, Ruth and Frances K. Harris and other members of the league made their points with voters. They spoke at union meetings, at school gatherings, at churches, even in the old red-light district.

"I went places that no other lady has ever been to in Galveston," Ruth Kempner recalled. "Including the five A.M. hiring houses down on Postoffice Street, and the whorehouses. In those days I drove a Buick convertible, and I drove down to the hiring halls across the street from the whorehouses, and I was beautifully received in all of them."

Ruth and two other league members, Frances K. Harris and Marilyn Schwartz, were elected to the commission to write a new city charter. Despite a well-financed campaign by the opposition, Galveston voters approved the new charter in April 1960, exactly a month after the sit-ins at the downtown lunch counter. Some members of the league fretted that the black students might become a side issue that would wreck their cause, but this didn't happen.

Though no woman had ever been elected to a governing body in

Galveston County, Ruth Kempner decided to run. During the campaign she raised more money from the old red-light district than any candidate in history. "I knew what to do with a precinct list," she smiled.

One of the highlights of the campaign was a face-to-face meeting between Ruth Kempner and one of the madams, Big Tit Marie, who—it was said—had a bosom on which you could have served coffee. This was before the days of television news, but there was a good turnout of photographers and reporters. It was an unforgettable sight—Ruth Kempner, pretty and petite in her simple cotton dress and no jewelry except her wedding ring, and the Amazonish madam, outfitted to the teeth in a blue brocade dress, a hat the size of a garbage-can lid, and enough jewelry and makeup to sink an ocean liner. Ruth made a short, to-the-point speech, addressed directly to the madam and other citizens of the district.

"But for the grace of God, I would be in one of your houses," Mrs. Kempner said. "I believe that people in your profession have a place, and have always had a place, in our civilization, and I'll do everything in the world I can to protect you. But I want you to know that I intend to have an honest police department. The first time a policeman is paid off, heads are going to roll."

Ruth was swept into office in 1960, as were six of the seven charter candidates who ran. Not only had Islanders elected their first female, they had also elected their first black since Wright Cuney: civil rights leader T. D. Armstrong. At a victory party at the home of Harris and Ruth Kempner, Ruth was offered the post of mayor. "Not on your life," she said. "I've got too much to do. The mayor's the greeter of the city, and I don't have time for that nonsense." At their first meeting the new council virtually rewrote Galveston's book of ordinances. Among other things, they revoked all the Jim Crow laws, putting an official seal on what Kelton Sams and his Central High students had already accomplished.

A year later a judge ordered the Galveston Independent School District to begin integrating, and by 1968 the schools were completely integrated. The medicine went down a lot easier when Islanders recognized that the number of talented football players switching from Central to Ball High School would guarantee Ball its best team in years. Doug Matthews, who later become Galveston's first black city manager, was captain of the school's first consolidated team in 1968. They finished second in the state.

The 1960 election was a landmark in Galveston history. It was a clear victory for the reformers and the progressives, but it was a personal and private victory, too, for the woman who had had the guts to out-Kempner the Kempners. "There never was a family that I admired more," Ruth Kempner said in an interview years later, "but I really do think they have to live up to me."

# 26

Bobby Moody was coming out first again. In the early 1970s, as Bobby's National Western Life Insurance Company was expanding, Shearn's Empire Life was in serious trouble, and so was his private bank, W. L. Moody & Son, Bankers, Unincorporated. Shearn was convinced that his troubles derived from a massive conspiracy cooked up by former Texas Governor John Connally, and including the Houston power structure, the Trilateral Commission, the Council on Foreign Relations, and 1972 presidential candidate (and former governor of Alabama) George Wallace. Incredibly, Shearn even believed his problems were somehow connected to the Watergate scandal. In his own mind Shearn Moody had more political enemies than Richard Nixon, *including* Richard Nixon. The motive for this conspiracy, Shearn maintained, was revenge for the lawsuit he had filed in 1970, which had the effect of blocking Connally's appointment to the board of the Moody Foundation.

The truth appeared to be far less complicated. The conspiracy, if that's what it was, started in March 1972, when Texas Attorney General Crawford Martin, a Connally protégé, happened to run into the attorney general of Alabama at a convention in San Antonio. Martin pulled his counterpart aside and told him; "You have an insurance company over there in Alabama that's about to collapse, and it's run by some pretty unsavory people." The company was Shearn Moody's Empire Life.

In April, Alabama insurance officials reexamined Empire Life's financial statement and downgraded the value of Shearn's interest in his grandmother's trust from $14.4 million to $4.4 million. With $10 million wiped off the ledger in a single stroke, Empire collapsed and was placed in receivership. The receiver, along with the shareholders, sued Shearn, charging him with fraud. In Texas the insurance commissioner filed a similiar lawsuit.

But things were going to get worse for Shearn Moody, a lot worse. Three months after his insurance company collapsed, representatives of the Securities and Exchange Commission entered Moody's private bank in Galveston with a subpoena for all his records. Investigators believed that Shearn was selling securities that were not fully covered. Because the private Moody bank was unincorporated, it wasn't backed by the FDIC, only by Shearn's personal wealth, which was recorded in the bank's statement of condition at $20 million. Even before his insurance company went belly-up, Shearn Moody wasn't worth anywhere near that much. In September 1972 the SEC regional office ordered the bank closed and placed in receivership.

Shearn had used the bank the same way the Old Man had used it, for pocket money. To his credit, Shearn made sure that when his bank failed nobody else lost money. Few people saw it, but Shearn had a generous side. He remembered with some embarrassment Old Man Moody's appalling cheapness, and told of a cross-country train trip with his grandfather when the Old Man flipped a paltry fifty-cent tip to a harried porter. Though only a teenager at the time, Shearn dug into his own allowance and gave the man twenty dollars. Later, when he became his own financier, his generosity took the form of allowing certain loyal associates to carry overdrafts at his private bank and to borrow large sums without collateral. State Senator A. R. "Babe" Schwartz, one of the many attorneys who served Shearn Moody, remembered that when the bank failed Shearn personally assumed the loans and overdrafts. "He charged them against future fees and salaries," said Schwartz, who had borrowed more than $200,000 from the bank.

His world falling apart, Shearn retreated behind the walls of his bayside compound. "He hardly ever left the Island," recalled Jim Wohlenhaus, Shearn's administrative aide in 1972. "He said he preferred to be a big fish in a little pond." Wohlenhaus and his family lived at the compound, along with a houseboy, a gardener, a chauffeur, and a former Las Vegas dancer and choreographer named

James Stoker. In court documents Stoker was always referred to as Shearn's "personal companion." An article in *Newsweek* reported that Stoker and Shearn lived together as "husband and wife," but Shearn denied that he was a homosexual, and told the magazine that Stoker was just a longtime employee and friend.

In the autumn of 1976 the suit filed against Shearn by the Texas Insurance Commission went to trial in federal district court in Dallas. During the months of pretrial hearings Shearn was deeply depressed: one day he looked out of his skyscraper hotel room in downtown Dallas, near the spot where John Kennedy was assassinated, and thought about jumping. But now that the trial date had arrived, he was more determined than ever to prove his innocence and bring down his enemies. "They made a terrible mistake," he said in a newspaper interview. "They shouldn't attack old money." Shearn was bursting to tell his side of the story, but attorney Roy Cohn had no intention of allowing Shearn to get near the witness stand—or for that matter near the courthouse. Cohn arranged for Shearn to be hospitalized in South Texas for the run of the trial, a ruse that Shearn's lawyers used many times to keep their client from shooting off his famous mouth.

Cohn's strategy was to attempt to convince the jury that the charge of fraud was laughable, just a misunderstanding brought about by Crawford Martin and other vindictive politicians. This was a contention Crawford Martin could not deny—the former attorney general had died of a heart attack a few days after a brutal deposition conducted by Cohn. If he couldn't make the jury swallow the Crawford Martin conspiracy theory, Cohn had an alternative strategy: to make them believe Shearn was merely the "titular head" of the errant insurance conglomerate. Shearn testified by deposition that he was no more than "the flag, the symbol" of the insurance conglomerate, and compared his role to that of the queen of England and the emperor of Japan.

But neither of Cohn's strategies got off the ground. Former Alabama Insurance Commissioner John Bookout completely destroyed the benign picture painted by the defense when he told the jury how Shearn had bragged about killing Crawford Martin. Lawyers for the plaintiffs then introduced a rambling memo that Shearn had written, outlining a scheme to subvert the law by buying up small insurance companies and milking them dry. The crusher was the testimony of a former Empire Life vice president, who recalled that when he warned Shearn that his disregard for the policyholders was unacceptable, Shearn replied, "Fuck the policyholders."

Cohn and the other lawyers knew by this time that they were going to lose: it was just a question of how much. The plaintiffs were willing to settle for $850,000, but Shearn had to agree before the jury began deliberations. Cohn telephoned Shearn and begged him—begged him repeatedly—to pay up and cut his losses. Shearn stubbornly refused. The jury found for the plaintiff, establishing Shearn's negligent mismanagement and breach of fiduciary duty, and set damages at $6 million plus interest.

After the trial Roy Cohn parted company with Shearn, not that Shearn's legal troubles were over. In the decade that followed, cases directly or indirectly related to Empire Life were appealed to the U.S. Supreme Court at least ten times: the paperwork connected with these cases filled a three-car garage. There were dozens of other lawsuits, too, some of them filed by Shearn Moody, some against. More determined than ever to recover his fortune—and to gain control of the Moody Foundation—Shearn went through more than a hundred different lawyers.

After Roy Cohn left, Shearn fell under the influence of another ambiguous figure, a former ANICO agent named Norman Revie. Cohn had originally hired Revie as a private investigator during the ANICO suits, but by 1975 Revie had become Shearn's administrative aide and guru. When people spoke of Shearn Moody, they also spoke of Norman Revie, as though the two were inseparable. A smarmy, heavyset man of mystery, Revie had collected crates of documents relating to Shearn's lost empire and had investigated most of Shearn's enemies. One thing that made him invaluable was his uncanny ability to keep track of all the paperwork and files. Revie wasn't a lawyer, but he acted as if he were—and in his company, so did Shearn. The two of them were constantly drafting quasi-legal documents, or tedious, laborious essays in which Shearn aired his views on the American judicial system or the U.S. Constitution.

INSIDE THE boardroom of the Moody Foundation, meanwhile, there was some fierce politicking going on. At stake was the mind and soul of the foundation's matriarch, Mary Moody Northen. For most of the 1970s the three trustees of the Moody fortune were Aunt Mary, Bobby, and Shearn. But Aunt Mary was in her mid-eighties: the day was approaching when she would be gone, and the nephews would have to decide on a replacement. On that day, or maybe sometime before that day, there would be a showdown. They couldn't both prevail. One or the other would have to capture Old Man Moody's title.

Shearn appeared to have the inside track, if for no other reason than he had the old lady's ear. It was Aunt Mary's habit to sleep until noon, then stay awake most of the night, a schedule that suited Shearn perfectly. Bobby and his second wife had eight children between them, and he didn't have time to stay up all night courting his aunt. Shearn, on the other hand, had nothing but time.

Seated in the parlor of the old family mansion, night after night, Shearn listened and Aunt Mary talked for hours about her papa, and about her dream of restoring the mansion and preserving her papa's vacation resort in Virginia. "I have to ask myself, what would Papa do?" she said again and again. She had become an Island icon, brought out for display at any number of public functions. There would be a sort of Alice in Wonderland befuddlement on her sweet face as some escort led her on stage to accept an award, or made sure she got to Ashton Villa in time to ring the bell on the Fourth of July. She was so conditioned to accept bouquets of flowers that when a bouquet of yellow roses meant for the female lead in a production at the amphitheater arrived, Mary just automatically stepped in front of the actress and accepted.

In her own way Mary Moody Northen was the most benevolent of the Moodys. In the years just after the Old Man's death, the trustess sat on their millions, partly because the estate was tied up in litigation—Moody suing Moody—but also because they felt no particular imperative to give. But starting about 1960 Aunt Mary changed that. As the board's senior member, she actively supported grants to build Moody libraries, dormitories, theaters, and field houses on college campuses all over Texas. Her only reservation was being certain that Papa would have approved, and making sure that Papa got the credit.

In 1969, however, Congress passed the Tax Reform Act, drastically altering the way foundations did business, and inadvertently setting the stage for a power play among the Old Man's heirs.

Among other things, the new law forced foundations to pay out minimum sums of their annual income and prohibited the socking away of large sums in real estate. The Moody Foundation was forced to sell millions of acres of ranch land that the Old Man had accumulated—mostly through repossessions—and invest the money in income-producing assets. Some of the Old Man's prized hotels, including the Baker in Dallas and the Stephen F. Austin in Austin, had to go. The Tax Reform Act also forced the foundation to sell its stock in the Moody National Bank, and to rid itself of all except 25 percent of its stock in ANICO.

"Mary Moody Northen couldn't understand how the government could force her to sell property when her father clearly intended otherwise," recalled Ed Protz, the Moody Foundation's grants co-ordinator from 1968 until 1982. "It pained her greatly that her father's will was being thwarted."

Bobby Moody had no problem understanding, however. This was the moment he had been waiting for, his opportunity to buy the Moody National Bank. Whoever controlled the bank also controlled ANICO. The Moody Foundation was a sort of Fort Knox where the family wealth was warehoused in perpetuity, but ANICO was the true cash cow of the Moody fortune, a company worth more than $3 billion. On paper Bobby wasn't all that wealthy. His insurance company, National Western, was an enormous success, but Bobby had signed away his interest in his grandmother's trust to make it so. Personally, he owned only 1.2 percent of ANICO stock. But the Moody National Bank owned 7 percent and controlled another 34 percent through the Libbie Shearn Moody Trust. Bobby already sat on the board of the Moody Foundation, which retained 25 percent.

When the foundation put the Moody National Bank up for sale in 1978, Bobby Moody was the high bidder at $4.6 million. Four years later he appointed himself chairman of the board of ANICO. Not yet fifty years old, Bobby Moody was almost as powerful as his legendary grandfather. He had the bank. He had ANICO. The only aspect of the Moody empire that he didn't control absolutely was the foundation. But he was working on it.

# 27

HURRICANE CARLA didn't do much physical damage to the Island, but the storm nearly finished it off psychologically. Carla began to cast her murderous eye on Galveston on Thursday, September 8, 1961, the sixty-first anniversary of the 1900 storm. For four days the storm lay offshore, feinting and turning, kicking up tides five to seven feet above normal.

Never before had a storm been so meticulously charted. A twelve-man crew from KHOU-TV in Houston set up shop on the fifth floor of the Post Office–Customs House Building on 25th Street, and a young anchorman named Dan Rather positioned himself next to the U.S. Weather Bureau's radarscope and broadcast almost continuously until the station lost its video signal Sunday night.

Carla was a massive storm, the largest and most powerful to hit the Texas coast in modern times. At one point it measured 400 miles across, and was driven by winds of 173 miles per hour. From Port Arthur west to Port Lavaca hundreds of thousands of people were evacuated, some of them to Galveston, where a sanctuary behind the seawall was considered safer than low-lying places on the mainland. A similar warning in advance of Hurricane Audrey in 1957 had gone largely unheeded, and more than 5,000 had died on the unprotected coast of Louisiana. By Sunday night there were more than 1,600 refugees crowded into the county courthouse on 19th Street, a building that had survived the 1900 blow. Floodtides were already knee-deep.

The storm finally committed itself Monday afternoon, crashing ashore southwest of Galveston, at Port O'Connor, the same path taken by two nineteenth-century storms that destroyed the port of Indianola. Galveston had been spared, or so everyone assumed. But now came another threat, one that nobody had anticipated: deadly tornadoes danced out of Carla's fury.

Early Tuesday a twister came in from the Gulf, just above the seawall, demolishing the Dreamland Café at 25th Street and veering along the west side of the Buccaneer Hotel. In its sporadic path the tornado ripped diagonally across Broadway, wrecking nearly two hundred houses and other buildings, and shearing the 23rd Street wall off the Bayshore Hotel while leaving furniture and occupants in place. Cutting through the heart of town, it missed St. Mary's Cathedral—but demolished the school next to it—then it headed toward the courthouse, where 1,600 refugees were huddled. County Judge Pete La Valle, who had been on his feet for forty hours trying to sort out and calm the refugees, had just stretched out on the top of his desk to take a nap when someone yelled, "Get down on the floor!"

"That was the first I knew of the tornado," he recalled. "There was a roar, then something that sounded like an explosion. Some people were knocked down twice. I rushed out into the courtroom. A lot of people were bleeding. We led them into the office of the tax assessor-collector, where we had set up a first-aid station earlier. I guess there must have been fifty hurt by flying glass, bricks, and wood. But within an hour everyone was treated."

A second tornado, less severe than the first, hit a few hours later, roaring in over the seawall between 82nd and 85th streets. It destroyed six houses and overturned some trucks. Much of the Island was flooded, and shrimp boats were washed up on 61st, blocking traffic for miles. The city had to do without power and water for several days, and city firemen were marooned for three days in the city auditorium. On the mainland whole villages were flattened, causing damages in the billions of dollars and killing dozens of people: it could have been thousands, except for the evacuations and the timely warnings broadcast by KHOU-TV. But on the Island only seven dead were attributed to the storm, and damage was in the area of $15 million.

Carla was perfidiously selective in what she destroyed. One of the refugees at the courthouse, a lawyer named Michael Kustoff, had left his chair to get a drink of water when the twister hit: the chair was reduced to splinters, but Kustoff suffered only a bruised ego when a Red Cross nurse tackled him and dragged him behind a desk. Miss Alice Block, a retired schoolteacher, refused warnings to leave her home at 4207 Avenue T. "It's just another hurricane," she said, noting that she and her parents had survived the 1900 storm by floating out to sea and back on a four-by-five-foot fragment of roofing. "I may be just a stubborn old woman, but I think I'll stay right here at home, thank you." When Carla had come and gone, Miss Block was still there, feisty as ever. In the tower at St. Mary's Cathedral, Mary, Star of the Sea, rode out another storm. But south of Broadway, in the historic plot bound by Avenues N to O, and 25th to 27th, two of the Island's most venerable institutions, the Ursuline Convent and Academy, were so seriously damaged that engineers doubted they could be restored.

In the months that followed, the Ursuline Convent and Academy became symbols of the Island's spirit, or lack of it. An editorial in the *Houston Post* noted that "no storm [has ever been able] to kill the spirit of perseverance in the face of adversity so characteristic of these sturdy islanders." But on the Island itself folks appeared not so sturdy, not so bold. Some people were ready to give up. Against the threat of tornadoes, the seawall had proved less than impregnable. Most people planned to stay, of course, but there was a palpable change in attitude, a loss of nerve, a rupture of values. Suddenly, people seemed tired of the past, tired of being reminded of their history and legacy. Until now homeowners had proudly preserved high-water marks and drainage holes from the 1900 storm, but in the backwash of Carla there was a citywide move to paint over the marks, fill in the holes, tear down, pave over, forget.

In part, this attitude reflected the urban-renewal mentality of the sixties, something that affected not just Galveston but all of Texas. You saw it especially in Dallas and Houston, a belief that new had to be better than old, an impulse to bury the past, to bulldoze, dismantle, sanitize, neutralize. It wasn't so much a need to build as it was a compulsion to destroy, to deny what was. In Galveston nobody went down to the Strand anymore, or even discussed it. The Wall Street of the Southwest was now the Bowery. A few artists, taking advantage of the cheap rents, lived in sparsely furnished studios on the upper floors of the old buildings, but by and large the Strand was populated by bums and derelicts. Once proud Hendley Row, the oldest stretch of commercial buildings on the Island, was known informally as the Wino Hilton.

Most of the buildings were as sound as the day they were built, and could be bought for as little as $10,000, but in the opinion of most Islanders they weren't worth the dynamite it would take to blow them up. The indifference was appalling. The same people who had the most to gain from a renaissance on the Strand—the ruling families, the snobbish BOIs, those who bragged that they were born with sand between their toes—the same crowd that should have been moving heaven and earth to restore the Island's grandeur, was the least interested.

The Moody Foundation was donating millions to colleges all over Texas, but until the late 1960s hardly anything to Galveston. When anybody did build, the resulting structure was apt to be a monument to blandness. The board of the Moody National Bank decided that its turn-of-the-century Classical Revival building on Market Street was too old fashioned, and moved a few blocks away to one of those brain-dead 1960s structures designed to look like a brick deposit box. The old bank with its Corinthian columns and terra-cotta glaze (which was supposed to pass for granite) was mostly facade—the Old Man had built it on the cheap—but at least it looked like a bank. By the grace of Mary Moody Northen, the old bank building on Market was spared the wrecker's ball and was turned over to the Galveston County Historical Society for use as a museum.

Brick-and-glass boxes, or their aesthetic equivalent, were popping up all over the Island. Broadway was becoming franchise row. Mary Moody Northen had a fit when they built a Dairy Queen next to the mansion, but apparently it never occured to her that she could easily have bought the same property. The Santa Fe Railroad shut down its Galveston operation and announced that the site of the historic Santa Fe Building might become a parking lot. The congregation of Temple B'nai Israel decided that its wonderful old Moorish-influenced synagogue was too outdated and over Ike Kempner's heated objection voted to sell the building to the Masonic Order. In redesigning the building to fit its needs, the Masons knocked off the temple's four Oriental minarets and plugged or plastered over its Gothic stained-glass windows and Moorish arches. What was happening to Galveston defied all logic—a people who had gloried for more than a century in Victorian splendor had decided to tear it all down and replace it with aluminum siding.

Though the battle to save the Ursuline Convent was mostly symbolic, and doomed from the start, it nevertheless produced a coalition of people who finally united to save Galveston from itself. Significantly, almost all of them were outsiders, people who had moved to the Island from other places. One of them was Sally Wallace, whose family owned the famed Lambshead Ranch north of Abilene. Sally and her husband Jack moved to Galveston in 1962 while the Island was still reeling from the effects of Hurricane Carla, and were instrumental in starting the preservation movement and keeping it alive. Another was Emily Whiteside, who came to the Island to head the Galveston County Cultural Arts Council. Another was Ed Protz, a sociologist and an expert on community planning who came from Atlanta to become grants coordinator at the Moody Foundation. And still another was Peter Brink, a Washington, D.C. lawyer (and the national treasurer of the Muskie for President campaign in 1971), who came to the Island in 1973 as director of the Galveston Historical Foundation (GHF).

Wallace, Whiteside, Protz, and Brink had a common interest in history and culture, and even more important, an outsider's perspective: they saw the Strand, for example, not as a row of decaying buildings, but as one of the greatest collections of Victorian architecture anywhere in the country. It was obvious to these people that Islanders were throwing away an incomparable treasure. Protz, who had watched Underground Atlanta develop and had seen what Gaslight Square had done for St. Louis, managed to convince board members of the Moody Foundation that there were worthy causes just outside their front door.

But it was late in the game: historic Galveston was in imminent danger of vanishing from the face of the earth. Property owners were desperate to sell, or find other ways to recover their investment. Bad faith was begetting bad faith, and tempers were running short. Already a number of nineteenth-century buildings had been leveled so quickly that preservationists never had a chance to protest. The historic Guild Building on Market at 21st had been replaced by an ANICO parking lot. The Wofford Building at 23rd and Mechanic had burned down mysteriously, right after the GHF got a court order to save it from the wrecking ball. Arson was suspected in several other fires, including one that destroyed a nineteenth-century boarding house at 25th and Market, killing more than a dozen people.

The Catholic diocese, insisting that the Ursuline Academy had been ravaged beyond repair, moved with unaccustomed swiftness to turn it over to the wreckers; now a century of tradition was merely a smudge on the ground. The saddest part was, there had been scarcely a murmur of protest. Many Islanders saw the Nicholas Clayton–designed academy as (in Ruth Kempner's words) "a red-brick monstrosity," though in its glory days the building had appeared as imposing and impressive as Notre Dame Cathedral in Paris.

The convent, a Louisiana-style stucco building that dated back to 1847, was less severely damaged, but the diocese wasn't sympathetic to the arguments of the preservationists. In a desperate attempt to buy time, Emily Whiteside convinced the nuns to let her use the convent for a summer arts program for young people, with the hope that the program might provide a permanent reason to spare the old structure. But it didn't work out. This was the early seventies, and the kids who took part in the program wore jeans and long hair and maybe smoked funny cigarettes, behavior that made the nuns very nervous. At the end of the summer the program was suspended and the building demolished.

But the loss of the convent had a galvanizing effect on the preservationists. It helped unite them under the banner of the Galveston Historical Foundation. The GHF wasn't a new organization. It had been around for years, in the hands of little old ladies who ratholed Mardi Gras souvenirs and donated family letters to the Rosenberg Archives. In 1957 the historical society purchased and restored the Samuel May Williams house. But this was a revival on a scale never dreamed of by old-time Islanders, an infusion of new blood and new ideas.

Ed Protz got the Moody Foundation to put up $250,000 seed money for a revolving fund, enabling the GHF to buy old buildings about to be demolished and hold them until someone came along willing to finance renovation. Peter Brink improvised a scheme by which the preservationists didn't have to buy the entire building, merely the easement on the facade: for a fraction of the purchase price the historical foundation could prevent a building from being destroyed. Jack and Sally Wallace put up the money to save Hendley Row from the wrecking ball after yet another mysterious fire destroyed its western section. Other organizations, such as the Kempner Fund, pitched in. The Junior League restored the Trueheart-

Adriance Building on 22nd, and the First National Bank Building around the corner on the Strand, which it then leased to Emily Whitehead's arts council.

In retrospect, the Galveston Historical Foundation's key move was hiring Peter Brink, who was thoroughly knowledgeable in the arcane field of fund-raising and grant-grabbing. Brink had a special feel for Galveston, for what it had been and what it could be, and he was able to pull several small, informal groups together under the GHF tent. Strengthed by a membership drive, the GHF created the East End Historical District, and the Silk Stocking Historical Precinct, and started a campaign to save Ashton Villa.

The villa of Miss Bettie Brown was about to be razed and replaced by a service station. Brink offered its owner, El Mina Shrine Temple, $100,000 for the old home, but the Shrine wanted twiced that much and began taking bids for the structure's demolition. Brink and his troops hurried down to the city council, where they lobbied through an ordinance that prohibited the defacing or destruction of historic structures more than a hundred years old. Over the furious objection of the Shrine, the city denied a demolition permit. Later the city bought Ashton Villa for $125,000, with help from the Moody Foundation, the GHF, and the Department of Housing and Urban Development. Today the villa is a museum, operated by the historical foundation.

Emily Whiteside was a dynamo in the movement, working ten and twelve hours a day on forty-seven different projects. She started an all-volunteer program, organized an arts festival on the Strand, secured grants from the National Endowment for the Arts, brought ballet companies and symphony orchestras to the Island, and combed the archives for clues to Galveston's buried and plastered-over history. One of the problems in bringing the performing arts to Galveston was the lack of a suitable auditorium: the largest assembly hall on the Island, the Moody Convention Center, was frequently booked for wrestling matches. Someone mentioned Martini's old State Theater, which most recently had been an X-rated-movie house. The theater shut down in 1974, and Emily was desperate enough to think it might be suitable.

Standing in front of the old theater, Emily saw what looked like a granite archway concealed beneath the rotting boards of the marquee. When she peeled back the boards, she saw letters carved in the Romanesque arch. Most of them had been broken away but she could make out one word—OPERA. A ghost breathed down the back of her neck as she realized that what she had discovered was the 1894 Grand Opera House, one of the few of its kind still in existence. This was one of the great finds of the restoration movement, and foundations got in line to back it. The Houston Endowment put up $250,000 to buy the building, and the Moody Foundation gave another $250,000 to stabilize it. Another $5 million was required to replace the theater's marble-tiled lobby, parquet floors, grand staircase, and other furnishings, and money came in from the Moodys, the Kempners, and many others from all across Texas.

The restoration movement proved to be contagious. All across the Island, people were painting, repairing, restoring. The Island had hundreds of raised cottages with gingerbread trim, many of them unique because it was the habit of nineteenth-century carpenters to make up the designs as they went along. Some of them had already fallen down from neglect, but many others were saved. The Galvez Hotel, which was allowed to run down under Moody ownership, was purchased by an investors' group and restored to its original splendor. George Mitchell, the son of a poor Greek immigrant, who had moved to Houston and made a fortune in oil, returned to the Island to buy twenty-two acres of old Fort Crockett and build the $36 million San Luis Hotel. Later Mitchell remodeled an old building, which he renamed the Tremont House, and led a movement to bring back Mardi Gras and to restore the old trolley line between downtown and the beach.

Eventually, forty buildings on the Strand were purchased and rehabilitated through the efforts of the Galveston Historical Foundation. Buildings that couldn't be fully restored were painted to look restored. The fourth floor of the Marx & Kempner Building had been lost in the hurricane of 1915, and with it much of the structure's charm. But in 1976 the city council approved a grant and hired New York muralist Richard Haas to paint a mural across the facade. Haas, who specialized in trompe l'oeil (fool the eye) paintings, borrowed details from Nicholas Clayton's original drawings, and painted what to the eyes of most passersby appear to be actual architectural details. As the old buildings returned to life one after another, the GHF raised more money to install historical markers and gaslights. Another Galveston newcomer, Evangeline Whorton, organized an annual celebration called the Dickens Evening on the Strand in which Islanders dress up in nineteenth-century costumes and make merry.

And still some Islanders didn't get it. "You people are crazy," a longtime Island resident told Ed Protz. "No respectable person will be seen on the Strand in daylight, much less at night."

The most controversial and bitterly devisive episode was the battle to save Pier 19 for the Mosquito Fleet. For more than a hundred years the colorful little shrimp boats had tied up at the pier at the foot of 20th Street, bow to stern with oceangoing tankers and freighters. In 1974, in what was essentially an act of desperation, the Wharf Board voted to evict the shrimpers. The prestige of the port was at an all-time low, and the board was grasping for a plan to improve its financial situation. The Mosquito Fleet wasn't paying its fair share of the rent, and port authorities wanted Pier 19 as a roll-on, roll-off loading dock for imported cars. The Wharf Board offered to move the shrimpers to new docks across the channel on Pelican Island. But the shrimpers rejected the offer, and the battle lines were drawn.

This wasn't just another skirmish between newcomers and old-timers, but a pitched battle for the soul of the Island. It pitted the Wharf Board, the business community, organized labor, the Chamber of Commerce, the *Daily News*, and the Kempners against a grass-roots movement of preservationists, Strand merchants, medical students and faculty, and street characters. The shrimpers chose Mary Moody Northen as their honorary chairman. Essentially, this was a reenactment of Galveston's oldest quarrel: is the Island a port, or is it a tourist mecca? Somehow it couldn't be both. The question was highly emotional, and plunged deep into the Island's psyche. The shrimpers were a quaint and picturesque lot— Italians, Greeks, Cajuns, and Hispanics mostly—simple men of the sea, drying spans of green and white netting on the riggings of their boats, while their womenfolk and children sorted the catch and laid it out for the inspection of passersby. Traditionally, Islanders had bought fresh seafood and other commodities right off the dock. The annual Blessing of the Fleet brought hundreds of tourists to the Island and was in its way a reaffirmation of Galveston's seafaring heritage.

But there was another side, less idealistic, more practical, and just as valid. Ruth Kempner articulated it in an interview. "The shrimpers are a bunch of thugs," she said. "They may be picturesque, but I've been on a grand jury and I can tell you that's as far as it goes. They are picaresque as well as being picturesque. What they are really doing is opening up Pandora's box of horrors. Without the Galveston wharves, Galveston doesn't exit. People might as well face that. There is no other excuse for Galveston's being except the wharves."

The Galveston Historical Foundation joined the fight on the side of the shrimpers, launching an advertising campaign and obtaining an injunction to block the eviction. The injunction not only halted the eviction, it impaired the Wharf Board's ability to issue revenue bonds, thereby obstructing other plans, including a proposal to install a grain elevator on Pelican Island. With its operation at a near standstill, the Wharf Board agreed to a public referendum. After almost three years of fighting, the voters settled the issue in 1977, voting by a margin of two to one to keep the Mosquito Fleet at Pier 19.

This was more than just a symbolic victory for the Galveston Historical Foundation. The referendum established that the electorate overwhelmingly supported a historic waterfront. The result is that Galveston has one of the few working ports in the country that manages to preserve a historical sense of time and place. The tall ship *Elissa* now has a permanent berth at Pier 21, next to the new Seaport Museum, and that 1877–vintage iron bark is as much a Galveston landmark as the seawall or the Strand. When a dry dock from Todd Shipyards broke loose in a spring storm, washing across the channel and slamming into *Elissa*, lawyers for the shipyard tried to claim that it was an act of God. They knew that they were in trouble, however, when a federal judge looked down from his bench and remarked: "God wouldn't do that to *Elissa*."

In the early 1980s the Kempners fought yet another losing battle with the preservationists and the GHF. This time the issue was whether or not Islanders wanted a port for supertankers on Pelican Island. Harris K. "Shrub" Kempner, Jr. was on the steering committee of the group that wanted the superport, though he recognized it was going to be a tough sell. The faculty and administration of the University of Texas Medical Branch was solidly opposed to the superport, which would have been located virtually in the medical school's backyard. Various environmental groups were automatically against any project that threatened to pollute Galveston Bay, as were commercial and sport fishermen. Shrub Kempner acknowledged that sleek, high-tech supertankers posed certain dangers, but argued that the alternative was a fleet of rust-bucket tankers sailing up and down the coast.

"I reminded people what happened with the *Burma Agate* and the *Mimosa* in 1979," Kempner said. This was a disaster fresh on every Islander's mind. Traveling at excessive speed four miles off Galveston, the freighter *Mimosa* rammed and gouged a hole in the side of the *Burma Agate*, which exploded in a ball of fire, killing thirty-two crewmen. Meanwhile, the crew of the *Mimosa* abandoned ship and left it running at full throttle. For hours the ship ran in circles, barely missing oil platforms and ships, until tugs ensnared its propeller with steel cables. The *Burma Agate*, which carried 400,000 barrels of oil, burned for sixty-nine days before it finally sank in forty feet of water. Part of the 250,000 barrels of oil it leaked into the Gulf floated into Galveston beaches.

Kempner's argument won out, or so it seemed. Voters approved the superport referendum by a comfortable margin. But that wasn't the end of the battle. Opponents demanded and got an environmental study, and used a number of legal maneuvers to delay the start of construction. When oil prices dropped in the early 1980s, changing market factors, Kempner and his group gave up the fight.

THE BATTLES fought by the Galveston Historical Foundation had a serendipitous benefit that went largely unappreciated at the time. They helped bring into the fold an invaluable ally—Mary Moody Northen. The grand dame of the Moody Foundation had always been interested in history—she ordered history books a dozen at a time—but had never considered how she might serve it. Ed Protz changed all that.

When Protz arrived as grants coordinator at the Moody Foundation in 1969, the board was in the habit of giving mostly bricks-and-mortar grants, constructing buildings with the name Moody over the front door, buildings that would have gotten built anyway. None of the Moodys ever demonstrated the sort of grand vision of, say, a Hugh Roy Cullen, who almost single-handledly built the University of Houston and the Texas Medical Center. The Moodys had as much money as the Cullens, but they chose to dribble it out to essentially inconsequential causes, many of them far away from Galveston. Imagine the impact if the Moodys had built a first-rate university on the Island, or a world-class art museum.

In the early seventies Protz began to guide the Moody board away from bricks and mortar, and in the direction of the arts and preservation. Without the revolving fund established by the Moody Foundation, the Strand wouldn't have been renovated. One of the most important Moody grants funded a project to buy and restore the Santa Fe Building, which anchored the Strand where it dead-ended at 25th Street. The railroad had already moved its regional headquarters off the Island, and was entertaining bids to have the handsome art deco building razed. Ed Protz and Bush Kempner, whose father I. H. had served on the board of the Santa Fe, went to Chicago to convince the president of the line to hold up demolition. Protz knew that Mary Moody Northen loved railroads, and sold her on the idea of using the old Santa Fe terminal to house a railroad museum. As a clincher, he suggested that she call the building Shearn Moody Plaza, in memory of her beloved brother.

Ed Protz and Mary Moody Northen traveled across the country in her LaSalle, visiting railroad museums and buying old locomotives and cars. Mrs. Northen preferred to drive at night, and Protz adjusted his schedule to hers. He drove, and she read railroad-buff journals and made notes. In Eugene, Oregon, they bought an entire privately owned railroad museum. They priced one of Lucius Beebe's private parlor cars, but decided not to buy. In the backyard of a farm house in East Texas they discovered a rusty engine once used by the Waco, Beaumont, Trinity & Sabine Railroad—in Mary Moody Northen's day some people called this line the Wobbledy, Bobbledy, Turnover & Stop. The old lady told Protz that when she was a young girl and people asked her name, she would tell them, "It's Mary and it's Elizabeth, too." That is why the locomotive on display now at the Railroad Museum is called the Mary & Elizabeth II.

Aunt Mary's nephews, Shearn and Bobby, were increasingly concerned over how much money she was spending—Shearn Moody Plaza alone cost the foundation $10 million—and how much she was influenced by Ed Protz. In 1982 they joined forces to have Protz removed from his position as grants coordinator. Protz wasn't fazed. He was already planning to resign and accept the position of director of the Mary Moody Northen Foundation. Technically, this foundation was created in 1963, but the old lady didn't get around to funding it until 1982. But suddenly the MMN Foundation was worth close to $40 million. That's how much she had saved from her inheritance, from her one-fourth interest in the Libbie Shearn Moody Trust, from dividends on her ANICO stock, and from other investments, including Moody National Bank shares purchased when they cost only a fraction of their eventual worth.

Shearn and Bobby Moody had spent so much time trying to outflank one another that they didn't notice, until it was too late, how Ed Protz had become Aunt Mary's friend, confidant, and proxy. Shortly after he was named director of the MMN Foundation, Protz was given power of attorney over the old lady's entire estate. That was the last straw as far as the Moody brothers were concerned. In 1983 they filed a petition asking that their aunt be declared incompetent. During the hearing Shearn and Bobby were particularly critical of Protz' role in dispensing the Moody fortune. "Protz has never had to go out and make a dollar in his life," the Moody brothers charged, as though they had. The court wasn't impressed with their pleadings. A judge ruled that Mary Moody Northen needed a limited guardian and appointed Ed Protz.

# 28

SHEARN MOODY had filed for personal bankruptcy in 1983, and was hiding out at a Moody-owned hotel in Washington, D.C., dodging subpoena servers and other real or imagined enemies. The bankruptcy trustee believed that Shearn and his aide Norm Revie had hidden funds in secret bank accounts in Liechtenstein, Costa Rica, and the Bahamas, and had put investigators on Shearn's trail.

Shearn's psychological dependency on Revie was starting to worry Shearn's friends. Revie had developed a Svengali-like hold over his boss. "Shearn won't take a leak without asking Norm," said one observer.

One family friend pointed out a convenient irony. Without Revie's close supervision, Shearn's problems might be even worse. Shearn had an affinity for lowlife, a long-running pattern of attaching himself to thieves and con men. Shearn's almost naive amorality, his sense that he was above the law, often resulted in some incredibly stupid stunts. When the Empire Life fraud judgment was being reviewed by the U.S. Fifth Circuit Court of Appeals, Shearn had the audacity to place personal calls to the judges. And when the case reached the Supreme Court, Shearn ordered sophisticated (and illegal) bugging equipment from Europe, and tried to lease office space across the street from the Supreme Court building, apparently to keep surveillance on the justices.

The fear that Shearn was losing touch with reality was reflected in his reckless use of the Moody Foundation to fund questionable projects. In the late seventies and early eighties he got millions of dollars in Moody grants for his pet charlatans, particularly those who carried the banner of the far right. His scheme to publish a book blasting the Texas insurance commissioner was so far-fetched it was comical. Shearn selected a former legislator and failed insurance executive named Jack Love as the book's author. Love would have been hard-pressed to write a coherent grocery list, much less a publishable book. Although Love went through $500,000 of his $750,000 Moody grant without producing a single page, Shearn nevertheless landed him a second grant of $500,000.

In 1981 Shearn arranged a $250,000 grant for Howard Phillips of Washington, the founder of the Conservative Caucus, to host a conference on Star Wars at the Galvez Hotel. The conference headliners included Senator Jesse Helms, Major General John Singlaub, and Washington journalist Jeffrey St. John, who spoke on "Restoring the Monroe Doctrine." One of the hosts of the conference was an ideologue named Doug Caddy, who lived in Houston and had acted as the Texas connection in order to make the conference eligible for a Moody grant.

Shearn was instantly captivated by Caddy, a dapper and immaculate figure who looked a little like G. Gordon Liddy without the hard edge. A lawyer and writer of right-wing books, Caddy had once shared offices with E. Howard Hunt at a Washington public-relations firm and for a time represented the original seven Watergate conspirators. Caddy's ideological contacts went way back. One year while an undergraduate at Georgetown University, he roomed with Tongsun Park, later infamous as the Korean influence peddler. Caddy was a disciple of William F. Buckley, too—he helped found Young Americans for Freedom in Buckley's living room. When Shearn learned that Caddy was a writer, he proposed that he help Jack Love with the insurance exposé. Love died a short time later, and Caddy inherited the project, eventually collecting $600,000 to finish that book and two others.

But Shearn had even bigger plans for Caddy, plans that involved tapping the millions stored away at the Moody Foundation. "Shearn asked me to set up a tax-exempt, nonprofit organization and apply for grants," Caddy said. "He told me that the Moody Foundation had $18 million a year to give away." Between 1982 and 1984 Caddy received nearly $3 million from the foundation.

Shearn's right-wingers made Bobby Moody and the staff at the

Moody Foundation nervous. Aunt Mary was off in her own world by this time and obviously wouldn't live many more years. In the meantime, Bobby was bending over backward to maintain cordial relations with his brother. Whatever Shearn wanted from the foundation, within reason, Bobby was willing to approve. The staff assumed that Shearn's grant applicants were being investigated by the foundation's lawyers, and lawyers assumed the staff was doing the investigating. In fact, the only person vouching for these people was Shearn himself.

Doug Caddy's last project for Shearn was a fiasco that could have sent both Caddy and Shearn Moody to jail. Since Empire Life still controlled 40 percent of Shearn's interest in his grandmother's trust, the company had taken out a $12 million insurance policy on his life. Shearn now believed that the Alabama insurance commissioner had hired the Mafia to kill him so that Empire could collect the insurance. Caddy's job was to go undercover and attempt to compromise the Alabama insurance commissioner with a cash bribe.

While Caddy was planning his move, Shearn was scheduled to appear at a hearing in bankruptcy court. Instead, Shearn decided to go back into hiding. Attempting to explain to the judge why Shearn wasn't in the courtroom, his lawyer let it slip that one of Shearn's agents was running a sting operation designed to expose the Alabama insurance commissioner. As it happened, a representative of the Alabama insurance commissioner was at that moment seated in the courtroom.

Though the mix-up could hardly be blamed on Caddy, Shearn was furious and quickly moved to cap Caddy's pipeline into the Moody Foundation. All things considered, Caddy had been a big disappointment to Shearn, who may have wrongly assumed that Caddy would be willing to kick back some of the grant money. Shearn found a new associate less squeamish than Caddy. His name was William Pabst, and he operated a shady organization called the Centre for Independence of Judges and Lawyers in the United States—CIJL for short. The CIJL was an organization devoted to helping those oppressed by the American legal system, or that's how it was presented to Shearn. At their first meeting Shearn poured out the pathetic story of the many ways he had been misused by the system. Pabst couldn't have been more sympathetic. He put a brotherly arm around Shearn's shoulders and said that it was damn well time to do something about that sitution.

For starters Pabst conducted a smear campaign against the judge in Shearn's bankruptcy case. With funds from a Moody grant he published a bound volume on the judge's alleged improprieties and distributed it at a judicial conference in Florida. Then he sent letters making similar allegations to the Department of Justice in Washington.

Pabst was no ideologue, but equal parts con man and crackpot. He sometimes pretended to be an attorney, and had once operated a law-school-diploma mill. At the moment, he was under indictment in Houston for swindling money from a charitable foundation operated by Atlantic Richfield. An expert on charitable, tax-exempt foundations, Pabst lectured on this subject at numerous conferences, many of them sponsored by his own bogus foundation, CIJL. As he educated people on the fine points of establishing foundations for the purpose of avoiding taxes, Pabst looked for likely recruits, innocent but greedy people willing to kick back most of the money and let Pabst worry about the details.

The conspiracy to swindle the Moody Foundation began in October 1984, and for many months worked to perfection. This is how it worked. Pabst recruited people like Dr. Robert D. Earl, a Houston dentist who wanted $600,000 to study, among other things, the dental malformations of convicts. The doctor's mission was to determine whether people who "look different" from the general population are more likely to end up in prison. One wonders what conclusions he reached after his dealings with Pabst.

Pabst helped applicants fill out the papers, and Shearn saw them through the process of approval. When Moody Foundation checks were issued, Pabst had them delivered to the applicants, who then wrote checks on their own foundations accounts—the foundations Pabst had helped them establish—made payable to people and groups they had never heard of. At first glance, the people that Pabst recruited appeared reputable, but their projects sometimes bordered on the ludicrous. A Republican party leader in Wharton County received a $375,000 Moody grant to "underwrite a program to develop human rights awareness," which included a booklet (written by Pabst) informing prospective jurors that most judges were not to be trusted. Another recipient got $150,000 to study dental problems of the Comanche and Karankawa Indians. Pabst arranged for the recipients to kick back up to 80 percent of the grant money to CIJL, or one of its dummy foundations. So smooth was Pabst's operation that even after he was convicted of the Atlantic Richfield swindle in May 1985 (and sentenced to ten years in prison), funds from the Moody Foundation continued to pour in on a regular basis. Shearn got to keep very little of the ill-gotten grant money: most of his share went to his lawyers, some of whom were part of the scam.

In October 1985, a year after Pabst began his scam, the spurned Doug Caddy decided to blow the whistle. He informed Moody Foundation attorney Buddy Herz that more than $500,000 in grants had gone not to their rightful recipients, but into the coffers of a phony corporation called CIJL, run by a convicted felon named William Pabst. Herz passed this information along to his boss, Bobby Moody. Both men knew that Shearn was close to a man named Pabst, but by this time they were numbed by Shearn's association with dubious characters. It never occurred to them that Shearn would go so far as to play fast and loose with the family foundation. A more logical conclusion, they agreed, was that Caddy was trying to shake them down.

Eventually, the foundation hired a law firm to look into Caddy's accusations. The investigation took nearly eight months and satisfied no one. While it supported Caddy's contention that grant money was being kicked back to Pabst, it concluded that Shearn had no knowledge of these illegal activities. And still the foundation hesitated.

Caddy brought the situation to a head by threatening to sue the foundation and, worse still, to take his accusations to the attorney general. At that point Bobby Moody decided that his only choice was to brief the attorney general himself.

A potential scandal at the Moody Foundation was a political hot potato in Austin. Attorney General Jim Mattox, who was mapping plans to run for governor, was a longtime friend of Shearn Moody. He had personally intervened in Shearn's bankruptcy case, and was frequently seen in public with Shearn and other members of the Moody family. Though Mattox later denied that he intentionally delayed looking into the case, an official investigation wasn't launched until nearly a year after Caddy first made his allegations.

Since the attorney general's office had no investigative force, the Moody Foundation was instructed to hire Clyde Wilson, the noted Houston private detective, who had recently exposed another charitable scandal involving the huge Hermann estate. Wilson agreed to take the Moody Foundation case, provided that he was permitted to submit any findings of criminal activity to the proper prosecutorial authorities, a condition the foundation accepted. Wilson was puzzled that Shearn, of all people, went along with his demands. After all, Wilson's probe of the Hermann Hospital trustees had caused them considerable embarrassment, and forced a few to resign. "I began to understand the next morning when Shearn visited my office and started talking about getting me a $400,000 grant," Wilson said later.

Shearn had once again badly misjudged the situation and the man. Clyde Wilson was as ornery as they come, a large, lean, mean maverick with a battered face and a glass eye that he enjoyed popping out and handing to first-time visitors. Clyde's credo was printed on a sign behind his desk: OLD AGE AND TREACHERY WILL OVERCOME YOUTH AND SKILL EVERY TIME. If Shearn hadn't realized that the game was over when Caddy blew the whistle, he certainly should have realized it when Clyde Wilson ushered him out the door.

During the autumn of 1986 Clyde Wilson submitted regular reports of his findings to the foundation, the attorney general of Texas, the U.S. attorney in Houston, and the district attorneys of Galveston and Harris counties. There was evidence that at least four Moody grant recipients had kicked back money to Pabst, apparently as much as $3 million. Within a few months Wilson had collected canceled checks and records and taken depositions from all the players, except Pabst, who had spotted trouble coming and skipped the country with most of the money.

In Houston, prosecutors at the U.S. Attorney's office were assembling evidence of fraud to take before a grand jury. A separate grand jury was looking into allegations that Shearn and Norman Revie had hidden funds in foreign banks to conceal them from his bankruptcy trustee and creditors. It had been more than three years since Shearn's initial bankruptcy filing, and not a penny had been paid to creditors. U.S. marshals seized Shearn's ranch and most of his assets, and the bankruptcy trustee filed a civil RICO suit, alleging that Shearn Moody was a racketeer. As was his custom in moments of crisis, Shearn went into hiding.

In August 1986 Shearn came out long enough to attend the funeral of his beloved Aunt Mary. During the weeks that Mary Moody Northen lay dying, Shearn became convinced that she was the target of a murder plot. In a letter to a local judge he attributed her pneumonia to "forced-feeding of soup in the bathtub" by her in-house staff, meaning by her guardian, Ed Protz, who had made his peace with Bobby but was still near the top of Shearn's enemies list. Shearn had photographs taken of his aunt on her deathbed and demanded an autopsy when she finally succumbed. His paranoia was characteristically ludicrous—the poor woman was 94, so frail and feeble at the end that she couldn't or wouldn't eat, or even open her mouth.

Mary Moody Northen's funeral would have done credit to a czarina. It was an echo of Galveston's glorious aristocratic past, choreographed by Ed Protz, with twenty-two rented limousines, an honor guard of cadets from Virginia Military Institute, and an assortment of patricians and dignitaries including Governor Mark White and Attorney General Jim Mattox. Radio station KGBC broadcast the service live. Islanders who had never met the grande dame face-to-face wept in the streets. The selection of Trinity Episcopal Church—instead of Moody Methodist Church—for Mary's last rites reflected one of those endearing little vendettas that made Island culture so fascinating: though the old lady's money built Moody Methodist into one of the finest churches in Galveston, she had a falling out a few years earlier with the leadership of the church, and vowed never to set foot inside as long as she lived, or in this case a little longer.

A soft rain was falling as pallbearers loaded Aunt Mary's casket into the hearse. Shearn stood on the steps of the church, a potty and rumpled figured in his mid-fifties, alone with his paranoia and a few loyal friends, comparing himself to Gandhi and still hoping to ward off disaster. Without warning, a U.S. marshal slipped through the crowd and slapped a document into Shearn's hands. It was a summons to appear before a grand jury in Houston. It was the beginning of the end.

After laying Aunt Mary in her grave, the family gathered in the conference room of the Moody-owned Ramada Inn on Seawall Boulevard for the reading of her will. Shearn held out a sliver of hope that Aunt Mary might remember him, but in true Moody form she left every penny of her estate to her foundation, headed by Shearn's nemesis, Ed Protz.

That same day Attorney General Mattox met with Bobby and Shearn. In Mattox' opinion the situation at the Moody Foundation was nearly out of control: one of the board's three members had just been buried, and another was about to be. From Bobby Moody's standpoint, however, this scenario couldn't have been neater. Replacing Mary Moody Northen was no problem. The only person Shearn and Bobby could agree on who was also acceptable to the attorney general was their mother, Frances Moody Newman, and she had expressed a willingness to serve. One can only imagine the vindication she must have felt. A more interesting problem was what to do in the eventuality that Shearn was indicted and convicted, as Bobby must have known he would be. In that case it would be the task of Bobby and his mother to boot Shearn off the board and name his replacement.

In the fall of 1987 Shearn was found guilty of seventeen counts of defrauding the foundation and sentenced to two concurrent five-year terms in prison. Two years after that both Shearn and Norm Revie were convicted of two counts each of bankruptcy fraud. In the spring of 1990 the Fifth U.S. Circuit Court of Appeals reversed Shearn's conviction for defrauding the foundation, on the grounds that the trial judge improperly failed to allow Shearn's lawyers to rebut testimony from a prosecution witness.

At this writing Shearn served his sentence on the other conviction, in a minimum-security prison in Fort Worth. Until his release in June 1991, he spent his days drafting and filing legal documents, dozens and maybe hundreds of them, challenging virtually every move by his bankruptcy trustee. But he was paying dearly for his contentiousness. Every time Shearn filed a document, the law firm for the estate answered with one of its own. A Houston law firm hired by the trustee billed the estate for 12,450 hours, at fees ranging from $85 to $225 per hour. In January 1990 the bankruptcy estate reported that it had yet to pay a single dollar to Shearn's creditors, but it had doled out more than $2 million to lawyers and accountants. Somewhere in the bowels of the earth Old Man Moody must be rattling his chains.

As for Bobby, he waited until Shearn was locked up, then appointed his son Ross to the vacant seat on the foundation board. Flanked by his mother and his son, Bobby Moody now controls every bit and parcel of the Moody empire.

# 29

LIFE IN Galveston today goes on much as it has for the last one hundred years. The changes are mostly cosmetic, a dab of concrete here, a layer of track there, a hotel, a pier, an artificial beach with white sand imported from Florida. The alterations come and go in a wink, impervious to the deception of time.

Quaint cottages raised on stilts sit jammed between splendiferous mansions and fields of tangled vines, and fishermen's beer joints lurk in the shadows of magnificent churches. A new house is anything built after 1950. Many neighborhoods still have their own taverns and family groceries, and some of the streets are still paved with pebbled asphalt rather than concete. It's hard to find a strip shopping center in Galveston, much less a mall.

Streetcars much like the cars of a hundred years ago shuttle along 25th Street, connecting the beach with the Tremont House and the Strand. The Strand sleeps most of the week, her Victorian face scrubbed and painted and waiting for the weekends. Down 21st Street, the Grand Opera House embraces the ghosts of Bernhardt, Booth, and Langtry. Along the docks a Russian freighter awaits attention. Lethargic hookers work the side streets and the seamen's bars, exactly as their professional ancestors did. Each evening at twilight the stubby little boats of the Mosquito Fleet return from the sea, a thousand squawking seabirds in their wake. And towering above it all, the ANICO Building, the city's only skyscraper, shimmers from the evening fog like an alabaster idol.

Viewed from the perspective of a widow's walk, the sandbar that is Galveston seems narrow and inconsequential, a comma of earth separating two great spans of water. Hurricanes have ravaged the Texas coast on an average of one every other year, and yet Islanders abide, shrug, mop up, collect their insurance, and rebuild, as though that were the natural order of things. In terms of the Island's overall economy, Hurricane Alicia in 1983 was a net gain.

Three times in recent years there have been moves to bring back casino gambling, and three times the voters have beat it back by a two-to-one margin. Each time the Kempners lead the opposition. "People in Texas seem to forget that we live here," says Shrub Kempner. "Casino gambling has absolutely ruined Atlantic City." Shrub's mother, the indomitable Ruth Kempner, remembers Galveston in the 1930s as the most romantic place in the world, sin and intrigue, music and moonlight walks on the pier, the smell of the surf. But it could never be like that again. "The Maceos were very paternalistic about Galveston," she says. "This was their home. Their children were brought up here. If we had an Atlantic City casino–type situation, we wouldn't have the Maceos, we'd have the international Mafia families that wouldn't give a damn what happened to this town."

Shrub is the elder spokesman of the family since his father, Bush Kempner, died in 1988. Bush was one of the Island's true gentlemen, accent on the gentle. He was a man of vision and courage. He died after sustaining a freak neck injury, crashing into the back wall of a tennis court, trying to return a high lob. When the doctors at John Sealy Hospital quoted the odds to Bush—even if he lived, he would be crippled for life—the old gentleman asked for time to visit with his children and grandchildren. Then he told them to pull the plug.

The Kempners, the Moodys and, in times past, the Sealys have taken a lot of heat for the way that subsequent generations have ruled—some would say stifled—the Island's economy and framed its social conscience. Writer Paul Burka, who was born on the Island but moved away in 1959, wrote not long ago:

"They (the three ruling families) shared the fatal preference for safety over risk that is the inherent weakness of dynasties after the first generation. This propensity for caution—the antithesis of the freewheeling, expansive philosophy of the rest of Texas—was augmented by the ever-present awareness of the sea and the knowledge that in Galveston investment was particularly precarious. As a result the families came to prefer monopoly over competition, lending over borrowing, and philanthropy over investment—all with tragic consequences for Galveston."

"Galveston banks have one of the lowest ratios of deposits to loans in the state," says one businessman. "It profits Bobby Moody and Shrub Kempner *not* to take risks. The Kempners' United States National—Islanders call it the Knee-Cap National—generates income out of its trust service, not from loans. Moody National is mainly a way for Bobby Moody to control ANICO."

Shrub Kempner acknowledges that Island banks have never "loaned up" the way banks have in other Texas cities, but then Island banks haven't been shutting down at the rate of three or four a day either. They have survived the decades by practicing caution, by looking in, not out. Kempner likes to remind people that when a promoter named J. R. McConnell came to the Island a few years ago, the Kempner bank was one of the few in Galveston that didn't get hurt.

At first reading, J. R. McConnell appeared to be the kind of legend that Galveston was made of, a comet who burst across the sky and vanished. In the mid-eighties, at about the same time that Shearn Moody was tapping his family's foundation for a few million, McConnell was putting together real-estate deals in Houston and Galveston for hundreds of millions. He had Islanders believing he was going to restore the Strand all by himself. A natural showman, McConnell brought in Johnny Cash and the Houston Symphony Orchestra to open one of his projects. Another project was to be a $900 million, 440-acre resort and golf course on the Island's east end.

McConnell declared bankruptcy in 1986, leaving partly finished condos littering the beach, and hundreds of millions of dollars in unpaid bills and bad notes. His empire was built on a pyramid of fraud, in which loans were obtained on the basis of property that either didn't exist, or had been previously sold. In the fall of 1987 he was indicted for fraud and jailed. Friendless and unable to make bail, McConnell tried to hang himself, but failed. Three months later, still recovering in the jail's hospital ward, he found a piece of electric cord, stripped the insulation off one end, wrapped it around his leg, and plugged the other end into a wall outlet. J. R. McConnell went out like he came in—in a spectacular flash.

McConnell made the mistake that others have made, the fatal presumption that this stretch of sand is a place to think big. On the contrary, those who have succeeded in Galveston are those who have learned to appreciate its limits. To paraphrase Colonel Moody, less is more for the rest of us.

Every inch of ground has been fought over for generations. Most of the Island's 61,000 people are squeezed behind the seawall—on the same piece of ground where most of them were squeezed before there was a seawall. The population hasn't changed significantly in fifty years. Employers who were the largest on the Island in the 1950s are still the largest. The single important new business—with the exception of the Galveston Historical Foundation—is a funeral home, funded by a bank in Missouri City, Texas. But the notion that the ruling families have somehow conspired to stunt growth is a canard. Galveston couldn't grow much even if it wanted to, and in its heart of hearts it doesn't want to.

Islanders have already stopped talking about J. R. McConnell and Shearn Moody. Those two rascals are just another chapter of history. Islanders have survived cannibal Indians, pirates, Civil War, acts of God, and scoundrels of all sizes and colors. They are not easily impressed.

What endures, what defies even the advance of time, is the Island itself. It is a mere sandbar, a ribbon of sediment, and it never promised anybody anything. People weren't even supposed to live here, but they have, and they do, and they will. Like the doomed fisherman said in the movie *Jaws*, it's only an island if you look at it from the water.

# *EPILOGUE*

IN 1995 A NEW PLAYER with an old familiar name swept into Galveston like an avenging angel, setting off the kind of firestorm that had once made the Island the most interesting and lively place in Texas. Tilman Fertitta, the 39-year-old great-great nephew of Papa Rose and Big Sam Maceo, seemingly came out of nowhere with a war chest of $40 million and some grandiose schemes to make Galveston better and within a few weeks had challenged Bobby Moody and the mighty Moody Foundation for the hearts and souls of Islanders.

The young Fertitta was born in June 1957, the same week that the attorney general shut down the Free State of Galveston and filed civil action against the Maceoes and their lieutenants, including Tilman's grandfather, Victor Fertitta, and his great-uncle Anthony Fertitta. By 1960, most of the family had scattered to the mainland or to other cities or states. Anthony moved to Las Vegas and into the legitimate casino business. So did Tilman's cousin, Frank. Tilman grew up in an affluent suburb of Houston but he must have known that his true destiny was back home on the Island.

A natural entrepreneur with a taste for flashy cars and expensive jewelry, Fertitta inherited the family's gift for high-rolling and risk-taking. In the 1970s he dabbled in clothing manufacturing and owned a chain of retail vitamin outlets and, for a time, profited from video arcade machines much as his ancestors once grew wealthy from slots and dice tables. Though heavily in debt by the mid-1980s, Tilman managed to buy controlling interest of Landry's Seafood Restaurant chain. Building new restaurants quickly and cheaply—including one on Galveston's Seawall Boulevard—he expanded Landry's into a $500 million enterprise, the second largest seafood chain in the country. "By the dawn of the nineties," Robert Draper wrote in *Texas Monthly* "[Fertitta] would [own] an empire as reflective of his day as insurance and energy were of the Moody and Mitchell era."

In 1995 Fertitta made his move on the Island, buying twenty-two acres of Galveston beachfront from George Mitchell, including the San Luis Hotel and the old Key Largo which Mitchell had purchased from Frank Fertitta eight years earlier. Tilman Fertitta envisioned an island paradise of the kind that those who lived here in the 1930s professed to remember—of bright lights, fast times and easy living. He poured millions into upgrading the sagging hotels, adding a first-class steak house at the San Luis, and sprang for the finest landscaping the Seawall had seen this century. Though few questioned Fertitta's good intentions, it was hard for some to accept that a descendant of Papa Rose and Big Sam Maceo came without an ulterior motive. Fertitta was also negotiating purchase of the entire waterfront at Kemah, the village at Clear Lake on the upper tip of Galveston Bay that the last of Jean Lafitte's pirates had settled. This deal kicked off a rumor that Fertitta was using mob money to establish a new gambling empire, but the notion was quickly dismissed.

Most observers saw Fertitta's bullish moves as a win-win situation. Draper wrote that, "Texas was civilized by daredevils like Tilman Fertitta who put everything they had on the line and wouldn't back down." Bobby Moody, however, appeared to have his doubts. In what some slanderers regarded as a retaliatory strike, Bobby announced that the Moody Foundation, which he controlled, would build a new 300-room "nonprofit" hotel on the grounds of Moody Gardens, the impressive theme park that the foundation funded in 1983. Originally created to rehabilitate victims of head injuries—such as Bobby's son, Russell—Moody Gardens became one of Galveston's major tourist attractions with its IMAX-3D theater, rain forest, NASA space museum and aquarium.

Fertitta believed, as did many others, that Moody's motives weren't altogether altruistic: the project would certainly benefit

Bobby's Gal-Tex Hotel Corporation, which would profit from managing the hotel. The foundation had also built a convention center at Moody Garden and this played into the larger equation. While the convention center cost the city nothing, its strategic location next to a "nonprofit" hotel that was exempt from federal and ad valorem taxes—and partially subsidized by the city—put hotels such as the two owned by Fertitta at an unfair competitive disadvantage.

At a Chamber of Commerce luncheon in November, 1996—at the Moody Gardens Convention Center, of all places—Fertitta launched an all-out attack on Galveston's tourist industry in general and Bobby Moody in particular. "I've been to forty-four states in the last few years," he told an audience of prominent business leaders, which included his father, Vic. "Galveston is definitely lagging behind all the other areas I've visited. We don't have amusement parks. We don't have golf courses. Our greatest asset is the beach, but it's also our greatest weakness." He pointed out the seedy novelty shops that line Seawall Boulevard, the weed-choked lots, and the procession of shabby hotels such as his father's Holiday Inn.

But Tilman saved his best shots for Bobby Moody. Though the Moody Foundation had contributed about $380 million to the Island in the past thirty years, Fertitta reminded his audience, the foundation has to give that money away. Unlike the patterns of generosity displayed by the other great Island families—the Sealys' noblesse oblige, the Kempners' discrete benelovence, and George Mitchell's lavishly expensive love affair with his native island—the Moodys have always given grudgingly and with expectation of a payback. From Fertitta's perspective the hotel-convention center was a sweetheart deal all the way.

On the surface, at least, Fertitta's message was directed to the practical side of the business community: if Bobby Moody is allowed to destroy competition, outside investors would avoid Galveston. But between the lines was a more subtle message: that his family was the spiritual opposite of the Moodys. The Ferittas and Maceos may have made their fortunes from gambling and prostitution, but nobody ever accused them of pinching pennies or of using charity to feather their own nests. Tilman was ready for a fight. Less than a week after his Chamber of Commerce speech, he sued the Moodys over the hotel-convention center arrangement. He also made clear that he would use his political influence—including the friendship and support of President Bill Clinton—to fight the foundation.

In the weeks that followed, the Galveston Daily News was flooded with letters supporting Tilman Fertitta. Old-timers hailed him as a giant killer and a hero, remembering gentler days when the charity and benevolence of the Maceos and Fertittas made life easy and pleasurable. After a while even George Mitchell hopped on the bandwagon for Fertitta.

A series of secret negotiations among Moody, Mitchell, Fertitta and the city eventually hammered out a compromise. In return for Fertitta dropping his suit, Moody made a number of concessions — offering equivalent discounts at Moody Gardens to all hotels, free transportation from hotels to convention center, and even offering to change its name from Moody Gardens Convention Center to Galveston Island Convention Center. For the first time in living memory, the Moodys had lost a power struggle in Galveston.

The mid-1990s clearly signaled a new day for the Island. Even as Fertitta was remodeling the San Luis and improving the landscaping along the Seawall, the city completed the grandest and most expensive ($6 million) beach renourishment program ever attempted on the Texas coast. As a feat of technology, reconstructing the beach was nearly as impressive as the building of the Seawall or the elevation of the Island.

For five months in the winter and spring of 1995 a dredge anchored off East Beach scooped sand from the ocean bottom and pumped it on shore, where bulldozers spread and leveled it. Eventually the work crew created a handsome 150-foot-wide strip of freshly dug sand that stretched from Tenth Street to Sixty-first Street, along the 10.4-mile Seawall. A spectacle to behold, the beach construction drew crowds of kibitzers daily, bolstering predictions that half a million new visitors would join the estimated seven million who flock to the Island each year. In two years, visitors would more than pay for the new beach through increased sales taxes and hotel bed taxes. "It's fascinating watching men and machines moving thousands of cubic yards of sand and never running into each other," Barbara Crews, mayor of Galveston in the mid-1990s, told me, shouting to be heard above the cacophony of engines, gears, gushing water and squawking seagulls. "It reminds people of a time when we used to have a beach, when you could actually drive your car along it."

City officials acknowledge that a category-four hurricane such as the three that ravaged Galveston this century will carry the new beach back out to sea. The Texas coast averages a hurricane every four years—the last was 1989—and is long overdue for a big blow. When it happens, Islanders will simply repeat the entire beach-renourishment process. "Do not forget," Crews told me, "that Galveston has started over before."

Many Islanders still profess a strong nostalgia for the rackets and the Free State of Galveston. "What people remember most about that era is that everyone who wanted a job had one," says A. R. "Babe" Schwartz, a former assistant district attorney and state senator, now a lobbyist for various Island interests. "The reason the rackets lasted so long," says constable Sam Popovich, the oldest lawman on the Island, "is that the biggest part of the people wanted it that way." Ten percent of the Island's adult population worked for the Maceos, and every merchant in town profited in some way from the rackets.

The Maceos changed the rules: the underworld became the overworld. Everyone cooperated and everyone made out. The Moodys, Sealys and Kempners—who owned all the banks on the Island—may not have socialized with the Maceos or Fertittas, but they did business with them. Not a single Galveston bank closed during the Depression. The Moodys' hotels were always full, even in the winter. By mutual agreement, the Maceos stayed out of the hotel business and the Moodys stayed out of the gambling business. Though cops and judges were generally corrupt, the Maceos maintained law and order with their own squad of vigilantes, known as Rose's Night Riders. No one in Galveston locked their doors in those days or feared to walk the streets. The Maceos were model leaders. They ran a clean game in a clean town, and anybody who didn't like it slept with the fishes.

Even as Tilman Fertitta was sounding out a new tomorrow, Islanders heard one final echo from the past. One morning in the winter of 1993, eighty-nine-year-old Vic C. Maceo walked into the office of certified public accountant Pete Miller, drew a .38 revolver from beneath his coat and started blasting in Miller's direction. Vic Maceo had somehow got it in his head that Miller owed him money from a real estate deal twenty-five years earlier!

"It was like a scene out of a bad movie," Miller said later, as doctors worked to repair a shattered bone in his upper arm and police booked Maceo for attempted murder.

Vic C. Maceo, also known as Little Vic to distinguish him from another cousin, Vic A. "Gigolo' Maceo, was the last of the old mobsters, a minor functionary in the Maceo organization. Nobody could explain why Maceo believed Miller owed him money from a long forgotten house sale, much less why the old gangster tried to take his revenge with a .38—though almost everyone agreed that it could only have happened in Galveston. Old-timers of the Little Sunday Morning Coffee Club, which meets every morning (except Sunday) at the Best Western Motel on Seawall Boulevard, speculated that some of Maceo's cronies had been ribbing him and suggesting that Pete Miller got the best of him in the deal. Years ago Miller was a busboy at the Balinese Room and later a cashier at the Studio Lounge, two of the Maceos' premier hangouts. The thought of getting suckered by a busboy must have been intolerable to a man like Vic Maceo.

"Little Vic was always a hothead," observed Angelo Montalbano, who in the old days had been a blackjack dealer for the Maceoes.

There was something wonderfully nostalgic—almost touching —about the shooting, though Pete Miller certainly didn't view it that way at the time. Little Vic arrived in a red sports car and wore a dark pin-striped suit and a dark fedora, just like gangsters in the movies. The gun that he used to wing Miller was so ancient that arresting officers had trouble shaking the copper-jacketed bullets from the chamber: bullets of that type haven't been used for years. As cops attempted to slap him in cuffs, the old mobster was heard to lament: "You don't handcuff a gentleman in this town!"

Though Pete Miller filed a civil suit, nobody had the stomach to put an 89-year-old man in prison, and eventually Islanders lost interest in the episode. In the end, a regular of the Little Sunday Morning Coffee Club speculated that the shooting had to do more with redemption than revenge. Vic was never much of a gangster. Maybe he was just trying one last time to get it right.

# INDEX

GARY CARTWRIGHT was born in Dallas and graduated from Texas Christian University. A prominent sportswriter for many years, he is the arthor
of *The Hundred-Yard War, Thin Ice, Blood Will
Tell, Confessions of a Washed-Up Sportswriter,
Dirty Dealing* and *HeartWiseGuy* and has written
and produced movies for CBS. He lives in Austin,
where he is a senior editor for *Texas Monthly*